D1759793

Ethical Intuitionism

Ethical Intuitionism:
Re-evaluations

Edited by

Philip Stratton-Lake

CLARENDON PRESS · OXFORD

This book has been printed digitally and produced in a standard specification in order to ensure its continuing availability

OXFORD

UNIVERSITY PRESS

Great Clarendon Street, Oxford OX2 6DP

Oxford University Press is a department of the University of Oxford.
It furthers the University's objective of excellence in research, scholarship,
and education by publishing worldwide in

Oxford New York

Auckland Cape Town Dar es Salaam Hong Kong Karachi
Kuala Lumpur Madrid Melbourne Mexico City Nairobi
New Delhi Shanghai Taipei Toronto
With offices in
Argentina Austria Brazil Chile Czech Republic France Greece
Guatemala Hungary Italy Japan South Korea Poland Portugal
Singapore Switzerland Thailand Turkey Ukraine Vietnam

Oxford is a registered trade mark of Oxford University Press
in the UK and in certain other countries

Published in the United States
by Oxford University Press Inc., New York

Contents

Contents

Notes on the Contributors

Robert L. Arrington is Professor of Philosophy at Georgia State University. His books include *Rationalism, Realism, and Relativism* and *Western Ethics*. He is co-editor (with H. J. Glock) of *Wittgenstein's Philosophical Investigations* and *Wittgenstein and Quine*, and (with M. Addis) of *Wittgenstein and Philosophy of Religion*. He is the editor of *A Companion to the Philosophers*.

Robert Audi is Charles J. Mach Distinguished Professor of Philosophy at the University of Nebraska, Lincoln. His books include *Action, Intention, and Reason*, *Practical Reasoning*, *The Structure of Justification*, *Religion in the Public Square*, and (as editor-in-chief) *The Cambridge Dictionary of Philosophy*.

Thomas Baldwin is Professor of Philosophy at York University. He is the author of *G. E. Moore*, and editor of the revised edition of G. E. Moore's *Principia Ethica*.

Roger Crisp is Fellow in Philosophy, St. Anne's College, Oxford. He is the author of *Mill on Utilitarianism*, and has translated Aristotle's *Nicomachean Ethics* for Cambridge University Press. He is subject editor (ethics) for the *Routledge Encyclopedia of Philosophy*, and has edited several collections in ethics and political theory.

Jonathan Dancy is Professor of Philosophy at the University of Reading. He is the author of *An Introduction to Contemporary Epistemology*, *Moral Reasons*, *Berkeley: An Introduction*, and *Practical Reality*. He is the editor of *Perceptual Knowledge*, *Reading Parfit*, and *Normativity*, and co-editor (with Ernest Sosa) of *A Companion to Epistemology*.

Stephen Darwall is John Dewey Collegiate Professor of Philosophy at the University of Michigan, Ann Arbor. He is the author of *Impartial Reason, The British Moralists and the Internal 'Ought': 1640–1740*, and *Philosophical Ethics*.

Berys Gaut is Lecturer in Moral Philosophy at St Andrews University. He is the co-editor (with Garrett Cullity) of *Ethics and Practical Reason* and (with Dominic Lopes) of *The Routledge Companion to Aesthetics* .

Notes on the Contributors

Allan Gibbard is Richard B. Brandt Distinguished University Professor of Philosophy at the University of Michigan, Ann Arbor. He is the author of *Wise Choices, Apt Feelings*, and co-editor (with Stephen Darwall and Peter Railton) of *Moral Discourse and Practice*.

Brad Hooker is Professor of Philosophy at the University of Reading. He is the author of *Ideal Code, Real World*, and is a co-editor (with Elinor Mason and Dale Miller) of *Morality, Rules, and Consequences* and (with Margaret Little) of *Moral Particularism*.

David McNaughton is Professor of Philosophy at Keele University. He is the author of *Moral Vision*.

Philip Stratton-Lake is Lecturer in Philosophy at the University of Reading. He is author of *Kant, Duty, and Moral Worth*, and is section editor (classical idealism) for *The Encyclopedia of Continental Philosophy*.

Nicholas L. Sturgeon is Professor of Philosophy at Cornell University. He has published widely on ethics, the empiricists, epistemology, philosophy of mind, and the history of ethics.

Introduction

It is generally agreed that certain forms of intuitionism[1] best reflect common-sense morality. One would have thought, therefore, that intuitionism has a certain default plausibility. But during the 1950s and 1960s intuitionism was rejected out of hand as an utterly untenable theory. How could a theory that aims to stick so closely to common sense come to be thought of as so implausible? Some criticized it on the ground that it succeeded in its aim of sticking closely to common sense too well, that it failed to tell us anything we do not already know, and is thus completely vacuous.[2] Others criticized it for the opposite reason: they objected to it, not because it expresses a series of obvious truths, but because it makes metaphysical and epistemological claims that are excessively extravagant,[3] and were thought to be patently false.

One would think that intuitionism could not be guilty of both charges, that it could not be criticized both for saying too little and for saying too much, though its critics managed to make both charges stick for more than two decades. Paradoxical as it may seem, however, we can see how intuitionism could be deficient in both of these ways. For the common-sense morality that intuitionists such as Price, Prichard, and Ross took so seriously is cognitivist, realist, and non-naturalist. Pre-reflectively, we have no doubt that our moral judgements express our moral *beliefs*, and that when these beliefs are true, this is because things are the way they represent them as being. To think of something as good or right is to think of it as having a certain quality, or character, namely that of being good or right.

Many thanks to Jonathan Dancy, David McNaughton, Keith Horton, and OUP's anonymous referee for helpful comments on earlier versions of this paper.

[1] As we will see, not all forms of intuitionism aim to reflect accurately the morality of common sense.

[2] See e.g. M. Warnock, *Ethics since 1900* (Oxford: Oxford University Press, 1968), 50; G. J. Warnock, *Contemporary Moral Philosophy* (London: Macmillan, 1967), 12–13; and A. MacIntyre, *A Short History of Ethics: A History of Moral Philosophy from the Homeric Age to the Twentieth Century*, 2nd edn. (London: Routledge, 1998), 254.

[3] W. K. Frankena, *Ethics* (Eaglewood Cliffs, NJ: Prentice-Hall, 1963), 86–7.

Introduction

Furthermore, although we may think that certain things are good because of their natural properties, pre-reflectively we do not think that goodness itself is a natural property. For, as Moore pointed out, for any natural property it is always an open question whether something that has that property is good. This openness shows that ordinarily we do not think of goodness as a natural property. Similar points can be made about rightness.

There is still substantial resistance to at least some of the central aspects of intuitionism, but its cognitivism, moral realism, and non-naturalism no longer appear to be the philosophical non-starters they were once thought to be. Furthermore, there has been a growing sense that we need to take our intuitions seriously.[4] The consequence of this is that there has been a renewed interest in ethical intuitionism over the last twenty years. A wide range of moral philosophers, from Aristotelians to rule-consequentialists to expressivists, Kantians, and deontologists, are beginning to look to the ethical intuitionists' work as a positive resource. It is, therefore, a good time to get clear on what it was the intuitionists said, and re-evaluate their contribution to our understanding of morality.

Different Types of Intuitionism

What, then, is intuitionism? Bernard Williams helpfully distinguishes between methodological and epistemological intuitionism. Methodological intuitionists maintain that there is a plurality of first principles that may conflict, and that no explicit priority rules for resolving such conflicts can be offered.[5] Examples of methodological intuitionism can be found in the work of Clarke, Price, Ross, and Ewing.[6] Epistemological intuitionism is the view that certain moral propositions are self-evident—that is, can be known solely on the basis of an adequate understanding of them—and thus can be known directly by intuition. Although all of the methodological intuitionists I mentioned are also epistemological intuitionists, not all epistemological intuitionists are also methodological intuitionists. Sidgwick

---

[4] This is, I believe, to a large extent due to the influence of Rawls's method of reflective equilibrium.

[5] B. Williams, 'What does Intuitionism Imply?', in Williams, *Making Sense of Humanity and Other Philosophical Papers 1982–1993* (Cambridge: Cambridge University Press, 1995), 182. Not all pluralists are methodological intuitionists, for a rationalized pluralism might have priority rules. Methodological intuitionists form, therefore, a subclass of pluralist theories.

[6] Prichard and McDowell may also be classed as methodological intuitionists, though moral principles do not seem to play any major positive role in McDowell's theory.

2

and Moore, for example, held that the plurality of moral principles that inform common-sense morality can be derived from a single consequentialist principle, yet also held that this first principle is known by intuition.

Sidgwick distinguishes three different types of epistemological intuitionism: Perceptional, Dogmatic, and Philosophical.[7] Perceptional Intuitionism is the view that it is particular moral judgements alone that are self-evident.[8] For Perceptional Intuitionists general rules can be formulated from such intuitions, but these rules will have little or no use in practical deliberation. Such intuitionists therefore tend to have a pretty low opinion of attempts to form our moral intuitions into a general system.

It is unclear what the distinction between Dogmatic and Philosophical Intuitionists is supposed to amount to in Sidgwick,[9] but he seems to hold that they are distinguished by what it is they appeal to in defending their claim that certain principles are basic.[10] Dogmatic Intuitionists defend the

[7] Williams distinguishes two forms of epistemological intuitionism: according to one, our intuitive knowledge is understood in analogy to mathematical knowledge; according to the other, it is understood in analogy to perception ('What does Intuitionism Imply?', 183–4). The former seems to correspond to what Sidgwick calls Philosophical Intuitionism, and the latter to Perceptional Intuitionism.

[8] *The Methods of Ethics*, 7th edn. (London: Macmillan, 1963), 99.

[9] At first sight it looks as though Dogmatic Intuitionists maintain that the principles of common sense are self-evident, and content themselves merely with enumerating and clarifying these principles, whereas Philosophical Intuitionists regard these principles as derived from some more basic, self-evident principle. This understanding of the distinction is suggested by Sidgwick's claim that Dogmatic Intuitionism amounts to 'an accidental aggregate of precepts, which stands in need of some rational synthesis' (ibid. 102). But this does not seem to be how Sidgwick understood the distinction, for he describes Dogmatic Intuitionists as not merely listing, but as ordering and systematizing the principles of common sense (ibid. 101). The distinction cannot be understood as one between methodological and non-methodological intuitionists either, for Sidgwick maintains that Philosophical as well as Dogmatic Intuitionists may be methodological intuitionists (ibid. 102). Furthermore, he clearly regarded Clarke as a Philosophical Intuitionist, and Clarke was a Methodological Intuitionist. At one point the difference between Dogmatic and Philosophical Intuitionists looks like one between those who seek the fundamental moral principle (or principles) within common sense, and those who deny that the basic principles can be found within common sense. This is suggested when he states that philosophical intuitionism, 'while accepting the morality of common sense as in the main sound, still attempts to find for it a philosophical basis which it does not itself offer' (ibid. 102). But, once again, this does not fit with the fact that he regards Clarke as a Philosophical Intuitionist, for he describes Clarke as trying 'to exhibit the more fundamental of the received rules as axioms of perfect self-evidence' (ibid. 104 n.), and thus as grounding morality on principles that can be found within common sense.

[10] In *The History of Ethics* Sidgwick states that although Price (a Dogmatic Intuitionist) thought that the principles of gratitude, veracity, fidelity, and justice are self-evident, he attempted to defend the view that these principles are basic by 'appeal to Common Sense rather than Reason' (*Outlines of the History of Ethics for English Readers* (London: Macmillan, 1954), 226). Sidgwick puts this point by talking of different ways of showing that certain principles are self-evident. But he thought that these principles can only be known self-evidently, i.e. non-derivatively, because they are basic.

view that certain principles are fundamental by reference to the deliverances of ordinary moral consciousness, whereas Philosophical Intuitionists defend this view by reference to rational insight.

It is common to regard intuitionists as merely listing the principles of common sense without any attempt to order them. Although there is some evidence that Sidgwick regarded Dogmatic Intuitionism in this way, this could not have been how he understood this view.[11] Indeed, there is no place for this form of intuitionism in Sidgwick's taxonomy, which is just as well, for no major intuitionist was content merely to list the principles of common-sense morality. The view that this was what many intuitionists were up to is pure myth.[12]

The Rises and Falls of Intuitionism

Sidgwick thought that Perceptional Intuitionism was pretty implausible, and so dismisses it fairly quickly as a respectable form of intuitionism. He gives Dogmatic Intuitionism more respect, but objects to it on the ground that it is 'difficult to accept as scientific first principles the moral generalities that we obtain by reflection on the ordinary thought of mankind, even though we share this thought'.[13] We have, therefore, to move beyond Dogmatic Intuitionism to Philosophical Intuitionism, according to Sidgwick.

Sidgwick does not, however, see the various phases, or periods, of intuitionism as developing historically from the crudest to the more sophisticated. On the contrary, he notes that the earliest form of intuitionism was philosophical, and that Dogmatic Intuitionism was a later development.[14] This is, he speculates, because of the doctrines to which intuitionists were responding at different times. In what he calls the first period, intuitionists were responding to Hobbes's philosophy, which tried to underpin common-sense morality with a principle of enlightened self-interest. Thus intuitionists like Cumberland and Clarke aimed to offer an alternative basis to common-sense morality. For Cumberland this basis is the common good of

There was, therefore, no important distinction in Sidgwick between showing that some principle is self-evident and showing that it is basic.

[11] See n. 9.   [12] See David McNaughton's contribution to this volume: Ch. 3.
[13] *The Methods of Ethics*, 102.
[14] Ibid., 103–4 n. He says nothing of perceptual intuitionism in this footnote.

all rational beings and for Clarke it is the more fundamental of the principles of common sense.[15] Since intuitionists of the first period aimed to underpin common-sense morality in some more basic principle, they could not appeal to common-sense morality in support of this foundation.

But the attempt to establish morality as a scientific body of truth based on self-evident axioms gradually fell into disrepute, and sentimentalism became the prevalent theory. It is against this empiricist view that the second period of intuitionism was a response. These intuitionists were keen to emphasize the cognitive element of moral consciousness, while meeting the empiricists on their own ground. They aimed to do this by attempting to show, 'among the facts of psychological experience which the Empiricist professed to observe, the assumptions he repudiated. And thus in Ethics it was led rather to expound and reaffirm the morality of Common Sense, than to offer any profounder principles which could not be so easily supported by an appeal to common experience.'[16] In his own philosophy Sidgwick attempted to re-establish the sort of Philosophical Intuitionism propounded by Clarke, though he did this not with reference to eternal fittingness, but to a consequentialist principle. His attempt to regenerate intuitionism did not, however, really bear fruit until the early part of the twentieth century. It is here in the work of Moore, Prichard, and Ross that we see what may be regarded as the third period of intuitionism.

It is tempting to regard the three main figures of this period as representing the three forms of intuitionism Sidgwick lists. At first sight Moore seems closest to the sort of Philosophical Intuitionism Sidgwick endorsed, Prichard seems to be a Perceptional Intuitionist, and Ross a Dogmatic Intuitionist. But although Moore's deontological theory makes him look like a Philosophical Intuitionist, his commitment to the doctrine of organic wholes means that the value of complex wholes cannot be inferred from the value of their constituent parts. We can only know the value of these wholes by intuition. Moore seems, therefore, committed to intuitive knowledge of a potentially infinite number of complex, particular goods, and in this respect seems more like a Perceptional Intuitionist than a philosophical one. Furthermore, it is not at all clear that Prichard was a Perceptional Intuitionist.[17] For although he talks of appreciating particular obligations in particular circumstances, he seems to have thought that through our appreciation of these particular obligations we can, through intuitive

---

[15] Ibid., 104 n.   [16] Ibid., 104 n.
[17] See Thomas Baldwin's contribution to this volume: Ch. 4.

5

induction,[18] come to know that all acts of this type are obligatory in this type of situation.[19] Finally, although Ross's frequent appeal to 'what we really think' makes him a Dogmatic Intuitionist, he thought basic moral principles are self-evident, and can, therefore, be seen as true by a proper understanding of them. Ross's intuitionism thus seems to have elements of both Dogmatic and Philosophical Intuitionism as Sidgwick understood these.

It was, for the most part, this mixture of Dogmatic and Philosophical Intuitionism that flourished in the first third of the twentieth century, and did not fall into disrepute until the late 1930s and 1940s. Just as the first period of intuitionism was replaced with the dominance of sentimentalism, so the third period would be replaced by different forms of non-cognitivism: emotivism, prescriptivism, and expressivism. Indeed, non-cognitivism would dominate moral philosophy of the twentieth century until the late 1970s, when various forms of cognitivism and moral realism began to reassert themselves. During this fallow period intuitionism seemed to be a completely dead force, to the extent that many could not understand why anyone ever took it seriously as a moral theory. Thus, for example, in 1967 G. J. Warnock wrote that 'Intuitionism seems, in retrospect, so strange a phenomenon—a body of writing so acute and at the same time so totally unilluminating—that one may wonder how to explain it, what its genesis was.'[20] What, then, were the arguments that were regarded as so damaging to intuitionism and led to its dramatic fall from grace? An important factor in the decline of intuitionism was its commitment to metaphysical and epistemological views that were regarded as both deeply implausible and unnecessary.[21] The key offensive metaphysical view was that moral judgements describe certain non-natural properties. Objections to intuitionists' epistemology focused on their claim that certain moral propositions are self-evident.

---

[18] Intuitive induction is direct inference from some particular fact to the strictly universal law that this fact instantiates. It is not to be confused with standard empirical induction. Unlike empirical induction, one need only be given one example of a principle to know by intuitive induction the universal principle. See C. D. Broad, *Five Types of Ethical Theory* (London: Routledge & Kegan Paul, 1930), 214.   [19] See Thomas Baldwin's contribution to this volume: Ch. 4.

[20] *Contemporary Moral Philosophy*, 16. Warnock attempts to explain this by maintaining that intuitionists lack curiosity and doubt.

[21] William Frankena wrote: 'an intuitionist must believe in simple properties, properties which are of a peculiar non-natural or normative sort, a priori or non-empirical concepts, intuition, self-evident or synthetic necessary propositions, and so on . . . all of these beliefs are hard to defend in the present climate of opinion' (*Ethics*, 86–7).

Non-Natural Properties

It is clear that intuitionists are committed to non-natural, normative properties. Is this commitment unsustainable? Frankena objects to the idea that ethical terms point to such properties on the ground that 'many philosophers cannot find such properties in their experience'.[22] But this objection is taking the perceptual language intuitionists often use far too literally. Intuitionists do not maintain that we experience moral properties in the way that we experience colour properties. Their claim is that when we think of something as being good, we are thinking of it not simply as being, say, pleasant, as the object of a first- or second-order desire, as promoting our interests, as having survival value, or as instantiating some very complex disjunction of natural properties, but as having a certain non-natural character. Their view is based, therefore, not on what we experience, but on what we *think*. Since the intuitionists' view is not intended to be supported by the supposed fact that we experience non-natural properties, the fact that some moral philosophers cannot find such properties in their experience raises no problem for the intuitionists' view.

The belief that we do think in this way is given great credence by Moore's open question argument. According to Moore, whenever we think of an object as being some natural way, as being pleasurable, desired, more evolved, etc., it always makes sense to ask: 'But is it good?' In this sense, all questions of the form 'X has some natural property, but is it good?' are open. What this openness seems to show is that it is one thing to think of something as being a certain natural way, and quite another to think of it as being good. For if we did think that goodness is identical with some natural property, N-ness, then the question 'X is N, but is it good?' would not have this open feel any more than the question 'A is an unmarried man, but is he a bachelor?' does.

But how is this argument supposed to work? Moore seemed to think that it works because analytical identities are obvious and uncontroversial. If Moore is right about this, then if goodness were analytically identical with some natural property (N), then the question 'X is N, but is it good?' would *not* have an open feel. But such questions do have this open feel, so goodness cannot be analytically identified with N-ness.

The trouble with this account of how the argument is supposed to work is that it is open to the objection that not all analytical claims are obvious

---

[22] Ibid., 87.

and thus uncontroversial.[23] But this objection can be avoided if we take up T. M. Scanlon's account of how the argument works. According to Scanlon the openness of the open question argument is explained with reference not to the supposed obviousness of analytical identity claims, but to the fact that judgements about what is good express conclusions about what would be reasons for acting or responding in certain (positive) ways. Natural facts may provide the ground for such practical conclusions, but judging that these natural facts obtain does not by itself involve explicitly drawing these conclusions. It is for this reason, therefore, that questions such as 'This is N, but is it good?' have an open feel. They have an open feel because when we decide that something is good, we conclude that we have reason to adopt some pro-attitude towards it, but in judging simply that it has some natural property, we have not yet formed a conclusion as to whether we have reason to adopt such an attitude towards it.[24] The open question thus forms an argument against any form of analytical naturalism not because if true such naturalism would be obvious, but because we think of goodness as a normative property and natural properties as non-normative.

A naturalist might accept this account of the open question argument, and even its conclusion, but deny that we can make any inferences about the way the world is from the fact that we think about it in certain ways. [25] For the way in which we think about the world is determined by our understanding of the concepts we use to describe it, and we cannot reliably infer that the world is a certain way from the fact that we conceive of it in a certain way. To think that one can make such inferences is to confuse words or concepts with properties,[26] analytical identities with synthetic identities. We know what we mean by certain concepts by a priori reflection, but the nature of the things to which these concepts refer can only be discovered by empirical investigation. We did not discover that water is H_2O or that heat is kinetic molecular energy by a priori reflection on what we mean by 'water' and 'heat', but by empirical investigation. Furthermore, we could not object to the view that heat is kinetic energy on the ground that this is not what we mean when we think of something as hot. But the intuitionists

[23] M. Smith, *The Moral Problem* (Oxford: Blackwell, 1994), 37–8.

[24] T. M. Scanlon, *What we Owe to Each Other* (Cambridge, Mass. Belknap Press, 1998), 96. This raises the question of how natural properties, goodness, and reasons are related to each other, to which I return later.   [25] See e.g. Allan Gibbard's contribution to this volume: Ch. 9.

[26] See e.g. Warnock, *Ethics since 1900*, 17, and H. Putnam, *Reason, Truth and History* (Cambridge: Cambridge University Press, 1981), 207. It should be noted that although Putnam thought that intuitionists such as Moore did confuse concepts and properties, he agreed with Moore that moral properties are non-natural properties (ibid., 211).

seem to object to a naturalistic account of moral properties in precisely this way.

There is, however, reason to think that intuitionists such as Moore and Ross did not confuse concepts and properties. For they were careful to distinguish an elucidation of the meaning of words and an account of the nature of the world with their distinction between proper verbal definitions and definitions of the sort they are interested in (i.e. metaphysical ones).[27] A proper verbal definition of 'good' is simply an account of how most people use the word, whereas a metaphysical definition is one that tells us the nature of the thing of which the concept is a concept.[28] This is not quite the distinction between an analysis of a concept and an account of the nature of a corresponding property, but it is close enough to give us reason to suppose that intuitionists such as Moore and Ross were aware of the distinction between concepts and properties that many think they simply conflate.

But although intuitionists may not have confused concepts and properties, they did seem to believe that there is a certain isomorphism between the structure of our concepts and the nature of the world, such that a proper analysis of our concepts would reveal to us the nature of the corresponding property or thing. This belief is not obviously confused, but the examples of heat and water seem to show that it cannot be accepted as it stands. Intuitionists need not, however, rest their view about the property of goodness on a general thesis about the relation of concepts and properties. All they need do is identify what it is about certain concepts, like the concepts of water and heat, that provides us with reasons to think that the corresponding properties are different, and then argue that these reasons do not apply to the concept of goodness.

With concepts of natural properties and substances like heat and water we have two reasons for thinking that the corresponding properties may be different. First, the concept of heat seems metaphysically superficial and incomplete. It tells us only about the characteristic effects heat has on us and other things, but nothing about its nature. The concept of water seems equally superficial, but for different reasons. This concept only picks out certain surface features of water, such as its being clear, odourless, tasteless, etc. It does not, however, tell us anything about the nature of the substance that has these features. Empirical science seems well suited to complete this

---

[27] See G. E. Moore, *Principia Ethica*, rev. edn. (Cambridge: Cambridge University Press, 1993), 60 and 63, and W. D. Ross, *The Right and the Good* (Indianapolis: Hackett, 1988), 1–2.

[28] Moore, *Principia Ethica*, 60. Moore makes this point with reference to the concept of a horse, though it is generally agreed that his example is not at all helpful.

picture by investigating the property that has these distinctive effects or surface features. In doing this, empirical science provides us with an account of heat and water that is metaphysically deeper than the one provided by the corresponding concepts.

Secondly, even if the concept of heat were not incomplete or superficial, in so far as it is a concept of a natural property, we have good reason to think that the empirical sciences are much better equipped than a priori reflection to discover the nature of heat. The same is true of the concept of water. In so far as this is a concept of a natural substance, the empirical sciences are far better suited than a priori reflection to tell us the nature of this substance.

These reasons do not apply to the concept of goodness. First, this concept does not seem to be metaphysically superficial or incomplete in the way that the concept of heat or water is. When we think of something as good, we do not think of it merely as having certain effects on us, or as picking out certain surface properties the property of goodness has, but think of it as having a distinctive characteristic. Not all intuitionists agreed with Moore that nothing could be said about the nature of this characteristic (though they all agreed that this is a non-natural property). A. C. Ewing, for example, maintained that the characteristic we have in mind when we think of something as being good is the property it has of being the fitting object of a pro-attitude. If this, or something like it, is correct, then the concept of goodness does not merely describe certain properties goodness has, but aspires to tell us what goodness is.[29] It does not, therefore, call for a metaphysically deeper account from some other source in the way that the concept of heat or water does.

Furthermore, if the open question argument shows that we do not think of goodness as a natural property, then we have no reason to think that the empirical sciences are better equipped than a priori reflection to tell us the nature of this property. On the contrary, we have good reason to think that empirical science is rather poorly equipped to do this job. In this respect the concept of goodness is, for better or for worse, like the concept of God. The only way in which we could know what it is that we are thinking about when we think about God is through a priori reflection on the concept of God. The concept of God is not only metaphysically deep, it is such that it would be crazy to think that empirical science could reveal an alternative,

---

[29] Ross would argue that something is only a fitting object of a pro-attitude because it is good (*The Foundations of Ethics* (Oxford: Clarendon Press, 1939), 278–9). This is, however, questionable. One might plausibly think that certain pro-attitudes are warranted simply by the fact that an action is kind, or considerate, rather than the fact that kindness and considerateness are good.

yet more accurate, account of God's nature. Similarly, the only way in which we could know what it is that we are thinking of when we think of something as good is by a priori reflection on the concept of goodness. Of course we could not know by reflection on the concept of goodness that this property is instantiated in the world any more than we could know by reflection on the concept of God that he exists (*pace* St Anselm and Descartes). But it is by a priori reflection on the concept of goodness that we know what it is we are looking for when we consider whether anything in the world is good—that is, whether anything instantiates the property of being good.

If our concept of goodness is not metaphysically superficial or incomplete, why do some metaphysicians believe that the property of goodness differs from how our concept represents it as being? If one accepts that the concept of goodness cannot be identified with the concept of some natural property, why think that empirical science can tell us anything about the nature of goodness? What drives certain philosophers to draw these conclusions is a deep-seated suspicion of non-natural properties. Sometimes this suspicion rests on a confusion of non-natural properties with supernatural, other-worldly properties. But others do not make this mistake, and rest their distrust of such properties on other grounds. In deciding whether we have good reason to think that the property of goodness (as well as other moral properties) differs significantly from the concept we have of it, we need to consider whether goodness as we ordinarily think of it is as mysterious as naturalists insist.

John Mackie famously argued that we have good reason to think that moral properties do not exist, because they are both metaphysically and epistemologically queer. 'If there were objective values, then they would be entities or qualities or relations of a very strange sort, utterly different from anything else in the universe. Correspondingly, if we were aware of them, it would have to be by some special faculty of moral perception or intuition, utterly different from our ordinary ways of knowing everything else.'[30] I put aside, for the moment, the epistemological issues Mackie raises, as I will address these later. For the moment I shall focus on the two metaphysical objections to non-natural properties Mackie raises. The first peculiarity, according to Mackie, seems to be that such properties would have to be utterly independent of our feelings and desires, yet able essentially to motivate us when perceived. Mackie writes: 'An objective good would be sought

---

[30] J. L. Mackie, *Ethics: Inventing Right and Wrong* (Harmondsworth: Penguin, 1977), 38.

by anyone who was acquainted with it, not because of any contingent fact that this person, or every person, is so constituted that he desires this end, but just because the end has to-be-pursuedness somehow built into it.'[31] And to-be-pursuedness is understood by Mackie to be a kind of power to motivate agents in certain ways. What generates the metaphysical queerness of moral properties is, therefore, a combination of the view that such properties are utterly distinct from us yet such that they must motivate when 'apprehended'. A second peculiarity stems from their consequential character. 'Wrongness', Mackie writes, must somehow be 'consequential' or 'supervenient'. An act is wrong because it is, say, a piece of deliberate cruelty. 'But just *what in the world* is signified by this "because"?'[32]

These points seem to tell against the idea that moral properties are non-natural properties, but I think the appearances here are deceptive. These points in fact tell against the view that moral properties are simple. It is the Moorean view that goodness is a simple property that implies that it must be utterly independent of us and our psychological states. This independence makes it very difficult indeed to see how it could be such as necessarily to call forth certain responses from us when apprehended. But intuitionists are not committed to the view that goodness is a simple property. Intuitionists such as A. C. Ewing and more recently John McDowell think that goodness is a complex property. Ewing maintains that to be good is to be the object of a fitting pro-attitude,[33] and McDowell holds that it is to be the object of merited approval.[34] As I understand the open question argument, goodness is best understood in terms of reasons rather than fittingness or meritedness. A plausible account of goodness in terms of reasons is provided by what Scanlon calls the 'buck-passing' account.[35] According to the buck-passing account of goodness, the fact that X is good is the fact that X has properties that give us reason to adopt some pro-attitude towards X. The buck-passing account of goodness goes some way to addressing Mackie's first metaphysical objection by allowing us to deny that moral properties must be utterly independent of us and our responses in order to be objective.[36] On this view, goodness cannot be objective in the

---

[31] Mackie, *Ethics: Inventing Right and Wrong*, 40. [32] Ibid., 11.

[33] A. C. Ewing, *The Definition of Good* (New York: MacMillan, 1947), 152.

[34] J. McDowell, 'Values and Secondary Qualities', in Ted Honderich, (ed.), *Morality and Objectivity: A Tribute to J. L. Mackie* (London: Routledge & Kegan Paul, 1985), 110–29.

[35] *What we Owe to Each Other*, 95 ff.

[36] McDowell makes this point with reference to his own account of value in terms of being the merited object of approval. In essence, however, his understanding of goodness is the same as the buck-passing account I endorse.

sense that it is utterly mind-independent, for this property cannot be under-stood without reference to certain psychological states (the pro-attitudes we have reason to adopt). It is, however, objective in the important sense that it is independent of how we as individuals happen to think or feel, and is thus there to be discovered.

But, Mackie might object, even if we are right that for X to be good is for it to have properties that give us reason to adopt some pro-attitude towards it, this would not explain how knowledge that X is good necessarily causes us to adopt some pro-attitude towards it. So this account fails to explain how an objective good would be sought by anyone who was acquainted with it. This is right, but does not cause a problem for a buck-passing intu-itionist. For the to-be-pursuedness that is built in to objective goodness is normative, not causal. If we come to believe that X is good, we may not be caused to pursue X, but we will believe that we have reason to pursue it, and this is all that is needed to capture the (normative) to-be-pursuedness that is built in to objective goodness.

It may be objected that we have still failed to capture the practical nature of evaluative judgements. For if such judgements describe how some aspect of the world is, and do not necessarily motivate us, it may be argued that we will have done all that reason requires of us simply in so far as we come to *believe* that X is good, and believing I have reason to pursue X is not pursu-ing X.[37] This argument, however, seems to me to be flawed. The fact that I think that evaluative judgements are property-ascribing statements does not commit me to the view that I have done all that reason demands simply in forming the *belief* that the pursuit of X by me is warranted. For if I fail to *act* in the light of this belief, then I will have failed to do what I believe the situation warrants, and this would be a form of *practical* irrationality. The practical nature of moral judgements need not, therefore, be captured by thinking of them as causing a kind of psychological push. It can be captured simply by noting that unless we *act* in the light of our moral beliefs—that is, in the light of our beliefs that certain practical responses by us are warrant-ed—we will be practically irrational.

One might have a sense that this account still seems too cognitive—that it does not capture the fact that morality is primarily about how we should act and feel, rather than about what we should believe. Moral judgements,

---

[37] This is the ground of Simon Blackburn's objection to 'Cornell Realists'. His main criticism of Cornell Realism is that by identifying moral properties with certain natural properties it makes moral judgement far too cognitive, and thus fails to capture our take on the bearers of those prop-erties (*Ruling Passions: A Theory of Practical Reasoning* (Oxford: Clarendon Press, 1998), 119–21).

it is said, 'do not seem to be mere property-ascribing statements, natural or non-natural; they express favourable or unfavourable attitudes, recommend, prescribe, and the like'.[38] Here the worry is that our account still represents moral knowledge as a kind of dry theoretical knowledge.[39] Someone might insist not only that certain feelings are rational *responses* to moral judgements, but that these judgements *express* these feelings.

But, as Ross pointed out, it is a mistake to think that we must choose between the view that moral judgements describe the world in certain ways and the view that they express our feelings. These are not exclusive options.

> . . . what we *express* when we call an object good is our attitude towards it, but what we *mean* is something about the object itself and not about our attitude towards it. When we call an object good we are commending it, but to commend it is not to say that we are commending it, but to say that it has a certain characteristic, which we think it would have whether we commended it or not.[40]

It may be, as Ross thought, that in judging that something is good or right we express feelings of approval, but this does not prevent such judgements from describing the world in some respect. There is nothing about intuitionism as such, therefore, that means that we must conceive of moral knowledge as a kind of dry, detached, theoretical knowledge. Intuitionists may, as Ross did, maintain that moral judgements in part express our attitudes towards certain things, and that to think of something as good or bad is to think of these attitudes as warranted by their objects. If all of this is right, then Mackie's first argument for the view that moral properties, as intuitionists understand them, are mysterious gives us reason to reject the view that these properties are simple. It does not, however, give us reason to abandon the view that they are non-natural properties.

Mackie's second metaphysical objection to the idea of moral properties focuses on deontic properties, but it applies equally to evaluative ones. Mackie objects that it is unclear what in the world it means to say that an act is wrong *because* it is cruel, or unkind, or selfish. Intuitionists certainly do not say enough about what the relation is between rightness and the ground of rightness (or between goodness and what makes something good). And, once again, their tendency to insist that rightness (and/or goodness) are

---

[38] Frankena, *Ethics*, 88.

[39] See e.g. P. H. Nowell-Smith, *Ethics* (Harmondsworth: Penguin, 1954), 41 and 48. For a Kantian form of the objection that realists reduce practical reason to theoretical reason, see O. O'Neill, 'Instituting Principles: Between Duty and Action', *Southern Journal of Philosophy*, 36, suppl. (1997), 79–96.   [40] Ross, *The Foundations of Ethics*, 255.

simple properties does not help them offer such an account. But Mackie presents no argument for the view that they *could* not say anything about this relation, and it is simply a mistake to think that intuitionists are committed to simple, indefinable moral properties. I have suggested that goodness is best understood as a complex property—that is, as the property of having properties that give us reason to respond in certain positive ways—and there are intuitionists who endorse a very similar view. I can see no reason why intuitionists cannot understand rightness as well as goodness in terms of reasons. Intuitionists could (and in my view should) embrace not only a buck-passing account of goodness, but also a buck-passing account of rightness.[41] According to such an account, the fact that φ-ing is right is the same as the fact that φ-ing has properties that give us conclusive reason to do it. Similarly, the fact that φ-ing is wrong is the fact that it has properties that give us conclusive reason not to do it. If intuitionists were to understand thin moral properties in this way, then they would be able to offer a plausible account of the relation that these properties stand to their ground. I will illustrate this point with reference to wrongness, but exactly the same account can be offered of rightness, goodness, and badness.

For cruelness, or selfishness, to *make* an act wrong is just for these features of one's action to be the reason-giving properties pointed to by the property one's act has of being wrong. To say that an act is wrong is to say that we have conclusive reason not to do it. To say that it is wrong *because* it is cruel is to say that it is the cruelness of this act that gives us conclusive reason not to do it—that is, that its cruelness is the property that has this reason-giving property. Intuitionists' tendency to insist that rightness and wrongness are simple properties obscures this, as it makes it seem as though there is a relation of wrong-making between the ground of wrongness and wrongness, and as Mackie points out, it is unclear what this relation could be. The buck-passing account of wrongness enables us to see that this relation is not one between some feature of the wrong act and its being wrong,

---

[41] Scanlon rejects a buck-passing account of wrongness (and presumably rightness) because he thinks that the wrongness of an act gives us a very strong reason not to do it, and this could not be the case if the wrongness of an act consisted in its having other properties that give us strong reasons not to do it (*What we Owe to Each Other*, 11). My view is that we should reject the idea that it is the wrongness of an act that gives us reason not to do it, at least if this is understood as a reason in addition to the reasons provided by the considerations that make the act wrong, though I cannot argue for this view here. Something like a buck-passing account of rightness can be found in John Balguy's intuitionism ('The Foundations of Moral Goodness', in L. A. Selby-Bigge (ed.), *The British Moralists: Being Selections from the Writers Principally of the Eighteenth Century* (New York: Dover, 1965), 191).

but between this feature and some agent or agents. Furthermore, this account enables us to see that this relation is a normative one—it is the property this feature has of standing in a reason-giving relation to some agent or agents. For intuitionists who adopt the buck-passing account of thin moral properties, therefore, there is no metaphysical mystery generated by the fact that these properties obtain *in virtue of* some other property.

Is there some other reason to think that the ordinary conception of moral properties, as it is captured by intuitionists, is mysterious and thus in need of revision? Geoffrey Warnock maintains that moral properties as intuitionists understand them are mysterious because nothing positive can be said about them. Intuitionists, he writes, insist that goodness and rightness designate properties, but do not tell us the nature of these properties: they insist there is a difference between these properties and other properties, but do not say what this difference is.[42] The first of these objections stems (once again) from the supposed simplicity of rightness and goodness, rather than from their non-naturalness. It is because they are simple that no definition of them can be provided. By itself, however, this does not make them mysterious. It may be that colour properties are simple in just the way we ordinarily think of them as being, but I do not think that if they were, their simplicity would make them mysterious.[43] Simplicity only implies indefinability, not mysteriousness. In any case, as I have stated, the idea that thin moral properties are simple is not essential to intuitionism. So even if simplicity did imply mysteriousness, the intuitionist view about moral properties need not imply any mystery.

Warnock seems to be on better ground when he objects to the intuitionists' view because they do not tell us what is distinctive of moral, as opposed to natural, properties. For it may be objected that if nothing can be said about what it is a for a property to be non-natural, it will not be at all clear what it is intuitionists are maintaining when they maintain that moral properties are non-natural. But Moore, at least, had a go at defining what it is for a property to be a non-natural property. According to Moore, natural properties are those with which the natural sciences and psychology are concerned.[44] If natural properties are those about which empirical investigation can inform us, then non-natural properties will be those about which the empirical sciences can tell us nothing.

[42] *Contemporary Moral Philosophy*, 13.

[43] It should be noted that intuitionists say many things about goodness and rightness, even when they insist that these properties are indefinable. See e.g. Ross, *The Foundations of Ethics*, 53 ff and 278–9.   [44] *Principia Ethica*, 92; see also p. 13.

Warnock might object that this is an inadequate account of the difference between moral and natural properties, but this would be a different objection. It is one thing to say that intuitionists tell us nothing about the natural–non-natural distinction, and quite another to say that what they tell us about this distinction is inadequate. It may be that Moore's account of the natural–non-natural distinction is inadequate, and that no satisfactory account of this distinction can be provided. If this is correct, then it will present a problem not only for intuitionism, but for naturalism also. For if the intuitionists' claim that moral properties are non-natural properties is empty or vague because they cannot provide a clear account of what it is for a property to be natural, then the naturalists' view that the only properties that exist are natural properties will be equally empty or vague. If, therefore, this is a problem for intuitionism, it is just as much a problem for naturalism.

In any case, it may be a mistake to become too obsessed with offering a *definition* of what it is for a property to be natural. There is a certain style of account of moral properties which is naturalistic. It is typically an account of moral properties in terms of either psychological states, evolutionary properties, causation and welfare or social stability, some functional property, or something of this sort. If we cannot provide an account of the natural, it is sufficient to maintain that moral properties cannot be identified with this sort of property or combination of such properties. This response is to some extent imprecise, but it is not so vague as to sap the intuitionists' view about the nature of moral properties of all content.

Critics of intuitionism fail, therefore, to show that moral properties as we ordinarily conceive of them are unacceptably queer or mysterious. Many of their objections stem not from the view that moral properties are non-natural, but from the view that they are simple. But intuitionists (and ordinary understanding) are not committed to the view that moral properties must be simple. If we abandon the view that moral properties are simple, and understand them in terms of reasons, they will no longer appear queer or mysterious.

I have claimed that there might be three reasons for thinking that the properties of goodness and rightness are different from our concept of them. We would have reason for thinking this if (1) our concept of goodness and rightness were metaphysically superficial or incomplete; (2) we thought of these properties as being such that the empirical sciences are best equipped to discover their nature; or (3) our concept of these properties represented them as being mysterious in some way. I have argued that none of these reasons apply to these moral concepts. If this is right, then the only reason one might have for supposing that goodness and rightness are different from the way we conceive of them would be a metaphysics which dogmatically insists that only natural properties exist, and that is no reason at all.

Self-Evidence

Intuitionists believe that certain basic moral propositions are self-evident, and thus can be known directly by intuition. It is this belief that William Frankena finds hardest to accept,[45] and many share his view. But care is needed here in getting clear what it is that is objectionable. For some it may simply be the view that we have knowledge in ethics, as some will maintain that we can have only moral opinions, and others will deny that moral judgements express cognitive states at all. But if it is accepted that moral judgements do express cognitive states and at least some of these amount to knowledge, the objection will be not that intuitionists think that we can know certain moral truths, but that they claim *a certain sort* of moral knowledge: self-evidence. It is this specific type of knowledge that is dismissed out of hand.

But despite the fact that the intuitionists' attachment to self-evident moral propositions has very often been dismissed out of hand, little care has been taken to get clear on what it is for a proposition to be self-evident.[46] It is worth while, therefore, spending some time clarifying this.[47] For a proposition to be self-evident is for it to be knowable on the basis of an understanding of it. So understood, there is no difference between a proposition's being self-evident and its being knowable a priori.[48] (It is partly for this reason that intuitionists so often compare basic moral propositions to mathematical ones.) Self-evident propositions are, therefore, something that most empiricists as well as rationalists can allow.[49] What

---

[45] *Ethics*, 88.

[46] Intuitionists are as guilty of this neglect as their critics, and as a result run together distinct claims.

[47] My understanding of the self-evident draws on Robert Audi's 'Intuitionism, Pluralism, and the Foundations of Ethics', in W. Sinnott-Armstrong and M. Timmons (eds.), *Moral Knowledge?* (Oxford: Oxford University Press, 1996), 101–36.

[48] Some define a priori propositions as those that can be known independently of experience, but this negative claim is true because the positive claim that a priori truths are knowable on the basis of an understanding of them is true.

[49] There is nothing in empiricism as such that rules out the idea that analytic propositions can be known a priori and are thus self-evident.

will divide them will not be a belief in self-evident propositions, but whether non-analytical propositions can be self-evident. What empiricists will find objectionable about the idea of self-evident moral propositions, therefore, is not the very idea of a self-evident proposition, but the idea that the sort of propositions intuitionists defend (synthetic ones) can be self-evident. For by their very nature (not as moral but as synthetic propositions) they cannot be self-evident, according to empiricists.

A common objection to the view that certain moral propositions are self-evident is the fact that there is disagreement about them.[50] But why should we think that disagreement about P undermines the view that P is self-evident? One might conclude that there are no self-evident moral propositions from the fact of disagreement if one supposed that a self-evident proposition must be obvious to all who consider it. But not all self-evident propositions are obvious. The propositions that 'Circles are figures bounded by a line that is equidistant from its centre', that 'All female mammals suckle their young', and that 'If all As are Bs, and no Cs are Bs, then no Cs are As' are all self-evident, but may not be obvious to everyone, at least at first sight. What we should conclude from the fact of disagreement is not that there are no self-evident moral propositions, but that if some are self-evident, they are not obviously true. But this conclusion in no way rules out the possibility of self-evident moral propositions.

It is sometimes thought that disagreement among intuitionists about basic moral propositions gives us good reason to suppose that these propositions are not self-evident.[51] Moore, for example, thought that it is self-evident that there is only one duty—the duty to produce as much good as possible—and that all other duties could be derived from this one. Ross, on the other hand, tells us that, despite a genuine attempt to see the self-evidence of this claim, he could not lose a sense that promise-keeping has a binding force that is independent of consequence-based considerations.[52] How could Moore and Ross come to differ in this way if basic moral propositions are self-evident?

The first thing to note is that Moore is making two claims here. The first is that our duty to promote the good is basic and is thus self-evident. The second is that this duty is the only basic duty we have. Having noted this, we can see that Moore and Ross agree about the first claim. Ross, of course,

[50] See e.g. McIntyre, *A Short History of Ethics*, 254.
[51] See Berys Gaut's contribution to this volume: Ch. 6.
[52] *The Right and the Good*, 40.

would claim that the duty to promote the good is only prima facie, but that is because he disagrees with Moore's second claim—that this duty is the only basic duty. Why did Moore think that this second claim is self-evident? This was because he held that the consequentialist duty is analytically true. If it is analytically true, then if some act is a duty it must be because it promotes the best outcome, for on this view its promoting the best outcome is what it is for this act to be a duty. But I think there is good reason to think that Moore did not reflect very carefully about this. If he had, he would have seen that his open question argument shows that while consequentialism might be true, it is not analytically true. The question 'Act X maximizes good, but is it right?' is as open as any such question about whether some natural property is good. If the latter openness shows that goodness cannot be analytically identified with any natural property, then the former shows that rightness cannot be analytically identified with the consequentialist principle. Indeed, Moore himself came to abandon his analytical consequentialism in his later work.[53] Now if consequentialism is not analytically true, I can see no reason to think that it is self-evident that the only basic duty we have is the duty to promote the good. It may be true that this *is* the only basic duty, but we cannot come to know this by attending to the proposition that states that it is. Moore thought that we could because he mistakenly thought that consequentialism is analytically true. But he could only have thought this through a failure to reflect carefully on what he was saying.

It may be objected that many people have a good understanding of the moral propositions intuitionists maintain are self-evident, but nonetheless insist that they are neither self-evident nor even true. Does this imply that these propositions could not be self-evident? First, as Robert Audi has pointed out, we do not need to know that P is self-evident to know that P on the basis of an understanding of it.[54] To believe a self-evident proposition is not to believe that it is self-evident, and is consistent with the belief that it is not self-evident. Consequently, the fact that many philosophers deny that certain moral propositions are self-evident in no way casts doubt on the view that they are.

Does the fact that one can have a good understanding of these propositions yet deny that they are true show that they cannot be self-evident? I do not see how it could. For a proposition to be self-evident is for it to be know-*able* on the basis of an understanding of it. It does not follow from this that

---

[53] G. E. Moore, *Ethics* (London: Oxford University Press, 1966), 22 and 27.
[54] 'Intuitionism, Pluralism, and the Foundations of Ethics', 106–7.

if P is self-evident and one understands P, then one will believe that P. All it means is that one's understanding of P provides a sufficient warrant for believing that P, not that one must recognize one's understanding as a sufficient warrant.

Some object to the idea that certain moral propositions are self-evident on the ground that this leads to dogmatism. Thus, for example, Korsgaard claims that all that intuitionists can do in the face of disbelief is insist that what they are saying is true,[55] and Nowell-Smith writes: 'If I do not recognize the truth of your statements of objective moral fact, you can do nothing to convince me by argument but are, like the subjectivist, thrown back on force or acquiescence.'[56] We should be on the guard against dogmatism, and be aware that many of our moral beliefs may be the product merely of upbringing, self-interest, or ideology. But a commitment to self-evident moral propositions does not make intuitionists especially vulnerable to dogmatism. For intuitionists do not dogmatically assert the self-evidence of anything that seems true to them, but claim this status only for those apparently basic moral convictions that survive careful reflection.[57] Such reflection is aimed at getting a clear understanding of the proposition in question in order to ascertain whether we really do think it expresses a morally basic truth. It also aims at providing arguments for its truth and self-evidence. If the proposition survives such reflection, then the intuitionist can do more than merely assert the truth of the proposition that someone else denies. He can take them through the form of reflection that convinced him of the truth and self-evidence of this proposition.

It may be thought that this is incoherent, that someone who thinks that P is self-evident cannot offer an argument for P.[58] But despite the fact that many intuitionists, as well as their critics, insist that no argument can be provided for a self-evident proposition, they are mistaken. For there is nothing about the fact that a proposition can be known solely on the basis of an understanding of it that rules out the possibility that it can be known in some other way as well, i.e. that it is epistemologically overdetermined.[59] It may be that not every self-evident proposition is

[55] C. Korsgaard, *The Sources of Normativity* (Cambridge: Cambridge University Press, 1996), 38.
[56] *Ethics*, 46.   [57] See my contribution to this volume: Ch. 5.
[58] M. Warnock seems to think this (*Ethics since 1900*, 53), as does Ross in *The Right and the Good*, 30. In an earlier paper, however, Ross seems to maintain that self-evident propositions can receive an independent justification. See his 'The Basis of Objective Judgements in Ethics', *International Journal of Ethics*, 37/2 (1927), 121.
[59] See D. O. Brink, 'Common Sense and First Principles in Sidgwick's Methods', *Social Philosophy and Policy*, 11 (1994), 179–201, for an alternative view.

epistemologically overdetermined, but the thought that some are is in no way absurd.

Some think that claiming the status of self-evidence for some of our moral convictions is simply an illegitimate way of parading subjective convictions as objective, rational truths.[60] But, as I have said, intuitionists are very careful which of their convictions they claim the status of self-evidence for. It is only those convictions that can plausibly be said to be basic that are even contenders for the status of self-evidence, and of these it is only those that survive careful reflection on their meaning and coherence that are claimed to be self-evident. Of course such reflection will not *guarantee* that these propositions are true, let alone that they are self-evident, but infallibility is too much to ask of any moral theory. All that can reasonably be asked is that sufficient care is taken to remove error and distorting influences, and there is nothing about the view that certain moral propositions are self-evident that rules out such care.

Mackie and others object to the intuitionists' epistemology on the ground that it assumes we have some strange faculty for perceiving moral properties. But it should be clear by now that no such faculty is assumed by intuitionists.[61] They claim that certain moral propositions can be known by intuition, not because they think we have such a sixth sense, but because they think these propositions are self-evident. Intuition is not for them a way of perceiving a property, but is a way of grasping the truth of certain (a priori) propositions. It might be thought that a priori knowledge in general presupposes a mysterious faculty of direct insight, but then one's objection is not to intuitionism as such, but to the very idea of a priori knowledge. Furthermore, I see no reason why we should think that a priori knowledge requires such a mysterious faculty. All it requires is the ability to understand and think.[62]

Once we get a clear understanding of what it is for a proposition to be self-evident then we can see that the intuitionists' view that certain moral beliefs are self-evident is not vulnerable to the sort of criticisms it is often thought to be, and is by no means obviously false. Furthermore, if certain

---

[60] R. M. Hare, for example, claims that 'intuitionism is nearly always a form of disguised subjectivism' ('Rawls' Theory of Justice', in N. Daniels (ed.), *Reading Rawls: Critical Studies on Rawls' 'A Theory of Justice'* (Oxford: Blackwell, 1975), 83). See also A. MacIntyre, *After Virtue: A Study in Moral Theory* (London: Duckworth, 1985), 17.

[61] See Roger Crisp's contribution to this volume: Ch. 2.

[62] See L. BonJour, *In Defence of Pure Reason: A Rationalist Account of A Priori Justification* (Cambridge: Cambridge University Press, 1998), 107–9.

moral principles have the kind of strict universality that intuitionists claim for them, then if we know them, this knowledge could not be empirical. For we could no more know by experience that certain acts are always prima facie wrong than we could know by experience that whenever we put two lots of two things together we will have four things. If, therefore, such moral principles are knowable, they could only be known a priori, and this was all the intuitionists were asserting when they asserted that they are self-evident.[63] Objections to the view that such principles are self-evident will have to deny either that these principles can be known at all, or that they have the kind of universal validity that means that they could only be known a priori. The first option seems epistemologically too pessimistic, while the second is not an epistemological objection at all, but the denial that there are strictly universal moral principles.

A Renewal of Interest

Although intuitionism has not achieved the sort of dominance it enjoyed in earlier periods, it is far from being the dead force it was thought to be in the 1950s and 1960s. On the contrary, there are a growing number of moral philosophers who are willing to defend important aspects of intuitionism and who may be seen as working within the intuitionist tradition.[64] Many factors contribute to this renewal of interest in intuitionism. One of the main factors is the gradual realization of the apparently irredeemable shortcomings of the sort of non-cognitivism that replaced the third period of intuitionism. In many ways, therefore, the contemporary renewal of interest in intuitionism is similar to that of the second period of intuitionism. It was recognized that morality could not be understood as the emotivists or prescriptivists understood it, and although expressivism retains a certain philosophical vitality which emotivism and prescriptivism have lost, it has only managed to survive as a form of quasi-realism—that is, by

---

[63] Things are complicated slightly by Ross's insistence that we can only know universally valid moral truths by means of intuitive induction from our knowledge of particular cases (*The Foundations of Ethics*, 170). But Ross seems to think that this process is a ladder that can be kicked away once we have climbed up it. For once we have got to the point where we can see the truth of some universal principle we no longer need to go through this process again, but can know it on the basis of an understanding of it.

[64] Robert Audi, Jonathan Dancy, John McDowell, David McNaughton, Derek Parfit, and David Wiggins.

looking as much like moral realism as it can while remaining within a Humean framework. With the demise of the dominance of non-cognitivism in ethics came a renewed belief that cognitivism and some form of moral realism are defensible after all. And once these views were no longer regarded as crazy, intuitionism could no longer be dismissed simply because it is committed to them.

Another important factor in the renewal of interest in intuitionism is a renewed confidence in the very idea of a priori knowledge as well as the distinction between the analytic and the synthetic. Quine's famous attack on the analytic–synthetic distinction in his 'Two Dogmas of Empiricism'[65] had the effect not only of leading many to regard *this* distinction with suspicion, but also to question the possibility of a priori knowledge. This was partly because of the empiricist view that only analytic truths could be known a priori, for if this view is correct, then if there are no analytical truths, nothing can be known a priori. Furthermore, some thought that Quine's holism caused problems for the a priori. If a proposition can be known a priori, then it is known independently of any experience. But if it is known independently of any experience, then no experience could falsify it. If, therefore, every proposition is revisable in the light of experience, then no proposition could be known a priori. As Katz puts it: 'With the collapse of the analytic/synthetic distinction and the eclipse of Carnap's logical empiricism, the way was open for a neo-Millian naturalism in which all truths are contingent (in the sense of being revisable on the basis of observation of nature), all objects are natural objects, and all knowledge is acquired on the basis of the empirical methods of the natural sciences.'[66] But more recently Quine's attack on the analytic–synthetic distinction has come to be regarded as less devastating than it first appeared. It may be devastating only for Carnap's conception of this distinction, but Carnap's conception of the analytic–synthetic distinction is not the only, or even the best, way of understanding the distinction.[67] Consequently, the intuitionists' view that basic moral propositions are synthetic a priori propositions could no longer be regarded as clearly hopeless simply in so far as it utilizes the concept of the synthetic.

---

[65] *Philosophical Review*, 60 (1951), 20–43; repr. in W. V. O. Quine, *From a Logical Point of View* (Cambridge, Mass.: Harvard University Press).

[66] J. J. Katz, *The Metaphysics of Meaning* (Cambridge, Mass.: MIT Press, 1990), 15. Katz goes on to argue that Quine's arguments against intensionalist theories of meaning are flawed.

[67] J. J. Katz, 'Some Remarks on Quine on Analyticity', *Journal of Philosophy*, 64/2 (1967), 36–52.

Furthermore, it has been argued that even if true, Quine's holism does not undermine the possibility of a priori knowledge. All that a priori knowledge implies is that a non-empirical justification can be provided for certain propositions, which, in the absence of opposing reasons, would be sufficient for knowledge. This is consistent with the view that experience could falsify these propositions. For experience may give us more reason to reject certain propositions than our non-empirical justification does for believing them.[68] On top of this, a growing number of philosophers have come to believe that we cannot do without a priori knowledge, and that some of this is synthetic.[69] So even if Quine's holism did render such knowledge impossible, this would give us reason to question his holism rather than a priori knowledge. There is, therefore, a renewed sense that we both need and have a priori knowledge. Many are still dubious that there are synthetic a priori *moral* propositions, but the fact that such knowledge is no longer ruled out simply in virtue of the fact that it is supposed to be synthetic and a priori means that the intuitionists' claim that certain moral propositions are self-evident cannot be dismissed without argument.

In Defence of Naivety

So far I have talked of the removal of obstacles to intuitionism. I shall finish with what I take to be a strong consideration in favour of the sort of Dogmatic Intuitionism Sidgwick thought was inadequate. In 1912 Prichard wrote that, because of growing dissatisfaction with moral philosophy, he was led to the view that the whole subject, as it is normally understood, rests on a mistake. Part of his dissatisfaction was that so many of the views and arguments in books of moral philosophy are 'so unconvincing and artificial'.[70] They are artificial in the sense that they do not gel with what we really think, as Ross would say. If asked why we think lying is wrong, we might point to the fact that in lying we betray the trust the other person has placed in us to tell the truth, or that we harm the other person in some way. If someone then went on to ask us what is wrong with harming, or betraying the trust of others, most would find it difficult to find something further to say.

---

[68] See A. Casullo, 'Revisability, Reliablism, and A Priori Knowledge', *Philosophy and Phenomenological Research*, 49 (1988), 187–213.　　[69] BonJour, *In Defence of Pure Reason*.

[70] H. A. Prichard, 'Does Moral Philosophy Rest on a Mistake?', in Prichard, *Moral Obligation: Essays and Lectures*, ed. W. D. Ross (Oxford: Clarendon Press, 1949), 1.

Introduction

To many it will seem as though we have already hit moral bedrock with considerations of fidelity and non-maleficence.

It might be argued that betraying the trust of others is wrong because in doing this we are acting on a principle that could not be willed as a universal law, or because a society in which trust is respected will be a happier society than one in which it is betrayed. But such Kantian and consequentialist support will strike us both as irrelevant and unnecessary. Pre-theoretically, we do not think that considerations of fidelity are morally salient for the reasons Kantians and consequentialists claim, but treat them as morally salient on their own account.

It is for this reason, I think, that intuitionists like Prichard think that so much moral philosophy is unpersuasive and abstract. It is not simply that we do not think in the way certain moral philosophers maintain, but that we cannot convince ourselves that we *should* think in this way. By insisting that ordinary moral thought be taken more seriously than it often is, the philosophy of intuitionists like Reid, Price, Prichard, and Ross avoid this artificiality. This is not to say that such intuitionists are hostile to theory. As we have seen, their ethical theories embrace distinctive meta-ethical and epistemological views. What they are opposed to is not theory as such, but a certain form of moral theory: a type of theory that opens up too great a rift between the way in which we actually think and deliberate and a theory that tries to make sense of this. In this they seem to be correct. One might be able to systematize our basic moral convictions by subsuming them under some single principle, but if we cannot convince ourselves that these convictions are true simply *because* they happen to fall under this principle, then the cost of such systematicity will be the sort of artificiality of which Prichard complains.

It is often objected (and not only by the critics of intuitionism) that it is illegitimate to give such an important role to the reflections of common sense. Moral theory, it is said, should not merely clarify common sense but criticize it in the light of independent theory. The trouble with this is that for such criticisms to have bite—that is, to be regarded as *good* criticisms—we must be able, after reflection, not merely to mouth their conclusions, but authentically to affirm them. If, for instance, we cannot give up our sense that promises have a special binding force that is independent of the good consequences a commitment to fidelity will bring, then we cannot accept that a theory which requires us to do so could be correct. As Ross puts it: 'to ask us to give up at the bidding of a theory our actual apprehension of what is [prima facie] right and what is [prima facie] wrong seems like asking people to repudiate their actual experience of

26

beauty, at the bidding of a theory which says 'only that which satisfies such and such conditions can be beautiful'.[71] Reference to what we really think would, of course, be inappropriate in science, for here we have a much more reliable method of discovering non-normative truths about the world. But we cannot establish moral truths by empirical research, or experiment. Such research may tell us, for example, that certain animals can or cannot feel pain, but it cannot tell us that these facts are morally relevant, that they give us moral reason to treat these animals in certain ways. The only way of establishing moral truth is by reflection on what we really think once the relevant concepts and principles have been clarified, distinguished from each other, and systematized. It must, of course, be allowed that this method will not *guarantee* truth, but this gives us no more reason to abandon this method in ethics than fallibility gives us good reason to abandon experiment and observation in the natural sciences.

The further we stand back from some practice, or phenomenon, the more it will appear absurd and senseless. If some practice appears to us in this way, the best we can hope for is some sort of external account of why people participate in this practice (ignoring, of course, their own explanations, which are thought to be hopelessly lost in the internal perspective). It is because modern critics such as Nietzsche, Marx, and Freud start from such a perspective that they believe that the only possible explanation of morality can be with reference to something like a will to power, ideology, or fear. But the error may lie not with those who stick closely to the pre-theoretical deliverances of common moral consciousness, but with those who stand so far away from the phenomena that these deliverances can only appear naive and mistaken. As Hegel wrote: 'If the fear of falling into error sets up a mistrust of Science, which in the absence of such scruples gets on with the work itself, and actually cognises something, it is hard to see why we should not turn round and mistrust this very mistrust. Should we not be concerned as to whether this fear of error is not just the error itself?'[72] Hegel's point here is not about ethics, but about the Kantian view that

---

[71] *The Right and the Good*, 40.

[72] G. W. F. Hegel, *The Phenomenology of Spirit*, trans. A. V. Miller (Oxford: Oxford University Press, 1977), 47. William James distinguishes between those who regard the chase for truth as paramount and those who regard the avoidance of error as more important. Having made this distinction, he expresses the same view as Hegel in regard to those who treat the avoidance of error as paramount. 'He who says, "Better go without belief forever than believe a lie!" merely shows his own preponderant private horror of becoming a dupe. He may be critical of many of his desires and fears, but this fear he slavishly obeys' ('The Will to Believe', in James, *The Will to Believe and Other Essays in Popular Philosophy* (New York: Dover, 1956), 18).

before we proceed to work out a system of philosophy we must come to an understanding of the faculty of cognition which is to form this system. But his point applies to ethics as well as to Kantian critical philosophy. The fear of error may be the error itself, for the desire to avoid mistakes and naivety may itself prevent us from getting at the truth. Intuitionists such as Price, Prichard, and Ross were more concerned to get at the concrete truth in ethics than to avoid error. It is this that so often makes their views on morality seem naive (especially from an Enlightenment perspective with its inherent horror of becoming a dupe) yet, at the same time, so refreshing.

Prospects for a Value-Based Intuitionism

Robert Audi

Throughout most of the twentieth century, and certainly since W. D. Ross published *The Right and the Good* in 1930, intuitionism has been standardly conceived as an uncompromisingly deontological theory. The concept of duty has been considered to be its central normative notion; and although Ross recognized the relevance of non-moral intrinsic values to what our duties require, he apparently regarded their bearing on moral conduct as derivative from their role in determining the content of some of our primary moral duties. Consider, for instance, the duty of beneficence, which reflects the positive value of pleasure: the enhancement of pleasure in the lives of others is among the central targets of beneficent conduct. Ross may have thought that since it is self-evident and unprovable that we have a prima facie duty of beneficence, neither considerations of value nor any other candidates for a more basic status ground this duty. Whether he was committed to precisely this inference or not, I want to explore the possibility that Rossian principles of prima facie duty can be grounded in considerations of value even if the principles are self-evident. In doing this I will assume, with Ross, both the plurality of basic moral duties and the possibility of non-inferential knowledge of principles expressing them. On both counts he differs from Moore, who (in much of his work) takes our specific duties to be grounded in promotion of goodness and our

This paper has benefited much from discussions with the other participants in the University of Keele conference entitled Re-evaluating Ethical Intuitionism, held on 3–5 June 1999, for which it was written. I also learned from presentations at Biola, Northern Illinois, and Santa Clara Universities, as well as from extensive comments by Geoffrey Sayre-McCord on a draft of my related paper 'A Kantian Intuitionism', at the Pacific Division of the American Philosophical Association in 1999. For helpful comments on earlier drafts I am grateful to Ruth Chang, Roger Crisp, Brad Hooker, Hugh LaFollette, Hugh McCann, and Philip Stratton-Lake.

Robert Audi

knowledge of principles of duty to derive from considerations regarding the relation between human conduct and the realization of intrinsic value.[1] On the first count, at least, Ross differs from Sidgwick as well.

Ross's intuitionism has some significant advantages over consequentialism; but Sidgwick and Moore, though consequentialists, must also be regarded as intuitionists at least in their countenancing non-inferential knowledge of some normative truths, and in one major respect their views have a strength that is missing from Ross's theory. I refer to their grounding of principles of conduct in a theory of value. This is a strength because it is desirable for an ethical theory to account for how morality contributes to human flourishing, to provide a basis for explaining the role of each of our major moral duties in making this contribution, and, more generally, to clarify the connection between the right and the good. The question I want to pursue here is whether, if we take a Rossian pluralistic theory of moral obligation as our model of intuitionism in ethics, we can preserve what is best in it, and perhaps strengthen it, by incorporating it in a wider theory that exhibits its basic, non-inferentially knowable principles of duty as in some significant way grounded in considerations of value. In the basic cases, I think, these considerations concern what is intrinsically good or intrinsically bad, in a sense that implies the provision of a reason for action: a broadly positive reason in the former case and a broadly negative reason in the latter.[2] Let us begin, then, with some fundamental points about reasons for action.

Intrinsic Value and the Grounding of Reasons for Action

I will assume that the notion of the intrinsically good is clear enough for the kind of work it will do here, and that, whatever kind of thing one may

---

[1] See e.g. H. Sidgwick, *The Methods of Ethics*, 7th edn. (London: Macmillan, 1907), bk. IV, ch. 1, where he calls utilitarianism the theory that 'the conduct which, under any given circumstances, is objectively right, is that which will produce the greatest amount of happiness on the whole' (p. 411); and G. E. Moore, e.g. *Ethics* (London: Oxford University Press, 1912, 1966), where he says that 'the total consequences of right actions must always be as good, intrinsically, as any which it was *possible* for the agent to produce under the circumstances' (p. 98).

[2] For a brief account of such values and their relation to reasons, see ch. 11 of my *Moral Knowledge and Ethical Character* (Oxford: Oxford University Press, 1997). A recent volume bearing on many of the difficult issues here is R. Chang (ed.), *Incommensurability, Incomparability, and Practical Reason* (Cambridge, Mass.: Harvard University Press, 1997); her instructive introductory essay bears particularly on the treatment of the organic element in reasons and values that is explored in this paper.

consider intrinsically good or intrinsically bad,[3] one is committed to taking things of this kind to provide a reason for action, specifically, some reason that is normative at least in the wide sense that it counts toward the justification of the action in question. For instance, if we regard pain as intrinsically bad, we are committed to supposing it provides (negative) reason for action, for example to taking an action's causing pain as a reason—though not necessarily an overriding one—to avoid performing that action. I also assume that moral considerations are reasons in this sense. Thus, if I believe that doing something would be unjust, I am committed to recognizing this fact as a reason to avoid the action; if you believe that an action is a fulfillment of a promise you made, you are committed to recognizing that fact as a reason to perform it. (I am not speaking of motivational reasons; I leave open here whether the kind of normative cognition in question necessarily motivates.)

Ross held that there is a plurality of grounds of duty. Some of these, such as unjust states of affairs and, on the positive side, promises one has made, clearly provide *moral* reasons for action.[4] Others, such as the possibility of improving people in respect of happiness or knowledge (a possibility crucial for understanding the duty of beneficence) do not obviously provide moral reasons; but, as Ross saw, they nonetheless can give rise to duties we naturally call moral, in a sense implying that degree of attentiveness to such considerations is a major factor in determining how moral a person is. Perhaps it is the associated *facts* that are the grounds of duty, for instance the fact that doing an extra seminar with one's students would enhance their knowledge. This interpretation of the Rossian position would yield a parallel to such cases as the fact that one has injured someone, which gives one a reason to make reparation, the fact that one can prevent an injustice, and so forth. It seems plain, moreover, that these grounds are considerations of value. Ross himself says that pleasure and knowledge, for instance, are among the things having intrinsic value. If they are, then (other things being equal) we are to promote them.

However anti-consequentialist Ross's overall view is, then, his theory

---

[3] Among the most plausible objections to its intelligibility is the idea that something can be good only qua *kind* of thing, pressed by, for example, Judith Jarvis Thomson in 'The Right and the Good', *Journal of Philosophy*, 94 (1997), 273–98. I accommodate what is plausible in this in 'Intrinsic Value and Reasons for Action', *Southern Journal of Philosophy* (forthcoming).

[4] It will be convenient here (and is consonant with normal English usage) to allow states of affairs, actions, and propositions to count as reasons for action. I have discussed reasons for action in detail in *The Architecture of Reason* (Oxford: Oxford University Press, 2001), esp. ch. 5.

apparently presupposes that considerations of intrinsic value play a role as, if not partially grounding duties (even basic prima facie duties), then at least as providing a way to see performance of duty as respecting or promoting something intrinsically good. His view is not, to be sure, that our duties are determined by facts about what kinds of deeds have the best overall consequences for promoting the plurality of intrinsic values he recognizes.[5] But one can deny that view and still hold that facts about the promotion of goodness (e.g. production of what is intrinsically good) and facts about the avoidance of evil (e.g. abstention from producing, or prevention of, what is intrinsically bad) are among the grounds of our duties.

Suppose, however, that one considers the place of moral norms in human life as a whole, which in turn requires considering the role of moral reasons for action in relation to other kinds of reasons for action. There is surely some plausibility in taking moral norms and rules as properly serving human flourishing or, if one finds some other positive term less problematic, human welfare, human good, or, say, the well-being of persons.[6] It is uncontroversial that the paradigms of morally right conduct consist in treating persons in certain ways (for instance, the ways that clearly accord with Ross's principles) and that the paradigms of immoral conduct consist in doing the opposite. Suppose we try to view a broadly Rossian intuitionism in the context of this conception of moral norms, and suppose we assume that we have a satisfactory way of determining our final duties given our prima facie ones. We can then begin to see how adhering to the framework of prima facie duties might conduce to human flourishing.

In explicating the determination of final duty, however, Ross left us with less than he might have. He said that it is practical wisdom that enables us to see what, finally, we ought to do. He was talking about overall duty and meant this to apply in moral matters. Even leaving aside non-moral conduct, such as the prudential or the aesthetic, is this as far as ethical theory can take us? I want to explore how far we might go beyond this or, alternatively, to

---

[5] One reason he holds this is that his principles would then be derivable from an overarching consequentialist one. Another is that he does not regard the question of what to do as in any sense quantitative, or at least quantitative in this way. I should add that the concept of promotion I use in connection with the intrinsically good must be understood broadly; for different goods various more specific terms are more accurate.

[6] The notion of well-being is of central importance in ethics for James Griffin and he has clarified it in his book *Well-Being* (Oxford: Clarendon Press, 1986). As William Frankena put a related point, 'morality was made for man, not man for morality'. See *Ethics*, 2nd edn. (Englewood Cliffs: Prentice-Hall, 1974), 44.

what extent we might specify how practical wisdom is to be applied, if we take values as a basis for duties.

Intrinsic Value and Prima Facie Duty

If, with Mill and the predominant strand in the empiricist tradition, one thought that there are no *moral* intrinsic values, one would find it easy to see how the deontologist in Ross might recoil from viewing our prima facie duties as grounded in values. For if intuitionist deontology represents anything above all else, it is a rejection of the idea that morality does not stand on its own feet. A number of convictions belong with this metaphor. Among the most important (found in Ross, Prichard, and others) is that moral judgments, even if their warrant requires factual grounds, need not be grounded in non-moral normative judgments. Ross emphatically rejected the idea that duty must be ascertained by determining the contribution of actions to the good. But this rejection is perhaps not as far-reaching as it seems. Consider virtue, which Ross took to include moral virtue. He regarded it as an intrinsic good, and promoting virtue is part of what the duties of beneficence and self-improvement require.[7] Here, then, is a class of duties that apparently have at least a partial value base. In any event, even apart from Ross's own theory of value, if we countenance moral intrinsic value, is there any reason to deny that injustice is a paradigm of an intrinsic moral evil and that adhering, against temptation, to sound standards of honesty is a paradigm of an intrinsic moral good, at least in the sense that there is non-instrumental reason to avoid the former and to achieve the latter?[8]

One could maintain that there is nothing of intrinsic value here, but only the fact that we take deeds of the kind (the act-type) in question to indicate basic reasons for action: that an act would be an injustice we consider a basic reason to avoid it; that another act would be honest we regard as a

---

[7] Ross says, for example, 'The first thing for which I would claim that it is intrinsically good is virtuous disposition and action, i.e., action, or disposition to act, from any one of certain motives of which at all events the most notable are the desire to do one's duty, the desire to bring into being something that is good, and the desire to give pleasure or save pain to others.' See *The Right and the Good* (Oxford: Clarendon Press, 1930), p. 134. He is not excluding *moral* virtue from his comment or even taking it as less valuable than nonmoral virtue.

[8] I here ignore the point that these might be better construed as *inherent* goods (i.e. goods that, though not necessarily intrinsic, are such that an appropriate experience of them has intrinsic value, as in the case of viewing a beautiful painting with aesthetic pleasure) since nothing in this paper turns on the distinction.

basic reason in favor of it; and so forth. For Ross, and for intuitionism as commonly conceived, justification simply ends here, and if this terminal status is explained at all, it is not by appeal to our reaching a justifying ground in something that has intrinsic value, but rather by appeal to our reaching something that is self-evidently a ground of duty.

I see no need to agree that justification must come to an end in this way, with the specification of an appropriate obligatory act-type or a Rossian ground of duty (if, in such matters, it ever must end at any particular place). It is surely plausible to say that, for instance, we have reason to be truthful because it is good to be so or, more specifically, because it is a way of according people a certain kind of respect. This is compatible with taking the fact that an action is truthful as *constituting* a reason to perform it; the point is that there can still be a ground for its doing so. Moreover, although in calling a veracious action a good kind of conduct we commit ourselves to there being a reason to perform it, this is not all we express. We leave open, indeed we perhaps even presuppose, that such deeds have admirable qualities and play a certain kind of role in human life. (Here I leave open the possibility of a noncognitivist account; a noncognitivist could accept this point and then try to explain why what we express by calling a deed good, or good *qua* according people respect, is more basic than what we express by saying simply that we have a reason to do it.[9])

It may be helpful to those of an empiricist bent to think about intrinsic value as belonging to experiences, as Mill did. We can be experientialists about the bearers of intrinsic value, however, without being hedonists about its nature. There are not only experiences of pleasure and pain but *moral* experiences, and some of these seem to have intrinsic value. Think of indignation that arises upon witnessing one person abusing another, or the sense of acting, against temptation, on a commitment to a promise, or the experience of suffering an injustice when unfairly excluded from voting on something that lies within one's competence. One could try to reduce these experiences to hedonic ones accompanied by a moral belief, say that the painful action in question is wrong; but I doubt that all of them will yield to such a strategy.

Furthermore, it seems plausible to consider at least some of these moral experiences to have intrinsic value and thereby to provide basic reasons for action. Indignation over wrongdoing can provide such a reason

---

[9] For a full-scale account of noncognitivism, see A. Gibbard, *Wise Choices, Apt Feelings: A Theory of Normative Judgment* (Cambridge, Mass.: Harvard University Press, 1990).

to reprimand someone; it can be a kind of moral distress that is relieved by the appropriate act (it can also, in a morally sensitive person, provide a reason by constituting a kind of evidence of wrongdoing). Here the reason for the reprimand might be to express one's indignation, and one might presuppose that this might change the conduct in question. The experience of being a victim of injustice is (as such) intrinsically bad; the experience of one's moral self-determination prevailing over temptation is intrinsically good. A single experience can, to be sure, have both intrinsically good and intrinsically bad aspects. Indignation as a moral experience can be intrinsically good in an overall sense, though the displeasure, often in the form of a felt resentment that sometimes goes with it, is intrinsically bad in its hedonic aspect. Indignation can also be, overall, intrinsically bad; it may be misplaced, as where a malicious tyrant is indignant over an underling's taking pity on an innocent prisoner who was to be tortured. Here it provides no moral reason for the agent to act.[10]

In my view, then, there are various kinds of things having intrinsic moral value, and some of them are experiences. Some of those experiences, moreover, such as indignation, illustrate the possibility that what is intrinsically good overall may have an intrinsically bad aspect or part.[11] Similarly, an intrinsic good can be a constituent in a state of affairs that is overall intrinsically bad. Consider a malicious man's enjoying his brutally bullying a female employee. His pleasure is utterly out of place and plainly undeserved. It is a good thing which he ought not to have. Taken in itself, the pleasure, *as* the kind of thing that 'makes his day' and is naturally and rationally sought for its own sake, is good; but because of what it is pleasure in, he ought not to have it, and his having it, construed overall, is an intrinsically bad state of affairs.[12]

---

[10] It might also be taken to provide a massively overridden reason here; nothing in this paper turns on which interpretation we take. Whether indignation provides a moral reason, as opposed to a more general practical reason, say on account of its unpleasantness as calling for relief, depends on whether, from the moral point of view, it has an appropriate basis. I have illustrated both indignation that evidences wrongdoing and indignation that is perversely determined by perceiving a good deed.

[11] Moore was unwilling to call these complex wholes good 'in themselves', since he restricted this term to what is 'ultimately good', i.e. intrinsically good and containing no parts that are not intrinsically good. See *Ethics*, esp. pp. 30–1. He apparently took 'in themselves' to entail goodness throughout, but that seems an artificial construction, and the indicated usage has not prevailed.

[12] What, then, of the case in which he enjoys what he falsely takes to be causing someone pain (and just hallucinates causing this)? Here it remains true that his enjoyment is intrinsically good, but the complex state of affairs, his enjoying the experience (as) of causing someone pain may still be intrinsically bad. (This might depend on, for example, whether he believes the person has masochistically asked for the painful action.)

Robert Audi

This is not to say that pleasure can occur without a determinate object whose nature bears on the overall value of a concrete pleasurable experience; but just as, in the abstract, one can take the fact that an act is of a certain kind, such as a promise-keeping, to have a moral weight even if the reason for action it provides may be overridden, we can take the fact that an experience is of a certain kind, such as a pleasure or a pain, to have an axiological weight even if the overall state of affairs in which it occurs has a greater opposing weight and the reason for action it provides may also be overridden. To illustrate, because the malicious man enjoys what he does, we view him even more negatively on account of his doing it, and we consider him, as a person, morally the worse for enjoying such a thing. Or, take a different case. A malicious, unrepentant murderer is living in hiding. His going unpunished is (morally) bad. But suppose he begins to enjoy life; the overall state of affairs, his going unpunished *and* enjoying his life, is intrinsically even worse than his simply going unpunished.[13]

The best way to explain these facts is surely to suppose that although there are some things, such as pleasure, that are intrinsically good—hence good on the basis of their non-relational properties—nonetheless, overall value, for instance that of a complex state of affairs like going unpunished and enjoying oneself, is not just the 'sum' of the intrinsic goods and evils of the elements or aspects of that state of affairs. If it were, then adding pleasure to the murderer's life would produce a better, not a worse, state of affairs. Moore and others have construed intrinsic goodness as organic in this way. I find this view quite plausible, and I take intrinsic goodness to be non-additive in the way illustrated by the case of a malicious man's coming to enjoy life.[14]

It is natural to take reasons for action to be grounded in elements having intrinsic value, including moral value (we need not claim that they cannot

[13] I am ignoring a distinction between the intrinsic and the inherent good, since it would complicate matters unnecessarily to observe it here. The distinction is developed in *Moral Knowledge*, ch. 11, where I indicate its application to cases of the kind in question.

[14] Moore formulated a 'principle of organic unities' in *Principia Ethica* (Cambridge: Cambridge University Press, 1903), e.g. p. 28, and reiterated a version of it in *Ethics*. In the light of an understanding of the organicity of value, one can see how Kant could both countenance intrinsic goods other than good will (including happiness) and yet say that 'a rational and impartial spectator can never feel approval in contemplating the uninterrupted prosperity of a being graced by no touch of a pure and good will' (*Groundwork of the Metaphysics of Morals*, 393). For detailed discussion of the principle of organic unities, see N. Lemos, *Intrinsic Value: Concept and Warrant* (Cambridge: Cambridge University Press, 1994), P. Stratton-Lake, *Kant, Duty and Moral Worth* (London: Routledge, 2000) ch. 8, and M. Zimmerman, *The Nature of Intrinsic Value* (Totowa, NJ: Rowman & Littlefield, 2001).

also be grounded in any other way, but I here ignore the possibility of such overdetermination). We would then expect that in a concrete case of action, what counts as overall reason for acting is an organic matter relative to the constituent reasons for or against the action. Now suppose we restrict attention to reasons of the kind that constitute (or at least generate) moral duty. We might now say that our overall duty is not just a matter of the number of reasons we have, nor of just the quantity of good we can produce—assuming that goodness can be quantified adequately—but of how all the relevant considerations fit together. This point is crucial in understanding such 'deontological constraints' as strong prohibitions of sacrificing one person for the sake of the general happiness.

Ross would not deny this organicity of overall duty, but he apparently thought that there is no general theory of value or of morality that adds significantly to the procedure of simply using practical wisdom to determine what one's final duty is. He was certainly committed to the unprovability of his principles of duty. To be sure, unprovability in a strict sense does not entail the impossibility of substantial support of a kind weaker than is provided by proof. But from the way Ross elaborates on his principles, I believe he intended to deny that we can in any sense establish them, or even justify them, on the basis of anything else, such as a comprehensive moral theory. There are, however, many kinds and degrees of justificatory support that one set of propositions can give another, and Ross apparently did not consider that this epistemological complexity raised by his position. Let us first explore the notion of proof.

Proof admits of weaker and stronger interpretations. Suppose we take as a rough necessary and sufficient condition for the kind of proving possible for moral principles that (*a*) one non-circularly infers the true proposition in question from one or more others that one either knows or truly believes with strong justification, and (*b*) one's premise set provides a cogent reason for the conclusion. This is *proof as sound justification*. This characterization—which corresponds to what seems the main everyday, non-technical notion of proof—leaves open whether such an inference must be (logically) valid, as it must be on a second, strong notion of proof that we obtain by adding a validity requirement to the one just sketched. This is *proof as sound deductive justification*. There is, however, a third notion of proof. In a somewhat loose use, one might prove a (true) proposition by showing that it is the only, or at least the best (and a good), explanation of some true proposition. Here we have *proof as sound abductive justification*.

If one views Ross in relation to Kant, one may naturally wonder whether some version of the categorical imperative might sustain a derivation of the kinds of moral principles Ross so plausibly defended or indeed of Ross's own. We can leave open whether such a derivation need be a proof, but a case can be made for the possibility of such a proof of the first of the three kinds just sketched. A broadly Kantian theory—though not necessarily one clearly attributable to Kant—can at least provide for some extension and unification of Rossian intuitionism.

A Kantian Integration of Rossian Principles

Suppose, then, that we take Rossian principles of duty to express central requirements for treating persons as ends—hence as having a kind of value—and for never treating them merely as means (for simplicity I restrict attention to just those principles Ross formulated). These ideas help to rationalize and interconnect Ross's principles. Moreover, a Kantian framework might help us in dealing with (even if it does not solve) a problem Ross acknowledged: deciding which of two conflicting duties (if either) is overriding.[15] Imagine that I am caught between helping a depressed friend and keeping an office hour. I might realize that my friend could have a breakdown and that only I can give comfort; I might see that if I miss the hour, my students will only have to make a needless trip to the campus and try again. Now suppose that, following Kant's categorical imperative—though not his own interpretation of it[16]—I consider both universality and intrinsic end formulations.[17] Kant's universality formulation (as I understand it) requires asking myself whether I can (rationally) universalize my maxim,

[15] In this and the next few paragraphs I draw on my paper 'A Kantian Intuitionism', *Mind*, 110 (2001), 601–35.

[16] I refer to Kant's widely known view, suggested in the *Groundwork of the Metaphysic of Morals* and other work of his, that a perfect duty, such as the duty to keep a promise, always outweighs an imperfect duty, such as the duty to help someone in distress. Since perfect duties can conflict, even if Kant were right about the former case, he would presumably need to appeal to the categorical imperative, in the way suggested in the text, to deal with those conflicts. I want to leave open, however, that other interpretations of the imperative are compatible with Kant's ethical writings overall.

[17] Kant apparently regarded these as equivalent, even if not *identical*, in content. I provisionally assume that, if only because the intrinsic end formulation provides the main materials needed for interpretation of the universality one, the equivalence claim is plausible. The falsity of this claim would not, however, substantially alter my project here, though I do think that apart from integration with the intrinsic end formulation (or some similar source of constraints) the universality one is of quite limited usefulness. Similar points seem to hold for the autonomy formulation: stressing that 'A rational being must always regard himself as making laws in a kingdom of ends which is possible through freedom of the will' (*Groundwork*, sect. 434), Kant says, 'the principle of autonomy is "Never to choose except in such a way that in the same volition the maxims of your choice are also present as universal law" ' (sect. 440).

which we might take to be roughly 'If my only means of keeping my friend out of danger is to miss my office hour, but in a way my students would not (at least on careful reflection about the facts of the case) resent, then I will miss it'.[18] Would universalizing this undermine the practice of keeping office hours? Surely not. Would my missing the hour in such a case offend a reasonable student? I believe not. If, however, I risked my friend's health to keep a promise of the relevant sort, I would apparently fail to treat the friend as an end in the relevant sense, the sense that implies (among other things) not only that I value my friend's well-being for its own sake but also that I am unwilling to forgo protecting it when I alone can do so, for the convenience of others (and indeed for any less than substantial reasons). Yet in breaking the promise I would not be using my students merely as a means; nor, given my explaining to them why I did not appear, would I fail to treat them as ends. I would not (at least in any obvious way) *use* them at all, as I would use someone by lying to get a loan.

Ross might say that these considerations add up to no more than rules of thumb to facilitate the use of practical wisdom. Practical wisdom is certainly needed to apply the categorical imperative. But surely we gain some help from it beyond what we derive from *theoretically unaided practical wisdom*: just getting the facts in conflict cases and trying to make a wise decision apart from reliance on such a principle (I leave aside the important question whether forswearing such reliance is even psychologically realistic).

Indeed, Ross himself would agree on one point that supports the applicability of the categorical imperative: if what we do is morally obligatory, it should in principle be describable in a way that is generalizable. For he regards moral properties ('attributes') as consequential upon natural ones, such as those involving the results of an action for pleasure and pain, approval and resentment. If it is natural facts, ultimately, that ground and justify our true moral judgments, it is plausible to hold that—in principle—one could describe these facts in a way that yields, for each sound moral

---

[18] I insert 'rationally' to capture Kant's intention and because it is in any case not plausible to think the requirement concerns either psychological or strict logical possibility; as is well known, in the *Groundwork* Kant grants that there is no inconsistency in universalizing the maxims corresponding to failure to do good deeds and to develop one's talents. In the application at hand we could be more cautious and say 'could not reasonably resent', but this may not be necessary for a sound maxim in such cases. A similar notion is illuminatingly discussed by T. M. Scanlon in connection with contractarian justifications. See e.g. his 'Contractarianism and Utilitarianism', in Amartya Sen and Bernard Williams (eds.), *Utilitarianism and Beyond* (Cambridge: Cambridge University Press, 1982), and his *What we Owe to Each Other* (Cambridge, Mass.: Belknap Press, 1998).

judgment, a non-trivial general description of its grounds. If they justify our judgment, then (on plausible assumptions) we can become aware of them through suitable reflection and, given sufficient conceptual clarity, formulate a description of them that expresses our justification.[19]

One might think that this is an unrealistic claim. But, for one thing, there is a *principle of discriminative threshold* operating: only factors one can discriminate can figure in the justificatory grounding of one's moral judgment. If an influence on moral judgment is below that threshold, it is at most a causal ground of the judgment. The discrimination need not be conscious; this is why we can properly disapprove of patronizing conduct on the basis of how it treats the person it is directed toward, and on the same basis can justifiedly judge that the conduct is wrong, even if, without special efforts, we cannot say what it is about the conduct that is objectionable, much less why it is patronizing. But I take it that if a ground of moral judgment is discriminable in the relevant way, then, at least through reflection guided by questions raised by oneself or someone else, one can in some way articulate the ground and bring it to bear in supporting the judgment. If this were not so, we would have to allow that moral judgments could be (justificationally) grounded in elements that are in a fairly strong sense inaccessible to the subject—something appropriate for a mere cause but not, I think, for a ground.[20] A ground of judgment, like a ground of action, should be one the agent is able to adduce in explanation or justification. If we do something for which we can find no such grounding element, we feel alienated from the action in a way we do not where we are acting as moral agents.

If grounds of moral judgment are accessible to the agent in the way I have suggested, then with suitable efforts one can produce some kind of account of why one holds an adequately grounded moral judgment (as opposed to one based on, for example, wishful thinking). If, in addition, one understands the relevant categories of moral appraisal—as one will if one has some command of the basic principles of prima facie duty—then one will by and large be able to produce a generalization in order to justify one's judgment by appeal to one or more of those duties. The generalization may be rough and ready, say that it is wrong to talk down to other

---

[19] This is a reference to the supervenience of moral properties, widely discussed in recent literature and explored in chs. 4 and 5 of my *Moral Knowledge*. The relevant passages in Ross are mainly in chs. 2 and 4 of *The Right and the Good*. See esp. pp. 33, 105, and 121–3.

[20] This would be quite all right for an externalist, reliabilist account of moral justification, but even then the relevant property must be *causally* discriminated, whether inaccessibly to consciousness (without outside help) or not.

people in a way that tends to hurt their feelings. Even a rough generalization like this, moreover, may be difficult to evoke from an ordinary person apart from some Socratic prodding or the development of some sophistication. Nonetheless, to make a moral judgment on a morally relevant ground is in part to be disposed to adduce the ground in a way that lends itself to at least rough generalization.

An Axiological Integration of Rossian Principles

If what I have so far suggested is plausible, we can see how Rossian principles of duty can be clarified, rationalized, and to some extent unified both by values and by wider moral principles. Might we not be able to retain Ross's principles of duty even if we take them to be grounded in certain values, as well as to be clarified by, and perhaps even derivable from, a version of the categorical imperative in the way I have described? It will help in answering this if we distinguish several kinds of grounding of principles.

In speaking of Rossian principles being grounded in certain values (or based on them, in a roughly equivalent terminology), I have in mind a kind of ontic grounding. To say that a (moral) principle is *ontically grounded* in a value is roughly to say that it is true at least in part because action in accord with the principle is at least a partial realization of that value. To say that a principle is *epistemically grounded* in a value (or in some other principle) is roughly to say that knowledge of, or justification for believing, the principle depends on knowledge of, or justification regarding, the grounding principle or value. And to say that a principle or, more accurately, a cognition (such as a judgment) with that principle as its content is *inferentially grounded* in another proposition is roughly to say that the first is held on the basis of the second (or cannot be properly held by the person in question apart from such an inferential connection). Overdetermination is possible within each category and across the categories. One element can be grounded in one way, or in more than one of these ways, and in either case it can be grounded on more than one other element.

In any of its forms, actual grounding should be distinguished from *groundability*. It may be in part because Ross and other intuitionists noticed that intuitively known moral principles are not inferentially *grounded* in other propositions—as they properly might be if the principles were epistemically dependent on other propositions—that they denied their epistemic groundability in any sense (their 'provability').[21] But the epistemic independence they insisted on is compatible both with inferential and epistemic groundability and with ontic grounding.

Supposing we can take Rossian principles to be grounded in certain values that provide basic reasons for action, it may still be unclear what the relevant values are. It is not enough to say, as Kant did, that persons have intrinsic value, particularly since some are so very bad (people can apparently even be 'no damned good'[22]). What is it about persons in virtue of which they must be treated as ends? Kant uses a number of notions. I want to consider one: dignity. This may in turn be taken to be based on autonomy, rationality, or other human characteristics, but the crucial point is that, being constituted in good part by moral rights, it is a moral value. In part, this is to say that in virtue of the dignity of persons we have *moral* reasons to act in a certain way toward them.

A second important point about dignity or indeed any comparably broad moral value that might ground the categorical imperative (such as 'worth') is that there is a far-reaching moral attitude that goes with it: respect for persons. If this is so, we might take both dignity and respect for persons as fundamental elements in a value-based intuitionism. Dignity is the overarching central value, and indeed its inherent goodness is intuitively knowable; respect is the central attitude.[23] May we not think of Rossian duty

[21] One may wonder why a cognition of a proposition that is epistemically dependent does not *have* to be inferentially grounded. The answer is that we can *have* a justification for a proposition, and even justifiedly believe it, without that justification's leading to our having a justified belief of a premise for the proposition. This would be a case of what, in 'Structural Justification' (repr. in R. Audi, *The Structure of Justification* (Cambridge: Cambridge University Press, 1993)), I called structural justification, to capture the idea that it resides in one's cognitive structure as opposed to the content of one's beliefs, say in dispositions to *form* beliefs, but not in actual justified beliefs. Structural justification is possible for a belief of a principle without that justification's figuring in any premise or being an inferential ground of the principle.

[22] The reference is to Nicholas Sturgeon's 'Moral Explanations', in David Copp and David Zimmerman (eds.), *Morality, Reason, and Truth: New Essays on the Foundations of Ethics* (Totowa, NJ: Rowman & Allanheld, 1985), where moral properties are taken to have explanatory power in a sense that is partly causal. My approach is compatible with elements of the moral realism defended by Sturgeon; the chief difference is apparently epistemological, but much of what I say could be detached from the rationalist epistemology that I am taking to be most natural, as well as historically dominant, for intuitionism. A similar compatibility might hold for the moral realism of Richard Boyd's related paper 'How to be a Moral Realist', in G. Sayre-McCord (ed.), *Essays on Moral Realism* (Ithaca, NY: Cornell University Press, 1988).

[23] This is not to say that there are no other good candidates to play the indicated roles. Moreover, dignity is presumably a higher-order value in the sense that beings have it on the basis of their capacity to realize other values, such as moral satisfaction, pleasure in contemplating goodness and beauty, and suffering in experiencing injustice to others or themselves.

principles (perhaps including some Ross did not formulate) as expressing prima facie requirements on respecting the dignity of persons? And is there not a notion of respect for persons—epitomized in treating them as ends and never merely as means—that properly goes with carrying out these duties? One dimension of respect for persons is, in Kantian terms, acting from duty in (at least some of) our relations with them. But there is a second dimension of respect for persons easily assimilated to the first but not reducible to it: doing one's duty toward someone else (and presumably toward oneself as well, assuming there are duties to oneself), whether the duties are Rossian or of some other moral kind, does not have moral worth (or at least suffers in moral worth) unless the deed is performed *with respect* for the person(s) in question.

Despite the naturalness of putting this second point in Kantian terms, it goes beyond the standard Kantian insistence that, to have moral worth, actions must be performed from duty. Actions performed from duty need not be performed with respect. The latter mode of action is not, for instance, equivalent to being performed *from* respect, where respect is conceived as an attitude yielding a motive of, say, reverence for persons or an intrinsic concern with their well-being. What motives underlie an action is determined by its ground; the manner of an action is largely determined by one's attitudes in performing it. There are, to be sure, ways of performing acts, including disrespectful ways, that tend to undermine any claim that they are done from duty; but in general the motive of an action does not foreclose the mode of its execution. The idea here is that even if an action is performed from duty—or from some other appropriate moral motive—if it is to have maximal moral worth it must also be performed respectfully, i.e. with an attitude that is part of, or adequately exhibits, respect for persons. It is not enough, for instance, to keep a promise out of a sense of obligation if one does it in a mean spirit, with a patronizing attitude, or with visible resentment that the promisee should expect it.

I do not find this requirement on respectful action—call it *the respectfulness requirement*—explicitly expressed in either Kant's *Groundwork of the Metaphysic of Morals* or Ross's *The Right and the Good*. If we distinguish the psychological side of moral theory—concerning moral requirements on the motivation and manner of obligatory conduct—from the more prominent normative problem of what act-types are obligatory or appropriate in the first place, Kant and Ross stand out in contrast to many moral philosophers in attending to the former. Among major ethical theorists since Kant, Ross is among the most instructive on the differences between the assessments of action in the two dimensions. But both are more illuminating on motive than on manner. It is fully in the spirit of both positions, however, to adopt the respectfulness requirement, and doing so helps to bring out the scope of the kind of grounding of moral conduct which a value base makes possible.

The notions of human dignity and respect for persons are to a certain extent open-ended. Their application is limited, however, in that they operate together and (so far as we work within broadly Kantian constraints) both are fruitfully understood in reflective equilibrium with the categorical imperative, which in turn must be understood in reflective equilibrium with what I am calling Rossian duties, even if not exactly the set of duties Ross formulated. As I understand human dignity, we would not possess it if we could not be moral agents, yet its basis is not only our capacity for moral agency and for the experience of moral value, but also our rational capacities and our distinctive kind of sentience. That we can reason, that we can pursue complicated projects, and that we can enjoy some things and suffer from others are among the capacities essential to our dignity. The kinds of things that we can enjoy or suffer from is important: we can be delighted by poetry, music, and conversation; we can smart from embarrassment and suffer moral anguish. In these and other capacities we have elements of dignity that the higher animals do not.

Suppose I have been right in thinking that Rossian principles can be integrated axiologically as well as deontologically. It still does not follow that one can deduce or even strongly justify Ross's principles from the categorical imperative itself or from any specific well-developed theory of value. I cannot show this in detail here, but perhaps I have said enough to establish that in the light of a plausibly developed interpretation of that imperative end of human dignity and respect for persons, such a unifying, grounding derivation is at least a reasonable hope. This kind of derivation (as suggested earlier) need not yield a strict proof, but does provide a connection strong enough for the grounding elements to supply both a justification and a partial explication of the principles grounded in them. There are at least two possibilities here. First, understanding the values—both negative and positive whose realization is central for human dignity helps us to justify and understand the categorical imperative; this, in turn, helps us to justify and understand Rossian duties. Second, one could proceed more directly, from an account of the relevant values to a kind of derivation of Rossian principles. In both cases, moreover, the grounding in question allows for related justificatory and explanatory connections running the other way: our understanding of Rossian duties helps us to justify and understand any overall moral directive that can ground them, as well as the values that account (or at least can account) for the place of all our duties in human flourishing.

Value-Based Intuitionism versus Maximizing Consequentialism

Since Moore's normative ethics is value-based and his metaethics is, in at least one way, intuitionist, it may be useful to note some differences between the kind of intuitionist theory sketched here and Moore's. First, although Ross agreed with Moore in taking self-evident principles to be unprovable, Moore was unlike Ross in not conceiving everyday normative ethical principles as self-evident. He may have thought it self-evident that we are to maximize intrinsic value, but he presumably thought (plausibly) that the application of this to everyday decisions requires that one determine (or in any case know) empirically the contribution of certain act-types to whatever has such value. More important, Moore's theory, like Sidgwick's, is apparently a maximizing consequentialism,[24] whereas on the value-based intuitionism I am sketching, in order to determine what is morally required of us we need not subordinate our conduct to any broadly quantitative standard, nor even, in general, ascertain the likely overall contribution of our options to the good. Even when we have occasion to conceive our options in the widest terms, we need at most to determine an appropriate way to respect the relevant intrinsic values. This can be a matter of the kind of act we are performing, conceived in relation to its appropriateness to human dignity, and in some cases it can be known non-inferentially and intuitively. There is no requirement to realize as much overall intrinsic goodness as we can. Often, we quite properly just do our salient Rossian duty. Thus, a problem that besets the maximizing consequentialist in attempting to distinguish the obligatory from the supererogatory is forestalled.[25]

To be sure, Moore's consequentialism is not monolithically quantitative, but organically so: producing maximal value in an overall, organic sense

---

[24] This maximization emphasis comes out in *Ethics*, e.g. in the optimality description of right action cited above.

[25] This is not to suggest that explicating this distinction is easy for any moral theory or that consequentialists have no resources for dealing with it. I discuss the problem for Kantian intuitionism in 'A Kantian Intuitionism'.

might require generating less sheer quantity of such particular goods as pleasures than would be achieved by some alternative action. As Moore put it,

In order to shew that any action is a duty . . . we must know accurately the degree of value both of the action itself and of all these effects [its effects broadly conceived]; and must be able to determine how, in conjunction with the other things in the Universe, they will affect its value as an organic whole. . . Ethics, therefore, is quite unable to give us a list of duties . . . [though] there may be some possibility of shewing which among the alternatives, *likely to occur to anyone*, will produce the greatest sum of good.[26]

Moore might grant, then, that in practice Rossian principles can be rules of thumb, but he would insist that they derive their moral authority entirely from considerations of overall goodness, as opposed to the kinds of deontic grounds Ross and other deontological intuitionists treat as self-evidently central for moral obligation. (It is true that one might be able to know that an act is a duty without being able to show this. But if Moore noticed this, he apparently did not think one could in this (presumably non-inferential) way know one's duties, or he would have spoken differently about the capacity of ethics to give us a list of duties.)

Ordinary problems of moral decision also tend to be more tractable on a value-based intuitionism than on a maximizing consequentialism. On the former view, in order to know one has a duty, it is not necessary that one even think of it or of duties of that kind as such that their fulfillment conduces to human flourishing. One certainly need not think of maximizing any value. To be sure, if we are making an actual choice between two otherwise equally acceptable options and it is plain that one of them conduces more to (say) human flourishing, we should choose that one. But it would be a serious mistake to infer from the defeating role of the (discernible) inferiority of an option in conducing to flourishing (or to any other value) that we must always positively aim at maximizing some value.[27] Adhering to a preferential standard of this sort in making concrete choices does not commit one to a maximizing standard as a general policy.

On the value-based conception of Rossian duties, both basic Rossian principles of duty and our specific duties under them can be known non-

---

[26] See *Principia Ethica*, 149.

[27] This is reminiscent of the error in epistemology of inferring, from the capacity of incoherence to defeat justification, that coherence is the ground of justification. Rejecting the fallacious inferences here does not, of course, commit one to denying that we should ever try to maximize or that coherence never plays a positive role in justification. Detailed discussion of the epistemological case is provided in my *Structure of Justification*, esp. chs. 3–4.

inferentially and in the intuitive, deontological fashion Ross described. Indeed, derivability of these principles from a more general one, such as the categorical imperative, or from a set of axiological standards, does not in the least imply that our justified confidence in the wider principle is any greater than in the derivable ones, and it may be less strong. Even among self-evident propositions there is considerable variation in justification for confidence in them. There is also variation in the related factor of the ease of their knowability.

A further contrast can be drawn on the plausible assumption that, for Moore, as apparently for Sidgwick and for utilitarianism generally, an over-all moral obligation to do something is a special case of having overriding practical reason ('best reason') to do it. A value-based intuitionism, as I conceive it, recognizing as it does distinctively moral values, and taking certain everyday moral duties as in an important sense basic, construes moral reasons more narrowly. Final moral duty may coincide with what one has best reason, overall, to do, but on an intuitionist view it is understood primarily in terms of grounds for moral action; and as Ross wisely noted in describing the scope of our duties, some intrinsic values, such as enhancement of one's own pleasure, apparently do not figure among the values central for moral duty.[28]

Here Ross (and certainly a value-based intuitionism of the kind I am sketching) is closer to Aristotle: we are to *realize* the good, for instance by developing virtues of character and doing beneficent deeds; we need not maximize it, say by doing as much overall good as we can by becoming self-less philanthropists at great cost in our personal happiness; and whether morally right conduct maximizes it is an empirical matter. The value-based intuitionism I have outlined preserves these and other elements in Rossian intuitionism: intrinsically good and intrinsically bad things are intuitively knowable as such; there are irreducibly moral values; final moral obligation need not be a case of what one has overall best reason (including non-moral reason) to do; it need not be determined either by quantitative weighting or by inference from an overarching principle like the categorical imperative; and there may not only be types of moral obligation that can be known a priori to be binding on us, there may in addition be an irreducible plurality of these. The most attractive and most distinctive features of Ross's ethics may be preserved by its integration with the wider framework introduced here.

---

[28] Ross notes this in connection with the duty of self-improvement. See e.g. *The Right and the Good*, 25–6.

Objections and Replies

Given some persisting stereotypes about intuitionism, the best way of clarifying the proposed theory in my limited space may be to deal with some objections. In some cases I will be defending a Rossian intuitionism and not specifically the project of constructing a value-based intuitionism. But even that modest effort should be useful: it is a good theory even in the version Ross presented in 1930, in *The Right and the Good*.

If the possibility of non-inferential knowledge of moral principles is important for intuitionism, have we not lost something by providing a value basis for the principles? Are they not at the mercy of the relevant derivations, so that, for instance, we cannot know what in general our duties are without considering the relation of our options to one or more basic values? One answer begins with the point that even if Rossian principles of duty are derivable from, and unifiable by appeal to, something more comprehensive, such as a theory of value or the categorical imperative, it does not follow that they cannot also be known non-inferentially or even be self-evident. Inferential and epistemic groundability do not imply either inferential or epistemic dependence. In my view, the principles are plausibly considered mediately self-evident (roughly, self-evident, but not knowable by us apart from reflection—possibly a great deal of reflection—on their content). Moreover, if, as I grant, they can be known apart from inferential derivation from something else, we may call them *epistemically autonomous*. This kind of autonomy is as much as Ross, as an intuitionist and moral philosopher, needed to claim for his principles.

It is important in understanding the epistemic autonomy of Rossian moral principles to see that it does not entail the *ontic autonomy* of the properties that figure in them. That is a matter of those properties being undetermined by possession of others. Ontic autonomy is not a status plausibly claimed for moral properties, since, as Ross saw, moral properties are 'consequential' (thus, in one sense, supervenient) properties.[29] Nor does epistemic autonomy imply the indefeasibility of our justification for the principles. That our justification can be non-inferential does not entail that no considerations drawn from the larger framework of values that provide a basis for the principles can undermine that justification or lead to modifications in our understanding of the principles.

---

[29] The truth of Rossian moral propositions, in which supervening moral properties figure essentially, is presumably consequential on natural properties in a derivative way. But it is no easy task to specify how the two kinds of dependency, that of properties and that of truth values, are connected, and the task need not be undertaken for purposes of this paper.

If, given the epistemic autonomy of Rossian principles, we can have non-inferential knowledge of our general duties and, given this, well-grounded subsumptive (hence inferential) knowledge of some of our specific duties as instances of the general ones, can we also have non-inferential knowledge of our specific duties? This question brings us to a second objection. If Rossian moral principles are self-evident, and especially if they are also derivable from something more comprehensive, can we account for the particularism of intuitionism as Ross presented it (and, I suggest, in its most plausible forms), i.e. for the view that it is through understanding a particular case of duty that we come to see ('apprehend') that a *kind* of deed—presumably a kind it saliently illustrates—is a duty? I take the apprehension in question to be a result of 'intuitive induction', not of induction by simple enumeration or any other kind requiring inference from premises that provide independent support for the kind of moral proposition in question. The point is that through understanding a particular case one sees something general, not that one generalizes from properties of particular cases of a given kind to properties of that kind of case. The latter form of generalization is possible, but not what Ross had in mind.[30]

A third objection to intuitionism in its rationalist forms concerns self-evidence. This notion, especially as applied to substantive, non-formal principles, has seemed to some to be mysterious. This is a very large issue, on which much can be said.[31] I shall confine my response to three points. First, in my view it is doubtful that we can account for knowledge of logic and pure mathematics without some notion of self-evidence (or at least a notion of the a priori that raises similar problems). Second, beliefs of self-evident propositions need not be considered justificationally indefeasible. As we know from studies in logic and mathematics, even what is a priori and necessary need not be such that one cannot lose one's justification for believing it. We may, for instance, discover errors in our crucial proof. Moreover, in part because theoretically adequate formulation of the moral principles in question should take place in a context in which reflective equilibrium has

---

[30] Ross characterized intuitive induction in more than one place. See esp. ch. 2 of *The Right and the Good*. I might add that the particularism referred to here is not the strong kind defended by Jonathan Dancy in *Moral Reasons* (Oxford: Blackwell, 1993). A brief appraisal of particularism is given in my 'Moderate Intuitionism and the Epistemology of Moral Judgment', *Ethical Theory and Moral Practice*, 1 (1998), 14–34.

[31] The notion of the self-evident is defended against many objections by Laurence BonJour, *In Defence of Pure Reason: A Rationalist Account of A Priori Justification* (Cambridge: Cambridge University Press, 1998), and for a more moderate account and other clarificatory moves, see my 'Self-Evidence', *Philosophical Perspectives*, 13 (1999), 205–28.

a major role, certain kinds of disequilibrium can defeat justification even where the proposition is true and justification for believing it can be restored. Third, and perhaps most controversial, even on an empiricist epistemology, as indeed perhaps along noncognitivist lines, one could maintain a kind of intuitionism much like the one sketched here. There would be difficulties in either case; but for certain empiricist views and even for certain noncognitivist positions, both a kind of non-inferential justification and a unification of a plurality of principles under a more comprehensive one would be possible.

A fourth objection is that the value-oriented Kantian intuitionism proposed ignores the need to countenance agent-relative reasons as constraints on conduct that would maximize intrinsic value yet be wrong because it uses someone merely as a means. Suppose I could save 100 innocent people from summary execution by terrorists if I executed one innocent person myself. May I not decline on the agent-relative ground that *my* deepest standards forbid so using a person as a means, even though I believe my doing so would add more to the intrinsic value in the world? (I presuppose that my deepest standards are rational.) A number of points must be made here.

To begin with, once we countenance moral values, it is arguable that the negative moral value of using someone merely as a means in this way is greater than the overall positive value produced. I think this may well be so, but it is not obvious that in all of the cases in question there will be such a difference in overall value. Suppose we change the example so that the number of innocent people saved from execution is 100 times greater or so that the innocent person I must execute would be forced, through brain manipulation, to coerce 100 people into using someone else merely as a means by killing that person to produce the amount of goodness I could produce in the first example. Might I still decline to step into this evil stream? Perhaps the answer is not clear, at least apart from further details (and details make an enormous difference in such cases); but let us assume that it is affirmative. If it is, might we not also reach it by considering the overall value of my options organically? In doing this, we must consider not just consequences of my options, in the sense of effects distinct from the actions that would produce them, but the actions *themselves*, which for a deontological theory may be inherently good or bad and will have specifically moral values or disvalues. Perhaps bringing about a great good, or even preventing a great evil, by doing something that sacrifices a person in a certain way is, overall, intrinsically bad or at least morally wrong. I cannot see why this should not be so. A single blemish can spoil an entire painting.

There is, however, a further question here: is the force of agent-relative reasons ultimately *derivative* from, or at least explainable in terms of, the results of an appraisal of one's overall reason for action, understood in relation to one's contribution to enhancing intrinsic value organically conceived? It is not obvious that the answer to this question is negative. We must not be misled by the term 'agent-relative': the agent and the specific situation of action are crucial, but only in a way that would have identical moral significance for any exactly similar agent in exactly similar circumstances. It is certainly not obvious that the force of agent-relative reasons is not derivative from the relevant agent's contribution to intrinsic value *together* with deontic considerations that are also organically conceived. A positive answer to either question would be explicable in relation to the value-based intuitionism I have presented; but even if the answers are negative, there is at least no good reason to expect a disparity between a sound moral judgment made on the basis of agent-relative reasons and a judgment properly made in the light of the same factual information on the basis of the theory I am presenting.

Related to the worry that the notion of self-evidence is at best mysterious are two objections posed by John Rawls: that intuitionism confronts us with brute facts where explanation should be possible, and that it offers too thin a concept of the person.[32] Let us consider these in turn.

The brute fact objection is perhaps invited by Ross's claim that his principles are self-evident and unprovable, at least if one assumes that any proposition having this status must simply be accepted as true by anyone who understands it. But, in addition to noting that 'mental maturity' is needed to see the truth of the principles in question, Ross acknowledges the defeasibility of the justification of intuitions (or 'convictions', as he also called them), even when he conceived these as beliefs of something self-evident.[33] I think, then, that it is some of Ross's epistemological pronouncements, rather than his actual application of his view of the epistemic or ontic status of moral beliefs, that lends plausibility to the brute fact objection. If one moves to the more systematic value-based theory sketched here, there is even less reason

---

[32] I take these from J. Rawls, 'Kantian Constructivism in Moral Theory', *Journal of Philosophy*, 77 (1980), 515–72; repr. rev. in Rawls, *Political Liberalism* (New York: Columbia University Press, 1993); see esp. pp. 91–2. The first objection is echoed by John McDowell in 'Projection and Truth in Ethics', in Stephen Darwall, Allan Gibbard, and Peter Railton (eds.), *Moral Discourse and Practice* (New York: Oxford University Press, 1997).

[33] Ross notes defeasibility when he compares moral convictions with sense perceptions, *The Right and the Good*, 41.

to call moral principles brute facts. Nothing in their nature prevents informatively deriving them from, or integrating them in relation to, other propositions; and, even apart from the explanation this can make possible, their conceptual complexity would make them appropriate objects of explanation by appeal to a significant range of clarificatory propositions.

One might think that even if moral principles are not brute, singular moral judgments must be, at least for a particularistic intuitionism. Here it is also important to see that despite appearances neither Ross's theory nor the wider theory developed here is acontextual, in the sense that it implies that, independently of circumstances, we 'just see' what we ought to do. To be sure, some factors, such as lying and promise-keeping, injury and relief of suffering, have a moral *bearing* in any context in which they occur, though it may be slight. But on Ross's view as well as on a value-based intuitionism, final duty is a contextual matter having to do with the overall composition of moral forces.

There is some reason to be sympathetic with Rawls's point that Rossian intuitionism presents a thin concept of the person. For Ross sometimes writes as if, quite apart from our sense of what a person is, we should simply see that the prima facie duties bind us. I believe Ross took it as obvious that persons have such good qualities as virtue and intelligence, qualities of which, as a great Aristotelian scholar if for no other reason, he surely had considerable understanding. But in my view the dignity of persons is multi-dimensional, involving at least rationality, normative judgment, sentience, and other values warranting respect for persons. These values governing moral obligation constitute a rich and open-ended array. If it turns out that Ross's intuitionism does not do justice to the concept of a person, the fault can be eliminated by the wider theory I have proposed.

It will be clear that I have sought to present an intuitionist theory that answers another criticism of Ross's intuitionism: the hodgepodge objection.[34] For if Rossian duties—possibly including some beyond those he

---

[34] This is treated by D. McNaughton, 'An Unconnected Heap of Duties?', *Philosophical Quarterly*, 46 (1996), 443–7, and Ch. 3 of this volume; B. Hooker, 'Ross-Style Pluralism vs. Rule-Consequentialism', *Mind*, 105 (1996), 531–52; and others. See also D. McNaughton and P. Rawling, 'On Defending Deontology', *Ratio*, 11/1 (1998), 37–54, both for interpretation of Rossian intuitionism and for criticism of an attempt (quite different from the approach outlined in this paper) to derive a related deontological standard from considerations of value. For critical discussion of Hooker's paper, see P. Stratton-Lake, 'Can Hooker's Rule-Consequentialist Principle Justify Ross's Prima Facie Duties?', *Mind*, 106 (1997), 51–8. A reply by Hooker follows in the same issue, and Hooker provides further defense of his view in *Ideal Code, Real World: A Rule-Consequentialist Theory of Morality* (Oxford: Clarendon Press, 2000).

formulated—are in some way derivable from considerations of value and unifiable in the light of a certain understanding of the categorical imperative, they are not a hodgepodge. This is not to imply that mere derivability implies unifiability; not all entailing premises can achieve unification of what they entail. Nor does unifiability require strict derivability. Illuminating interconnections among principles are possible apart from deducing them from a common set of premises.

One might, however, grant that the theory I propose succeeds in providing for a good measure of unification of Rossian duties, but still wonder whether it implies something Ross plausibly denied: that there is really only one duty. In denying that there is just one, Ross was thinking of Moore and other maximizing consequentialists, but might it not be claimed that the theory I have sketched simply represents Rossian duties as expressing ways, say, to respect the dignity of persons?

I do not deny that Rossian duties can be seen in this light. But it is not as if we had a conception of (for instance) dignity as a one-dimensional quantity to be maximized. Dignity is an open-ended notion whose content is in part given by the duties that it demands we fulfill.[35] In any case, suppose that the *property* of being a prima facie duty were equivalent to a 'single' deontic property (something I certainly do not claim). One candidate would be the disjunctive property of being either a duty of fidelity or one of beneficence or . . . and so on for all the first-order prima facie duties. A more economical candidate, and one more in keeping with the theory outlined here, would be the property (belonging to act-types) of constituting a way of morally respecting the dignity of persons, as do truthfulness, beneficence, and the other obligatory act-types. The *concept* of a prima facie duty need not be simply the disjunctive one in question, nor need the concepts of each of the duties in question be tied directly to that of respecting the dignity of persons. Let me explain how this can be so.

I take duties to be individuated quite finely, at least as finely as intentions, which are among the psychological elements crucial in representing to moral agents the objects of their duties. The duty to A, then, is not the same duty as the duty to B, unless the act-concepts in question are equivalent. Thus, an elementary geometry student's duty to draw an equilateral triangle is not identical with a duty to draw an equiangular one (and a beginner

---

[35] This can give rise to a circularity problem if there is no way to understand it apart from the duties, but that is not so; nor is it the only basis for knowledge of those principles (as it could not be if they are self-evident).

may not even see the connection). Moreover, clearly the disjunctive property just specified (that of being a prima facie duty of fidelity or one of beneficence or . . . and so on for all the first-order prima facie duties) is intelligible only on the basis of an understanding of its several disjuncts. The least deontologically pluralistic outcome we would have, then, would still preserve conceptual independence of the first-order duties: for each of them, one could have a concept of it, and indeed a non-inferential knowledge that people are subject to it, without taking it to be an instance of respecting the dignity of persons, indeed probably without even having the relevant concept of dignity; and this could hold even if there is either an ontological equivalence between being a prima facie duty and being a duty of respecting dignity, or an ontological dependence of the former duty on the latter. Such theoretical equivalences and dependences need not affect the ordinary morally sensitive agent, the kind whose reflective confidence in moral matters is an essential starting point for any particularistic intuitionism.

Clearly, then, there can be a multitude of distinct duties even if they can all be integrated in the light of certain values, such as those essential for the dignity of persons, and can be exhibited as consequences of more basic duties. Duties are as multifarious as intentions. In neither category is there any reason not to see some of the elements as grounded, in one or another of several ways, in more basic elements in the same category, nor, for either duties or the corresponding intentions, is there any bar to viewing their fulfillment as a realization of various kinds of value.

Conclusion

If I have been right in the main ideas suggested here, we can retain the attractive features of a Rossian intuitionism and still extend the theory to a more comprehensive, better-unified view. There can be a comprehensive principle, which may or may not be non-inferentially knowable, that can unify first-order principles of duty without implying that they are not themselves non-inferentially knowable and in that way epistemically independent. There can also be values associated with such a principle which can do two things: they can indicate how adhering to the principle conduces to human flourishing, and they can provide some help in dealing with conflicts of prima facie duties. The intrinsically good and intrinsically bad things in question can be non-inferentially and intuitively known to be good or to be bad, as some of the principles that reflect them can be non-inferentially and intuitively known to be true. And, without the burden of having to maximize any value or set of values, moral agents can see themselves as promoting the good in fulfilling their moral obligations.

Overall duty, like overall reason for action, is commonly a matter of an organic composition of basic prima facie reasons; and though the fulfillment of an overall duty can be seen to realize values, and its existence can even be ontically grounded in considerations of overall value, it is not an additive result even with respect to a plurality of values as components. Despite this ontological complexity, it is often quite obvious what one's final duty is. Even where duties conflict, it may still be plain that one should, for instance, tell the truth or help a suffering friend. In many such cases (though not in all) one may have a moral intuition that constitutes a kind of non-inferential knowledge of final duty. When there is a conflict of duties that leaves it at least initially unclear what to do, if we have practical wisdom we can often determine our final duty without the help of theory. But theory is available to assist practical wisdom in recalcitrant or borderline cases. It can play this role even for a person of practical wisdom who is highly intuitive. This is not a one-way street, however: the exercise of practical wisdom—which often leads to plausible and highly stable intuitions in moral matters—may also extend our theory. Intuitions about cases, like principles of general obligation, retain moral and epistemic authority; but intuitions about cases may also be corrected by a good theory, even though, without them, we could neither develop a good ethical theory nor adequately conduct our moral life.

Sidgwick and the Boundaries of Intuitionism

Roger Crisp

In the mid-1980s I attended a series of graduate seminars, run by Derek Parfit, on Sidgwick's *Methods of Ethics*. Parfit began the first seminar by claiming that the *Methods* was the greatest book on ethics ever written. This was not to say that Sidgwick was the greatest moral philosopher ever, since he had had the advantage of reading the works of past philosophers.[1] Parfit went on to describe the common experience of thinking of some philosophical point, and then later finding it in Sidgwick. This struck a chord with me at the time. Writing a thesis on utilitarianism, I had found a central claim in my argument anticipated by Sidgwick—and, to make matters worse, hidden deep in a footnote.

Of course, one reads Sidgwick primarily not to avoid reinventing the wheel, but to seek the illumination of his 'pure white light'—to use the phrase used of him by a British philosopher overheard by Blanshard.[2] Sidgwick came after the great seventeenth- and eighteenth-century debates between the intuitionists of the moral sense school, such as Shaftesbury and Hutcheson, and the rational intuitionists, Cudworth, Clarke, Price, and others. His aim was to follow Aristotle, by reflecting upon the common-sense morality of his day in order to make it as consistent as possible, and to seek whatever justification might be available for elements within it:

For helpful comments on earlier drafts, I am grateful to Robert Audi, Brad Hooker, Derek Parfit, Bart Schultz, Robert Shaver, those who attended the University of Keele conference entitled 'Re-evaluating Ethical Intuitionism', held on 3–5 June 1999, and an anonymous reader for Oxford University Press.

[1] Similar views were held by C. D. Broad and Brand Blanshard. See Broad, *Five Types of Ethical Theory* (London: Routledge & Kegan Paul, 1930), 143; Blanshard, *Reason and Goodness* (London: George Allen & Unwin, 1961), 90–1.

[2] B. Blanshard, 'Sidgwick the Man', *Monist*, 58 (1974), 349.

to expound as clearly and as fully as my limits will allow the different methods of Ethics that I find implicit in our common moral reasoning; to point out their mutual relations; and where they seem to conflict, to define the issue as much as possible. In the course of this endeavour I am led to discuss the considerations which should, in my opinion, be decisive in determining the adoption of ethical first principles.[3]

A 'method' is a rational system for determining whether a proposed action is right or not. Sidgwick considers three main methods—egoism, intuitionism, and utilitarianism—and sought to show that the last two could, contrary to common belief, be reconciled. Because of his insight, impartiality, and exactingness, he was able to produce a version of intuitionism which, its boundaries duly drawn, and cleared of a misconception, should find more agreement among contemporary thinkers than the views of any of his predecessors, and is at least a serious contender for the strongest version of intuitionism yet developed.

1. Intuition, the Radar View, and Intuitions

Whatever intuitionists believe, presumably they must think that human beings possess 'intuition'.[4] It is commonly thought that intuition must be, as J. L. Mackie put it, 'some special faculty of moral perception . . . utterly different from our ordinary ways of knowing everything else'.[5] This was clearly the position of the moral sense theorists. Hutcheson, for example, suggests that 'the Author of Nature . . . has given us a moral sense to direct our actions . . . a determination of our minds to receive the simple ideas of approbation or condemnation from actions observed antecedent to any opinions of advantage or loss to redound to ourselves from them'.[6] But because a rational intuitionist might also posit some special rational faculty, let me call this the *radar view* of intuition. As bats have radar, so we have our special moral faculty.

---

[3] H. Sidgwick, *The Methods of Ethics*, 7th edn. (London: Macmillan, 1907), 11; cf. pp. 373–4, quoted at p. 67–8 below. In this paper I shall restrict myself to the account of intuitionism offered by Sidgwick in *The Methods of Ethics*. References are to the 7th edition.

[4] It is here worth noting the view of John Grote that 'The word "intuition" . . . is a most misleading word: for by its reference to sight it inevitably suggests an object supposed to exist standing off from us and independent of us, than which nothing can be supposed more incongruous with the notion of immediate thought . . . in fact, it is almost the most confusing word in all philosophy' (*Exploratio Philosophica*, ii (Cambridge: Cambridge University Press, 1900), 147 and 203).

[5] J. L. Mackie, *Ethics: Inventing Right and Wrong* (Harmondsworth: Penguin, 1977), 38.

[6] J. B. Schneewind (ed.), *Moral Philosophy from Montaigne to Kant*, 2 vols. (Cambridge: Cambridge University Press, 1990), 510.

Roger Crisp

Sidgwick does believe that intuition is a 'faculty'.[7] Compare what Socrates says in connection with knowledge and belief in the *Republic*:

Let us class together as 'faculties' the powers in us and in other things that enable us to perform all the various functions of which we are capable. Thus I call sight and hearing faculties . . .
And should opinion be classified as a faculty?
Yes, it is the power which enables us to hold opinions.[8]

Intuition for Sidgwick is a doxastic faculty,[9] nothing more, or less, than a capacity for forming beliefs of a certain kind, with the possibility thereby of acquiring knowledge. He is not committed to the radar view.[10] The analogy he draws—absolutely standard in the rational intuitionist tradition, and rooted in Aristotle's *Ethics*—is not with sense perception, but with the quasi-perceptual, intellectual understanding characteristic of disciplines such as mathematics.[11] To use Aristotle's example, as one sees for oneself that a triangle is the last mathematical object, so one sees (morally) P.[12] Consider this from Sidgwick: 'the propositions, "I ought not to prefer a present lesser good to a future greater good," and "I ought not to prefer my own lesser good to the greater good of another," do present themselves as self-evident; as much (*e.g.*) as the mathematical axiom that "if equals be added to equals the wholes are equal." '[13] Sidgwick draws a contrast between the a priori character of moral intuition and the a posteriori nature of sense experience.[14] Some moral intuitions might, however, be held not to be a priori: consider the intuition that I must keep

---

[7] *The Methods of Ethics*, 5 and 275.

[8] Plato, *Republic*, trans. D. Lee, 2nd edn., (Harmondsworth: Penguin, 1974), 477c–e. The word translated as 'faculty' is *dunamis*, which may also mean 'capacity' or 'power'. Indeed the verb translated here with the notions of enablement and power is *dunasthai*.

[9] *The Methods of Ethics*, 28.

[10] Robert Audi notes, approvingly, that neither is Ross. See Audi, 'Intuitionism, Pluralism, and the Foundations of Ethics', in W. Sinnott-Armstrong and M. Timmons (eds.), *Moral Knowledge?* (Oxford: Oxford University Press, 1996), 106. I am indebted to Audi's article, and see my project in relation to Sidgwick as similar in aim and outcome to his study of Ross. It is worth noting that the radar view was denied also by Alexander Smith and William Whewell; see J. Schneewind, *Sidgwick's Ethics and Victorian Moral Philosophy* (Cambridge: Cambridge University Press, 1977), 107.

[11] For doubts on the appropriateness of the analogy, see B. Williams, 'What does Intuitionism Imply?', in Williams, *Making Sense of Humanity and Other Philosophical Papers 1982–1993* (Cambridge: Cambridge University Press, 1995), 183–4; Audi, 'Intuitionism, Pluralism, and the Foundations of Ethics', 114. For a view on the relation of intuitionism and rationalism, see A. Donagan, 'Moral Rationalism and Variable Social Institutions', in P. A. French, T. E. Uehling, Jr., and H. F. Wettstein (eds.), *Midwest Studies in Philosophy, 7 Social and Political Philosophy* (1982), 3.

[12] Aristotle, *Nicomachean Ethics* 1142ª23–30.

[13] *The Methods of Ethics*, 383; cf. pp. 229, 338, 507.   [14] Ibid., e.g. p. 98.

this particular promise.[15] Still, it is fairly clear that Sidgwick himself took intuitions (proper) to be synthetic a priori truths—that is, substantive truths that can be known merely by the proper understanding of them. This is probably because he was considering intuitions as possible foundations for a universal philosophical ethical theory, as a method, not as a particular response to individual situations.[16]

What is the P that is seen intuitively? Sometimes Sidgwick implies that it is the property of rightness or reasonableness, as instantiated in some action or rule.[17] More often, however, it is a proposition to the effect that some action or rule is right or reasonable.[18] Sidgwick would probably not have seen an important difference between intuiting such a property and intuiting such a proposition.[19] For he would have been prepared to elucidate seeing F-ness in some object O as seeing that O is F, that is, as acquiring the belief that O is F.

Again, as standard in the tradition, Sidgwick distinguishes intuitive beliefs as non-inferential.[20] My belief that I should help Ms Jones, based on my beliefs that one should help people in need, and that Ms Jones is in need, is not intuitive. But my belief that, *ceteris paribus*, one should help people in need may be intuitive, if it is not inferred from some other belief or set of beliefs.

It is common to hear the claim that intuitionists are committed to 'entities or qualities or relations of a very strange sort, utterly different from anything else in the universe'.[21] But just as it may be a mistake to link intuitionism too quickly with the radar view, so it is unwise to saddle it, as an epistemological thesis, with any metaphysical commitment to (for example) non-natural properties.[22] Indeed Sidgwick himself, unlike Whewell perhaps, need not be seen as committed to any form of 'Platonist' metaphysics, but merely to the idea that there are reasons for action.[23] Likewise, a philosophical naturalist may accept intuition if she allows that we have the capacity to form non-inferential beliefs about what it is ultimately right or reasonable to do. Whether the objects of those beliefs can be

---

[15] The example is from Audi, 'Intuitionism, Pluralism and the Foundations of Ethics', 109.

[16] Cf. Sidgwick's doubt about whether Perceptional Intuitionism counts as a method, quoted in Sect. 4, below.   [17] *The Methods of Ethics*, 77.

[18] Ibid., pp. xviii–xix, 5, 28, 77, 98, 101.   [19] Cf. ibid., 2.

[20] Cf. Audi, 'Intuitionism, Pluralism, and the Foundations of Ethics', 109, 131–2 n. 18. Strictly, of course, it is propositions that are inferred from other propositions.

[21] Mackie, *Ethics*, 38.

[22] Cf. Audi, 'Intuitionism, Pluralism, and the Foundations of Ethics', 122.

[23] See Schneewind, *Sidgwick's Ethics*, 222 and 303–4.

understood naturalistically or not is a metaphysical question, to be kept apart from epistemology or psychological questions concerning moral phenomenology.

2. The Hotline View

We have seen that, while remaining within the broadly intuitionist tradition, Sidgwick denies the radar view. He denies also what one might call the 'hotline view', according to which beliefs based on moral intuition are self-evident in the sense of self-guaranteeing or indefeasible.[24] The hotline view can be found explicitly stated in the majority of intuitionist writers before Sidgwick, including Suárez, Grotius, Pufendorf, Locke, Clarke, and Shaftesbury.[25] The following from Clarke is pretty typical:

These things are so notoriously plain and self-evident that nothing but the extremest stupidity of mind, corruption of manners, or perverseness or spirit can possibly make any man entertain the least doubt concerning them. For a man endued with reason to deny the truth of these things is the very same thing as if a man that has the use of his sight should at the same time that he beholds the sun deny that there is any such thing as light in the world.[26]

This form of dogmatism tends to rest on the view that knowledge of morality is given by God to all human beings, and indeed that such knowledge provides evidence of God's existence. Denial, then, is close to heresy. As he retreated from theism, so Sidgwick distanced himself from the hotline view:

By cognition I always mean what some would rather call 'apparent cognition'—that is, I do not mean to affirm the *validity* of the cognition, but only its existence as a psychical fact, and its claim to be valid . . . I wish . . . to say expressly, that by calling any affirmation

---

[24] See Audi, 'Intuitionism, Pluralism, and the Foundations of Ethics', 107. Again, Sidgwick was anticipated by Alexander Smith. See Schneewind, *Sidgwick's Ethics*, 87. Note that Sidgwick does accept that moral beliefs can be self-evident in a different sense: see below.

[25] See e.g. Schneewind (ed.), *Moral Philosophy from Montaigne to Kant*, 73 (Suarez: 'indubitably true by the light of faith'); p. 94 (Grotius: 'fundamental conceptions which are beyond question'); p. 164 (Pufendorf: 'the common and important provisions of the natural law are so plain and clear that they at once find assent, and grow up in our minds, so that they can never again be destroyed'); p. 185 (Locke: 'moral principles require reasoning and discourse . . . to discover the certainty of their truth'); p. 493 (Shaftesbury: 'Sense of right and wrong therefore being as natural to us as natural affection itself, and being a first principle in our constitution and make, there is no speculative opinion, persuasion, or belief, which is capable immediately or directly to exclude or destroy it').

[26] Ibid., 296–7.

as to the rightness or wrongness of actions 'intuitive', I do not mean to prejudge the question as to its ultimate validity, when philosophically considered: I only mean that its truth is apparently known immediately, and not as the result of reasoning.[27]

There is, I suspect, little need for me to defend the wisdom of Sidgwick's rejection of the hotline view. Stripped of its theological grounding, and regardless of the success or otherwise of the Cartesian project, the view that certain moral principles are indefeasible is nothing more than bluster. It is disappointing, then, to find it in the work of Prichard, along with the idea that, though someone who disagrees with him about ethics is not a heretic, she is a less 'developed moral being'.[28] Prichard's own hotline view rests not on theology, but on the semantic point that knowledge must be true and so (Prichard argues) cannot be doubted, which can of course be rather easily sidestepped by speaking only in terms of beliefs (or by noting that knowledge can anyway be doubted). Ross clearly owes a great debt to Prichard, one that he acknowledges in the preface to *The Right and the Good*.[29] But as far as I can see Audi is right to claim that Ross nowhere commits himself explicitly to the hotline view. Unlike Moore, however, Ross does not deny it. Moore follows Sidgwick: 'in every way in which it is possible to cognize a true proposition, it is also possible to cognize a false one'.[30] Among those recent writers who see themselves as successors to Ross, Jonathan Dancy does not commit himself either way, while David McNaughton explicitly allows that any moral belief may justifiably be questioned.[31]

To return to Sidgwick. Though he gives up the hotline view, he emphatically does not give up the idea that intuitions—genuine intuitions—are self-evident.[32] Genuine moral intuitions, then, are self-evident, non-inferential

---

[27] Cf. *The Methods of Ethics*, 34 n. 2, 211; cf. 2. Note the 'only'. Sidgwick here restricts himself to something like the narrow definition of intuition I am recommending. As we shall see, he does not always respect this restriction.

[28] H. A. Prichard, 'Does Moral Philosophy Rest on a Mistake?', in Prichard, *Moral Obligation: Essays and Lecturers*, ed. W. D. Ross (Oxford: Clarendon Press, 1949), 9 and 14–15.

[29] W. D. Ross, *The Right and the Good* (Oxford: Clarendon Press, 1930), p. v; for Prichardian influence, see e.g. p. 12.

[30] G. E. Moore, *Principia Ethica* (Cambridge: Cambridge University Press, 1903), p. x; cf. p. 75. Moore is particularly keenly aware of the difficulty of holding the view that intuitions are self-evident as non-inferential, while using as evidence for such intuitive propositions the fact that they appear self-evident: 'By saying that a proposition is self-evident, we mean emphatically that its appearing so to us, is *not* the reason why it is true: for we mean that it has absolutely no reason' (ibid. 143; cf. p. 145). (We should understand 'reason why it is true' as 'reason why we are justified in holding it to be true'.)

[31] J. Dancy, *Moral Reasons* (Oxford: Blackwell, 1993); D. McNaughton, *Moral Vision* (Oxford: Blackwell, 1988), 156.

[32] *The Methods of Ethics*, 211–12. The distinction between genuinely and apparently self-evident

moral beliefs, and they provide the hope of axioms on which to ground a scientific ethics. More on self-evidence, and ethics as a science, below.

Sidgwick commonly speaks of certain intuitions as 'fundamental'.[33] He should not be understood to be importing any kind of strong foundationalism.[34] First, recall his denial of the hotline view. Second, consider the role he gives to common-sense morality (CSM) as a test for our moral intuitions (more on this below). Sidgwick's claim is best taken to be merely that certain intuitions are more important than others in moral justification, or in developing a moral theory.

Sidgwick from the start of the *Methods* assumes 'that there is something under any given circumstances which it is right or reasonable to do, and that this may be known'[35]—and that this knowledge is acquired at least in part through exercise of the intuitive faculty. Intuitionism as he understands it is the view that knowledge of moral truth can be obtained through intuition, i.e. that some of our ultimate and underived moral beliefs may be true and justified. It is, then, a form of ethical cognitivism. Intuitionism should not, however, be tied to cognitivism so tightly; all it requires is *beliefs* (or perhaps 'cognitions') of a certain kind, which may then be interpreted in line with either cognitivism or non-cognitivism.[36] The methodology of self-evidence (see Section 6, below) can, in fact, be detached from any cognitivist implications, and turned into a first-order set of recommendations about how to decide what to do. If second-order claims may be insulated from first-order, as many non-cognitivists believe, there is nothing to prevent a non-cognitivist's advocating that we aim to construct a system of moral beliefs which, as far as possible, meets the conditions of self-evidence, and then to live by that system. Indeed at times Sidgwick himself appears to think that any first-order view, to be at

---

intuitions can be found at pp. 374–5. On apparent self-evidence, see Audi, 'Intuitionism, Pluralism, and the Foundations of Ethics', 114 and 132 n. 24. Audi suggests that the use of 'self-evident' of false beliefs is non-standard. But presumably he would not object to a distinction between genuine and apparent self-evidence, genuine self-evidence then being at least a prima facie basis for knowledge. (Audi prefers that we describe beliefs anyway as (at best) only derivatively self-evident, self-evidence proper being a chararacteristic of the content of beliefs.)

[33] *The Methods of Ethics*, pp. xviii and xxi.

[34] *Pace* T. H. Irwin, 'Eminent Victorians and Greek Ethics', in B. Schultz (ed.), *Essays on Henry Sidgwick* (Cambridge: Cambridge University Press, 1992), 304. Cf. my 'Griffin's Pessimism', in R. Crisp and B. Hooker (eds.), *Well-Being and Morality: Essays in Honour of James Griffin* (Oxford: Clarendon Press, 2000), 116–21. [35] *The Methods of Ethics*, p. vii; cf. p. 33.

[36] Cf. Audi, 'Intuitionism, Pluralism, and the Foundations of Ethics', 123.

all respectable, must rest on a fundamental intuition[37] (see e.g. the discussion of hedonism on p. 98).[38]

3. Who is Not an Intuitionist?

Which philosophers deny intuitions? Hume might, at first blush, be thought a paradigm non-intuitionist. But consider Hume's famous passage on exercise:

Perhaps, to your . . . question, *why he desires health*, he may . . . reply, that *it is necessary for the exercise of his calling.* If you ask, *why he is anxious on that head,* he will answer, *because he desires to get money.* If you demand *Why? It is the instrument of pleasure,* says he. And beyond this it is an absurdity to ask for a reason. It is impossible there can be a progress *in infinitum;* and that one thing can always be a reason, why another is desired. Something must be desirable on its own account, and because of its immediate accord or agreement with human sentiment and affection.[39]

Hume's suggestion that something must be desirable on its own account is not implausibly taken to be a belief, indeed a non-inferential one. It would be 'absurd' to seek a further reason for it—that is, it is self-evident. Hume would indeed have to be taken to claim that we have this belief only because pleasure 'recommends itself' to our sentiments, 'without any dependence on the intellectual faculties'. But the belief would not be inferred from the feelings; it could not be. So Hume may be understood as an intuitionist.

Continuing to seek opponents to Sidgwick, we may examine the controversies in nineteenth-century ethics to which he was party. A key debate was that between the intuitionists and the inductivists. Sidgwick, however, saw clearly that this debate rested on a confusion.[40] The inductivists believed that 'right and wrong, as well as truth and falsehood, are questions of observation and experience'.[41] They saw themselves in opposition to the intuitionists, who accepted 'a natural faculty, a sense or instinct, informing us of right and wrong'.[42] But once it becomes clear that there is

---

[37] Cf. D. D. Raphael, 'Sidgwick on Intuitionism', *Monist*, 58 (1974), 407.

[38] It should be noted that Sidgwick here insists on cognitivism as well as the meeting of the four conditions, because he thinks that normative truths are not reducible to natural truths. But what I am suggesting is that cognitivism and the conditions can be prised apart.

[39] D. Hume, *An Enquiry Concerning the Principles of Morals*, ed. T. Beauchamp (Oxford: Clarendon Press, 1998), app. 1.19.   [40] *The Methods of Ethics*, 97–8.

[41] J. S. Mill, *Utilitarianism*, ed. R. Crisp (Oxford: Oxford University Press, 1998), 1. 3. 19–21.

[42] Ibid., 1. 3. 2.

a difference between the claim that there is a special faculty of intuition, and the claim that normative views require at least one ultimate, non-inferential normative proposition as their foundation, the intuitionist–inductivist debate collapses.

Might it be possible to deny the non-inferentiality of moral beliefs, suggesting, perhaps, that each belief rests on others? This leads to a Sextian regress of justification, of course, but as a psychological view it might still be true.[43] Hume and many other people, however, provide counter-examples.

The only clear opponents to the Sidgwickian version of the view that we have moral intuition, and moral intuitions, are likely to be those who deny the existence of any moral beliefs, such as strict emotivists.[44] Sidgwick's argument against strict emotivism is a powerful one, and was employed later against Ayer and others: 'The peculiar emotion of moral approbation is, in my experience, inseparably bound up with the conviction, implicit or explicit, that the conduct approved is . . . right—*i.e.* that it cannot, without error, be disapproved by any other mind.'[45] Note that we are not here concerned with the matter whether the conduct approved really is right or not, merely with the question whether human beings have the capacity to acquire such beliefs or convictions. Sidgwick's introspective claim seems to constitute a good counter-example to strict emotivism. What is required is some plausible account of the nature of Sidgwick's experience, and of how he came so seriously to misinterpret it. I know of no such account.

To summarize the argument so far. Moral intuition is the capacity to form non-inferential, self-evident beliefs that certain actions, rules, or whatever are right or reasonable, and moral intuitions are such beliefs. The claim that we possess such a capacity should be kept apart from any other thesis, such as the radar view, the hotline view, or non-naturalism. So understood, the view that we have moral intuition is likely to be widely accepted.

---

[43] See Sextus Empiricus, *Outlines of Pyrrhonism*, trans. J. Annas and J. Barnes as *Outlines of Scepticism* (Cambridge: Cambridge University Press, 1994), 1. 15. Partly because of limitation of space, I am being somewhat brusque with coherentism here. But I should register my belief that coherentism can avoid regress only through the introduction, at some level, of non-inferential groundings (in other words, by moving in the direction of foundationalism).

[44] See e.g. A. J. Ayer, *Language, Truth, and Logic* (Harmondsworth: Pelican, 1971), 142. Cf. Allan Gibbard: 'To call something rational is to express one's acceptance of norms that permit it' (*Wise Choices, Apt Feelings: A Theory of Normative Judgment* (Oxford: Clarendon Press, 1990), 7). Gibbard has pointed out to me that more subtle versions of emotivism or expressivism may use the term 'intuition' to refer to a certain set of moral utterances which can then be understood according to the theory. But it may be that the Sidgwickian argument to follow in the text provides at the least a phenomenological hurdle for such a view to jump.

[45] *The Methods of Ethics*, 27; cf. pp. 35, 211.

4. Perceptional Intuitionism

As is well known, Sidgwick offers a threefold characterization of the forms of intuitionism: Perceptional (PI), Dogmatic (DI), and Philosophical (PHI). Let me now consider how he distinguishes them.

One relevant contrast, which has already been touched upon in the weight attached to non-inferentiality above, is that between immediacy and non-immediacy. Sidgwick says of PI: [It] may be called, in a sense, 'ultra-intuitional', since, in its most extreme form, it recognizes simple immediate intuitions alone and discards as superfluous all modes of reasoning to moral conclusions: and we may find in it one phase or variety of the Intuitional method,—if we may extend the term 'method' to include a procedure that is completed in a single judgement.'[46] The contrast here, then, is between a form of intuitionism that puts all of its weight on the intuition that φ-ing is right or reasonable, and a form that, though allowing such an intuition, draws its conclusions about what to do on the basis of some kind of reasoning. This perhaps explains why Sidgwick chooses also to characterize PI in terms of its object, namely, particular actions. For a version of intuitionism that put all of its weight on the intuition that a certain rule was right or reasonable, and then rejected any mode of reasoning to a conclusion about what to do, Sidgwick may be thinking, would be odd indeed: its rules would never find any application.

Again, however, distinctions are getting entangled with one another. It is worth keeping the immediate–non-immediate distinction apart from that between action-focused and rule-focused theories. As Sidgwick allows, the action-focused view he describes is only one version of such a view. We can imagine an action-focused view that puts a lot of weight on the exercise of reasoning. Similarly, though an ultra-intuitional version of DI—a version of intuitionism that concerns moral rules—is unlikely, it is not impossible. It may be claimed that one can intuit immediately the correct moral rules, and equally immediately in any situation see which rule is relevant, and even which means to take to one's goal.

Intuitionism is an epistemological theory, a theory about how we should reach our moral conclusions. The immediate–non-immediate distinction does capture something epistemological, namely, the weight to be placed

---

[46] Ibid., 100. PI is an extreme form of 'situation ethics' or 'particularism', since it advocates judging each case entirely on its merits, and without any use of moral principles. Less extreme versions of each view respectively may be found in, for example, J. Fletcher, *Situation Ethics* (London: SCM Press, 1966), ch. 8; Dancy, *Moral Reasons*, ch. 4.

on intuition in relation to rational argument. A theory that allows for a lot of reasoning between fundamental intuition and action does not, however, seem to differ importantly from a theory that allows for less reasoning, if both theories place all the justificatory weight upon the intuition about what is ultimately right or reasonable.

Sidgwick's focus on the action–rule distinction, then, has little to do with epistemology or intuitionism. There is an obvious and important distinction between claims about the justificatory weight to be put on beliefs acquired in a certain way, and the content of those beliefs. Above I suggested that the claim that we possess the faculty of intuition should be understood as epistemological or psychological, and not as metaphysical. A corollary of that, of course, is that intuitionism should be seen as an epistemological and not a metaphysical thesis. The moral of Sidgwick's attempt to distinguish PI from DI using the action–rule distinction is that intuitionism should also be kept apart from first-order ethics.[47] And it is in first-order ethics that claims about whether we should focus on actions, rules, virtues, characters, or whatever belong.

The same is true of several other distinctions Sidgwick uses to characterize forms of intuitionism. For example, he distinguishes intuitionism concerning rightness or reasonableness from intuitionism concerning goodness.[48] There may well be a large difference between right-centred and good-centred ethical views, but this difference seems independent of epistemology. The same is true of the distinction between views according to which rightness can be intuited of action independently of consequences, and views that deny this.

There is an obvious danger in failing to keep first-order views and epistemological views apart, namely, some first-order view may be rejected for irrelevant epistemological reasons, or some epistemological view may be rejected for irrelevant first-order reasons. Sidgwick himself provides an example, aspects of which we have already discussed. At page 97 Sidgwick contrasts the 'Intuitional' view that certain consequences are 'judged to be good *immediately*' with the view that such consequences are to be judged 'by inference from experience of the pleasures which they produce'. Now this may be taken to be a contrast between an intuitionist and a non-intuitionist view, and it could be that someone who favours intuitionism might therefore reject the view about inference from experience. But Sidgwick himself goes on to show

---

[47] Cf. Broad, *Five Types of Ethical Theory*, 206; Audi, 'Intuitionism, Pluralism, and the Foundations of Ethics', 102.   [48] *The Methods of Ethics*, 3, 103, 105, 391.

that views such as the inference view themselves require a fundamental intuition (to the effect, in this case, presumably, that it is ultimately reasonable to judge the value of consequences by inference from the pleasures that they produce). And it has to be admitted that in this passage Sidgwick makes it less clear than he might that he is not contrasting intuitionism with non-intuitionism, since he suggests that classing the immediacy view as 'Intuitional' is to claim that 'the results in question are judged to be good *immediately*, and not by inference from experience of the pleasures they produce'.

5. Dogmatic Intuitionism, Philosophical Intuitionism, and Common-Sense Morality

DI is a pluralistic view based on the morality of common sense. Given that one must not allow its intuitionist credentials to rest on its pluralistic content, let me now consider the difference between the second and third 'phases' of intuitionism, between DI and PHI.

One obvious way in which one might attempt a distinction between these two views would be to concentrate on their respective attitudes to CSM.[49] DI requires us to begin *and* end with common-sense morality, and indeed to remain within its boundaries throughout our inquiry.[50] We may be unsatisfied with PI's potential for arbitrariness and inconsistency, and seek, perhaps in addition to intuitions concerning particular actions, intuitions concerning 'general formulae'. Such general rules are easy to find, and the task of DI is to clarify them and make them more precise, so that they may serve as 'scientific axioms'. This is what Sidgwick himself attempts on behalf of DI in III. 2–10.

A radical version of PHI might perhaps eschew putting any weight at all on CSM, advising us to attempt to free ourselves from any potential for bias from ingrained prejudice by distancing ourselves from our everyday moral beliefs. This is not Sidgwick's version. His third phase of intuitionism also begins with, or emerges out of, CSM. Sidgwick admits, that is, that he is inclined broadly to accept CSM. But Sidgwick's conception of philosophy itself is different from that which he sees as undergirding DI:

we conceive it as the aim of a philosopher, as such, to do somewhat more than define and formulate the common moral opinions of mankind. His function is to tell men what

---

[49] Ibid., 214–16.   [50] I take it that this is why Sidgwick calls it dogmatic.

they ought to think, rather than what they do think: he is expected to transcend Common Sense in his premises, and is allowed a certain divergence from Common Sense in his conclusions . . . we should expect that the history of Moral Philosophy—so far at least as those whom we may call orthodox thinkers are concerned—would be a history of attempts to enunciate, in full breadth and clearness, those primary intuitions of Reason, by the scientific application of which the common moral thought of mankind may be at once systematized and corrected.[51]

The difference between DI and PHI, then, is that the advocate of DI takes the commonly accepted moral rules as the 'basis on which his own system is constructed',[52] beginning, that is, on the assumption that a tidied-up set of the rules of CSM will be the result of reflection. The aim of moral philosophy, according to DI, is to *formulate* CSM using the intuitional method.[53] PHI, however, seeks to get behind CSM, and to systematize and correct it.[54] One's conclusions are still constrained by CSM, however, and 'flagrant conflict with common opinion' must be avoided.[55] In this sense, Sidgwick's version of PHI is a version of Aristotelian dialectic.[56] The general idea is that CSM, as a whole, has some initial authority. It is, presumably, conceivable that it might have to be junked, but that possibility is highly remote. One then seeks self-evident background intuitions about what is right or reasonable, and these should explain, systematize, and justify (much of) CSM. If one's background intuitions are seriously inconsistent with CSM, or some of its core principles, that is highly likely to count against them. But if they are not, then those aspects of CSM which are inconsistent with one's principles may be rejected, while conflicts in CSM may be resolved, and gaps filled in, using the background principles.

It is worth noting that this procedure is not quite a version of what Rawls calls reflective equilibrium.[57] Rawls's method requires one to test one's

---

[51] *The Method of Ethics*, 373–4.   [52] Ibid., 373.

[53] Sidgwick almost certainly has Whewell in mind; see Schneewind, *Sidgwick's Ethics*, 108.

[54] *The Methods of Ethics*, 374; cf. p. 102.   [55] Ibid., 373 and 400.

[56] See Aristotle, *Nicomachean Ethics* 1145ᵇ1–7. Like Aristotle, Sidgwick does not restrict himself to seeking coherence in the set of views constituted by common sense and philosophy, but develops his own positions, which are then tested against common sense and philosophy. Cf. Schneewind, *Sidgwick's Ethics*, 48.

[57] See John Rawls, *A Theory of Justice* (Cambridge, Mass.: Harvard University Press, 1971), 20–1 and 48–51. At p. 51 n., Rawls quotes *The Methods of Ethics*, 373–4, as evidence of Sidgwick's holding something close to the reflective equilibrium view. On this, see P. Singer, 'Sidgwick and Reflective Equilibrium', *Monist*, 58 (1974), 490–517. Unlike Singer, I do not accept that Sidgwick appeals to common-sense morality only as part of a rhetorical strategy. Nor do I see that pp. xv–xxi of *The Methods of Ethics* justifies Russell Hardin's interpretation of Sidgwick as committed to reflective equilibrium; see Hardin, 'Common Sense at the Foundations', in B. Schultz (ed.), *Essays on Henry Sidgwick* (Cambridge: Cambridge University Press, 1992), 146.

principles against one's considered and confident moral convictions. For example, the principles delivered in the original position might be tested against our confident conviction that religious intolerance is unjust. Both principles and convictions are provisional, and if there is a mismatch one goes back and forth between principle and convictions, modifying either as seems appropriate, until one reaches equilibrium.

Sidgwick's method differs from this in several ways. First, he draws no distinction between principles and considered convictions. Convictions, if they are properly considered, will be self-evident, and thus constitute principles.[58] Second, in any plurality of principles one seeks consistency between them. One way to do this might be to seek some new self-evident principle, on the basis of toing and froing between reflection on the conflicting principles, which might enable one to abandon both of the original principles. But another might be to engage in further independent reflection on each principle, in the hope of seeking consistency through detecting merely apparent self-evidence in the case of one or more of the inconsistent principles.[59] Finally, though one is required to test one's own principles against CSM, CSM need not be taken to be 'considered'. Indeed, Sidgwick does not think it is. Aristotelian dialectic requires testing one's conclusions against the views not only of the wise, who have considered beliefs, but also of the many.[60] If I think P, and nearly everyone else has thought and continues to think not-P, I should—if I have no more reason to think that I am right—be reduced 'temporarily to a state of neutrality'.[61] It turns out, as we shall see shortly, that Sidgwick's requirement that we compare our own conclusions against CSM is itself part of his account of self-evidence, and hence of his account of intuitionism itself.

Sidgwick's attempt to distinguish two phases of intuitionism, DI and

[58] Unless, of course, they are merely convictions concerning particular cases. But if one wishes to give weight to convictions concerning particular cases, and restrict their being universalized into principles, it is unclear why one should be interested in principles.

[59] Rawls does in fact allow that mere knowledge of our principles may suggest 'further reflections that lead us to revise our judgments' (*A Theory of Justice*, 49). This seems to allow that even perfect reflective equilibrium is unstable, and one might wonder whether the point at which instability sets in is not the point at which a Sidgwickian epistemology appears attractive.

[60] Aristotle, *Nicomachean Ethics* 1098^b27–9. I have already mentioned Sidgwick's reference to the views of the many at *The Methods of Ethics*, 373 and 400. At pp. 384–6 he appeals to the views of the wise—in particular, Clarke and Kant—in support of his own. He does not discuss the fact that at least certain other respectable philosophers would disagree with him. Because of the appeal to the views of the many, I am unable to accept T. H. Irwin's claim that 'Sidgwick intends to reject any role for moral beliefs [Irwin means, I think, "common-sense moral beliefs"] in specifying the first principles' (Irwin, 'Eminent Victorians and Greek Ethics', 304).

[61] *The Methods of Ethics*, 342. See the discussion of 'consensus' below.

PHI, again runs together first- and second-order positions, and thus fails successfully to characterize any difference in intuitional method. Let us assume that PHI sets certain standards for intuitions to meet, and recommends that we seek to hone our intuitions in the hope that they may meet the standards (this is, of course, exactly what Sidgwick himself claims, and I shall discuss the standards below). DI as formulated above treats CSM as its 'basis', in the sense that it sees the job of philosophy as the formulation of CSM and no more. But there is nothing to prevent the view that CSM's general principles are correct being an intuition that meets all the relevant standards. The view that these principles are correct is a first-order view, in other words, and does not capture anything specific to any form of intuitionism.

6. Self-Evidence

The real difference between intuitionisms—or rather applications of intuitionism—in Sidgwick rests on the notion of self-evidence. Indeed Sidgwick himself claims that the move through his three phases is a move towards greater 'certainty'.[62] But differences here are best captured initially not in the form of any threefold schema, but on a spectrum of more and less self-evidence. We might then want to suggest that the difference between DI and PHI in relation to the self-evidence of their intuitions is such a large one that they deserve their respective titles.

Sidgwick sets out four conditions for genuine self-evidence, an intuition's self-evidence increasing to the extent that it meets any of these conditions. They are:[63]

Clarity. 'The terms of the proposition must be clear and precise.' That is, we must be clear about their sense. We must also, in the case of ethics, be clear about the precise practical implications of the proposition.[64] The aim is to ground ethics on scientific axioms that will deliver unambiguous practical conclusions in particular cases. III. 2–10 represent Sidgwick's attempt to discover whether such axioms are available through a formulation of CSM.

Reflection.[65] 'The self-evidence of the proposition must be ascertained by careful reflection.' An intuition is not a gut reaction or instinct, but a belief

---

[62] *The Methods of Ethics*, 214–15.
[63] Ibid., 338–42; cf. p. 100; Schneewind, *Sidgwick's Ethics*, 267 ff.
[64] See e.g. *The Methods of Ethics*, 215.
[65] Cf. Audi, 'Intuitionism, Pluralism, and the Foundations of Ethics', 112, 116, 118, and *passim*.

which to 'careful observation' presents itself as a dictate of reason. Note that, in so far as it is an intuition, it must not be a conclusion arrived at on the basis of rational argument, whether deductive, inductive, or of any other kind, since self-evident intuitions stand on their own, providing, if required, the ultimate premises for such arguments. I take it that much of the reflection in question will concern the origin of the intuition: Is it a product of my upbringing? Am I merely adopting it unthinkingly on the basis of societal authority? Does it rest on my subjective likes and dislikes? Much of course also will concern the content of the proposition itself. But it might concern also the implications of the proposition, and whether they can be accepted (as, for example, in Sidgwick's dialectical testing against CSM of apparently self-evident principles). Ultimately, I am seeking to vindicate my beliefs, to reassure myself that I believe P because it is indeed the case that P. In general, we can see here Sidgwick's attempt to avoid Bentham's and Mill's criticism of intuitions as mere prejudices.[66] The notion of the synthetic a priori also seems to be in play, in that self-evidence must be based on *reflection* and not, for example, on the marshalling of empirical evidence.

Consistency.[67] 'The propositions accepted as self-evident must be mutually consistent.' In the III. 11 analysis it is unclear whether Sidgwick is speaking of logical or practical consistency. The first would rule out as self-evident, for example, the two logically contradictory propositions 'One should always be spontaneous' and 'One should always be reflective', if held in that form by a single person. Practical inconsistency would rule out not only such sets of propositions, but also, for instance, 'One should always be kind' and 'One should always be just', if a case can be imagined in which the demands of justice conflict with those of kindness. The conclusion of the *Methods*, in which Sidgwick discusses attempts to make egoism and utilitarianism practically consistent, suggests he had the practicality test in mind.

Consensus.[68] 'Since it is implied in the very notion of Truth that it is essentially the same for all minds, the denial by another of a proposition that I have affirmed has a tendency to impair my confidence in its validity.'

---

[66] See Schneewind, *Sidgwick's Ethics*, 134 and 179.

[67] Cf. Broad, *Five Types of Ethical Theory*, 159; W. K. Frankena, 'Sidgwick and the History of Ethical Dualism', in B. Schultz (ed.), *Essays on Henry Sidgwick* (Cambridge: Cambridge University Press, 1992), 457–8.

[68] Cf. Audi, 'Intuitionism, Pluralism, and the Foundations of Ethics', 111.

Sidgwick does not go as far with Aristotle as to say that what seems so to all is so.[69] Mere consensus provides no positive support for a proposition's self-evidence. But it is 'an indispensable negative condition of the certainty of our beliefs'. If others disagree (rationally) with a belief of mine, it can no longer be said to be self-evident, even if it meets the other tests for self-evidence. This is so, however, only 'if I have no more reason to suspect error in the other mind than in my own'. Reasons for suspicion arise, I suggest, either if the other mind contains thoughts with an equal claim to self-evidence, or if the other minds are those of nearly everyone.[70]

PHI, then, amounts to the following view. We have intuitive moral beliefs, and some are more reliable than others.[71] Any philosophically respectable conclusions about how we should act must meet the conditions of self-evidence. They should be clear, reflective, consistent, and meet with consensus on the part of the many and the wise, and possess these qualities above certain thresholds. Further, the greater the extent to which they exceed the relevant thresholds, the more self-evident and hence reliable they are.[72]

---

[69] Aristotle, *Nicomachean Ethics* 1172^{b}36–1173^{a}1.

[70] Note that we have to understand self-evidence as a property like, for example, happiness. I may have some happiness in my life, but it may not be a happy life. Likewise, a belief may have some degree of self-evidence—i.e. it may to some extent meet some of the four conditions—but not be self-evident.

[71] Schneewind (*Sidgwick's Ethics and Victorian Moral Philosophy*, 201) claims that Sidgwick distinguished DI from PHI by claiming that PHI alone does not supply substantive recommendations in particular cases (see e.g. *The Methods of Ethics*, 379). But of course Sidgwick's intuitions do deliver utilitarianism, which is one of his methods. The tenor of Sidgwick's argument strongly suggests that what rules out DI is its failure to meet the four conditions. In particular, the 'accidental aggregate of precepts' composing CSM cannot be self-evident if it lacks an underlying explanation (cf. ibid. 102).

[72] Let me briefly return to Audi's intuitionism, or 'ethical reflectionism' as he sometimes calls it. Audi himself puts four requirements on genuine intuitions ('Intuitionism, Pluralism, and the Foundations of Ethics', 109–11): (i) non-inferentiality; (ii) firmness (i.e. non-hesitancy); (iii) comprehension; (iv) pre-theoreticality. Obviously Sidgwick will agree with the non-inferentiality requirement, and his conception of intuitions as self-evident beliefs commits him to the firmness requirement. The comprehension requirement is close to Sidgwick's clarity requirement. Finally, I believe Sidgwick would also accept the pre-theoreticality requirement, since the whole point of attempting to achieve self-evidence is to ground ethical science. Likewise, I see no reason to think that Audi will object to Sidgwick's requirements, though he may agree with my criticism in the text below of Sidgwick's interpretation of the clarity and consistency requirements. It is worth noting that Audi does not take intuitions to have self-evident objects, but does suggest that if conditions like these are sufficient for justification for P, then P is self-evident.

7. Philosophical Intuitionism and Judgement

How plausible is PHI? In the case of consensus, Sidgwick's Aristotelianism is mild enough. He does not claim that one has to give up one's background intuitions if they are at odds with the equally self-evident views of others or with widely held if less than self-evident views. It is only their claim to certainty that is lost, and to deny this seems the most obstinate dogmatism.[73]

Sidgwick attaches little weight to any beliefs of one's own that will not stand up to scrutiny in the light of the four conditions, or to any belief that is not widely held. Whether he is right about this is not, I suggest, an a priori matter, though his proposal does have an initial attraction. Sidgwick has in mind an end to inquiry, through the attaining of a satisfactory set of self-evident principles. If one developed such a set, and found that one's views were at odds either with non-self-evident beliefs of one's own or those of a few others, it might be considered intellectually complacent to end one's inquiry there. But my guess is that Sidgwick's implication is correct: it would be wiser to move on to some other activity.[74]

The reflectiveness requirement might seem more doubtful. It could be argued that, to understand ethics, one must engage with real life, and judge in the heat of battle rather than the cool of the study. But Aristotle's view seems more plausible that, though ethical understanding may indeed involve grasp of 'first principles' through moral education and experience, philosophical progress can be made only through philosophy. What about claims such as those of Bernard Williams that reflection destroys knowledge?[75] This criticism, along with Williams's criticisms of systematic ethical theory, do not apply at the level of the reflectiveness requirement in Sidgwick's intuitionism. As I have already suggested, Sidgwick's view that CSM is to be systematized need not itself be seen as a commitment of PHI. Even Williams may count himself as an intuitionist in Sidgwick's sense; indeed his first-order ethical views, arguably, may meet the four conditions of self-evidence to a greater extent than Sidgwick's own first-order views.

---

[73] This is one of the fences, indeed, at which Sidgwick's own dualism of the practical reason falls, the other being the consistency condition. Cf. M. G. Singer, 'The Many Methods of Sidgwick's Ethics', *Monist*, 58 (1974), 446. At p. 446–7, n. 28 Singer attributes the point originally to James Seth.

[74] Schneewind suggests that Sidgwick did not fully appreciate the implications of the scientific model of ethics for his views of moral progress, in particular the fact that no view in science is final (Schneewind, *Sidgwick's Ethics*, 214). But why should Sidgwick not have assumed that both science and ethics could come to an end, even if both are at present far from doing so?

[75] B. Williams, *Ethics and the Limits of Philosophy* (London: Fontana, 1985), ch. 9.

Roger Crisp

There is, however, a problem with the clarity and consistency conditions.[76] Sidgwick runs together clarity of sense with precision of practical
implication, and this caused him both to misunderstand those of his opponents who allowed a central place to judgement, and to miss the possibility
of resolving the dualism of practical reason that leads him to despair. We
may agree that we ought to be as clear as possible about the meanings of
terms we employ in our ethical discourse. And we may even agree—as does
Aristotle[77]—that we should make our moral principles as precise as possible. But we should not go to excess in drawing analogies between ethics and
science. Science's aim is to be comprehensive in explanation. If some event
occurs that is not covered by the explanatory principles of some particular
science, then, to that extent, that science has failed. One cannot leave it up
to the individual observer to make up his or her own story about what has
happened. Sidgwick sees ethics as aiming to be comprehensive in justification, to provide in advance a mechanism for deciding what to do in any situation that may arise.

In science, post hoc and therefore ad hoc explanations are unacceptable.
But in ethics post hoc justification may well be something not only acceptable, but unavoidable. As Williams puts it, 'judgement is constantly
required'.[78] It is here that Sidgwick most clearly distances himself from
Aristotle and identifies himself with nineteenth-century proponents of the
scientific method in ethics. But, as Aristotle said, in any area we should seek
principles which are only as precise as they need to be. A carpenter needs
only to be able to draw a right angle, not to understand its geometry.[79]

Sidgwick fails to see the implications of the unavoidability of ethical
judgement. His aim is a monistic principle, with clear prescriptions in every
case. Even in the case of utilitarianism alone, however, he will face problems. First, as Ross noticed, utilitarianism is not a monistic view.[80] It consists of two principles—maximize pleasure and minimize suffering—and
these must be weighed one against the other. Further, even the assessment
of pleasure itself is pluralistic, requiring (at the very least) the weighing of
the factors of intensity and duration. Again, applying any such principle,
even if it stands on its own, will in each case require a sensitivity to the
salient features of human well-being that could not be captured in any set of
principles, however long.

[76] Cf. my 'Griffin's Pessimism', 122. [77] Aristotle, *Nicomachean Ethics* 1165ª34–5.
[78] Williams, 'What does Intuitionism Imply?', 189.
[79] Aristotle, *Nicomachean Ethics* 1098ª29–32.
[80] W. D. Ross, *The Foundations of Ethics* (Oxford: Clarendon Press, 1939), 89.

What Sidgwick disparages as 'aesthetic intuitionism',[81] then, is unavoidable.[82] Nor is it clear why Sidgwick is so against the use of judgement in particular cases when it is clearly required in the application of PHI's methodology. In the case of Sidgwick's own pair of principles, for example, judgement might decide in any particular case how much weight to attach to promoting the general good vis-à-vis the agent's own well-being. And the same goes for the application of the larger set of principles that emerge from reflection on CSM.

Here, then, Sidgwick took one step backwards, leaving it to Ross to reiterate Aristotle's point that 'judgement lies in perception'.[83] Freed of the mistaken emphasis on practical precision, however, Sidgwick's intuitionism provides a powerful method for the resolution of debates in normative ethics, though much remains to be done in working out the details and implications of his conditions for self-evidence.

I began by mentioning Parfit's account of the experience of arriving at some philosophical point only to find that Sidgwick had got there first. Let me end with a comparison of the conclusions of their books. Famously, Sidgwick ended the first edition of the *Methods* thus: 'the prolonged effort of the human intellect to frame a perfect ideal of rational conduct is seen to have been foredoomed to inevitable failure'. Contrast Parfit's final sentence: 'Non-Religious Ethics is at a very early stage. We cannot yet predict whether, as in Mathematics, we will all reach agreement. Since we cannot know how Ethics will develop, it is not irrational to have high hopes.' Here, then, is at least one thought Sidgwick did not anticipate.

---

[81] *The Methods of Ethics*, 228.

[82] Sidgwick almost certainly saw Aristotle as an aesthetic intuitionist; cf. Irwin, 'Eminent Victorians and Greek Ethics', 293.

[83] Aristotle, *Nicomachean Ethics* 1109^{b}23; Ross, *The Right and the Good*, 42.

An Unconnected Heap of Duties?   3

David McNaughton

Despite its name, the school of ethical intuitionism which flourished
between the world wars, and whose greatest proponents were H. A.
Prichard and W. D. Ross, was not distinguished from its competitors by a
distinctive epistemology. The dispute between intuitionism and its main
rival, the utilitarian tradition, revolved around the issue of whether there
was more than one fundamental moral principle.[1] The utilitarian tradition in ethical thought can be represented as holding that there is just one
fundamental duty or moral principle: the duty of beneficence. In the
hands of G. E. Moore, whom Ross and Prichard saw as their main opponent, the theory had developed into a sophisticated consequentialism
which subscribed to a pluralist account of the good. Even so, in determining which action is right, only one consideration is relevant: which
action will produce the most good? Ethical intuitionism rejected this
monism about what makes right actions right as over-simple, and insisted
that there are a number of distinct and irreducible basic duties or moral
principles, all of which can be relevant in determining whether some
action is right. Both parties to this debate were taken to agree that an ethical theory rests on intuition, by which was meant no more than that the
most basic ethical principles, since they could not be inferred from more
basic ones, must be self-evident.

I am grateful to members of the philosophy department at Keele University, to Brad Hooker, and
especially to Jonathan Dancy and to an anonymous referee for the *Philosophical Quarterly* for helpful advice on an earlier draft of this paper.
   This paper was first published in *Philosophical Quarterly*, 46 (1996), 433–47.
   [1] This point is made with clarity and force by Prichard's pupil J. O. Urmson ('A Defence of
Intuitionism', *Proceedings of the Aristotelian Society*, 75 (1975), 111–12).

It has become commonplace to dismiss the deontic pluralism of an ethical intuitionist such as Ross fairly briskly, for a variety of reasons. In this paper I examine two main charges. First, intuitionism is held to be unsystematic, offering us merely a 'heap of unconnected duties' with no unifying rationale. Thus D. D. Raphael complains that, while intuitionism 'gives a reasonably accurate picture of everyday moral judgement . . . it does not meet the needs of a philosophical theory, which should try to show connections and tie things up in a coherent system'.[2] Second, intuitionism can give nothing in the way of general guidance to the agent who is faced with a conflict of duties, because it refuses to rank duties in order of importance or stringency.[3] In fact Ross, who offers the most fully worked-out version of intuitionism, does offer a systematic justification for the list of fundamental duties he puts forward, and does claim that some duties are more stringent than others. To the best of my knowledge, Ross's remarks on these topics have not been much discussed in the standard literature. This is due, in part, to the failure of many critics to read Ross with either the care or the sympathy with which they would approach other major writers in the subject. I shall argue, firstly, that Ross has an entire answer to those who maintain his theory is unsystematic; second, that Ross fails to sustain his claim that some duties are more stringent than others, but that this is not a defect in his theory.

1

We can expand the first complaint as follows. Common-sense morality appeals to a large variety of moral principles, which have no discernible structure. Intuitionism does not attempt to systematize ordinary morality, but simply mirrors it. An intuitionist, such as Ross, merely presents us with a more or less arbitrarily selected list of the more common (prima facie) duties, and announces them to be self-evident. Since there is no structure to this list, there seems to be no explanation of why some items are on the list and not others, and therefore no room for rational debate in the event

---

[2] Raphael, *Moral Philosophy* (Oxford: Oxford University Press, 1981), 55. H. W. B. Joseph may also well have had Ross in mind when he stated that 'our obligations are not a heap of unrelated obligations' (*Some Problems in Ethics* (Oxford: Clarendon Press, 1931), 92). A similar terse dismissal can be found in R. Attfield, *A Theory of Value and Obligation* (London: Croom Helm, 1987), 105–6.

[3] The classic contemporary version of this complaint is voiced by Rawls (*A Theory of Justice* (Cambridge, Mass.: Harvard University Press, 1971), 34).

of disagreement about what should be included. Given the unavailability of reasoned discussion we simply have one bare intuition pitted against another. Even a philosopher who admits that we may eventually have to appeal to intuition may rightly feel that this is too quick. Moral theory should facilitate reasoned debate, not forestall it. Indeed, in the absence of such structure it is doubtful whether intuitionism, unlike utilitarianism, can lay claim to be a moral *theory* at all.

Such a criticism fails to recognize that philosophical intuitionism does seek to systematize common-sense morality, and in much the same way as many utilitarians have tried to do. For it seeks to show that the plethora of precepts which constitutes common-sense morality can be derived from a very small number of self-evident basic duties. 'The general principles which [intuitionism] regards as intuitively seen to be true are very few in number and very general in character.'[4] Both utilitarianism and intuitionism can therefore be seen as sharing the theoretical goal of explaining and justifying our everyday moral judgements by appeal to the fewest number of most general principles. In this sense, intuitionism is as much engaged as is utilitarianism in constructing a moral theory; they only differ over how many basic principles they need to accomplish the task.

In fairness to his critics it must be admitted that Ross does not explicitly state in his famous exposition of his theory in chapter 2 of *The Right and the Good* that his theory has this explanatory structure, but it is implicit throughout his long and detailed discussion. He begins by offering a categorization or division of prima facie duties for which he does not claim 'completeness or finality' but which he maintains is not 'arbitrary' because 'Each rests on a definite circumstance which cannot seriously be held to be without moral significance.'[5] Subsequent discussion makes it clear that this list of prima facie duties is a first shot at a complete list of basic and underivative duties.[6] As Ross points out, it is slightly misleading to think of these as distinct or fundamental *duties*, since on Ross's account prima facie duties are not strictly duties at all, 'but something related in a special kind of way to duty'.[7] One's duty proper is what one ought actually to do, all things con-

---

[4] Ross, *The Foundations of Ethics* (Oxford: Clarendon Press, 1939), 190. Sidgwick also saw this as the aim of philosophical intuitionism. See Sidgwick, *The Methods of Ethics*, 7th edn. (London: Macmillan, 1967), 102.

[5] Ross, *The Right and the Good* (Oxford: Clarendon Press, 1930), 20.

[6] That Ross admits any basic principles is denied by Jonathan Dancy in 'An Ethic of Prima Facie Duties', in P. Singer (ed.), *A Companion to Ethics* (Oxford: Blackwell, 1991), 219.

[7] Ibid., 20.

sidered, in some particular situation. The list might more accurately be thought of as a list of fundamental morally relevant characteristics of actions; of features of actions which are right- or wrong-making characteristics which always carry weight when we are considering whether a particular action is right or wrong.[8] With that proviso, here is my summary of the items on Ross's original list.

1. Duties resting on a previous act of my own. These in turn divide into two main categories:
   (a) duties of *fidelity*; these result from my having made a promise or something like a promise;
   (b) duties of *reparation*; these stem from my having done something wrong so that I am now required to make amends.
2. Duties resting on previous acts of others; these are duties of *gratitude*, which I owe to those who have helped me.
3. Duties to prevent (or overturn) a distribution of benefits and burdens which is not in accordance with the merit of the persons concerned; these are duties of *justice*.
4. Duties which rest on the fact that there are other people in the world whose condition we could make better; these are duties of *beneficence*.
5. Duties which rest on the fact that I could better myself; these are duties of *self-improvement*.
6. Duties of not injuring others; these are duties of *non-maleficence*.

This list is only provisional; Ross goes on to discuss whether it can be further reduced by showing that some of these duties are not really basic. Since the dialectic of the argument dictates that a duty cannot remain on the list if it can be shown to be derivative, we need to know what it is for one duty to be derived from another.

Unfortunately, Ross gives no systematic account of the relation of derivation, but one can be gleaned from scattered remarks throughout the text. After reviewing and revising his list of basic duties, he writes: 'These seem to be, in principle, all the ways in which *prima facie* duties arise. In actual experience they are compounded together in highly complex ways.'[9] He then gives as an example the citizen's duty to obey the laws of her country. That duty 'arises from' (at least in the ideal case) three basic duties: gratitude, fidelity, and beneficence. We should be grateful for the benefits we have received from the state; we have made an implicit promise to obey by

---

[8] Philip Stratton-Lake drew my attention to this point.   [9] *The Right and the Good*, 27.

retaining permanent residence in a country whose laws we know we are expected to obey; beneficence also requires us to obey the laws because they are 'a potent instrument for the general good'. Ross later[10] gives a similar account of the duty not to lie. He claims that this duty, which he does not sharply distinguish from the duty of veracity, stems from two of the basic duties on his list: those of non-maleficence and fidelity. To lie to someone is (normally) to do an injury to that person (and perhaps to others). In addition, Ross holds that communication standardly presupposes an implicit mutual undertaking by all parties that they will use language to convey their real opinions. In such cases, to lie is to breach this implicit promise. We show what is wrong with lawbreaking and lying by showing that to act in these ways is, normally, to be in breach of more than one of our fundamental duties.

In his discussion of both these cases, Ross makes it clear that there can be special circumstances in which some of the considerations which count against acting in these ways do not apply. In such cases, the force or bindingness of the duty in question may be weakened. For example, a very bad government will not be promoting the general good, and then there will be no duty arising from considerations of beneficence to support it. In the case of lying, the presupposition that there is a mutual agreement to make true assertions can lapse. If someone is a habitual liar, then she has announced, by her actions, her refusal to be bound by this implicit contract, thus releasing others from their obligation to honour it. Similarly, if I am in a strange society and know nothing of their social practices, not even whether they are friendly or hostile, then there is no such implicit understanding. In Ross's opinion, a large part of the stringency of the duty not to lie stems from the supposed implicit promise; where it is not present then the obligation not to lie is much weakened.[11]

Although Ross does not discuss this point, it seems perfectly possible that there might be cases where none of the considerations which normally make lawbreaking or lying wrong apply. For example, if I play a game of Cheat with my children, I must lie, because that is part of the game. On Ross's account of what makes lying wrong, it may be that there is absolutely nothing wrong with lying in such cases. The tacit agreement to tell the truth is explicitly cancelled in such games and it is at least arguable that I am, in this context, doing no harm whatever to my children in lying to

---

[10] *The Right and the Good*, 54–5.   [11] Ibid.

them.[12] Similarly, there can surely be governments so bad that there is nothing to be said in favour of obeying them, and everything to be said against.

If there are circumstances, such as playing Cheat, where the fact that saying something would be a lie does not furnish any reason whatever for not saying it, then in what sense can it be said, as Ross does, that there is a duty not to lie? On Ross's official account of prima facie duty, refraining from lying cannot be such a duty because, as we saw, that would imply that lying was universally a wrong-making characteristic; that it always counted against an action that it involved lying. But this claim is arguably false; it does not count at all against my playing Cheat with my children that we shall all lie as hard as we can. In the case of derivative duties, such as the duty not to lie or to obey the law, we must say rather that it is only normally or standardly that we have a prima facie duty to act in this way.

If the duty not to lie is understood in this way, can we still maintain *of a particular act* that it is prima facie wrong in virtue of being a lie? We might be tempted to interpret Ross's account of lying as holding that in a normal case, where it does count against an action that it would involve lying, the act is prima facie wrong, *not* in virtue of being a lie, but in virtue of its being a case of promise-breaking and causing harm. But this, I think, is a false contrast. Acts can get to be instances of promise-breaking or maleficence in a number of ways. It may be true of some particular act that it is in virtue of its being a lie (rather than, for example, the non-payment of a debt) that it is an instance of promise-breaking and maleficence. If this is right, then the fact that *this* act is a lie may make it prima facie wrong, even though there can be acts which, though they involve lying, are not made prima facie wrong by that fact. On this interpretation, lying is not a fundamental moral consideration (which is why it does not occur on the list of basic duties) but not all morally relevant considerations need be fundamental. The fact that some act is a lie can still be a reason why that act is prima facie wrong.

The examples of derivative duties we have so far considered are cases where our prima facie duties are, in Ross's words, 'compounded together in highly complex ways'. But derivative duties need not be complex in this manner. For some kind of action may be a derivative duty in virtue of its falling, in standard cases, under just one basic duty. Take the duty a child has to honour its parents; it might plausibly be claimed that this duty rests on the single basic duty of gratitude. As in the previous examples, there

---

[12] For a different account of why there is nothing wrong with lying in these cases, see J. Dancy, *Moral Reasons* (Oxford: Blackwell, 1993), 60–1.

could be exceptional cases where there was not even a prima facie duty to honour one's parents. Where the child had received nothing from its parents there would be, on this view, no duty to honour them. Ross gives another example himself in his discussion of punishment. He dissents from the common intuitionist view that there is 'a fundamental and underivative duty' to reward the virtuous and punish the innocent. Rather, he claims, the state of affairs in which the good are happy and the bad unhappy is better than the reverse. Since we have a general duty of beneficence, we have a duty to bring about the better state of affairs. 'The duty of reward and punishment seems to me to be . . . derivative. It can be subsumed under the duty of producing as much good as we can.'[13] There may be cases where no good would come of punishing (perhaps because the wrongdoer has suffered enough) and here punishing would not be even prima facie right.

In sum, derivative duties are not on the list of basic duties because the characteristic by which they are picked out is not itself morally fundamental, nor does it entail the presence of a morally fundamental characteristic. They still count as duties, however, because acts having that character normally or standardly have one or more of the morally fundamental characteristics that figure on Ross's basic list.

Being underivative is not, however, sufficient for inclusion in Ross's list of basic duties, for he is also striving for as high a level of generality as possible. Thus there may be duties which are not derivative in the sense just defined, but are not on the list because insufficiently general. Thus it is plausible to hold that the fact that an act would be the paying of a debt always counts in its favour. Here, the reason why we are unable to imagine a particular case where debt-paying is not prima facie right may be supposed to lie in the fact that one could not be in debt unless one had made an (implicit) promise to repay. That an act is a paying of a debt thus entails that it is the keeping of a promise. The duty to pay debts will then not appear on the list of basic duties because it is only a specific instance of the more general duty of fidelity.

I am not here concerned to defend Ross's analysis of any of these duties; I cite them merely to illustrate his general approach. With the two distinctions between derivative and underivative duties and between more and less general underivative duties now in place, we can now see how one might make a case for amending Ross's list. Challenges can come from one of two directions. It may be claimed either that the list needs shortening because it

---

[13] *The Right and the Good*, 58.

contains some duty that is not really basic, or that the list needs lengthening because it leaves out a basic duty.

The list needs shortening if it can be shown to contain duties that are either derivable from other duties on the list, or are insufficiently general in form. The latter challenge will have been made out if it can be shown either that one duty on the list is just a specific instance of a more general basic duty, or that two of the putative basic duties are just specific instances of one wider inclusive basic duty. Immediately after drawing up his initial list Ross embarks on a discussion to see if it can be made more 'systematic'. His conclusion is that the list does need shortening, and his discussion provides two examples of the latter kind of challenge at work.

First, he considers whether beneficence and self-improvement are distinct duties.[14] The main reason for thinking that they are lies in the fact that, while we have a duty to give others pleasure, as well as to make them knowledgeable and virtuous, we normally think we have no corresponding obligation to give ourselves pleasure. Ross discusses whether the belief that we have no duty to give ourselves pleasure arises merely from the fact that it is redundant to require us to do something which we are already (too) strongly motivated to do. If we think, as Ross is inclined to, that there is in fact a duty to give ourselves pleasure, a duty which it is rarely if ever necessary to invoke, then categories 4 and 5 can be merged under the wider head of universal beneficence.

Second, Ross argues that the duty of justice is simply a specific instance of the general duty to bring about the good since, as we saw when discussing punishment, Ross's view is that the distribution of goods in accord with merit is a specific kind of good. So Ross's final list is whittled down to five: the duty to bring about as much good as possible, under which now fall justice, beneficence, and self-improvement, and the distinct duties of non-maleficence, fidelity, gratitude, and reparation.[15]

The other way to criticize the list would be to claim that it is too short, because there are underivative moral considerations that have not been included. We should note that, in order to exclude some putative basic duty from the list it would have to be shown that it is *wholly* derivative. Thus lying should only be excluded if our moral objection to lying rests solely on the fact that lying would normally involve us in breaching other duties, such as fidelity and non-maleficence; the claim must be that the mere fact that an act is a lie carries no independent moral weight, however slight.

---

[14] Ibid., 24–6.   [15] Ibid., 27.

Critics of intuitionism are wont to point out that different intuitionist philosophers cannot agree about which are the basic duties, as if this were itself a sufficient refutation of the theory. But this would only be an objection to intuitionism if the theory held that the contents of the list should be immediately obvious, which it does not. What is important is that there should be some rational and principled way to settle such disputes, and this is what I have tried to show. There is no need to resort to a blank appeal to intuition. Nor should we imagine that intuitionism of this stripe need be conservative. Nothing in Ross's procedure prevents moral criticism of the prevailing mores of a society.

It may, of course, be that there is no one way of structuring these duties that will be uncontroversially the right one. That is not, however, a matter that can be determined in advance. Moreover, the discovery that there were several possible ways of carving up the territory between which it was hard to decide would itself constitute important philosophical progress.

A critic of Rossian intuitionism might now complain, rather more cautiously, that while Ross's list is by no means an arbitrary heap, the basic duties are still unconnected, and that this is a weakness in his theory. But why might one think it a weakness? One suggestion might be that the simpler a theory is the better and, all else equal, the fewer independent axioms, postulates, or underived principles to which it appeals the better. The intuitionist need not deny this, but he will point out that there are other desiderata for a theory, among which fitting the facts and explanatory adequacy rank highly. Ross's main complaint about consequentialist theories is that they oversimplify and thus fail to account convincingly for the nature of our moral thought. By this he means, not only that they deliver counter-intuitive verdicts in particular cases, but that they give a distorted account of the reasons we would offer for those verdicts.[16] Nor is it always the case that the theory with the fewest underived principles is the simplest; for simplicity at the level of principle may lead to complexity at a higher level.

The second suggestion might be that a theory which admits the existence of distinct and irreducible moral principles gains in systematic unity if those principles are generated by some unitary justificatory procedure, as is the case perhaps with Kantianism, or with rule-consequentialism. To this Ross might reply that he also offers a single test. The difference between his test and the Kantian one is that the latter is atomistic, generating each principle independently of the others, whereas his is holistic, testing each principle by

[16] *The Right and the Good,* 19 and 37–9.

seeing whether it can be derived from the others. But why should a holistic test be less systematic than an atomistic one?[17] The real worry here, I suspect, may be about not the lack of systematic unity in Ross's theory, but the perceived need for a justificatory grounding for each duty. But that is, of course, just to beg the question against the intuitionist who maintains that these basic duties stand in no need of grounding.

A third worry might be that duties that are distinct and irreducible may also be disparate, having nothing significant in common, except that they are all duties. But of course they may have a great deal in common, and if they do, then the theory would have a further unity. Ross in fact seems to suggest at various points[18] that at least some, and perhaps all, of our duties, both basic and derivative, do have something in common; they rest on relationships between persons, each different relationship generating a different duty. Positional duties, contractual duties, and duties of special relationship are the model here. Of the seven basic duties which Ross has on his original list, three—fidelity, gratitude, and reparation—seem to fit this description neatly. The others, however, raise problems. In order for me to have a duty of beneficence, non-maleficence, or justice towards some particular person or group, it does not have to be the case that I previously stood in any particular relationship to them; it is enough that they are in need, or that they could be harmed, or that goods are unjustly distributed among them. Nor, in the case of duties of self-improvement, is it clear what it means to talk about my relationship with myself. These difficulties may or may not be soluble; my only purpose here was to illustrate how it might be that distinct duties may yet have some common structural element that gives them a unity.

My conclusion is that intuitionism, at least in Ross's version, is not systematically less unified than its major rivals. If there are objections to it, they lie elsewhere.

II

I turn now to my second topic, the issue of what Ross has to say about the respective ranking of the basic moral duties in cases of moral conflict. Ross rejects what he calls 'out-and-out intuitionism', which says that there are

---

[17] I owe this point to Jonathan Dancy.   [18] e.g. *The Right and the Good*, 19 and 22.

absolute duties that should be fulfilled irrespective of the consequences.[19] Duties are prima facie for Ross; where they conflict we have to decide, in each particular case, which is here the weightiest. Now Ross's view commits him to the wholly plausible claim that the stringency of a duty can vary from one occasion to another. Some promises, for example, are solemn and binding, and ought only to be broken, if at all, in the most serious circumstances; others are less weighty and can more easily be overridden by other considerations. Ross is standardly interpreted as claiming that a conflict between duties in a particular case can only be resolved by determining what weight those duties carry in that case; nothing *in general* can be said about the relative weight of different kinds of duty. Even as careful a commentator as Audi makes this claim. '[Ross] seems committed to the view that ethical generalizations do not *independently* carry evidential weight in such conflicts. One should not, e.g., appeal to a second-order generalization that duties of justice are stronger than duties of fidelity.'[20]

This interpretation runs counter to the text. On several occasions Ross explicitly claims that one duty is more binding or more stringent than another, although no very clear overall picture emerges of their precise relations. Both fidelity[21] and non-maleficence[22] are held to be more stringent than beneficence. Later on he adds to the list of more stringent duties, albeit in a cagey remark:

For the estimation of the comparative stringency of these *prima facie* obligations no general rules can, so far as I can see, be laid down. We can only say that a great deal of stringency belongs to the duties of 'perfect obligation'—the duties of keeping our promises, of repairing wrongs we have done, and of returning the equivalent of services we have received. For the rest, 'the decision rests with perception'.[23]

Ross appears, therefore, to be trying to find room for a position midway between the complete generalism of absolutism (or indeed of a lexical ordering of duties) which gives no consideration to the circumstances of the particular case, and a doctrine of prima facie duties that makes the outcome of any conflict depend solely upon the wholly individual circumstances of the particular case. That midway position is intended to allow us

---

[19] See Ross, *The Foundations of Ethics*, 79.

[20] R. Audi, 'Ethical Reflectionism', *Monist*, 76 (1993), 297. I have been equally at fault in this regard: see my *Moral Vision* (Oxford: Blackwell, 1988), 198. B. Gaut ('Moral Pluralism', *Philosophical Papers*, 22 (1993), 17–40) is an honourable exception to the general rule.

[21] *The Right and the Good*, 19. [22] Ibid., 22.

[23] Ibid. 41–2. The quotation (which appears in the original Greek in Ross) is from Aristotle, *Nicomachean Ethics* 1109^{b}23 and 1126^{b}4.

to say something about the ranking of duties in general which falls short of absolutism: namely, that some kinds of basic duty might be thought to be, in their intrinsic nature, more weighty than others. This does not mean that the less weighty duty will never win out, only that it starts with an initial handicap which it will have to work hard to overcome. In deciding what to do, it seems, we must take into account not only how weighty an instance of each particular duty we have in the case before us, but also the *general* weight that is to be given to each of these duties.[24]

This doctrine of 'double weighing' is hard to grasp in the abstract; it is not clear what it means, still less whether we hold such a view. Ross supplies a couple of examples which are supposed to do the double duty both of illustrating the claim and of showing that the particular moral judgements we make commit us to it. His first claim is that the duty of non-maleficence is recognized both as distinct from and as more binding than the duty of beneficence. 'We should not in general consider it justifiable to kill one person in order to keep another alive, or to steal from one in order to give alms to another.'[25] But this example will not help Ross to illustrate the claim that non-maleficence is the more stringent duty because, as I shall now go on to show, we only need the claim that non-maleficence is *distinct* from beneficence to explain our judgement in this case.

In any choice I make, considerations of beneficence are always relevant, because what I choose will have some influence on the well-being of others. Where beneficence is the only relevant duty, then the right action is completely determined by the amount of good I can produce: the right action is the one that brings about the best state of affairs. If two courses of action produce the same amount of value, then, from the point of view of beneficence, there is nothing to choose between them.

Ross holds, of course, that there are other duties, such as fidelity and non-maleficence, distinct from beneficence, which have to be taken into account where relevant. Since they are distinct duties, they must carry independent weight in determining which action is my duty proper, though what weight they will have in the particular case will depend on the circumstances. Two consequences follow. First, where the balance of good between the two courses of action is (roughly) equal, the other duty will be decisive, because beneficence will not favour one course over the other.

---

[24] For a more recent attempt to argue, like Ross, that different kinds of duty have different weights, see K. Baier, *The Rational and the Moral Order* (La Salle, Ill.: Open Court, 1995), 71–6.

[25] *The Right and the Good*, 22. Nor did Ross change his view in his later work; see *The Foundations of Ethics*, 75.

Second, where the balance of good, and therefore beneficence, counts morally in favour of one course of action, but some other duty, say the duty to keep promises, counts against doing it, then beneficence will only win out if it has sufficient weight to outweigh the other duty in this case. But the weight that we should give to the duty of beneficence in any particular case depends solely on the surplus of good produced by following one course of action rather than another. So beneficence will only win out over the other duty if the course of action favoured by beneficence will produce a considerably better state of affairs than that which will result if we act in accordance with the other duty. In fact, it will have to produce a surplus of good sufficiently large for us to judge that, in this case, the good to be achieved outweighs all the weight against that course which stems from the fact that it would involve a breach of the other duty.

These consequences follow simply from the fact that, on Ross's view, the other duties are *distinct* from beneficence. In weighing up what to do, one must take account not only of how much good will be produced, as the duty of beneficence requires, but also of the independent weight of the other duties. There is thus no need to bring in any doctrine about one duty being weightier than another at the general level in order to explain, for example, why it is wrong 'to kill one person in order to keep another alive, or to steal from one in order to give alms to another'. We do think it wrong to kill one person to save another, but that may simply be because, given that the benefit to one is roughly counterbalanced by the loss to the other, the duty not to harm tells against killing the one, but not against failing to save the other. (If we think that the benefit and loss are not equal, this will be because we think being killed is a greater evil than not having one's life saved, and that will not help Ross's case.) Similar remarks will be true, not just of conflicts between fidelity or non-maleficence and beneficence, but of a conflict between beneficence and any other duty.

This diagnosis is confirmed when we see that Ross claims that the distinctness of fidelity and beneficence *alone* is sufficient to account for our judgement in a structurally similar case.

. . . if . . . I could bring equal amounts of good into being by fulfilling my promise and by helping someone to whom I had made no promise, I should not hesitate to regard the former as my duty.[26]

Ross's other example seems to get us closer to what we need.

---

[26] *The Right and the Good*, 18.

We . . . think . . . that normally promise-keeping, for example, should come before benevolence, but that when and only when the good to be produced by the benevolent act is very great and the promise comparatively trivial, the act of benevolence becomes our duty.[27]

One way of understanding this remark is as follows. We are to imagine separate rankings of instances of both duties in order, from the least to the most weighty instances. We then claim that a beneficent action can only make a breach of fidelity right when it is located significantly higher on its scale than the breach of fidelity is on its scale. But it is not clear that we can make any sense of these cross-scale comparisons. To mention just one obvious difficulty: in order to know roughly how high up the scale one is, one must have a sense of where its top is as well as its base. Since, however, there seems to be no limit to the amount of benefit that might flow from a single action, there is no top to the scale of beneficence. If there is no measure of how high one is on that scale, then an act cannot be significantly higher on it than it is on the scale of fidelity. So we are still no nearer making sense of the idea that one duty is in itself more binding than another.

Ross's remarks could be taken to suggest a different interpretation that would, finally, give us a sense in which one duty might be more stringent than another. The claim that the promise must be 'comparatively trivial' might naturally be read as meaning, not that it is trivial as compared with the substantial amount of good which might be achieved, but that it is trivial *compared with other promises*. So understood, this would impose an additional condition that must be met before it could be our duty to break a promise. Not only must the balance of good greatly favour the breaking of the promise, but the promise itself must not be of a particularly serious, solemn, or binding kind. On that interpretation, where a promise is particularly solemn and binding, no amount of good to be achieved, however great, could make it our duty to break it.

Since, on Ross's view, the weight to be accorded to a duty is not just a function of the good produced, there does not seem to be anything in Ross's system that prevents him claiming that serious cases of promise-breaking could have a moral weight that could not be outweighed by any amount of good to be achieved on the other side. Nevertheless, it seems to me unlikely that Ross actually held this view; there is no other textual evidence for it. Moreover, it is a position that does not seem to me very attractive with regard to promise-keeping. Most of us feel that there are situations in which

---

[27] Ibid., 19.

it would be right to break a promise, however solemn. In the case of non-maleficence, however, there does seem a case for claiming that it is intrinsically weightier than beneficence in the sense just defined. For while it can be right to inflict some comparatively slight harm in order to secure a great good or avert a disaster, it may be that it can never be right to inflict a very serious harm, such as killing an innocent child, to achieve a good end. Here the end really cannot justify the means in any circumstances.

Such a position might make room, within a system of prima facie duties, for something like an absolute constraint against killing the innocent. (The fact that Ross is opposed to 'out-and-out intuitionism' is further reason to think that he cannot be advocating this view.) For, while the duty not to harm in general is only prima facie, the duty not to inflict certain serious kinds of harm, such as killing the innocent, would be one that cannot be overridden. Moral considerations on the other side would not be *silenced*, however. On this view, the fact that killing an innocent person would do good will always be a reason in its favour; it will just be that it will never be strong enough to override the duty of non-maleficence in this case.

We have had great difficulty in finding an interpretation of Ross's claim that some duties are more stringent than others which made sense and which there was good reason to think that Ross held. It seems best, therefore, to suppose that Ross was just confused when he thought that he needed, in order to explain our moral judgements, to claim not only that there were duties distinct from beneficence, but also that the former were more stringent than the latter. We are left, then, with the claim that all we can do, when faced with a moral conflict, is to look carefully at the particular case in all its complexity and form a reasonable judgement as to which duty (or duties) carry the most weight.

Does his failure to come up with any general guidance as to how to resolve moral conflicts constitute a complaint, as his critics seem to suppose, against Ross's system, as distinct from a complaint against Ross's account of his own system? I think not. It is only a complaint against intuitionism that it does not offer any general guidance about what to do in a situation of moral conflict if one thinks that this is a reasonable job to expect a moral theory to do. Ross has a much less ambitious picture of the role of moral theory than that. The job of moral theory is simply to see which general account of the nature of our duties (and of goodness) gives the best overall picture of our moral thinking. There is no question of theory revealing answers to moral questions that cannot otherwise be answered, or justifying what would not otherwise be justified. In particular, where there are puzzling moral conflicts, moral theory will not help to resolve them. This does not mean that we must simply blankly 'intuit' what to do in such cases, or else make an arbitrary decision. Deciding what to do in complex cases involves discernment, sensitivity, and judgement, but those skills have to be exercised at the level of the particular case. To look to abstract theory to help out is to look in the wrong place. If Ross is right in this, as I believe he is, then it is not a defect in his theory that it turns out after all to have nothing general to say about the relative stringency of our basic duties.[28]

III

The heart of most objections to intuitionism lies in the belief that it is a profoundly anti-theoretical ethical view. This claim is partly true and partly false; intuitionism seeks to perform some but by no means all of the tasks that are often demanded of moral theory. One such task is to reveal the structure of our moral thought, to impose order and systematic unity on what otherwise seems rather unstructured and even inchoate. Here, as I have tried to show, Ross's theory does as well as its rivals. A second task is that of justification. Different theories construe this task differently. On Ross's theory, it is not a matter of finding or constructing a justification for our moral beliefs, which might otherwise remain unsupported. It consists, Ross claims, in showing both that the general principles of duty (the items on the basic list) are self-evident and that we bring our knowledge of those general principles to bear on each particular case. Since almost all morally significant acts will fall under more than one of these principles, we cannot have more than probable opinion about what is the right thing to do in any particular case.[29] The third task some have hoped that a moral theory might perform is to supply guidance in making difficult moral choices. I hope I have shown that, on Ross's account of moral judgement, this is a task that moral *theory* cannot perform. To complain, therefore, that Ross's system fails to perform it is to miss the point of his theory.

---

[28] I try to defend this claim in *Moral Vision*, esp. ch. 13. For Ross's defence of a 'bottom-up' moral epistemology, see *The Foundations of Ethics*, pp. 168–73. For an even more radical insistence on the primacy of the particular, see Dancy, *Moral Reasons*, esp. chs. 4–6.

[29] *The Right and the Good*, 32 and 42.

The Three Phases of Intuitionism

Thomas Baldwin

I

In *The Methods of Ethics* Sidgwick distinguishes between three 'phases' of intuitionism, the 'Perceptional', the 'Dogmatic', and the 'Philosophical' phase.[1] For Sidgwick these phases have a teleology—they are 'three stages in the development of Intuitive Morality';[2] but one does not have to endorse his teleology to find his threefold distinction helpful in the context of critical reflection on ethical intuitionism.

Sidgwick of course interprets intuitionism broadly—as a form of reasoning concerning the 'moral maxims which reflection shows to possess ultimate validity'[3]—so that he can interpret the utilitarian's judgement that pleasure is the ultimate good as an 'intuition'. But he begins with the familiar interpretation of intuitionism as the view that we can have knowledge of right and wrong action without reference to the consequences of action. 'Perceptional Intuitionism', as the name implies, is the view that this knowledge of right and wrong is comparable to our ordinary perceptual knowledge of things. Hence it rests on the claim that the moral judgements on which we should place most confidence concern the particular situations we experience: 'it is always the rightness of some particular action that is held to be immediately known'.[4] Thus the thought is that, when turning the corner of a street and encountering someone who has fallen over, we can see at once that we should offer to help. We do not need to reason our way to this practical conclusion by reminding ourselves of the principle that

---

[1] H. Sidgwick, *The Methods of Ethics*, 7th edn. (London: Macmillan, 1907), 102.
[2] Ibid.   [3] Ibid., 383.   [4] Ibid., xxv.

we have a duty to help those whom we find in distress. On the contrary, this principle commands assent only in so far as it is confirmed by our moral perceptions in particular cases. So, according to the perceptional intuitionist, it is a mistake to pay much attention to such principles; what matters is 'the proper development of the practically important faculty manifested or exercised in particular moral judgements'.[5]

'Dogmatic Intuitionism' is the name Sidgwick gives to the view that the moral judgements on which we should place most confidence are, by contrast, the principles affirmed by 'common sense'. Sidgwick discusses this position in book III of *The Methods of Ethics*, and the fact that he gives this book the general title 'Intuitionism' is an acknowledgement of the fact that this is the position advocated by those, such as Whewell, who are standardly thought of as intuitionists. As Sidgwick sets out the dogmatic intuitionist's common-sense principles, they mainly concern our duties, though he adds a brief discussion of the virtues—chapter 10 of book III has the rather dismissive title 'Courage, Humility etc.'. Overall he famously characterizes the 'morality of Common Sense' as 'a collection of such general rules, as to the validity of which there would be apparent agreement at least among moral persons of our own age and civilization, and which would cover with approximate completeness the whole of human conduct.'[6] There is much here that one might want to question, and the last clause is especially unsatisfactory: does Sidgwick just mean that common-sense moral principles apply throughout human life? Or does he mean (as his words more naturally suggest) that they positively regulate the whole of human conduct? Under this second interpretation the requirement is clearly excessive: it is a matter of common sense that, on the contrary, many of the principles which regulate human affairs are not moral principles at all (e.g. traffic regulations). So dogmatic, common-sense intuitionism is best understood without a commitment to 'cover with approximate completeness the whole of human conduct', whatever exactly this amounts to.

In accordance with his teleological schema Sidgwick of course rejects dogmatic intuitionism along with perceptional intuitionism (which is only very briefly discussed) in favour of his third type, 'Philosophical Intuitionism'. The mark of this position is that although it incorporates some respect for common sense, its primary aim is to articulate principles that are intrinsically self-evident: the philosophical intuitionist seeks to find principles with the following four features:

---

[5] Ibid., 100.   [6] Ibid., 215.

Thomas Baldwin

1. the concepts involved should be clear and distinct;
2. the principles should be reflectively self-evident;
3. the principles should be consistent;
4. the principles should command general consent.

Sidgwick explicitly alludes here to Descartes,[7] and the connections are obvious if one thinks of Descartes's 'Rules for the Direction of the Mind' and the conception of 'intuition' developed there in Rule 3 ('intuition is the indubitable conception of a clear and attentive mind which proceeds solely from the light of reason').[8] It is, then, because he finds the morality of common sense lacking in these respects that he is led to articulate his own more abstract principles as a distinct and superior form of 'Philosophical Intuitionism' which generalizes the earlier understanding of intuitionism to include knowledge of good and evil as well as of right and wrong.

II

Before considering further these three types of intuitionism which Sidgwick distinguishes, however, I want to say a little about Moore's form of ethical intuitionism since one of the difficulties inherent in Moore's position can be identified by reference to Sidgwick's threefold classification.

As a pupil of Sidgwick Moore follows him in conceiving of ethical intuitions, fundamental ethical propositions, as self-evident truths. Moore's hostility to 'naturalism' of course leads him to emphasize that these are truths whose truth cannot be derived from truths concerning our psychology, sociology, metaphysics, etc. Though the emphasis here is new, there is no disagreement on this point with Sidgwick. But there is sharp disagreement concerning the identity of these propositions. Most of Moore's intuitions are much less abstract than Sidgwick's philosophical intuitions; for example, Moore's intuitions include the proposition that the intrinsic value of aesthetic consciousness is greatly enhanced where it is informed by knowledge concerning the things appreciated.[9] The explanation for this difference is that Moore's principle of organic unities implies that complex

---

[7] *The Methods of Ethics*, 338–9.

[8] René Descartes, *Philosophical Writings*, i, ed. J. Cottingham, R. Stoothof, and D. Murdoch (Cambridge: Cambridge University Press, 1985), 14.

[9] G. E. Moore, *Principia Ethica*, rev. edn., ed. Thomas Baldwin (Cambridge: Cambridge University Press, 1993), 245–8.

94

situations, including complex states of consciousness, are in principle liable to have a degree of intrinsic value as wholes which is not determined by the intrinsic value of their 'parts'—i.e. the intrinsic value of their constituent features. Hence the specification of the intrinsic value 'as a whole' of a complex is a fundamental ethical proposition, i.e. an intuition. Thus Moore's claim that knowledgeable aesthetic appreciation is of much greater value than uninformed aesthetic appreciation rests on the intuition that the former state of consciousness has much greater intrinsic value as a whole than the latter, even though knowledge itself has little or no intrinsic value.

As a result, for Moore, new intuitions, i.e. fundamental ethical propositions, are in principle needed in all cases of moral reflection in order to assess the value as wholes of the potential consequences of the courses of action available to one. These intuitions are plainly not those of Sidgwick's philosophical intuitionist; equally, they are not those of Sidgwick's perceptional intuitionist: for Moore's intuitions, although necessitated by the complexities of new situations, are inherently general: they concern the intrinsic value of types of situation, however complex.[10] Finally, as the example above shows, Moore differs also from standard 'dogmatic' intuitionists in denying that his intuitions concern our familiar duties and obligations; he regards our beliefs concerning these as much too deeply infected by local perspectives to warrant the status of ethical intuition.[11] Hence Moore's ethical intuitions do not belong within Sidgwick's threefold classification: they lack the abstract rationality of Sidgwick's philosophical intuitions, the common-sense support of standard intuitions, and the immediacy of perceptional intuitions. As a result Moore's intuitionism appears literally dogmatic: not only is his foundationalist conception of ethical intuition such that there is nothing to be said in favour of any such intuition, it is also apparent that there is nothing to be said to explain why our beliefs about them are likely to be true. In addition Moore's combination of the principle of organic wholes with his ideal utilitarianism is especially problematic: the need to bear in mind the possibility of fresh intuitions concerning the relative intrinsic value as wholes of the complex situations which are among the consequences of action undermines the possibility of systematic utilitarian practical reasoning .

As I have indicated, the main source of this difficulty is Moore's principle of organic wholes. It may well be the case that there are good reasons for accepting that there is an irreducible plurality of goods and evils, but it is

---

[10] Ibid., 170–1.   [11] Ibid., 198 and 209.

surely mistaken to attempt to deal with the complications of moral deliberation in a complex world by relying on the availability of indefinitely many fundamental ethical intuitions concerning the relative intrinsic value of complex situations. It is one of the strengths of standard common-sense intuitionism that it does not require an analogous thesis concerning the existence of intuitions about the relative obligatoriness of different duties to handle the issue raised by conflicts of duty. Instead, as we shall see, it invokes a distinct conception of the practical wisdom of the person who has to make judgements in situations of this kind.

Nonetheless, Moore's introduction of his principle of organic wholes was not unmotivated. For it was an attempt to insert into a utilitarian theory the kind of consideration which intuitionists standardly contrast with utilitarian reasoning, that which concerns the way in which certain duties or obligations are intrinsically 'fitting' to situations of certain types without reference to the consequences of action. This is especially clear in Moore's discussion of punishment. Moore argues[12] that combining what he acknowledges to be the intrinsic evil involved in punishment with the intrinsic evil of the criminal's crime produces a 'whole' which is sufficiently good 'as a whole' to sustain a total evaluation of a situation involving crime and punishment as one which is less intrinsically evil 'on the whole' than the evil of the crime by itself. Moore's reasoning here is not utilitarian and he sees himself defending a retributive theory of punishment.[13] On the face of it, however, the reasoning Moore offers is not attractive—how can two evils *literally* make a good? But if we think of this application of Moore's principle as a way of inserting into a utilitarian theory the intuitionist's conception of punishment, according to which crimes 'deserve' punishment—where 'desert' is precisely a case of the non-consequential 'fitting' relation,—then, I suggest, we can see what is going on, though, it has to be added, to sympathize with Moore's reasoning at this point one has to adopt an ethical point of view which conflicts with his ideal utilitarianism.

III

Returning now to Sidgwick's three types of intuitionism, I start with some comments on Sidgwick's own favoured type: 'Philosophical Intuitionism'.

---

[12] *Principia Ethica*, 263.   [13] Ibid., 269.

As I mentioned, Sidgwick characterizes this position in Cartesian terms: ethical intuitions are to be intuitions of the kind commended by Descartes. Sidgwick imposes this demand in the name of 'science', by which he means Cartesian science, founded upon self-evident principles which employ clear and distinct concepts, not the kind of speculative theoretical science with which we are now familiar. The motivation for this imposition of scientific rigour is, not surprisingly, the pursuit of knowledge: right at the start of *The Methods of Ethics* Sidgwick remarks that

the student of Ethics seeks to obtain systematic and precise general knowledge of what ought to be, and in this sense his aims and methods may properly be termed 'scientific'[14]

and later in the book he endorses a conception of Moral Philosophy as an attempt

to enunciate, in full breadth and clearness, those primary intuitions of Reason, by the scientific application of which the common moral thought of mankind may be at once systematized and corrected.[15]

It is then in the name of science so conceived that he finds the common-sense principles of dogmatic intuitionism wanting:

It is only being maintained that the objects of these [sc. moral] impulses do not admit of being scientifically determined by any reflective analysis of common sense.[16]

This conception of ethics as a Cartesian science can be thought of as motivated by a thesis which has been a familiar feature of the intuitionist tradition from Clarke until the twentieth century, namely that fundamental ethical truths have a status as a priori truths of reason comparable to truths of mathematics. For where fundamental ethical truths are so conceived it is natural to expect that claims to knowledge of them are to be legitimized by bringing them together into a system which is based upon some self-evident 'primary intuitions of Reason' and which yields a means for deriving other principles from them. This quasi-mathematical conception of ethical truth does not, however, appear to constitute Sidgwick's own starting point. Instead he seems to be primarily guided by the methodological assumption that if a theorist in the field of ethics is to have anything to add to common sense, his work must yield a precise system whose foundations give it the status of genuine science, and which can therefore be employed to resolve the difficult practical questions to which common sense offers no precise guidance. The ethical theorist will have failed in his task if his reflections

---

[14] *The Methods of Ethics*, 1.   [15] Ibid., 373-4.   [16] Ibid., 360.

lead him to the view that in hard cases there is no way to improve upon the judgements of the man of practical wisdom; for what was wanted was a precise statement of the reasons which are to guide judgement in such hard cases.

Although, as I have indicated, Sidgwick's aspiration in this area does not seem to be based upon the familiar comparison between ethical and mathematical truth, his position can be compared to Frege's simultaneous insistence that scientific knowledge, particularly in mathematics, requires a logical system which provides precise rules for determining when inferences are valid: it is not sufficient to rely on the good sense of mathematicians. The difference between Frege and Sidgwick, however, lies in their achievements. Notwithstanding Russell's discovery of the contradiction inherent in his system, Frege did create a logical theory which provides 'systematic and precise general knowledge' of deductive inference. Indeed his logic constitutes what one might call, in Sidgwick's terms, an ethics of deductive inference. The results of Sidgwick's own painstaking inquiries, by contrast, are meagre and unpersuasive. At the end of his attempt to vindicate his hedonist theory of the good all he can offer is the consideration that estimates of potential happiness do at least provide a 'common standard' for comparing competing values such as Virtue, Truth, Freedom, and Beauty;[17] and he finds in his famous 'Concluding chapter' that he has to leave the conflict between rational egoism and rational universalism unresolved.

Could one hope to do any better? Since Sidgwick's philosophical intuitionism rests upon the prospect of drawing substantive conclusions from 'primary intuitions of reason', the Kantian project of expounding practical reason might be regarded as a form of philosophical intuitionism, and contemporary Kantians such as Christine Korsgaard will maintain that one can precipitate significant moral principles out of a conception of moral normativity grounded in the possibility of rational agency.[18] It would, however, be a mistake to treat the Kantian project as a straightforward case of Sidgwickian philosophical intuitionism. For Sidgwick has no general theory of practical reason within which he seeks to locate his ethical intuitions; instead he just aims to find some fundamental ethical propositions which meet his Cartesian standards of rigorous science. Nonetheless, it is worth exploring the way in which Sidgwick's approach to ethics can be enriched by taking over aspects of a Kantian conception of practical reason, and I

---

[17] *The Methods of Ethics*, 405–6.
[18] C. Korsgaard, *The Sources of Normativity* (Cambridge: Cambridge University Press, 1996).

shall attempt this by considering briefly Thomas Scanlon's formulation of a 'contractualist' position in *What we Owe to Each Other*.

Scanlon's work deals with that central area of morality which concerns the relatively impersonal duties and obligations which we owe each other just because we recognize each other as responsible moral subjects, and not because of some special personal relationship, such as friendship. Scanlon maintains that the way to think about the scope of these duties is to set the question of their delineation in the context of attempts to justify our conduct to others; and, further, that when we think about this requirement we see that it implies that our conduct should accord with principles which no one could reasonably reject as a basis for informed and uncoerced general practice.

Thus Scanlon, like Sidgwick, subjects our common-sense intuitions of right and wrong to a test of reason. Unlike Sidgwick, however, Scanlon does not propose his test as a quasi-Cartesian method of doubt, founded on the presumption that moral principles should be self-evident to all reasonable people. Instead he argues that it provides a way of organizing reflections on this central area of morality because it starts from the conviction that it is where we recognize that we could not justify to others some proposed course of action which involves them that we are motivated not to act in this way. Hence, Scanlon argues, we can use the demand for reason inherent in the requirement that we be able to justify ourselves to others as a way of sharpening our moral reflections.

As Scanlon recognizes, and discusses at length, because we can only justify ourselves to others where they do not have reasonable grounds for rejecting the principle which guides our action, much of the substance of his position depends on what may be advanced as a 'reasonable' ground for rejecting a principle for action. It would clearly render the position uselessly circular if the fact that a putative principle permitted agents to act wrongly were to be adduced as a reasonable ground for rejecting it; for the procedure is supposed to help us identify what courses of action are wrong. That dead end might encourage the view that reasonable grounds for rejecting a proposed principle should always be couched in terms which involve some relatively straightforward interests such as Rawls's primary goods[19] to which one can appeal without threat of circularity. But Scanlon rejects this option for the reason that it would impose too crude an understanding of the structure of moral reasoning.[20]

[19] Rawls, J, *A Theory of Justice* (Oxford: Clarendon Press, 1972), 92–5.
[20] T. M. Scanlon, *What we Owe to Each Other* (Cambridge, Mass.: Belknap Press, 1998), 214 ff.

This point can be illustrated by considering an issue which has been recently a matter of some concern: whether teachers have a duty not to enter into sexual relationships with their students even when there is an emotional relationship between them. Scanlon's procedure enjoins us to think about this matter by asking whether one can reasonably reject a principle which permits such relationships. Once one thinks about the power structure inherent in the relationship between teacher and student and about the values inherent in an educational situation which is supposed to be developing and liberating the capacities of students, one can readily find reasonable grounds for rejecting such a principle. But it is also clear that the grounds being invoked here are not just primary goods: they allude at a basic level to such matters as individual freedom, but the reasons are then filled out with specific reference to the normative structure of educational institutions and relationships, and in this respect the debate draws on moral principles which inform our understanding of these institutions and relationships. To rule these considerations out of play because they concern more than primary goods would impoverish our reasoning in the name of an unnecessary attempt at a foundationalist reconstruction of moral reasoning.

Again, take a different case—that of euthanasia: is this wrong? Is there a principle permitting it in certain situations to which no one can reasonably reject? Here matters can seem very simple: those who uphold the sanctity of life will give this as their reason for rejecting such a principle. But Scanlon will set that aside as a refusal to allow that a principle prohibiting euthanasia needs to be justified to those most intimately involved in the situation. The debate will then focus on whether there are reasonable grounds to reject a principle which permits suitably voluntary, well-informed, and independently supervised procedures for euthanasia. Again it is clear that one cannot do justice to the complexity of the relevant considerations if one restricts oneself to primary goods such as the absence of pain and human dignity, important though they are. For the difficult issues concerning euthanasia arise from the responsibilities of medical professionals towards those in their care and the duties of trustees towards those who have entrusted this life-and-death decision to them at a time when their own state of mind is affected by serious pain and its consequences. Once again, we cannot do justice to the complexity of the issue without taking these moral considerations into account.

Scanlon himself remarks that 'a sensible contractualism, like most other plausible views, will involve a holism about moral justification: in assessing one principle we must hold many others fixed. This does not mean that these other principles are beyond question, but just that they are not being questioned at present.'[21] So Scanlon's procedure is a way of organizing and correcting our informal common-sense moral judgements by subjecting them to a holistic discipline that is governed by the demand of reason that we be able to justify ourselves to others. We have therefore travelled some way from Sidgwick's abstract Cartesian project; but precisely by filling out the demand of reason as the constraint of reasonable justification to others Scanlon shows that it can be used to impose more order on one part of common-sense morality than Sidgwick seems to have supposed possible. It is, however, worth bearing in mind that Scanlon restricts himself to that part of morality in which we concern ourselves with those duties and obligations which 'we owe to each other'. Thus he excludes the duties inherent in friendship and love, and equally does not cover such matters as gratitude. So it is also by restricting the scope of his theory to rather less than the full range of moral duty as conceived by traditional intuitionists that Scanlon finds a space for productive critical argument which falls between Sidgwick's all too abstract level of reflection and an unsystematic description of our moral common sense.

IV

Having considered Sidgwick's 'philosophical' critique of common-sense morality from above, I turn now to consider the critique from below, i.e. the critique in the name of what Sidgwick calls 'Perceptional Intuitionism'. Sidgwick does not set out this position in any detail, nor does he identify any philosopher in particular as a 'Perceptional Intuitionist', though in the light of his developmental conception of the three phases of intuitionism one should probably think here of early moral sense theorists such as Shaftesbury. But someone to be considered in this connection is Sidgwick's great critic F. H. Bradley, who insists in his famous paper 'My Station and its Duties' that 'We know what is right in a particular case by what we may call an immediate judgement.'[22] Bradley's position is, however, complex, since he also holds that moral judgement involves an 'intuitive subsumption, which does not know that it is a subsumption'.[23] This enigmatic phrase is explained in the following passage from a long footnote to it:

[21] *What we Owe to Each Other*, 214.
[22] F. H. Bradley, *Ethical Studies*, 2nd edn. (Oxford: Clarendon Press, 1927), 194.
[23] Ibid., 196.

But the ordinary moral judgement is not discursive. It does not look to the right and left, and considering the case from all its sides, consciously subsume under one principle. When the case is presented, it fixes on one quality in the act, referring that unconsciously to one principle, in which it feels the whole of itself, and sees that whole in a single side of the act. So far as right and wrong are concerned, it can perceive nothing but *this* quality of *this* case, and anything else it refuses to try to perceive.[24]

Hence it looks as though Bradley does not deny that there are general principles concerning the moral significance of the 'qualities' of action; what he denies is that we consciously invoke such principles in reaching our moral judgements. Instead, from the perspective of judgement, priority lies with the verdict concerning the particular case in hand, and it is only by subsequent reflection that we can abstract the principle involved.

The immediacy of our moral judgement in particular cases was also emphasized by another Oxford philosopher, albeit someone of a very different metaphysical temperament: H. A. Prichard. Prichard ends his paper 'Does Moral Philosophy Rest on a Mistake?' with the following remark: 'if we do doubt whether there is really an obligation to originate A in a situation B, the remedy lies not in any process of general thinking, but in getting face to face with a particular instance of the situation B, and then directly appreciating the obligation to originate A in that situation'.[25] In Prichard's case the significance of this contrast between 'general thinking' and 'getting face to face with a particular instance' is again primarily epistemological. Just before the quoted passage Prichard has been discussing scepticism about knowledge of mathematics and arguing that the only way to deal with sceptical doubts is to return to a particular case, such as whether $7 \times 4 = 28$, and then ask oneself if one really has any doubts about the point in question—with a clear implication that one does not (the line of thought here is more familiar to us from Moore, who famously argued that the best response to the sceptic's 'general thinking' is precisely to return to particular certainties such as that 'this is a hand'). Similarly, therefore, Prichard holds that the only way to deal with moral scepticism is to get oneself 'face to face' with a particular situation and then acknowledge the obligation inherent in that situation.

Yet there is a further question which can be raised here, namely whether moral judgement involves a commitment to underlying general principles which spell out the moral significance of general features of the world, even

---

[24] *Ethical Studies*, 197.
[25] In *Moral Obligation: Essays and Lectures*, ed. W. D. Ross (Oxford: Clarendon Press, 1949), 17.

if our recognition of them has to be distilled from our immediate judgements in particular cases. In thinking about this question it is useful to replace Sidgwick's name 'Perceptional intuitionism' with the contemporary term 'particularism', and then to distinguish the position of an 'epistemological particularist', whose position permits, though it does not require, a commitment to general principles, from that of the 'moral particularist', who rejects it.

For the epistemological particularist who is not a moral particularist (such as Bradley), our moral consciousness is primarily exercised through our responses to particular situations, but the moral judgements involved bring with them a commitment to general principles concerning the moral significance of features of the situations in question. The initial attention to the particular is required to provide exemplary material for the exercise of our moral consciousness; but, if we reflect, we should then be in a position to undertake what C. D. Broad, following W. E. Johnson, calls an 'intuitive induction' whereby, having understood in this particular case why there is, say, a duty not to violate someone else's confidence, we appreciate that the duty holds generally.[26] Moral particularists, by contrast, reject the presumption that our moral judgements concerning particular situations bring with them any commitments to underlying general principles concerning the significance of features of the case. They hold that the recognition that some particular betrayal of confidence was wrong does not bring with it a commitment to thinking that such betrayal is generally wrong. Perhaps there are inductive 'rules of thumb' to be discerned, but in general the structure of morality is not rule-governed (notice that in this respect moral particularism resembles that most general of 'general thinkings': act-utilitarianism!).

Once this distinction is drawn, it is, I think, clear that Prichard, like Bradley, is not a moral particularist. In the passage quoted above he describes how, having got ourselves 'face to face' with a 'particular instance' of situation B and appreciated the obligation to originate A in that situation, we are led to acknowledge what must be a general obligation to originate A in situation B, since A and B are types, not tokens. It is also clear, however, that it is moral particularism that is the really challenging position here, since the defender of common-sense intuitionism can adapt his epistemology to accommodate the epistemological particularism of Bradley and Prichard (I say more about this later).

---

[26] C. D. Broad, *Five Types of Ethical Theory* (London: Routledge & Kegan Paul, 1930), 214.

Moral particularism has, I think, only recently received a full statement and defence, from Jonathan Dancy in his book *Moral Reasons*. Dancy offers two arguments for the moral particularist position: one arises from a consideration of the structure of moral reasoning, of the ways in which in some cases reasons do not merely outweigh others, but actually 'silence' them. The second argument arises from what is held to be an inconsistent triad concerning moral reasons: cognitivism, internalism, and moral 'generalism' (the denial of moral particularism).

The first argument starts from the thought that because the moral generalist holds that moral reasons (duties, obligations, etc.) are determined by general principles, the generalist must hold that they function as weights that are placed in the scale of deliberation whenever the appropriate feature is present, so that even when outweighed by more powerful contrary considerations, they still constitute 'prima facie' reasons for courses of action. This, Dancy argues, is unacceptable: in some cases reasons of one kind can be completely undermined by other reasons in a way which is captured only by the moral particularist who focuses on the structure of the morally relevant considerations on a case-by-case basis and therefore avoids the presumption that a consideration which is a reason in one case should be a reason in all similar cases.

As a particularist, Dancy of course seeks to substantiate this (general) line of argument by particular examples. Here are three typical ones: one concerns pleasure:

the fact that an action will give pleasure can be a reason for doing it or for approving of it when done. But it can also be a reason for disapproving of it. . . . If I tread on [a worm] with pleasure or to give you pleasure, my action is the worse for it.[27]

The second example (reminiscent of Prichard's favourite example) concerns the duty to return a book one has borrowed:

I borrow a book from you, and then discover that you have stolen it from the library. Normally the fact that I have borrowed the book from you would be a reason to return it to you, but in this situation it is not. It isn't that I have *some* reason to return it to you and more reason to put it back in the library. I have no reason at all to return it to you.[28]

The third concerns lying: Dancy points to the fact that there are games in which one is required to lie, and comments, 'That an action is a lie is commonly a reason not to do it; here it is a reason in favour of it.'[29]

---

[27] J. Dancy, *Moral Reasons* (Oxford: Blackwell, 1993), 56.   [28] Ibid., 60.
[29] Ibid., 61.

These examples certainly show that moral reasons are not always straightforward; but whether they are convincing as objections to moral generalism is more disputable. The first example draws on a familiar anti-hedonist point—that the value of a pleasure depends on the value of that in which pleasure is being taken. No moral generalist who allows that in some cases the prospect of pleasure is a reason for action need be committed to the unqualified hedonism which disputes this point. The second example is equally inefficacious: the duty to return what one has borrowed rests on the presumption that the item borrowed either belongs to, or is rightly under the care of, the person from whom one has borrowed it. In the case envisaged this presumption is undermined by the discovery that the book has been stolen from the library. So the duty simply lapses, without any significant threat to the generalist. Thus the generalist can handle these cases by observing that moral principles, like laws, are typically complex and qualified. Where they do not apply, they do not sustain moral reasons for action despite the fact that the cases involved have some similarities with cases to which they do apply.

The third example shows that some moral principles do not apply in playful situations and thereby indicates a different kind of condition on the application of moral principles. This is a threat to the generalist only if moral generalism is taken to require that moral principles be unconditional in their application once due account has been taken of their presuppositions and qualifications. But need a generalist accept this requirement? It is worth exploring this type of case a bit further. In Dancy's example of a game whose rules involve the suspension of the normal principles of honesty (Cheat), no player is harmed by being deceived (except in so far as they lose the game); for the beliefs expressed in the game have no application outside the context of the game. By contrast, because the results of physical injury, unlike deception, cannot be confined within a playful context, the moral prohibitions on physical injury remain in force within games (even if the players consent to their suspension). In between these two areas of morality there are areas of conduct, e.g. involving sexual behaviour, where the limits of what is acceptable within a game are open to argument—we have the conception of a game's 'getting out of hand' where some of those participating engage in forms of conduct that other players do not regard as permissible within the game (the plays of Alan Ayckbourn often include games which get out of hand in this way).

Thus what emerges is that in games and other playful situations players can consent to the temporary suspension of some of the moral principles which regulate 'conventional' morality, though an important characteristic of these cases is that once the game is over it should be possible to return to normal life without any injuries as a result of participation in the game. Are there implications here which threaten the moral generalist, as Dancy maintains? The conclusion to be drawn is surely that there are not: for the considerations which determine whether or not a conventional moral principle is suspended are all inherently general—they concern the rules of the game, the consent of the players, and the absence of long-term injury. Admittedly, their application in a particular situation, e.g. where a game threatens to get out of hand, may well involve the exercise of judgement; but it is no part of the moral generalist's position to hold that the application of general moral principles to particular situations is an entirely straightforward matter.

Dancy's examples draw on the fact that moral reasoning is not the unconditional application of simple-minded, unqualified, moral principles. In his discussion of the structure of reasons for action Scanlon makes a similar point; but although Dancy's examples were intended to support his moral particularist thesis, Scanlon's treatment of it provides support for the moral generalist.[30] Scanlon begins, as Dancy does, by observing that reasons for action are sometimes not just outweighed, but completely undermined: for example, if one is involved in making an appointment to a post, one has to bracket considerations arising from one's friendship with some of the candidates, even though in normal life we see nothing objectionable in doing favours for one's friends—indeed it is part of friendship that one should be disposed to do things on behalf of one's friends which one would not do for others. Scanlon takes it that this point illustrates the fact that reasons for action are like reasons for belief, whose evidential significance can also be undermined once background considerations are introduced—e.g. once it is discovered that a witness has been lying or that some forensic equipment was unreliable. Thus the possibility of undermining reasons for action points to the fact that reasons for action, including moral reasons, are like reasons for belief in that they stand in logical relationships with other propositions; in both cases, where a situation is such that the presupposition of a reason is violated, it follows that the reason does not apply in that situation.

The reason that this comparison between reasons for action and reasons for belief provides support for the moral generalist is that in offering reasons

---

[30] *What we Owe to Each Other*, 52 ff.

for belief we offer considerations which provide support in virtue of general connections (logical, causal, conventional, etc.) between the supposed facts in question—we are 'theoretical' generalists. There is no tension at all in this case between the existence of underlying general connections and the complex structures of implications and presuppositions as a result of which reasons for belief can be completely undermined (indeed it is hard to make particularism with respect to reasons for belief altogether intelligible). But if this is the situation in the case of reasons for belief, there is every reason to expect that reasons for action are similar in this respect.

So far I have sought to show that Dancy's examples do not make a convincing case for moral particularism. But what of his alleged inconsistent triad: cognitivism, internalism, and moral generalism?[31] Dancy develops the point by reference to Ross's conception of a prima facie duty: he argues that (i) generalists can conceive of moral reasons only as 'prima facie'; but (ii) such reasons fail the 'internalist' demand that they should be capable of motivating action by themselves, without drawing on some background desire to be moral, precisely because their 'prima facie' status implies that they lack the capacity by themselves to determine the will. Because they are, so to speak, only tentative input into the determination of action, they cannot by themselves motivate action in the way that internalism requires.

One reply to this challenge will be to ask why it is supposed to be so imperative to be an internalist. Externalism is not an intrinsically absurd doctrine and can be defended in the light of a suitable account of moral motivation.[32] But it is not necessary to take this line. An alternative response for the generalist who seeks to be an internalist will be to reject Dancy's imputation to him of Ross's conception of a prima facie duty, since it does not readily accommodate the conditional applicability of moral principles discussed just now. But in the present context it is not even necessary to make this move: the point of Ross's 'prima facie' qualification is just that moral duties are not in all cases overriding, since where there is a conflict of duties at least one duty will, inevitably but rightly, remain unfulfilled. Internalism, however, is not the untenable doctrine that moral reasons, such as duties, are in all circumstances overriding. It is just the thesis that duties are intrinsically motivating, and there is no inherent conflict between this thesis and the recognition that sometimes this motivation is

---

[31] *Moral Reasons*, 93.

[32] Philip Stratton-Lake, 'Why Externalism is not a Problem for Ethical Intuitionists', *Proceedings of the Aristotelian Society*, 99 (1999), 77–90.

overridden by other, more powerful, contrary moral motivations. So there is no inherent conflict between internalism and generalism.

V

It is time now to turn to the position of Sidgwick's 'Dogmatic Intuitionist', the defender of moral common sense, and I begin by briefly making a case for the generalist aspect of this position. In deliberating what to do, comparing the merits and defects of different possible courses of action available to us, we necessarily consider only types of action, not particular tokens of these types. The actions we subsequently perform are tokens; but in deliberating we concern ourselves with what is then merely possible, and we can evaluate these possibilities only by reference to the general types they would instantiate; for, as mere possibilities, they are conceived of only as possible instantiations of types. But if we can only evaluate these possibilities, morally as well as in other respects, by reference to the general types they instantiate, it must be possible for us to draw on general moral principles which specify the moral value of the features by which the types are defined (alleviating distress, breaking a promise, etc.). Hence if we are to be able to deliberate morally, our moral concepts must permit us to place confidence in general moral principles.

The particularist may respond that his position allows us to use inductive methods of generalization, and thus to place confidence in moral considerations arising from particular situations we have previously encountered. In assessing this, however, one must distinguish epistemological particularism from moral particularism. As I observed earlier, the moral generalist can accept epistemological particularism and invoke intuitive induction as our way of discriminating the general principles inherent in our convictions concerning the particular situations we encounter. What is distinctive about moral particularism is the disavowal of any such intuitive inductions of general principles. So, for the moral particularist, the only generalization from particular cases that is permitted is of inductive rules of thumb, concerning what we have reason to expect concerning situations of various familiar types. But this does not provide an adequate basis for the role of moral considerations in practical deliberation. It suggests that in order to be confident that nuclear warfare would be wrong, we have to have had experience of nuclear warfare. Furthermore, although past experience of murders does indeed suggest that the fact that a future action involves the deliberate killing of another is a reason for expecting that it too will be wrong, this inductive reasoning will not imply that this fact is itself a reason for the action's being wrong. But it is this latter consideration which enters into ordinary practical deliberation and moral judgement.

This is especially clear in cases of moral conflict such as abortion. In cases of this kind the conflicting reasons do not undermine each other and the agent has to choose the lesser of the two evils—e.g. a foetus is aborted in order to alleviate the distress of a young woman who has been raped. The combination of features here does not just provide reasons both for thinking that the action is good and for thinking that it is bad; it implies that the action itself is both good and bad. Moral conflict is not a conflict of evidence concerning the evaluation of a particular situation; it is a conflict of values inherent in that situation. It is easy to see how this conflict of values can arise from different general moral principles that apply to different features of the situation. What is impossible to understand is how there can be conflicting particularist moral evaluations of it.

Yet although the existence of moral conflict is a consideration which counts in favour of the common-sense intuitionist's moral generalism, it is less clear what account he should give of the ways in which we resolve these conflicts. He can of course point to the familiar considerations which we employ when we think about them: which outcome will lead to more serious harm? how easy will it be to make amends later? which personal relationship is more important? which person will understand our apologies and be more forgiving? and so on. But the theoretical presuppositions of these considerations are not so clear. One obvious suggestion is that in invoking them we presuppose that there is a principled way of resolving moral conflict. For the generalist who is a common-sense intuitionist, however, this suggestion must be wrong, at least where it implies that conflict between moral principles is always to be resolved by reference to higher-order principles. For that approach gives these higher-order principles the kind of priority which leads back to a version of Sidgwick's philosophical intuitionism, and the common-sense intuitionist will reject such a position.

The defender of common sense must hold that our common-sense practices of dealing with moral conflict are not attempts at subsumption or qualification of the moral principles involved; instead they are essentially methods of damage limitation. Thus he will agree with Ross[33] that the

---

[33] W. D. Ross, *The Right and the Good* (Oxford: Clarendon Press, 1930), 41–2.

resolution of moral conflict depends on the sensitivity and good sense of the agent involved, and that at this point there is a kind of practical 'know-how' (practical wisdom) which is not a matter of deferring to some more fundamental intuition but the exercise of judgement concerning the case in hand. Hence a question that now arises is whether the defender of common sense, having rejected a commitment to authoritative higher-order principles, is required to accept that this reliance upon the exercise of practical wisdom in resolving moral conflicts amounts to inserting an element of moral particularism within the account.

It would not be fatal for the position if it did, for it would not imply that it is incorrect for the common-sense intuitionist to give priority to the general moral principles whose conflict provides the occasion for the exercise of this particularist practical wisdom. But in fact even this admission of a role for particularism can be qualified. For the agent who resolves a moral conflict thereby sets a precedent which suggests a way of coping with similar cases; so his judgement in this case brings with it a commitment to a general principle, albeit a poorly specified one which simply applies to 'situations like this' and implies that in order to justify contrary judgements in apparently similar cases it is necessary to introduce further distinctions, as in legal reasoning within a common law system. In some cases it may be that the experience of moral conflict and its resolution leads to the conceptualization of distinctions which remove the conflict by motivating a qualification of the moral principles involved; but the defender of common sense will offer no guarantee that this can always be achieved (contrast euthanasia and abortion here: we are surely on the way to developing a conception of conditions under which euthanasia is morally permissible; but abortion remains justifiable only as the lesser of two evils).

What is indisputable is that the common-sense intuitionist who acknowledges this irreducible role for practical wisdom in resolving moral conflict introduces an element of epistemological particularism into the position. As I have already stressed, there is no inconsistency here, but it is worth noting that the context for this commitment is different from that envisaged by Prichard and Bradley, in the passages discussed earlier, when they encourage us to get 'face to face' with a situation in order to appreciate its moral significance. For their cases are supposed to be sufficiently unproblematic that we can use them to repel sceptical doubts. Indeed not only do they concentrate on such cases, Bradley at least fails to allow properly for others. For when we think of hard cases, such as those familiar from discussions of abortion, Bradley's emphasis on our 'immediate judgement' and his disparagement of discursive reflection is plainly unsatisfactory. These hard cases are not the abstract creations of sophistical philosophers, but part of the texture of ordinary life, and once we find ourselves enmeshed in one, we cannot without bad faith avoid doing precisely what he tells us not to do: looking 'to the right and left, and considering the case from all its sides' while reaching our practical conclusion.

This blindness to hard cases is, of course, no reason to reject Bradley's emphasis on our 'immediate judgement' in straightforward cases, which Prichard invoked in order to counter philosophical scepticism. Indeed it is effective for this purpose as a way of reminding us of the kinds of things we do actually feel and think. But unless one can supply some further account of the authority of common sense, a position which simply sets out the common-sense convictions arrived at by intuitive induction from our convictions in particular cases will invite Sidgwick's characterization of it as 'dogmatic'. For it will appear to be a sociological document rather than a critical elucidation of morality.

The remaining challenge to the common-sense intuitionist, therefore, is to find a way of meeting this requirement without legitimizing Sidgwick's demand that one 'enunciate, in full breadth and clearness, those primary intuitions of Reason, by the scientific application of which the common moral thought of mankind may be at once systematized and corrected'.[34] As I indicated earlier, Scanlon's approach offers one way forward here, since, without appealing to self-evident 'intuitions of Reason' as foundations, he draws on the condition of reasonable justifiability to others as a way of refining our common-sense judgements of right and wrong into a coherent set of rules that are to govern our impersonal dealings with one another. But Scanlon specifically restricts his approach to the morality of what we 'owe to one another', and, thinking about morality more generally, the response to Sidgwick must be that since human affairs are not systematic it is a mistake to think that the ordinary, common-sense morality which regulates and inspires human affairs needs to be 'systematized' (and then 'corrected'). Instead, in developing a critical appraisal of it, the place from which to start is with the thought that our common-sense moral judgements concerning our duties, responsibilities, and virtues are embedded in a largely implicit understanding of our culture and institutions: the family, place of work, school, shop, hospital, neighbourhood, state, etc. So a critical understanding of these judgements needs to be informed by an explicit

---

[34] *The Methods of Ethics*, 373–4.

Thomas Baldwin

understanding of these institutions and their place in human life, together with an awareness of the possibility of organizing human affairs in other ways. In thinking, for example, about the duty of gratitude, we have to think about the place of gifts within our culture and the contexts within which acts of kindness are welcomed—and also those in which they are inappropriate or worse. No abstract Kantian or utilitarian principles will help us here; what is required instead is both a localized understanding of the human significance of gratitude in our culture, together with a historical and anthropological understanding of the place of gifts and gratitude in other cultures.

This can at first sound like a surrender of moral theory to sociology and politics. But it need not be a surrender as long as the social and political theory involved is critical, as indeed most such theory is: feminist theories of the family are a good example. The implication of such an approach, however, is that intuitionist moral theory needs to abandon much of its characteristic purity in order to recolonize the moral sciences from which it was expelled at the end of the nineteenth century by the late Victorian positivists. In calling for this, however, I think I am in fact merely describing something already well under way—as 'applied ethics'. However, this label seems to me terrible: it goes with the mistaken Sidgwickian faith in a domain of pure systematic science which can then be applied to concrete problems (think, as ever, of the mathematical analogy, of pure and applied mathematics). Redescribed, however, as 'moral science' this is the way for common-sense intuitionism to rediscover and validate itself.

Pleasure and Reflection in Ross's Intuitionism   5

Philip Stratton-Lake

Ethical intuitionists build their moral theory on a set of general moral convictions about the right and the good, which they regard as self-evident. This epistemology and associated methodology has, however, come under serious criticism. Two common objections are that it is dogmatic and especially vulnerable to bias. Both of these worries focus on the supposed self-evidence of the moral convictions on which intuitionist theories rest. It is claimed that intuitionists are dogmatic because the supposed self-evidence of their basic moral convictions means that if someone does not see the truth of these propositions, then all the intuitionist can do is dogmatically assert that they are true. Christine Korsgaard, for example, says that if one asked an intuitionist whether one really ought to do some particularly demanding act, all he can say is 'simply "Yes". That is, all he can say is that it is true that this is what you ought to do.'[1] It doesn't help to say to someone who denies that some moral proposition is true, that it is self-evident, for if they deny that it is true, they will, a fortiori, deny that it is self-evident. Staring at the proposition doesn't help.

The charge of bias springs from the same source. The worry is that if we base our moral theory on moral convictions we regard as self-evident, then these basic convictions will never be subjected to scrutiny. Consequently, they may do little more than reflect views that we find

I would like to express my gratitude to Robert Audi, Roger Crisp, Jonathan Dancy, and David McNaughton for helpful comments on an earlier draft of this paper. I also benefited from discussion of this paper at research seminars at the philosophy departments of Trinity College Dublin and the University of Reading.

[1] C. Korsgaard, *The Sources of Normativity* (Cambridge: Cambridge University Press, 1996), p. 38; see also p. 32, and P. H. Nowell-Smith, *Ethics* (Harmondsworth: Penguin, 1954), 46.

subjectively compelling, but which express prejudice, or the social position we occupy, rather than genuine rational insight. This criticism can be found, for example, in R. M. Hare.[2] Indeed, Hare goes so far as to say that 'intuitionism is nearly always a form of disguised subjectivism', making moral truth depend upon what we happen to believe.[3] I think that the charges of both dogmatism and bias are at best exaggerated, and that this can be seen in W. D. Ross's ethical intuitionism.

Self-Evidence and Reflection

Ross's intuitionistic methodology does not treat moral intuitions as brute givens that cannot be questioned. Rather, it is our moral convictions after reflection that form the basis of his moral theory. Such reflection is required because self-evident moral propositions are not obvious in the sense that anyone who understands them will immediately assent to them. Ross maintains that a moral proposition is self-evident,

not in the sense that it is evident from the beginning of our lives, or as soon as we attend to the proposition for the first time, but in the sense that when we have reached sufficient mental maturity and have given sufficient attention to the proposition it is evident without any need of proof, or of evidence beyond itself.[4]

Self-evident truths need not be obvious, and obvious truths are not necessarily self-evident.[5] Ross clearly thinks that self-evident moral propositions are not obviously true to every one. They will not, for example, appear true to someone who has not achieved 'sufficient mental maturity'.[6] But even if one has reached the appropriate level of maturity, the truth of these propositions may not be apparent at first sight. His point here is not that their self-evidence may not be apparent at first sight, but that their truth may not be

[2] 'Rawls' Theory of Justice', in N. Daniels (ed.), *Reading Rawls: Critical Studies on Rawls' 'A Theory of Justice'* (Blackwell: Oxford, 1975), ch. 4. See also A. MacIntyre, *After Virtue: A Study in Moral Theory* (London: Duckworth, 1985), 17.

[3] Hare, 'Rawls' Theory of Justice', 83. For a sympathetic treatment of this worry in relation to the a priori in general, see L. BonJour, *In Defence of Pure Reason: A Rationalist Account of A Priori Justification* (Cambridge: Cambridge University Press, 1998), 133–7.

[4] W. D. Ross, *The Right and the Good* (Indianapolis: Hackett, 1988), 29.

[5] Obvious but non-self-evident truths are everyday empirical truths, such as that if I drop something, it will fall.

[6] It should be noted here that Ross is talking of *mental* maturity, rather than *moral* maturity. One has achieved such maturity when one is able to think in general terms. See e.g. *The Right and the Good*, 33.

evident at first sight, and one does not need even to have the concept of self-evidence in order to know some self-evident proposition.[7]

The truth of such a proposition is only apparent after one has considered it with sufficient attention, and this attention involves various forms of reflection. This can be seen, for example, in Ross's discussion of the intrinsic deontic status of promises. He writes: 'it seems, on reflection, self-evident that a promise, simply as such, is something that *prima facie* ought to be kept, and it does not, on reflection, seem self-evident that production of maximum good is the only thing that makes an act obligatory'.[8] Ross's intuitionism rests not on a set of unquestioned moral convictions, but on those that we hold after reflection. What form does this reflection take? In Ross it involves considering particular cases, various thought experiments, and a consideration of the degree to which these intuitions cohere with our other moral convictions. We can see the way in which consideration of particular cases figures in such reflection in Ross's discussion of the universal principle of fidelity.

The general principles of duty are obviously not self-evident from the beginning of our lives. How do they come to be so? The answer is, that they come to be self-evident to us just as mathematical axioms do. We find by experience that this couple of matches and that couple make four matches, that this couple of balls on a wire and that couple make four balls: and by reflection on these and similar discoveries we come to see that it is of the nature of two and two to make four. In a precisely similar way, we see the prima facie rightness of an act which would be the fulfilment of a particular promise, and of another which would be the fulfilment of another promise, and when we have reached sufficient maturity to think in general terms, we apprehend prima facie rightness to belong to the nature of any fulfilment of promise.[9]

Thought experiments also play an important role in Ross's reflection on his moral convictions. In considering whether something is good in itself, for example, we have to ask ourselves whether we think it would be good even if it existed alone, or whether when we compare two worlds which differ only in respect to this putative good we think that one world is better than the other.[10]

---

[7] See R. Audi, 'Intuitionism, Pluralism, and the Foundations of Ethics', in W. Sinnott-Armstrong and M. Timmons (eds.), *Moral Knowledge? New Readings in Moral Epistemology* (Oxford: Oxford University Press, 1996), 106–7.

[8] *The Right and the Good*, 40.

[9] Ibid., 32–3.

[10] Sometimes the isolation test—the question of whether we would consider something good even if it existed quite alone—does not make sense, as certain things cannot be conceived of as

Reflection on particular cases and thought experiments enable us to attain an adequate understanding of the proposition in question. An adequate understanding of some moral conviction will also involve a clear grasp of certain distinctions. For example, to achieve an adequate understanding of one of Ross's prima facie duties one must at least be clear about the distinction between prima facie duty and duty proper, between what makes an act right and what it is for an act to be right, and between what it is for an actually right act to be prima facie wrong and for an actually wrong act to be prima facie right. Failure to get clear on these distinctions will mean that one does not have an adequate understanding of the general concept of a prima facie duty, let alone some principle that involves this concept.

Finally we have to ask ourselves whether our moral convictions are coherent and consistent.[11] It may turn out that some of our moral convictions are inconsistent, or incoherent. In such a situation one at least of our convictions must be given up. Both inconsistency and incoherence among moral convictions give us reason to reject at least one of these convictions. Do consistency and coherence give us positive reason to believe in these propositions? The mere fact that an intuition is consistent with our other moral convictions does not seem to give us any reason to believe it, though the fact that it coheres with our other moral convictions may give us such a reason. Although Ross thinks that inconsistency and incoherence among our moral intuitions would give us reason to reject some of these, he does not explicitly consider the issue of whether coherence between certain moral propositions gives us reason to believe them. This issue was, however, considered by A. C. Ewing. For Ewing our moral judgements are ideally coherent if and only if they 'form a system such that they are not divisible into logically independent groups but help confirm one another's truth, and that none of them could be false while all the others . . . remained true'.[12] He held that the fact that an ethical judgement coheres with our other ethical judgements in a way that brings us nearer to such an ideal system gives us positive reason to believe that judgement.[13] Ewing did not, however,

---

existing in isolation. It is difficult to see how to make sense of a pleasure existing without at least a consciousness of that pleasure, or virtue without someone whose virtue it is, except perhaps as uninstantiated universals. But it is not the universals that are thought to be intrinsically good but their instances. The two-world thought experiments are not, it seems to me, so vulnerable to such an objection and for the most part succeed in achieving what the isolation test was designed to show.

[11] Coherence is standardly thought to be more than mere consistency, though it is not always clear what this something extra is. See R. Audi, *Epistemology: A Contemporary Introduction to the Theory of Knowledge* (London: Routledge, 1998), 192 ff.

[12] A. C. Ewing, *The Definition of Good* (New York: MacMillan, 1947), 91.   [13] Ibid.

think that coherence by itself can provide justification. It is not coherence with any sort of ethical judgement that provides justification, for coherence with false moral beliefs would give us reason to reject, rather than accept, a moral proposition.[14] Thus, Ewing writes: 'just as the coherence test will not work in regard to theoretical judgements unless we admit that there are truths based on sense experience with which the judgements have to cohere, so it will not work in ethics unless there are ethical truths apprehended intuitively with which other ethical judgements may be expected to cohere'.[15] For Ewing, then, the fact that a moral proposition coheres with our moral convictions only justifies us in believing that proposition on the condition that we have some independent (non-coherence-based) justification for believing the propositions with which it coheres. Self-evidence provides this independent justification. Thus, coherence cannot replace self-evidence in ethics, but can provide an epistemic supplement to it, according to Ewing.

Although Ross did not consider whether coherence can provide positive justification for a moral belief, there is nothing in his ethical theory which prevents him from endorsing Ewing's view. Ross could, then, regard considerations of coherence not only as a negative test of our moral convictions, but as providing positive support to them also.

It may be objected that Ross could not think of coherence as providing such justification for self-evident moral propositions, for these propositions are supposed to be self-justifying. But there is nothing about the view that certain moral propositions are self-justifying that means that they cannot be justified in other ways. All that is needed for a proposition to be self-evident is that a certain epistemic route is available. But the availability of this epistemic route in no way rules out the possibility of other epistemic routes.[16]

Why is coherence needed for self-evident propositions if an adequate understanding of them is sufficient to ground knowledge? The answer to this is that we do not need this extrinsic justification for self-evident propositions. If it were needed, then P could not be self-evident, for then an adequate understanding of P would not be sufficient to know that P. But

---

[14] Ibid., 92.   [15] Ibid.

[16] Russell held that although there are certain self-evident propositions which neither need nor can be proved, we can have extrinsic reason to believe at least some self-evident propositions. He maintains that although the propositions of arithmetic can all be deduced from the general principles of logic, 'the simple propositions of arithmetic, such as "two and two are four", are just as self-evident as the principles of logic' (*The Problems of Philosophy* (London: Oxford University Press, 1913), 112).

although this sort of extrinsic justification is not needed to know basic moral propositions, it is nevertheless good if it is available. We have to concede that many propositions have appeared self-evident to many people that have turned out to be false—that is, we must concede that a proposition may falsely appear self-evident. Consequently, anything that gives us further, i.e. extrinsic, reason to think that some apparently self-evident moral proposition is true is useful. Reflection on the coherence of our moral convictions provides this extra reassurance (though there is no reason to think that coherence is the only form such reassurance may take). Since the reasons that coherence provides are not needed to know the truth of self-evident propositions, but (given our fallibility) it is good if we have such reasons, reflection on the coherence of some putative self-evident truth with our other convictions may be called 'epistemically supererogatory'. And the epistemically supererogatory in no way threatens the self-evidence of the proposition it supports.

In *The Right and the Good* Ross seems to rule out the idea of epistemically supererogatory justification when he writes that with self-evident propositions 'we are dealing with propositions that cannot be proved, but that just as certainly need no proof'.[17] But the sort of justification coherence provides falls a long way short of a proof. Furthermore, in an article published in 1927 (three years before *The Right and the Good*) Ross states that 'the fact that something can be inferred does not prove that it cannot be seen intuitively'.[18] If P can be seen intuitively it can be known directly on the basis of an adequate understanding of it, and thus does not need further argument to justify a belief in it. But if P can be inferred from other propositions, then such extrinsic justification is available, even though it is not needed. It seems, therefore, that Ross would be perfectly happy with the idea that coherence provides us with epistemically supererogatory reasons to believe in self-evident propositions, though, as I have pointed out, he only considered inconsistency and incoherence as providing negative epistemic reasons.

It is only convictions which survive the three forms of reflection described above that are putative self-evident truths, and thus can form the basis of an intuitionist theory. I say 'putative' since some of them may not be basic, and thus will be grounded in some more fundamental consideration or principle[19]. It is only the basic moral principles that can be

---

[17] *The Right and the Good*, 30.
[18] 'The Basis of Objective Judgements in Ethics', *International Journal of Ethics*, 37/2 (1927), 121.
[19] This is Ross's view about lying.

self-evidently true, for since the considerations referred to in these principles are morally salient on their own account rather than because they instantiate some other consideration, the truth that they are moral considerations, or that they are morally relevant, must be believed self-evidently.

The fact that it is only those moral convictions which survive reflection that form the basis of ethical intuitionist theories should cast doubt on the view that the methodology of ethical intuitionism is dogmatic, or unenlightened, and especially vulnerable to bias. The moral convictions on which an intuitionist moral theory rests are far from being an arbitrary set of strong moral beliefs members of our society happen to have. Rather, they are a set of pre-theoretical convictions that have survived fairly rigorous inspection. It seems to me that such principles, or truths, are at least as good a starting point for a moral theory as anything else that is available, and are better than most.[20]

What I want to do now is show how demanding and rigorous such reflection can be by tracing Ross's reflection on the conviction he had, and many share, that pleasure is good on its own account and not merely for the sake of something else. Ross was aware that this good is unlike the other goods he lists in certain respects, and that these respects cast doubt on its claim to be intrinsically good. Nonetheless, in *The Right and the Good* he maintained that pleasure is, with certain qualifications, intrinsically good. But he was not happy with his attempt to deal with these problems and returned to this issue in *The Foundations of Ethics*. Here further reflection led Ross to abandon his earlier strongly held conviction that pleasure is (with certain qualifications) intrinsically good, and that this is self-evident. He now argues for the contrary thesis that pleasure is an extrinsic good. By tracing the process of reflection that led Ross to abandon his earlier conviction we will see that his intuitionism has the resources to reject widely shared moral convictions, and these resources provide a good response to the charge of bias. Furthermore, since the basic moral convictions on which Ross builds his theory are subjected to such reflection, he can do more than dogmatically assert that those that survive are true. If someone doubts their truth, he can take them through the same process of reflection that led him to retain them.

---

[20] I take seriously Prichard's worry that non-intuitionist theories appear artificial, or abstract. The idea here is not so much that they do not reflect the way we actually deliberate, but that we cannot convince ourselves that we ought to deliberate in the way these theories recommend. See my Introduction to this volume.

The Argument that Pleasure is Intrinsically Good

Let me start with the reflections that Ross believed support the view that pleasure is intrinsically good. He offers three arguments for this view. The first is based on a thought experiment of the sort Moore made familiar. Ross maintains that if we imagine two worlds, or, as he puts it, 'two states of the universe', one including widespread and intense pleasure, and the other widespread and intense pain, yet containing the same amount of virtue (which Ross has already argued is intrinsically good), we cannot doubt that the former world is better than the latter, and this gives us good reason to believe that pleasure is intrinsically good.[21]

One might object that what we are being asked to imagine here is impossible on the ground that virtue always tends to promote general pleasure, so the two worlds could not differ so drastically in terms of pleasure and pain if they both contain the same amount of virtue. But Ross quite rightly rejects this objection for two reasons. First, he points out that pleasures and pains can be caused by things other than virtuous actions, such as disease and natural disasters, and that these can explain the difference of pleasure and pain in the different worlds.[22] Second, even if we think that such states of the universe could not exist, the supposition is a legitimate way of vividly bringing us to see something which is really self-evident—that pleasure is intrinsically good.[23]

The second way of getting us to see that pleasure is intrinsically good is by considering our attitudes towards cruelty and kindness. Kindness, for Ross, is the desire to give pleasure to others, and cruelty, the desire to inflict pain. We approve of the former, and disapprove of the latter. But, he maintains, these attitudes can only be explained on the assumption that we think that pleasure is good and pain bad, for it is only on this assumption that we would approve of a desire to give pleasure to others and disapprove of a desire to inflict pain.[24]

Ross considers the objection that we disapprove of the desire to inflict pain not because we think that pain is bad, but simply because it is unpleasant. A similar response might be made in relation to our approval of kindness. In response to this Ross insists that apart from the thought that pain is painful he has the further thought that 'a state of affairs in virtue of being painful is prima facie[25] (i.e. where other considerations do not enter into the

---

[21] *The Right and the Good*, 135. [22] Ibid., 134.
[23] Ibid., 135. [24] Ibid.
[25] I shall return to the notion of prima facie goodness below.

case) one that a rational spectator would not approve, i.e. is bad; and that similarly our attitude towards kindness involves the thought that pleasure is good'.[26] This response is not, however, wholly persuasive. First, one might object that it seems little more than an assertion that his objector is mistaken. Second, one might object that if we approve of kindness because it produces something that is intrinsically good (pleasure), then we should admire not only acts that make others happy, but also those that make the agent happy, for these acts also produce pleasure. There is, however, nothing admirable about such acts. But even if these objections are conceded, Ross could maintain that his other arguments give us good reason to believe that pleasure is intrinsically good.

His third argument is that the thought that virtue deserves to be rewarded by happiness, and vice with unhappiness, assumes that happiness is good and unhappiness bad.[27] Kant claimed that happiness is not good, but is merely a source of satisfaction to the individual. But Ross notes that this claim does not fit with Kant's view that the union of virtue with happiness is not merely 'the object of the desires of rational finite beings', but something that approves itself 'even to the judgement of an impartial reason' as 'the whole and perfect good'; a good that is better than virtue alone. Furthermore, Kant maintains elsewhere that happiness is a conditional good, something that is good only on the condition that it is deserved, i.e. if the agent has a good will. This implies that when the condition is satisfied, happiness is not merely desired, but is also good. In the end, then, Ross maintains that even the most austere moralist must acknowledge that 'while virtue alone is morally good, deserved happiness. . . is not merely a source of satisfaction to its possessor, but objectively good'.[28]

These arguments show that Ross can do more than dogmatically assert that pleasure is good to someone who denies this, even though he thought that it is self-evident that pleasure is good. What he can and does do is bring to their attention considerations that will enable them after reflection to see that this proposition is true.

The reflection to which we must submit our moral convictions before they are incorporated into an intuitionist theory not only involves attending to the sort of considerations I have mentioned so far, but also involves considering how our moral convictions cohere. This critical form of reflection

---

[26] Ibid., 135.

[27] Ibid., 135–6. Like many other intuitionists, Ross was content to take over the utilitarian account of happiness as pleasure and the absence of pain. This seems to me a wholly inadequate account of happiness, but I do not wish to challenge it here.   [28] Ibid., 136.

undermines further the charge of dogmatism and enables intuitionists like Ross to deal with the charge of bias. For Ross is content to consider not merely those arguments that support his conviction, but also considerations that raise doubts about it. In *The Right and the Good* Ross tries to deal with these doubts by insisting that we do have a prima facie obligation to promote our own pleasure, and by introducing the notion of prima facie goodness. But these attempts to deal with the difficulties with the thesis that pleasure is intrinsically good are quite unsatisfactory. In *The Foundations of Ethics* Ross came to recognize this and abandoned his earlier view. It is to these further forms of reflection on the value of pleasure that I now turn.

A Duty to Promote our Own Pleasure?

The difficulties with the thought that pleasure is intrinsically good first arise in chapter 2 of *The Right and the Good*. We have, Ross, maintains a prima facie duty to promote the good, so if pleasure is intrinsically good, we have a prima facie duty to promote it whenever we can. But although we do seem to have a prima facie duty to produce pleasure for others, 'it is by no means so clear that we recognize a duty to produce pleasure for ourselves'.[29] Ross thinks that this anomaly can be explained. First, the thought that some act is a duty requires, he writes, a certain amount of reflection on our part, and so does not normally arise in relation to a type of act which we are already strongly inclined to do. It is for this reason that a highly sympathetic person does not tend to think of helping others as a duty. Since she is already strongly inclined to do such acts, the thought that she is duty-bound to perform them never occurs to her. The same is true, Ross maintains, in relation to the duty to promote our own pleasure. 'We are all', he writes, 'impelled so strongly towards the promotion of our own pleasure that we do not stop to ask whether it is a duty or not.'[30] Second, since dutiful actions often involve giving up some pleasure that we desire, we come by a natural association of ideas to think of duty and pleasure as opposed. It is for this reason, he suggests, that the idea that we have a prima facie duty to promote our own pleasure may seem counter-intuitive even when we reflect on the matter.

Ross maintains that the only grounds for objecting to this are (1) that

---

[29] *The Right and the Good*, 24.   [30] Ibid. 25.

pleasure is not good,[31] (2) that there is no prima facie duty to promote as much good as we can, or (3) that although we ought to promote other intrinsic goods we are not required to promote our own pleasure even though this is also intrinsically good. Ross rejects (1) as he thinks that we have good reason to think that pleasure is intrinsically good. He thinks that (2) is too implausible to be considered, and as a result dismisses it out of hand.[32] He rejects (3) on the ground that he thinks that it leads to paradoxical consequences; for he thinks that it implies that 'if a man enjoys giving pleasure to others or working for their moral improvement, it cannot be his duty to do so'.[33]

Now these arguments are far from compelling, and Ross himself seems less than convinced by them, for immediately after putting forward these arguments he notes that it is a very stubborn fact 'that in our ordinary consciousness we are not aware of a duty to get pleasure for ourselves'.[34] Such stubborn facts of our ordinary moral consciousness are normally given great weight by Ross, and he is only able to persevere with his view that we do have a duty to promote our own pleasure in the face of such a recalcitrant moral consciousness by thinking of all pleasure as intrinsically good, and of the fact that we have a prima facie duty to promote the good. 'It is only if we think of our own pleasure not as simply our own pleasure, but as an objective good, something that an impartial spectator would approve, that we can think of the getting it as a duty.'[35] Furthermore, in *The Foundations* Ross completely ignores this earlier argument. There he states that the view that we have no duty to maximize pleasure for ourselves 'seems to be so clear as not to need argument'.[36] The fact that he so easily abandoned his earlier attempt to explain away this strong intuition suggests that he was never quite comfortable with this explanation in the first place.

Undeserved and Vicious Pleasures

We have seen that Ross held that the thought that pleasure is intrinsically good is assumed by those who think that it is better that virtue be rewarded

---

[31] He actually says that (1) is the denial that pleasure is prima facie good, a term he only explains in ch. 5. I shall discuss this notion later.

[32] On this Ross seems to me to be mistaken. We might think that friends are good things, but that we should not sacrifice one friendship simply because by doing so we could make two more friends. This is part of Scanlon's argument against the conception of goodness as 'to be promoted'. See *What we Owe to Each Other* (Cambridge, Mass.: Harvard University Press, 1998), 88–90.

[33] *The Right and the Good*, 25. [34] Ibid., 25–6.

[35] Ibid., 26. [36] *The Foundations of Ethics* (London: Clarendon Press, 1939), 273.

with happiness than not. Ross notes also that the notion of merit raises difficulties for the view that pleasure is intrinsically good. He writes, 'while this conception implies the conviction that pleasure when deserved is good, and pain when undeserved bad, it also suggests strongly that pleasure when undeserved is bad and pain when deserved is good'.[37] Although thoughts about merit may lead one to think that some pleasures are good, namely the deserved ones, they also lead one to the view that pleasure is not always good. A vicious act is bad: a vicious act rewarded is even worse. The view that pleasure is not always good is further supported by the fact that the value of pleasure and pain seems to depend on the value of that which pleases or pains us. 'We think that the pleasure taken either by the agent or by a spectator in, for instance, a lustful or cruel action is bad; and we think it a good thing that people should be pained rather than pleased by contemplating vice or misery.'[38] It seems therefore that pleasure is not always good and pain not always bad. Ross does not tell us why he thinks that this casts doubt on the view that pleasure is intrinsically good, but he most likely has in mind Moore's view that if something is intrinsically good, then 'anything exactly like it must, under all circumstances, possess it in exactly the same degree'.[39] This follows from the claim that something's intrinsic value depends solely its intrinsic nature. If this is correct, then if something has exactly the same intrinsic nature, then it must have exactly the same intrinsic value.[40] The problem with undeserved and vicious pleasures is that there is little reason to think that they could not have the same intrinsic nature as a deserved or innocent pleasure. One might argue that the nature of the pleasure is determined by the thing one gets pleasure from, so that a vicious pleasure could not have the same intrinsic nature as an innocent, let alone a virtuous one. I think this is mistaken, but I do not need to argue for this to show that Ross has identified a real problem with the view that pleasure is intrinsically good. For although a vicious pleasure might not be able to have the same intrinsic nature as a virtuous or innocent one, there is no reason to think that this is true of undeserved and deserved pleasure. For since these

---

[37] *The Right and the Good*, 136.   [38] Ibid., 137.

[39] G. E. Moore, 'The Conception of Intrinsic Value', in Moore, *Principia Ethica*, rev. edn. (Cambridge: Cambridge University Press, 1993), 287.

[40] I agree with Jonathan Dancy that the notion of 'dependence' is too indiscriminate, and that something's intrinsic value is best understood as value it has *in virtue of* its intrinsic nature (see his 'The Particularist's Progress', in B. Hooker (ed.), *Particularism* (Oxford: Clarendon Press, 2000), 140–1, and 'On the Logical and Moral Adequacy of Particularism', *Theoria*, 3 (1999), 212–24). This is not just a verbal change, but has substantial implications. I do not, however, intend to go into this here.

differ only in relation to desert, they could, as well as having the same duration, intensity, and feel, be caused by the same object. But, Ross maintains, they would differ in value. If pleasure is intrinsically good, then in such cases the undeserved pleasure must have the same value as the deserved one. Since they do not, pleasure cannot be intrinsically good.

Ross attempts to resolve this problem by introducing the idea of prima facie goodness. Ross begins by reminding us that, strictly speaking, it is not certain things that are good or bad, but certain states of affairs, or what he calls facts.[41] He then goes on to say:

> If we look at the matter thus, I think we can agree that the fact that a sentient being is in a state of pleasure is always in itself good, and the fact that a sentient being is in a state of pain is always in itself bad, when this fact is not an element in a more complex fact having some other characteristic relevant to goodness and badness.[42]

When we are considering the question of whether undeserved pleasure, or pleasure in cruel activities, is good (in relation to moral beings), we are considering the goodness of one of these 'complex facts', and this total fact is, Ross maintains,

> quite inadequately described if we say 'a sentient being is feeling pleasure, or pain'. The total fact may be that 'a sentient and moral being is feeling a pleasure that is undeserved, or that is the realization of a vicious disposition', and though the fact included in this, 'that a sentient being is feeling pleasure' would be good if it stood alone, that creates only a presumption that the total fact is good, and a presumption that is outweighed by the other element in the total fact.[43]

Ross is here attempting to resolve the difficulty with respect to pleasure by understanding the intrinsic goodness of pleasure in analogy with the intrinsic prima facie rightness of fidelity, beneficence, non-maleficence, etc. But it is not quite clear how the analogy with prima facie rightness is supposed to work. If the analogy is taken strictly, then Ross's view will be that any state of affairs that included pleasure will in this respect be good, although the value of this aspect of the total situation may not succeed in making the total state of affairs good if it is outweighed by the disvalue of some other aspect. So if it weren't for the fact that a vicious disposition (bad) is part of the total fact, then the total fact would be good, and if the pleasure's being undeserved (bad) were not a part of the total fact, then also the pleasure would succeed in making the state of affairs good. So the thought is that each of the basic goods always has the same evaluative weight, and thus

---

[41] *The Right and the Good*, 137.   [42] Ibid.   [43] Ibid.

always makes the total state of affairs better; and although the total fact that pleasure in some cruel activity is bad, this does not imply that the pleasure involved is bad, but only that the cruelty brings more disvalue to the total situation than the pleasure brings value. This atomistic conception of the value of pleasure means that we can hold onto the idea that pleasure is always good.

But although there is evidence to suggest that Ross did understand the prima facie nature of the value of pleasure in this atomistic way,[44] it is not the only way in which he understood it. Immediately after he introduces the analogy with prima facie rightness he says that 'a state of pleasure has the property not necessarily of being good, but of being something that is good if the state has no other characteristic that prevents it from being good'.[45] Here the prima facie goodness of pleasure is not understood atomistically, but holistically. According to the holistic view, pleasure is what Kant would have called a conditional value. If something is conditionally good, then it will not always be good, for any value it has will depend upon the condition, whatever that is, being satisfied. According to the atomistic understanding of prima facie goodness the pleasure in some cruel activity is still good, though the total state is bad because the value of the pleasure is outweighed by the disvalue of the cruelty. According to the holistic interpretation, this pleasure is not good at all, but is made bad by its being a pleasure in some cruel activity. This contrast can be put another way. According to the atomistic interpretation, the total state of affairs is the better for the presence of the pleasure, while according to the holistic interpretation, it is the worse. The same applies for undeserved pleasure.

Which of these two possible accounts of prima facie goodness is the better? The atomistic understanding of the prima facie nature of the value of pleasure fails adequately to deal with the problem it was designed to solve. The problem was not a doubt about whether the disvalue of cruelty or of undeservedness outweighed the value of pleasure. The serious doubt raised about the intrinsic value of pleasure stems from the fact that in such a complex state of affairs the pleasure itself seems bad—that is, that the total situation is made worse, rather than better, by the presence of the pleasure. On the atomistic interpretation this is simply denied, and hence can hardly count as solving the problem.[46]

---

[44] This is supported by the earlier quotation where he talks of the value of the pleasure being 'outweighed' by the disvalue of the vicious act. See also his discussion of commensurability of pleasure and virtue (*The Right and the Good*, 150 ff.).   [45] Ibid., 138.

[46] Furthermore, Ross has not shown that something's being undeserved is intrinsically bad, and does not argue for this.

It would seem, therefore, that the holistic account of prima facie goodness is better. But this understanding of the value of pleasure does not deal with the problem either. For the problem introduced by undeserved pleasures and pleasures in cruel activities is that they strongly suggest that pleasure is not always good, which it should be if it is intrinsically good. The holistic sense of prima facie goodness does not help Ross at all with this problem, for it simply reinforces the view that is causing the problem—namely, the view that pleasure can sometimes be bad.

Ross might have tried to deal with this problem by utilizing Moore's doctrine of organic unities. It is true that Ross spends some time in chapter 3 of *The Right and the Good* attacking this doctrine, but he does not end up rejecting it: all he concludes is that the doctrine is far more limited in its application than Moore thought, but 'its truth in the abstract seems unquestionable'.[47] How then might this doctrine help with the worry that pleasure seems intrinsically good, but is not always good?

Moore's doctrine rests on a distinction between intrinsic goodness and (what Ross later called) contributive goodness.[48] For something to be intrinsically good is, according to Moore, for its goodness to depend solely on its intrinsic nature. For something to be contributively valuable is for it to stand in a better-making relation to the whole of which it is a part. Contributive value is, therefore, a relational form of value. Moore's doctrine is that the contributive value of parts stands in no necessary relation to their intrinsic value. A part may be intrinsically good, yet contribute disvalue to the whole, be intrinsically bad, but contribute value to the whole, or contribute value even though it has neither intrinsic value or disvalue. Moore maintains that the intrinsic value of identical parts must always remain the same, for reasons already mentioned. But since their contributive value is extrinsic, their contributive value may change from context to context.

Now it may seem that Ross could utilize this doctrine to deal with the problem raised by the fact that pleasure does not seem always to be good. For he could then maintain that although pleasure is intrinsically good wherever it is instantiated, the value that an instance of pleasure contributes to some overall state of affairs may vary. If one takes pleasure in the well-being of others, then one's pleasure will be not only intrinsically good but also contributively good. The presence of this pleasure not only is good by itself, but also makes the whole situation better. This is not the case where

---

[47] Ibid., 72.   [48] Ibid.

one takes pleasure in the suffering of others. The fact that one gets pleasure from other people's suffering is not a redeeming feature of the situation, but actually makes things worse. Nonetheless, Ross could maintain that although the contributive value of pleasure has changed, its intrinsic value remains unaltered. The pleasure itself remains intrinsically good even though the situation is made worse by its presence. If this works for vicious pleasures, then it should also work for undeserved ones.

But I think there is good reason to think that the doctrine of organic wholes is incoherent. It is incoherent because it cuts off intrinsic value from any reason-giving relation. On this Moorean picture the reasons we have to act or respond in certain ways are determined wholly by contributive value. If something is contributively good, then we have reason to pursue it, promote it, endorse it, or, in general, to welcome it. If something is contributively bad, then we have reason to avoid it, abolish it, condemn it, or in general regret its presence. The fact that the same thing might be intrinsically good or bad does not seem to imply that we have any further reason to welcome or avoid it. Suppose we think that pleasure is intrinsically good, and that when it is pleasure in other people's suffering it is contributively bad (it makes things worse). If there is some necessary connection between intrinsic value and practical reasons, then in such a situation we would have to say that the fact that this instance of pleasure is contributively bad means that we have reason to disapprove of it, but the fact that it is intrinsically good means that we have reason to welcome it. But there seems to be no reason whatsoever to welcome this pleasure. To think that there is is to think that the fact that the agent feels pleasure is a redeeming feature of the situation. But this thought is ruled out by the fact that its presence makes things worse, that it is contributively bad. For this reason I think we should reject the doctrine of organic wholes as incoherent.

Ross's View in The Foundations of Ethics

We have seen that Ross could only sustain the view that pleasure is intrinsically good in *The Right and the Good* by a half-hearted attempt to maintain that we have a prima facie duty to promote our own pleasure, and by an unsuccessful attempt to introduce the notion of prima facie goodness. In *The Foundations of Ethics* he returns to the problem of the value of pleasure—a problem he describes as 'one of the most puzzling problems in the whole of ethics'.[49] Indeed, during the five years that separate the two works[50] further reflection revealed a number of other difficulties with the thesis that pleasure is intrinsically good. The first is that in relation to other goods, such as moral dispositions and actions, and intellectual and artistic activities, we can replace the term 'good' with 'admirable' or 'commendable', but we cannot do this in the case of pleasant experiences. 'There is nothing admirable or commendable in the mere feeling of pleasure.'[51] The second is that other goods reflect well on their owner, whereas this is not the case with pleasure.

While we call a man good, or at least admirable (for 'good' as applied to men tends to be limited to moral goodness) in respect of his actions and dispositions and in respect of his intellectual or artistic activities, any goodness that pleasure may be supposed to have is not in this way reflected on its enjoyer. A man is not good in respect of the mere fact of feeling pleasure.[52]

The third is not new, but can be found, albeit in a different form, in *The Right and the Good*. It is that although we have a prima facie duty to promote the good, we do not have a prima facie duty to promote vicious pleasures. Ross does not explicitly refer to his attempt to deal with this problem in *The Right and the Good*. He does, however, consider a response that looks very much like the one made by him there—that is, the idea that pleasure is prima facie good in the atomistic sense. He says: 'With regard to immoral pleasures, it might be said that they are good qua pleasures but bad qua immoral, and that their badness qua immoral outweighs their goodness qua pleasant, and that this is the reason why we are never bound to produce them or aid in their production.'[53] Ross rightly notes that this response is inadequate, but for reasons other than those I mentioned earlier. Ross points out that this view cannot explain why we are never bound to promote immoral pleasures. For if the pleasure were great and the immorality minor, then the value of the pleasure could outweigh the disvalue of the immorality; and assuming we have a duty to promote the good, we would, in such circumstances, be bound to promote immoral pleasure.[54]

Ross also mentions the fact that we have no obligation to bring about

[49] *The Foundations of Ethics*, 271.

[50] Although *The Foundations* was published in 1939, the lectures on which it is based were given in 1935–6.　　　　　　　　　　　　　　　　　　[51] *The Foundations of Ethics*, 271.

[52] Ibid.　　　　　　　　　　　　　　　　　　　　　　　　　　　　[53] Ibid., 274.

[54] Ross considers someone who says that no amount of pleasure could outweigh the disvalue introduced by any degree of immorality, but he rejects this as 'impossible' if the value of pleasure and virtue are on the same scale, as they would have to be if they were both intrinsically good (ibid. 275).

pleasure for ourselves as an objection to the view that pleasure is intrinsically good. Strangely he makes no reference to his earlier attempt to deal with this objection in *The Right and the Good*. His view now seems to be that the weight of evidence against the thesis that pleasure is intrinsically good means that we should not attempt to explain away these difficulties, but accept the view to which they inexorably point[55]—namely, that pleasure is not intrinsically good. This seems to me the right way to go, for if we do have a prima facie duty to promote our own pleasure, then sometimes this will be our actual duty. If we fail to do our actual duty, then we have reason to feel guilty. But it is hard to believe that we ever have reason to feel guilty about the fact that we have failed to take an opportunity to get pleasure for ourselves. One might of course regret this failure, but guilt seems wholly inappropriate. If this is right, then it cannot be the case that we have a prima facie duty to promote our own pleasure.

The Extrinsic Value of Pleasure

As we have seen, reflection on the value of pleasure eventually led Ross to abandon the intuition that pleasure is good in the same sense that virtue and knowledge are good. He does not, however, go so far as to claim that pleasure never has any value. All he denies is that when it is good it is intrinsically good.[56] In what sense, then, does Ross regard pleasure as good? Ross maintains that pleasure has a distinctive form of extrinsic value which, unlike intrinsic value, can be defined. He defines the goodness of pleasure as the property of being a worthy object of satisfaction.[57]

---

[55] Thus, for example, in relation to the problem that vicious pleasures introduce, he says, 'if this were all, it might be possible to modify the statement that pleasure is good, by saying "pleasures that are not manifestations of a bad moral nature are good"' (ibid. 272). This was the line he took in ch. 5 of *The Right and the Good*. But in *The Foundations* he goes on to note that 'against this suggestion a fresh difficulty arises' (p. 272).

[56] Michael Zimmerman has argued that pleasure is intrinsically good, but that its intrinsic value depends on the intrinsic value of its intentional object ('On the Intrinsic Value of States of Pleasure', *Philosophy and Phenomenological Research*, 41/1–2 (1980), 26–45). Ross could not accept this, as it would commit him to the view that the intrinsic value of two instances of pleasure could be different even if their intrinsic nature were identical.

[57] What does it mean for such satisfaction to be a worthy response? At various points Ross treats 'worthy' as synonymous with 'justified', 'proper' (*The Foundations of Ethics*, 276), and 'fitting' (p. 278). Elsewhere he states that the fact expressed by saying that innocent pleasures of one man are worthy objects of sympathetic satisfaction 'is plainly only another way of saying that the satisfaction an other takes in such things is morally suitable, or right' (ibid. 279). Ross prefers his view to be

Virtue and knowledge are worthy objects of admiration, but this is not what it is for them to be good. For Ross, the property of being a worthy object of admiration and that of being intrinsically good are distinct properties that are necessarily coinstantiated in virtue and knowledge. He maintains that these properties must be distinct, as he thinks that virtue and knowledge are worthy objects of admiration because they are good.[58] In the case of pleasure, however, the property of being a worthy object of satisfaction and of being good are identical.

The sort of satisfaction at issue cannot be just any old satisfaction, since the pleasure an agent produces for himself is a worthy object of satisfaction, and we have as much reason to be satisfied with our own innocent pleasures as we do with others'. But Ross wants to avoid the idea that our own pleasure is good. This is because if our own pleasure is good, then this will generate a prima facie obligation to produce it, an obligation which Ross had rightly come to think does not exist. So the satisfaction at issue must be of the sort that one cannot feel in relation to one's own pleasures. Only then can it capture the asymmetry of the deontic relevance of one's own and others' pleasures. The sort of satisfaction that embodies this asymmetry is, Ross claims, sympathetic satisfaction. For 'sympathy, by its very nature must be of one man with another, and cannot be felt by a man for himself'.[59] If to think that pleasure is good is to think that it is a worthy object of sympathetic satisfaction, and such satisfaction can be felt only towards other people, then, Ross argues, we cannot think that our own pleasure is good. Consequently, we cannot think that we have a prima facie obligation to promote our own pleasure.

This account of the value of pleasure seems to resolve the other difficulties with the view that pleasure is intrinsically good. The second problem is that not all pleasures are good. Some pleasures, such as pleasure taken in what is bad, and undeserved happiness, are bad. In *The Right and the Good* Ross attempted to deal with this problem by maintaining that pleasure is prima facie good. But we saw that this notion is ambiguous, and that neither

expressed using the concept of rightness, as this means that we can define the goodness of pleasure with reference to rightness; something Ross regards himself as already having shown to be the fundamental (and thus indefinable) concept in ethics.

[58] Ibid., 278. I think this is mistaken. Although we must think that the object of what we admire is good, we think our attitude is warranted not by the goodness of its object, but by the properties in virtue of which this object is good, such as the property of being selfless, courageous, or kind. If asked why I admire some individual I would not reply by saying 'because she is good', but would cite these other features. Furthermore, once I have cited these I would not, for the sake of completeness, need to add 'and because she is good'.   [59] Ibid., 276.

way of understanding it deals satisfactorily with the problem. But if we think that the goodness of pleasure consists in its being a worthy object of sympathetic satisfaction, the fact that not all pleasures are good is easily accommodated. For those that are bad will be those towards which it is inappropriate or wrong to feel sympathetic satisfaction. It is not appropriate to feel satisfied with the fact that someone is getting pleasure from some vicious activity, or that someone who does not deserve happiness is happy. Not all pleasures are good because not all pleasures are worthy objects of satisfaction for others. And if it is true that some pleasures are bad, this will explain why we have no prima facie obligation to bring about vicious or undeserved pleasures.

The third and fourth problems Ross identified with the view that pleasure is intrinsically good is that whereas the term good can be replaced with admirable, or commendable, in relation to other goods, this is not true of pleasure, and that although the value of intrinsic goods is reflected in their possessor, the mere fact that I am feeling pleasure in no way casts me in a positive light. These disanalogies can be explained by the fact that, unlike virtue and knowledge, pleasure is not an intrinsic good. Intrinsic goods are worthy objects of admiration, whereas the extrinsic value of pleasure means that it can only be a worthy object of satisfaction.

Pleasure and the Prima Facie Duty to Promote the Good

I think that much of this is correct, though I think that Ross was mistaken in thinking that his account of the value of pleasure explains the asymmetry in deontic relevance of one's own and others' pleasure. Ross thought it did because he claimed that the thought that pleasure is good is the thought that it is a worthy object of sympathetic satisfaction, and since I cannot feel such satisfaction for my own pleasure, I cannot think that such satisfaction is worthy in relation to my own pleasure. This seems to me to be mistaken. I can think that my own pleasure is good on this account even if I cannot feel sympathetic satisfaction towards my own pleasure. For I could think that my pleasure is a worthy object of sympathetic satisfaction for others, and thus that it is good. But if my own pleasure is good in the sense that it is a worthy object of sympathetic satisfaction (for others), and if I have a prima facie obligation to promote the good, then it must be the case that I have a prima facie obligation to promote my own pleasure as well as others'. Therefore,

Ross cannot rely on this account of the value of pleasure to explain why we have no prima facie duty to promote our own pleasure.

In the light of this failure Ross has only two options. The first is to argue that the extrinsic value pleasure has is not really a form of goodness at all.[60] The second is to abandon the view that there is a prima facie duty to promote the good. My view is that the second alternative is the better option, first, because I do not see how one could plausibly maintain that the value of pleasure as Ross understands it is not really a form of goodness, and second, because Ross had already moved some distance away from the conception of value that underpins the prima facie duty to promote the good—namely, the teleological conception of value.[61]

According to the teleological conception of value, to be good is to be 'to be promoted'. Given the teleological conception of value it is very difficult to avoid the conclusion that we must have a prima facie duty to promote the good, for if the good is to be promoted, then what we ought (prima facie) to do is promote it. Ross was already moving away from this conception of value in thinking of it as something to be admired, or to feel sympathetic satisfaction towards, rather than simply as something to be promoted. Nonetheless, he still held onto the prima facie duty to promote the good, a prima facie duty that was shaped by the very conception of value from which Ross was already beginning to depart. Once he has moved this far away from the teleological account of value in his reflections on the value of pleasure, what he should do is question whether the proposition that there is a prima facie duty to promote the good retains its self-evidence. Once we have abandoned the teleological conception of value, we should at least consider whether we need to revise the content of this duty. For if we abandon the view that there is only one appropriate response to value, namely, promotion, then if there is a prima facie duty in relation to the good, it should reflect the plurality of different responses that are appropriate. Promotion will be one of the appropriate ways to respond to value, but it will not be the only one.

But I think that reflection on the value of pleasure requires us to do more than simply revise this prima facie duty. For if there is a prima facie duty to respond to value in certain ways, whatever those ways are, then any failure to respond in the appropriate way would be a moral failure. Yet what

[60] In a talk on Prichard in Oxford in May 2000 Jonathan Dancy maintained that instrumental value is not a form of value and ascribed this view to Ross. If he is correct, then it may be that other forms of extrinsic value are not really forms of value.
[61] I take this notion from Scanlon, *What we Owe to Each Other*, 79–87.

reflection on the value of pleasure shows is that not all such failings are moral failings. If this is right, then reflection on the apparent self-evident proposition that pleasure is intrinsically good should lead us not only to deny that this proposition has the status it appears to have, but also to reject the prima facie duty to promote the good (as well as any modified version of this duty), and the attempt to derive the duties of beneficence, justice, and self-improvement from this duty.[62] This is not because happiness, justice, and virtue are not good, but because our failing to respond to such goods in the appropriate way need not always be a moral failing.

Conclusion

What all of this shows is how rigorous and demanding reflection on our moral convictions can be within an intuitionist moral theory. It led Ross to abandon his earlier conviction that pleasure is intrinsically good, and although his reflections did not take him this far, it undermines the view that we have a prima facie duty to promote the good and that the prima facie duties of beneficence, justice, and self-improvement are grounded in this. However, my primary aim in this paper has not been to argue for some particular view on the issue of the value of pleasure, or the prima facie duty to promote the good, but rather to show how demanding the sort of reflection to which intuitionists such as Ross insist we must submit our moral convictions can be.

I began by mentioning two related problems many have with ethical intuitionism: the charges of dogmatism and bias. The assumption underpinning the charge of dogmatism is that intuitionists cannot offer any argument for their basic moral convictions because they regard them as self-evident. But a proposition is self-evident just in case we can know it on the basis of an understanding of it, and the possibility of this epistemic route in no way rules out the possibility of other epistemic routes. Ross was aware of this in his 1927 paper, and although he claimed that no proof could be offered for such propositions in *The Right and the Good*, the forms of reflection that persuaded him that certain of our moral convictions are self-evidently true (consideration of particular cases, thought experiments, and coherence) can be offered as reasons to someone who does not see the

---

[62] In *The Right and the Good* Ross argues that these three principles can be reduced to one (p. 27).

truth of these propositions. Of course, citing these considerations may not succeed in convincing someone of the truth of some proposition. But that is not the point. The point is that the belief that such propositions are self-evident does not mean that they can only be dogmatically asserted against those who fail to see their truth.

The charge of bias is also based upon the assumption that intuitionists build their moral theories on a set of unquestioned moral convictions which may do nothing more than reflect the moral outlook of some particular society. It should be clear by now that this assumption is false. Ross does not base his intuitionist moral theory on a set of unquestioned moral convictions, but rather on a set of convictions that survive rigorous reflection. I have tried to show how demanding such reflection can be by focusing on the question of whether pleasure is intrinsically good. We have seen that although he thought he could deal with the difficulties such reflection raised in *The Right and the Good*, further reflection forced him to abandon his earlier conviction that pleasure is intrinsically good. It is true that most of his moral convictions survived such reflection, but I have argued that he should have carried this critical reflection further and questioned not only the view that pleasure is intrinsically good, but also the view that we have a prima facie duty to promote the good. Furthermore, the issue is whether intuitionists have the resources seriously to question their basic moral convictions and thus to avoid parading a set of local opinions as universally valid moral truths. The fact that Ross was forced to abandon even one of his deeply held moral convictions is a sufficient proof that intuitionists have such resources.

Of course it may be pointed out that although intuitionists do not uncritically accept any moral convictions that come their way, they cannot eliminate the distorting influence that one's upbringing, environment, and other factors might introduce. Nonetheless, intuitionists are in no worse a position than any other objectivist moral theory in this respect, and the fact that intuitions enter into their theory in a very structured and systematic way puts them in a better position than many in this respect.

It may be thought that in defending intuitionism from the charge of dogmatism and bias in this way we lose the thought that intuitionism presents a distinctive moral theory. Of course, if intuitionism can only be distinctive by being dogmatic and biased, its distinctiveness seems no great loss. But I do not think we lose its distinctiveness in defending it from these charges. For although intuitionists such as Ross thought that arguments can be offered for basic self-evident ethical truths, they do still maintain that these basic truths are self-evident, that they lead to a pluralist moral theory,[63] and that what makes them true are certain non-natural properties. I do not claim that to be an intuitionist one must endorse all of these views. Sidgwick and Moore, for example, are not pluralists, but are (epistemic) intuitionists. Nonetheless, these three characteristics are sufficient by themselves to make Ross's intuitionist moral theory a distinctive view in ethics. Intuitionists neither need, nor endorse, unquestioned moral convictions.

---

[63] It is true that Moore was not a pluralist about the right, but he was a pluralist about the good.

Justifying Moral Pluralism　　　6

Berys Gaut

1. Two Concepts of Intuitionism

The term 'ethical intuitionism' is one which has acquired a variety of uses over the course of its history. Two are salient for my purposes here. On the one hand, it has been used to denote a moral theory which holds roughly that there is an irreducible plurality of moral principles, a view which I shall term 'moral pluralism' or simply 'pluralism'. On the other, it has been used to denote a theory in moral epistemology, a type of foundationalist theory which holds that all immediately justified moral beliefs are self-evident, a view which I will term 'epistemic intuitionism', or simply 'intuitionism'. The fortunes of these two doctrines have been strikingly dissimilar. Moral pluralism has been attractive to many philosophers, capturing as it appears to do the structure of our normative moral views; epistemic intuitionism, on the other hand, has been widely rejected. Yet both doctrines were held together by self-styled intuitionists, such as W. D. Ross, seeming to form an indissoluble whole in their thought; and the attractions of Ross's pluralism have consequently been somewhat occluded by the distrust felt towards his intuitionism.

I intend to examine the relation between moral pluralism and epistemic intuitionism, particularly as they figure in Ross's theory. Is intuitionism a defensible doctrine, in terms of which an adequate justification of pluralism can be cast? Or ought pluralism to be justified by means of a different epistemic structure? I will argue for the latter option: I thus aim to preserve much of the superstructure of Ross's moral pluralism, while shifting it to a

I would like to thank the participants in the University of Keele conference entitled Re-evaluating Ethical Intuitionism, held on 3–5 June 1999, and members of the philosophy departments of Durham University and of the University of Maryland at College Park, for their comments on this paper. I am also grateful to Garrett Cullity, Mark Nelson, and Robert Stecker for their written comments.

new justificatory foundation, the structure of which is not correctly described by an intuitionistic epistemic theory. The upshot will be a justification of moral pluralism radically different from, and, hopefully, better than, that advanced by Ross.

2. Ross's Moral Theory

Moral pluralism is the theory that there is a plurality of first-order moral principles stating what one has moral reason to do; that these principles may conflict in their application to particular cases; and that there is no higher-order moral principle which in each case of conflict ranks one first-order principle above another. What one has to do in such cases is to employ one's judgement about what one has most reason to do, a judgement which escapes codification by principles.

Cases of principles conflicting should not be understood as generating contradictions; so pluralism must be formulated using something like aspect-terminology or *pro tanto* principles. For instance, a particular action might be held to be right *in so far as* it is an instance of keeping a promise, but wrong *in so far as* it is involves neglecting to help someone who needs help. The agent must then make the *all things considered* judgement about whether it is right or wrong *simpliciter*, and so judge what she morally ought actually to do. Note that each of the *pro tanto* principles specifies a different ground for a moral judgement: in the example, keeping a promise is a ground for holding an action to be right, while neglecting to help someone who needs help is a ground for holding an action to be wrong.

Ross's moral theory is a kind of pluralism. Its core notion is that of 'prima facie' duties, though the phrase is somewhat misleading, since it suggests an epistemic notion. What he actually means is, I believe, something very similar to the *pro tanto* notion outlined above.[1]

Generically, Ross's theory is a pluralistic theory. Specifically, it is a deontological theory, in the sense that it holds that 'right' cannot be defined in terms of 'good', nor can rightness be non-analytically reduced to some function of goodness. Within this deontological framework Ross ultimately counts as basic the following five principles specifying duties: a general obligation to bring about as much good as possible (under which

---

[1] See, for instance, his claim that a prima facie duty is 'a parti-resultant attribute' (W. D. Ross, *The Right and the Good* (Oxford: Clarendon Press, 1930), 28).

he subsumes duties of beneficence, justice, and self-improvement), and four special duties: duties of fidelity (to keep promises, including the implicit promise not to lie), of gratitude, of reparation for harm done, and of non-maleficence.[2] From these duties, all other prima facie duties can, he believes, be derived.[3]

How does Ross justify this pluralistic theory? He appeals frequently to 'direct reflection on what we really think'[4] or to 'what most plain men think'.[5] But this, of course, cannot be the whole of the method, for plain men disagree on some moral issues. Ross writes in the introduction to *Foundations of Ethics*:

We must start with the opinions that are crystallized in ordinary language and ordinary ways of thinking, and our attempt must be to make these thoughts, little by little, more definite and distinct, and by comparing one with another to discover at what points each opinion must be purged of excess and mis-statement till it becomes harmonious with other opinions which have been purified in the same way.[6]

And in *The Right and the Good* he writes of rejecting some moral convictions as illusory, because they are in conflict with others which stand better the 'test of reflection'.[7] What we seem to be dealing with here, then, is something like the method of reflective equilibrium, before the term was coined.

Now this might seem surprising, since it is often held that reflective equilibrium is a coherence method of justification, yet Ross is an epistemic intuitionist, and intuitionism is a foundationalist theory of justification. But, as Robert Audi among others has noted, there isn't any contradiction here.[8] There are various ways to bring out the consistency. Here is one way to do so: reflective equilibrium is not a *theory*, but a *method*, of justification; it tells

---

[2] Ibid., 21–7.

[3] For a useful discussion of the extent to which Ross manages to subsume other duties under these basic ones, and so to achieve a large degree of unity in his moral system, see D. McNaughton, 'An Unconnected Heap of Duties?', *Philosophical Quarterly*, 46 (1996), 433–47 (repr. as Ch. 3 in this volume). [4] *The Right and the Good*, 23.

[5] Ibid., 28.

[6] W. D. Ross, *The Foundations of Ethics* (Oxford: Clarendon Press, 1939), 3.

[7] *The Right and the Good*, 41; the full passage runs: 'the moral convictions of thoughtful and well-educated people are the data of ethics just as sense-perceptions are the data of a natural science. Just as some of the latter have to be rejected as illusory, so have some of the former; but as the latter are rejected only when they are in conflict with other more accurate sense-perceptions, the former are rejected only when they are in conflict with other convictions which stand better the test of reflection.'

[8] See R. Audi, 'Intuitionism, Pluralism, and the Foundations of Ethics', in W. Sinnott-Armstrong and M. Timmons (eds.), *Moral Knowledge? New Readings in Moral Epistemology* (Oxford: Oxford University Press, 1996), 107–8.

Berys Gaut

one how to justify one's moral beliefs, by attempting to render consistent one's moral principles with one's judgements about particular cases. It presupposes that justification of an individual belief increases as its coherence with other beliefs increases. But appeal to reflective equilibrium as a method does not entail the theoretical claim that coherence with other beliefs is the *only* source of justification of a belief. Use of the method is consistent with there being other types of justification besides coherence: one could, for instance, hold that the inputs to reflective equilibrium, considered judgements, are justified non-inferentially, say, on quasi-perceptual grounds. On such a view reflective equilibrium would be a kind of device for correcting quasi-perceptual errors. So use of reflective equilibrium is consistent with foundationalism.

Foundationalism I will understand as the claim that all mediately justified beliefs owe their justification ultimately to immediately justified beliefs. A belief is mediately justified if it is justified by virtue of its relation to other justified beliefs (for instance, because one can infer the belief from them). A belief is immediately justified, in contrast, either if it is self-evident (as are arguably the basic truths of mathematics and logic), or if it is justified by some other state, which is not a belief: for instance, an experience of some kind, such as a perception or an emotion.[9] From the fact that there are two kinds of immediate justification, it follows that there are at least two kinds of foundationalism. One, intuitionism, holds that all immediately justified beliefs are self-evident. The other, experiential foundationalism, as I will call it, holds that all immediately justified beliefs are justified by experience, and none of them are self-evident. Coherence theories, in contrast, hold that there is no such thing as immediate justification: any belief is justified by its coherence with other beliefs.

Ross is an intuitionist about the basic prima facie duties: he holds, for instance, 'That an act, *qua* fulfilling a promise . . . is *prima facie* right, is self-evident.'[10] Our grasp of self-evident truths he calls 'intuition', but nothing he says commits him to the view that this is a special faculty. Intuition is simply a direct apprehension of what is self-evident, and is an exercise of reason, in the same way that our grasp of basic mathematical truths is an exercise of reason. As we have seen, something like reflective equilibrium is

[9] This account is based on that of W. P. Alston, 'Foundationalism', in Jonathan Dancy and Ernest Sosa (eds.), *A Companion to Epistemology* (Oxford: Blackwell, 1992), 144–7. However, Alston also seems to require that immediately justified beliefs are not also mediately justified, since he regards the justificatory relations between 'foundation' and 'superstructure' as one-way. But it is consistent with foundationalism as I am construing it to hold that every immediately justified belief also has a distinct, mediate, justification.   [10] *The Right and the Good*, 29.

required to remove contradictions and unclarities in ordinary moral con-sciousness. But having done this ground-clearing work, simply by reflection on the fundamental moral principles specifying prima facie duties, one can grasp their truth. Such reflection may have to be hard and sustained, taking place over many years, but in the end it alone will suffice to grasp the truth of the basic moral principles: it is 'an absolutely original and direct insight into moral principles',[11] and the knowledge it yields is certain.[12]

Thus one's knowledge of the basic moral principles is self-evident and certain, as Ross also thinks is true of our basic mathematical knowledge. Indeed, the analogue between mathematical and basic moral truths for Ross is very close, and helps lend credibility to the self-evidence of our knowledge of prima facie duties: both mathematical and moral truths, he holds, are objective, a priori, necessary, and non-analytic.

Finally, all of the above holds only of our knowledge of prima facie duties. Our knowledge of which particular act we should perform, when that act is both prima facie right and prima facie wrong, is only a matter of probable opinion, being neither self-evident nor certain. Here he cites Aristotle's remark that 'The decision rests with perception' (*aisthesis*).[13] The reason for this is part-ly that the balancing of prima facie rightness and wrongness is a complex mat-ter, requiring grasp of the details of the situation: 'what I have to do is to study the situation as fully as I can until I form the considered opinion (it is never more) that in the circumstances one of them is more incumbent than any other'.[14] It is also because one of our prima facie duties is to produce as much good as possible, and one cannot know for certain what effects an act will pro-duce indefinitely into the future, so one cannot be certain as to how much weight this duty has in its application to a particular act.

3. The Problem of Self-Evidence

The basic pluralistic structure of Ross's theory has a great deal of plausibil-ity as an account of our normal moral commitments. One may of course

---

[11] *The Foundations of Ethics*, 172.

[12] Ross also appeals to what he terms 'intuitive induction' (ibid., 170), that is, the process of first grasping the prima facie rightness of certain act-types as they are instantiated in particular acts and then apprehending that the principles expressing these duties are true in their complete generality. However, intuitive induction appears simply to be a claim about the order of discovery, not of jus-tification: in the end, one knows the truth of the principles by directly reflecting on them in their full generality. [13] *The Right and the Good*, 42.

[14] Ibid., 19.

object to details of the particular principles which Ross acknowledges. For instance, his view that justice is a matter of distributing pleasure or happiness in accordance with the merits of different people[15] is, apart from its coarseness as a theory, simply an elision of questions of justice with questions of desert. But I am interested here not in finessing the details of the theory, but in evaluating its broad structure, and in particular in determining how its pluralism can be grounded in terms of a different justification structure than intuitionism. Of course, it might be that the alternative justification proposed here is correct, as is also Ross's own justification: that is, it might be that pluralism is epistemically overdetermined. But I am going to argue that there is reason to reject Ross's intuitionism.

Ross claims that the principles of prima facie duty are self-evident. Now if a proposition is self-evident, one might suppose that there should be a high degree of convergence on the fact that it is self-evident. For it might seem that the self-evidently true is what is obviously true, and if something is obviously true it is obvious that it is obviously true. If this were correct, it would be hard to argue that even the five basic moral principles that Ross cites are self-evident.[16] For many philosophers reject moral intuitionism: while perhaps agreeing that, say, harming others is prima facie wrong, they maintain that this is not self-evidently so. Utilitarians would try to justify the claim by deriving it from considerations of maximizing the general welfare, Kantians would try to justify it in terms of the categorical imperative: for both, our knowledge of the moral principle is not self-evident, but derived from some other, more basic, principle. Other philosophers hold that our knowledge of the proposition about harming is experiential. Even some moral intuitionists would deny that the proposition about not harming is self-evident: instead, some other kinds of proposition are, according to them, self-evident. Moore, for instance, was an intuitionist like Ross, but he held that *no* moral principle telling us what we ought to do is self-evident; rather, it is only certain judgements about what is good in itself, about what ought to be, that are self-evident.[17] So there is widespread disagreement about which, if any, moral principles are self-evident. Contrast this with the genuinely self-evident (because in this case analytic) proposition that all bachelors are unmarried. Here there is widespread agreement not just on

---

[15] *The Right and the Good*, 21.

[16] Of course Ross allows that the application of these principles can lead to judgements that are not self-evident: that in cases of conflict, for instance, the decision rests with perception, as we noted above.

[17] G. E. Moore, *Principia Ethica* (Cambridge: Cambridge University Press, 1903), 148.

the truth of this proposition but also on the fact that it is self-evident. That is not the case with propositions about moral duties. How then can the Rossian intuitionist claim that they are self-evident?

The intuitionist's best response is to deny that the self-evident is to be identified with the obvious. So a proposition might be self-evident, but not obvious; and that explains the failure of philosophers to agree that it is self-evident. In developing a reconstructed Rossian intuitionism, Robert Audi gives a plausible example of a proposition that is not immediately obvious, but is self-evident—that if there have never been any siblings, there have never been any first cousins.[18] And Audi characterizes the self-evident in general in a way which allows self-evident truths not to be immediately obvious. He defines self-evident propositions as 'those truths such that (1) if one (adequately) understands them, then by virtue of that understanding one is justified *in* believing them, and (2) if one believes them on the basis of (adequately) understanding them, then one thereby knows them'.[19]

So mere reflection on a self-evident proposition alone, independently of any justificatory relations it may possess to other propositions or to any experiences, is sufficient for knowing it, according to this account. But the proposition need not be obviously true: reflection on the proposition may have to be hard and sustained in order to come to understand it adequately.

Now this account of the self-evident is clearly congenial to Ross's own account of self-evidence, for as already noted Ross thinks that there is an important role for something like reflective equilibrium in clarifying concepts and judgements, rendering different people's judgements consistent, and rejecting some as illusory. So he can not believe that it is simply obvious what our prima facie duties are—some ground-clearing may well be required before one can apprehend the self-evidence of a moral proposition. Ross believes that it can be quite hard to grasp what is self-evident. After announcing that the fact that certain actions are prima facie right is self-evident, he continues, 'not in the sense that it is evident from the beginning of our lives, or as soon as we attend to the proposition for the first time, but in the sense that when we have reached sufficient mental maturity and have given sufficient attention to the proposition it is evident without any need of proof, or of evidence beyond itself'.[20]

The claim that the self-evident is not what is obvious is correct. But does

---

[18] Audi, 'Intuitionism, Pluralism, and the Foundations of Ethics', 114.

[19] R. Audi, *Epistemology: A Contemporary Introduction to the Theory of Knowledge* (London: Routledge, 1998), 95. [20] *The Right and the Good*, 29.

this point adequately answer the objection that if basic moral duties are self-evident, then why have so many philosophers, including some intuitionists, denied this? On a broadly Rossian account of self-evidence, we should say that those who deny that some moral duties are self-evident have failed adequately to understand the propositions about these duties: for if they had properly understood them, they would have grasped that they were self-evident. Or to put the matter directly in Ross's own terms, we should say that they lack sufficient mental maturity or have paid insufficient attention to the propositions. But such failures of understanding or reflection are scarcely credible as explanations of why many philosophers have denied the self-evidence of these propositions. Moore, for example, was at least as talented a philosopher as Ross, and appears to have given morality as least as close a scrutiny as Ross did. So his failure to grasp the purported self-evidence of moral duties is not plausibly traced to any failure of understanding or attention on his part. On any normal, non-question-begging account of what it is to understand a moral proposition, we can safely assume that Moore understood these propositions. So the self-evidence view does not have a plausible theory of error to explain why the deniers of self-evidence have failed to grasp the purported self-evidence of these propositions. It cannot trace such failures to failures to conduct long chains of deductive reasoning correctly, or to appreciate subtleties in one's moral experience correctly, for in so far as one grasps the self-evidence of these propositions, one does not rely on long chains of reasoning or on appeal to experience, but simply on reflection on the nature of the propositions considered in themselves. If one holds that a proposition is self-evident, one automatically restricts the sources of errors that may mislead thinkers about it. In contrast, the deniers of the self-evidence of moral propositions have a plausible theory of error to explain the views of intuitionists: our conviction of the truth of certain core moral propositions is so firm that it can easily come to seem to us that these propositions are self-evident, even when they are not in fact knowable apart from their relations to other propositions or experiences.

Defenders of Ross might insist that all this objection shows is that Moore and others failed to give moral propositions the attention required to show that they are self-evident. But this simply begs the question: for this reply identifies the requisite degree of attention in terms of whatever is required to show that the propositions are self-evident.

So the objection is this: though a self-evident proposition need not be obvious, it is plausibly one such that understanding that proposition alone, independently of any justificatory relations it may have to experience or to any other propositions, is sufficient to know it. But then failures to grasp its self-evidence must be put down merely to failures to understand that very proposition, rather than its perhaps complex relations to experience or to other propositions (which would give more scope to allow failures of understanding). Provided that cognizers understand the proposition, then they will grasp that it is self-evident. That is what we find with the proposition that if there have never been any siblings, there have never been any first cousins, which is indeed self-evident. But that is not what we find with the propositions about moral duties; and on any normal criterion of understanding a proposition, people who do understand these propositions nevertheless deny that they are self-evident. Unless we simply set the criterion for what it is to understand a proposition question-beggingly high, then we have grounds for denying that these propositions are self-evident.

4. An Alternative Justification for Pluralism

So we have some reason to reject the intuitionist epistemology which underpins Ross's pluralism;[21] but how might one justify pluralism, and what would be the epistemic structure of such a justification?

4.1. Reflective Equilibrium and Epistemic Theories

The place to begin the justification is by appeal to reflective equilibrium, something akin to which, as we have already seen, is a core part of Ross's methodology. Ross deploys it to argue that a pluralistic theory best captures the shape of our ordinary moral commitments. In particular he calls attention to what he terms 'the highly personal character of duty',[22] that is, the fact that many of our duties reflect the multiple relations in which we stand to others. He complains of Moore's ideal utilitarianism that it 'seems to simplify unduly our relations to our fellows', treating them merely as possible beneficiaries of our actions, whereas in fact they stand in multiple relations to us—as promisees or promisers, spouses, children or parents, friends, fellow countrymen, and 'each of these relations is the foundation of a *prima facie* duty'.[23] This is a core insight of pluralism—that our moral

---

[21] Objections can also be raised to Ross's claims that moral propositions are necessary and known a priori, but I will not examine these here. [22] Ibid., 22.
[23] Ibid., 19.

reasons reflect the multiple relations in which we stand to others, that this is a fundamental reason why our ordinary morality is pluralistic, and is one reason why we should suppose that our morality will remain pluralistic even after it has been subject to continued reflective improvement.

Here is not the place to develop that thought fully, but let me give a sketch of how a defence of pluralism by use of reflective equilibrium would proceed.[24] Common-sense morality is at least on its surface pluralistic—it countenances a plurality of principles, giving reasons not to kill, not to lie, not to steal, reasons to help others when they are in need, and so forth. Reflective equilibrium operating on these commitments will seek to clarify them, to make moral principles and judgements about particular cases consistent, and in its wide version, to render moral commitments in general consistent with non-moral beliefs, such as those about the nature of persons and of society. We have several reasons to believe that this process of reasoned improvement would not result in endorsement of one overarching moral principle, from which all our judgements could be derived, but would still countenance a plurality of principles. One reason already noted is the plurality of significant relations in which we stand. Such relations ground a set of agent-relative principles: for instance, I have reasons to help my children, friends, and spouse, reasons which are grounded on the relations in which these people stand to me. These reasons are in a perfectly good sense impartial: each person has reason to give special help to those in these kinds of relations to her; but it is not the case that, say, I hold that everyone else has special reason to help *my* children or friends. Given their interconnection with personal relationships, agent-relative reasons go deep, which is one reason for thinking that views which take one agent-neutral principle as fundamental, such as standard forms of consequentialism, are in the end unable to account for the shape of our moral commitments. Many of the moral dilemmas we face represent conflicts grounded on the different relations in which we stand, such as that of the father who debates whether to turn in his criminal son to the police: he faces a conflict between the demands of parenthood and of citizenship.

The moral reasons we acknowledge are not merely agent-relative; the principle of beneficence is an agent-neutral one—an agent has a reason to help any person in need. That principle is again deeply grounded, reflecting our cognitive grip on the fact that the suffering of others is as real as our own, and

---

[24] The account sketched in Sect. 4.1 is drawn from my 'Moral Pluralism', *Philosophical Papers*, 22 (1993), 17–40, and my 'Rag-Bags, Disputes and Moral Pluralism', *Utilitas*, 11 (1999), 37–48. The claims are defended in much greater detail in these papers.

146

that if some good outcome can be achieved by an action, such as the relief of suffering, then this is a reason to perform the action. And the existence of agent-neutral as well as agent-relative reasons gives grounds for thinking that a simple monistic theory cannot capture the complexity of our moral views.

Of course, none of this is meant to be decisive in favour of pluralism: one can always accept that one should systematically ignore or alter one's considered moral judgements when they clash with one's favoured monistic theory. But since reflective equilibrium is a method employed and endorsed by several kinds of moral philosophers, including many utilitarians and Kantians, they should have reasons to be chary of too systematic a sacrifice of considered judgements to principles. And the considerations adduced above suggest that the pluralist has good reasons to be hopeful that she should win the battle against the monistic views of these rivals, since—to put it at its simplest—she starts with the built-in advantage that the input to reflective equilibrium is a pluralistic morality, and not the monistic views which these alternatives favour.[25]

There are reasons to believe, then, that use of reflective equilibrium as a justificatory method operating on our common-sense moral commitments will favour a pluralistic moral theory. But what reason is there to believe that the resulting convictions are fully justified? Perhaps we have merely rendered more orderly a set of unjustified moral convictions.

Reflective equilibrium, as we have noted, is compatible with both foundationalist and coherence theories of epistemic justification. For moral epistemology, coherentism may appear an attractive option: on this view, one would hold that reflective equilibrium is a complete method for moral justification, and that therefore the justification of our moral beliefs is entirely a matter of coherence with our other beliefs—that is all the justification that they need or could possess. However, for the usual reasons to do with the regress argument and the logical possibility of maximally internally coherent but false and unwarranted sets of beliefs, I do not believe that we should go down the coherentist route. As Brandt has argued, there is no reason to hold that more coherent sets of beliefs are more justified than less coherent ones, 'unless some of the beliefs are initially credible—and not merely initially believed—for some reason other than their coherence, say, because they state facts of observation'.[26]

---

[25] A defence of pluralism should also show that it does not suffer from the defects, such as being overly conservative and being a mere ragbag of different principles, which are commonly alleged against it. Pluralism is defended from such objections in my 'Rag-Bags, Disputes and Moral Pluralism'.

[26] R. B. Brandt, *A Theory of the Good and the Right* (Oxford: Clarendon Press, 1979), 20.

Berys Gaut

Foundationalist justifications in contrast attempt to give an account of this initial credibility, but appear untenable as theories of moral knowledge. A great deal of our knowledge of the world depends on our experiential contact with it, including saliently our perception of it. But how could we be said genuinely to experience values? In explaining our apparent experience of such things as chairs, rocks, and atoms, we must appeal to the existence of these entities to explain the experiences, and so the genuineness of the experiences is vindicated. But such appeal is neither plausible nor necessary in the case of our apparent experience of values: the appeal is not plausible, since science seemingly does not countenance the existence of entities such as values, and it is not necessary, since appeal simply to our *beliefs* about values can explain our apparent experience of values.

There are of course other domains of knowledge where the experiential contact thesis also appears to lack application, such as mathematics, where talk of experiencing abstract numbers looks to be untenable. It was this mathematical model to which Ross appealed; but, as we have seen, that model should be rejected for morality, because of the lack of self-evidence in the moral case.

So both the main options for a foundationalist justification appear to be ruled out. I am going to argue, however, that we do have experiential contact with moral values, and therefore that one can coherently maintain a moral epistemology which is a type of experiential foundationalism: we experience values, including moral values, and we can have immediate justification for our views about them. And one can use this claim to argue that we have knowledge of moral reasons.

4.2. A Value-Grounded Theory of Moral Reasons

Reasons and Value

Consider the following biconditional: an agent has a normative reason to φ iff φ-ing is good. This biconditional, perhaps with some refinements, could be endorsed by a wide variety of theorists about practical reason, including neo-Humeans, Kantians and Aristotelians. It captures a connection between having a reason and being valuable which is plausible, but not objectionably strong: the biconditional holds that an agent has *a* reason to perform an action if it is good, though not necessarily an *overriding* reason to perform it. Not every thinker about reasons would

148

endorse the biconditional, but it is a solid enough claim to serve as our starting point.[27]

Within this broad agreement, however, there is a fundamental disagreement about which half of the biconditional should be read as having priority. Theorists, such as Aristotle, who hold a *recognitional* view of the relation between the faculty of practical reason and value hold that the role of practical reason is to recognize whether an action is valuable, where the action's being valuable is constituted independently of rational choice. Such a view has a *value-grounded* conception of practical reasons, interpreting the biconditional as holding that an agent has reason to perform an action because that action is good. In contrast, theorists such as Kant who hold a *constructivist* view of the relation between practical reason and value maintain that an action's being valuable is constituted by its being the object of rational choice. Constructivists have a *reason-grounded* conception of value, interpreting the biconditional as holding that an action is good because one has reason to perform it.[28]

There are good grounds for favouring a recognitional model of the relation between value and practical reason, and therefore a value-grounded conception of practical reasons.

First, a constructivist in holding that the (practically) good is simply what is the object of rational choice inverts the natural understanding of why we make the choices we do: we say that we choose something *because* it's good—because, say, it's more pleasant, or intellectually more rewarding, or richer and deeper than the alternatives.

Further, in claiming that goodness is constituted simply as the object of rational choice, the constructivist shoulders the burden of giving an account of practical reason which abjures ineliminable reference to evaluative states of affairs. Historically the most influential way of doing this is by proposing purely formal criteria for being rational (such as the universalizability of one's reasons, adoption of those reasons autonomously, etc.) and holding that actions are valuable when they are (using these

---

[27] Ross, interestingly, would deny the biconditional. He argues that even when applied only to actions, 'right' does not mean the same as 'morally good' and more strongly that 'nothing that ought to be done is ever morally good' (*The Right and the Good*, 4). If this is correct, then we have a counter-example to the biconditional; for the rightness of an act is a type of reason to perform it, and moral goodness is a type of goodness. I believe that Ross's claim should be rejected, since it rests on the false premiss that one can never be obligated to have a motive, though I will not argue the point here.

[28] For the recognitional–constructivist distinction, see Introduction, esp. sect. I, in G. Cullity and B. Gaut (eds.), *Ethics and Practical Reason* (Oxford: Clarendon Press, 1997).

criteria) rationally chosen. But some of the actions passing this test are clearly not valuable, may even be damaging to the agent, and are on intuitive grounds deeply irrational. An agent who after due rational reflection (on formalist criteria) decides that what she most wants to do is to devote her life to reciting every second name in all the phone books in the world, and decides to sacrifice to this aim all other goods, such as significant relationships, the pursuit of knowledge (other than of phone numbers), and so forth, would, on this constructivist picture be doing something which was valuable, and which she had most reason to do. Any model of practical reason which produces such a result has gone radically wrong.[29]

Alternatively, the constructivist may note that to be rational is to have a propensity to recognize and respond to reasons, and then give not a formal but a substantive account of what reasons we have; he then reduces talk of goodness to talk of reasons. Scanlon has recently proposed a version of this view, which he terms the 'buck-passing' account of what is valuable. According to this view, 'being valuable is not a property that provides us with reasons. Rather, to call something valuable is to say that it has other properties that provide reasons for behaving in certain ways with regard to it.'[30] Scanlon includes under reasons for behaving not just reasons for acting towards the thing in a variety of ways (promoting it, or preserving it, etc.), but also reasons for adopting certain attitudes towards it (admiring it, or respecting it, etc.).

Scanlon advances two considerations for the buck-passing view. First, he notes that if one says that one has reason to choose something because it is valuable, then the question arises of why one judges that it is valuable. In answering that, one is led to cite some natural facts about the object that give one reason to choose it—e.g. I have reason to visit a resort because it is pleasant, and I have reason to applaud a discovery because it casts light on the causes of cancer. But having cited the natural facts as the grounds of my choice, appeal to the property of being valuable is rendered redundant: 'These natural properties provide a complete explanation of the reasons we have for reacting in these ways to things that are good or valuable. It is not clear what further work could be done by special reason-providing properties of goodness and value, and even less clear how these properties could provide reasons.'[31] Second, he says that given the sheer variety of things

---

[29] For a fuller critique of this version of the constructivist model, particularly in its Kantian form, see my 'The Structure of Practical Reason', in Cullity and Gaut (eds.), *Ethics and Practical Reason*.

[30] T. M. Scanlon, *What we Owe to Each Other* (Cambridge, Mass.:Harvard University Press, 1998), 96.

[31] Ibid., 97.

that are good and the variety of grounds one cites for their goodness, there doesn't seem to be a single reason-providing property that is common to all the different things that are called 'good'.

Scanlon's second argument clearly fails: after all, it is commonly and correctly held that goodness is a supervenient property, so there is no problem with acknowledging the variety of objects and properties on which it supervenes. His first argument is more weighty. He says that it is mysterious how goodness could ground reasons: but given the plausible aprioricity of the biconditional, we may simply be dealing with a conceptual connection here. More tellingly, Scanlon says that *goodness* drops out as redundant in explaining one's choices, since for any reason to choose or admire some object, one can always cite as a complete explanation of one's choice a natural property which the object possesses. Were that true, it would indeed tell in favour of the buck-passing view. However, it is not true that one can always cite a natural (in the sense of non-evaluative) property as a complete explanation of the ground of one's choice. Even his own example of choosing a resort because it is pleasant doesn't cite a natural property. The pleasant isn't what *causes* pleasure, since one may take pleasure in what isn't pleasant, and not take pleasure in what is pleasant. The pleasant is a species of the good.[32] And similar remarks apply to several other grounds one may cite in explaining one's reasons for choosing certain objects. My reason for looking at a painting may be because it's beautiful. But I cannot fully specify the grounds I have for calling it beautiful in terms of the natural properties of the painting: the beautiful cannot be exhaustively specified in terms of some set of non-evaluative properties of the painting. So in such cases there must be an ineliminable reference to what is valuable in explaining one's reasons for choice, and then one can give a partial specification of the grounds for one's judgement of why something is valuable by citing some of the natural properties of the object. It turns out then on closer inspection that one cannot eliminate reference to values in giving a full explanation of one's reasons for choosing.

Experiencing Value

Given these problems with constructivism, we have reason to adopt a recognitional model of the relation between the faculty of practical reason

---

[32] Scanlon (ibid., 96), holds that 'X is pleasant, but is it good?' is an open question; but if true, this merely proves that the pleasant is not identical with the good, not that the pleasant is not a species of the good. For in posing the question, we may mean to be inquiring whether X is good all things considered.

and value, and therefore a value-grounded conception of practical reasons. So we should hold that moral reasons are grounded on values. And moral epistemology becomes then a question of how we know what is valuable. But how is this possible? Let us begin by noting the kinds of things that people say about what is valuable, before we raise any philosophical questions about them; that way we can get a clearer view of the phenomena which need to be justified, or to be explained away.

Consider first prudential values—what makes a person's life go well for her. How does a person know that her life is going well? Primarily it is through what she feels: she enjoys life and finds it deeply satisfying. Here pleasure should not be thought of merely as a feeling, but as a sign of things going well. One's pleasure in something can be subjected to critical reflection: perhaps it is based on misconceptions about the object in which one is taking pleasure, or too shallow an appreciation of it, for instance. One kind of affective state—emotions—has a particularly close connection to value; for emotions are partly constituted by evaluative thoughts about their objects. To fear something involves thinking of it as dangerous; to envy someone for something involves thinking of them as possessing something worth having; to be ashamed of something involves thinking of that thing as shameful; and so on. An important way in which we know what is valuable in our lives, then, involves the having of emotions.

Prudential values also have explanatory power. We can explain in part why one person's life is going well and another's life is going badly: such things as accomplishments, deep personal relationships, and pursuit of knowledge tend to make lives go well.[33] This is not a trivial claim, resting for instance on the fact that 'accomplishment' means something worth doing: for we know the kinds of things that count as accomplishments (and sustained chanting of the telephone directory does not). And lack of accomplishments and of deep personal relationships can explain why someone's life is going badly, and why she feels a sense of emptiness.[34] We have a large amount of knowledge about what makes lives go well, drawing not just on obvious facts about the fulfilment of basic human needs for sustenance, shelter, and so on, but also on the sustained experience and reflection of many generations, incorporated in our common-sense evaluations and judgements, and in our art and literature.

---

[33] In fact, it is in terms of these basic goods that we understand the rationality of certain pursuits—that is why, for instance, reading out every second word of all the telephone directories in the world is not a rational occupation.

[34] James Griffin, *Value Judgement: Improving our Ethical Beliefs* (Oxford: Clarendon Press, 1996), ch. 4.

Similar points to those just made about prudential values apply to the moral case. A salient way in which we know that something is morally bad is because we feel moral outrage or disgust at it, and are strongly disposed to judge it bad; conversely, moral goodness is the object of our feelings of moral approval and pleasure. And here again, the emotions play a central role in our cognition of value because of their conceptual connection to evaluations: guilt involves the thought of having done something morally wrong, and anger the thought that someone else has done something wrong. These affective reactions are again subject to reasoned criticism, to ascertain whether we really have grasped the relevant features of the case properly; and this process of reasoned criticism is simply the application of the familiar processes of reflective equilibrium. Furthermore, just as we can advance well-grounded explanations in the prudential case, so we can in the moral case: slavery was abolished because it was evil, and people eventually came to recognize that it was so; liberal regimes tend to flourish because they allow people to lead good lives, securing basic human goods such as freedom and exercise of the capacities for self-realization.

It is not surprising that similar affective and explanatory accounts can be given for prudential and moral values, since moral values are deeply implicated in prudential values. A prudential value such as having good friendships implies the recognition of certain moral values: a good friend is one who cares for you for your own sake, not merely instrumentally; so one must be capable of recognizing the non-instrumental value of others' lives in order to participate in friendships. The same point applies to other similar fundamental human goods, such as participating in loving relationships and in communities of various kinds. Ross is indeed correct in calling attention to 'the highly personal character of duty'.

The entanglement of moral with prudential values is not confined, however, to the class of relationships with others. It is also implied in one's self-concern. When I want my life to go well, I want my life to be *good for me*. But this notion is not *merely* an egoistic and agent-relative notion: i.e. one which grounds egoistic agent-relative reasons (though that undoubtedly is a large part of its meaning). For if it grounded only egoistic reasons, then I should judge that no one else had reason to help me (unless they wanted to do so), no matter how great my suffering, and no matter how little effort were required by them to help me. On this view, even if I were dying at the roadside in the burning wreck of my car, and drivers passing by could save my life simply by calling the emergency services on their mobile phones, they would have no reason to do so. But clearly my self-regard isn't like that: I do believe that others in this situation have *some* reason to help me. My prudential concern involves a notion of agent-neutral value (that is, the kind of value which grounds agent-neutral reasons) which makes at least some claims on others. My concern with my own life manifests itself then not just in the claim that it is good-for-me, but also in the claim that it is good *simpliciter*.[35]

Value and Biology

These remarks so far have been at the level of recording ordinary evaluative practices; they illustrate the extent to which we talk of experiencing not only prudential but also moral values, and of how these can be explanatory of our feelings and actions.

We need now to confront the philosophical objection that this appearance of experiencing values and of values being explanatory is illusory. Confining ourselves to the sphere of human action and experience reviewed above, that objection is hard to sustain. Suppose one claims that all that has been shown is that values play no role in explanation, since it is merely agents' *beliefs* about values which explain their actions and feelings—for instance, a person's belief that her life lacks accomplishment is what explains her sense of emptiness. But this is unconvincing: sometimes the best explanation for why someone believes that they have accomplished nothing is indeed that they have accomplished nothing.[36] So in respect of human experience, we have reason to believe that values are explanatory, because appeal to them forms part of the best explanation of why we have some of the beliefs and feelings that we do.

However, a more general objection can be raised: this apparently explanatory role in respect of human experience cannot be a genuine one, since values never are genuinely explanatory, for humans are part of nature, and values have no explanatory role in nature in general. In reply to this broader worry, I want briefly to sketch out a response which gives some grounds for querying the view that values have no explanatory role in nature in general.

I suggest that when we get puzzled as to how there could be values in the world, values there to be experienced, we tend to be operating with an

---

[35] Suppose in contrast that someone claimed that her life were valuable only for herself. In some unusual cases—maybe she has sunk so low, become so degenerate, or depraved—we might agree with her. But in standard cases we could correctly hold that she was wrong: her life had some value *simpliciter*. In ordinary evaluative discriminations we hold that someone who understands the value of her life only in agent-relative terms has made a mistake.

[36] See Griffin, *Value Judgement*, 63.

impoverished conception of nature, and therefore of naturalism. We tend to think of nature as that studied by physics; but nature includes more than this—it includes *living* nature. Value is a concept which has its application to living things and their products. We can talk, for instance, of a plant having good roots only because it has certain goals (to grow, to self-maintain, to reproduce, etc.), goals determined by its nature as a living being, and roots are good when they are such as to enable the plant to attain these goals. Appeal to value here is explanatory: the roots may grow in one direction rather than another, say, because the soil in this direction is better for the plant. Of course, such explanations must also appeal to the mechanisms by which a living being advances towards its goals: but that is to explain how ends, the realization of which is good for the organism, are reached; it is not to remove the explanatory role of value.

Value then has its primary application to living beings. But it also has a derivative application to artefacts, that is, to things made by living beings to serve certain ends. We judge a beaver's dam to be good because it serves the ends of the beaver, to make a pool of still water in which to swim and hunt. In the same way, human artefacts are good when they fulfil the ends for which humans made them. Of course, we individuate and define artefacts by the ends which they serve: dams are defined by their end of damming water. But artefacts have these ends only because a living being made them to serve those ends.

An important value category is that of need. This may seem surprising, since the concept of need looks non-evaluative: for instance, the claim that a plant needs water to live might not seem to involve any evaluative concepts. However, when we talk of needs as applied to living beings, we are always implicitly appealing to what living beings need *in order to flourish*, i.e. in order for their lives to go well. It is perfectly coherent to say of a plant, which is alive but is stunted because it is in dry conditions, that it does not have as much water as it needs. So the notion of need refers to what is required in order not merely to live, but in order to flourish. And note too that the notion of need is explanatory: a plant sends out roots because it needs sustenance from the soil; an animal goes hunting because it needs food; and so on. Health is an evaluative concept too, and can figure in explanations, such as that an animal did not survive because it was unhealthy.

The concept of value applies, then, to living nature, and importantly for our present claim is explanatory. In contrast it plays no explanatory role for non-living nature: the movements of the planets cannot be explained in terms of the satisfactions of their needs: they have none, for they have no goals. Because values can enter into explanations, they can also be known by cognitively sophisticated creatures. Values can satisfy the experiential contact claim. And human beings, as living beings who are also rational beings—that is, beings capable of recognizing and responding to available reasons and therefore to values—are capable of knowing about values. As noted above, a prime way in which humans can know about values is through their affective and more particularly emotional responses, corrected by processes of reflective equilibrium in the light of all available relevant considerations. Given the centrality of value to living beings, it is hardly surprising that we should have evolved cognitive and emotional capacities capable of grasping how to lead our lives well.

My suggestion, then, is this: our pre-reflective assumption that we can experience values is correct. We do so by employing our affective capacities, corrected by rational reflection. That we can experience values is just what one would expect when a living being becomes a rational being. Moral deliberation proceeds by reflective equilibrium as its method, but what grounds the method is the fact that we can experience what is valuable and what is not. Experiential foundationalism is the epistemic theory that best represents the structure of the justification of our moral commitments; reflective equilibrium is the method of moral deliberation; and, as I earlier argued, moral pluralism is its outcome.

4.3. Clarifications and Objections

The biological conception of value can easily be misconstrued. What it claims is that a large and significant class of biological explanations—explanations, that is, about living creatures—are value-involving: they appeal to evaluative states of affairs to explain why some living being behaves in a certain way or has a certain structure. Values figure in biological explanations, including in those that do not involve human beings. Because of this explanatory role of values, we can also invoke values in explaining why we have experiences as of things being valuable (both prudentially and morally). So we can save the appearances: the experiences can be veridical.

The biological conception of value does not claim that we can simply read off facts about what we ought to do from facts about human nature—though human nature does to a large extent constrain what counts as our good: the good life for a human is different from the good life for a fish. Still less does it claim that humans have a function. It does not claim that all values are derived from needs (though needs play an important role which has been surprisingly neglected by philosophers)—needs are a relatively straightforward example of how biological categories are value-involving. Nor is the biological conception of value supposed somehow to supplant the use of reflective equilibrium in deliberation about values. On the contrary, that procedure is an essential component in deliberating about what we should do, and can take us far beyond its experiential input, as can that use of reflective equilibrium which operates on perception and yields science.

Needless to say, there are several possible objections to the justification of pluralism defended above, and I cannot address them all here. So let me briefly consider just two objections: the first is to the biological conception of value; the second is to the value-grounded conception of reasons.

First, the explanatory success of microbiology and evolutionary theory surely show that one can eliminate reference to values in explaining the structure and behaviour of living things: modern scientific biology, as opposed to the kind of 'folk biology' explanations to which I have just drawn attention, sweeps away talk of goals and values in biology. Values we have learned are not genuinely explanatory at all.

In reply, first note that microbiological processes can not by themselves fully explain the structures and behaviour of organisms: such explanations will explain, say, *how* a plant manages to grow towards the light, detailing the cellular mechanisms involved in this movement, but not explain *why* it grows towards the light—why it has those mechanisms. (Indeed, if we think of microbiology as giving an account of organic mechanisms, then the very idea of a mechanism presupposes some end or function, an explanation for which has to be given.) So the crucial issue concerns the role of evolutionary theory, which does seek to explain basic structures and processes. Evolutionary theory makes two central claims: first, that there is a 'tree of life', i.e. that different species have common ancestors, which entails the fact of evolutionary change—that there has been fundamental change in lineages leading from ancestors to descendants. Second, evolutionary theory holds that natural selection plays some role in explaining this evolutionary change, that is, in explaining speciation, extinctions, and the evolution of new phenotypic characteristics in species (that is, in explaining the morphology, physiology, and behaviour of organisms).[37] Given its explanatory role, it is natural selection that represents the challenge to value-involving explanations.

---

[37] See Elliott Sober, *Philosophy of Biology* (Oxford: Oxford University Press, 1993), chs. 1 and 5 for an informative account of evolutionary theory and adaptationism.

That the basic claims of evolutionary theory are true is, I think, indisputable. But it is important to realize that biologists disagree about the importance of natural selection in evolution. Adaptationists, such as Maynard Smith, hold that the *only* (or only significant) explanation of evolutionary change is natural selection; evolutionary pluralists, such as Lewontin and Gould, hold in contrast that natural selection is merely one of many factors that explain evolutionary change. If adaptationism is false, there is at least room to hold (though it is of course not thereby entailed) that some of the other explanatory factors for evolutionary change are value-involving. And, as noted earlier, we confidently employ biological explanations which appeal to evaluative concepts, such as health and need.

However, suppose for the sake of argument that adaptationism were true. Is it the case that the explanations given by natural selection do not involve values? On the face of it, this is not so: writers on evolution frequently make evaluative claims, holding for instance that natural selection causes characteristics of organisms to evolve because such characteristics are good for those organisms. But on closer inspection these evaluative claims are given a reduction to non-evaluative vocabulary: what is good for an organism is a matter of its fitness, and this is identified, roughly, with its probability of survival and leaving a high number of offspring. So, one may object, it turns out that natural selection explanations are not, despite appearances, value-involving. However, this would be a mistake: if I successfully reduce evaluative properties to non-evaluative ones, I claim that the two kinds of properties are identical; but if property P is identical to property Q, then if the former has explanatory power, *ipso facto* the latter does too. Hence if adaptationism were true, it would show that we should be value-reductionists. So, far from value-reductionism proving that values have no explanatory power, it provides one kind of explanation of how it is possible for values to have such power. And of course philosophers have often taken to be a salient advantage of reductionism that it secures the epistemology of values. The truth of adaptationism would in short show the truth of value-reductionism, but would not undermine the epistemology of value or the claim that explanations are value-involving.[38]

---

[38] However, if adaptationism is false, we have no good reasons, I would argue, to be value-reductionists; the view thus defended here is what Griffin calls 'expansive naturalism', the claim that 'values are, without reduction, also part of the natural world' (*Value Judgement*, 62). While Griffin seems to confine his support for this view to values which explain human actions and feelings, my suggestion is that we have reasons to believe that irreducible values are to be found more broadly as properties of living beings, not just human beings.

The second objection to the justification of pluralism defended here concerns whether the value-grounded conception of reason is consistent with moral pluralism. For surely the value-grounded conception is fundamentally a teleological one, and thus a kind of consequentialism, inimical to the deontological structure of Ross's theory. Thus the resulting theory might be pluralist, the objection goes, but only in the sense that it is a kind of consequentialism which acknowledges a plurality of competing values. But then we would have something akin to Moore's theory, ideal utilitarianism, which Ross took as his main target of attack.

The reply is that the theory advanced here is indeed teleological in a broad sense—in the sense that it interprets the biconditional so that an agent has reason to perform some action because the agent's performing that action is good. It is also teleological in the sense that it gives epistemic priority to the valuable over what we have reason to do. But the value-grounded conception of reason and the epistemic priority of the valuable do not entail consequentialism. The biconditional holds that we have reason to perform some act because that act is good. What makes that act good might be the fact that it has good consequences. If we held that the *only* thing that made an act good were the goodness of its consequences, then we would indeed have some kind of consequentialism. But it is consistent with acceptance of the value-grounded reading of the biconditional to hold that some acts are *intrinsically* good, considered quite apart from their consequences. And what the intrinsic goodness of an act might consist in is the fact that it is the keeping of a promise, or the expression of gratitude for some favour received, or any of the other features which Ross claims make actions prima facie right. So the broad sense in which the value-grounded theory is teleological is consistent with the rejection of consequentialism and the espousal of a version of moral pluralism.

5. Ross and Aristotle

I have argued, then, that Ross's epistemic intuitionism should be abandoned as a justification-structure for moral pluralism; instead we should justify pluralism using reflective equilibrium, a value-grounded conception of reasons, and a biological conception of value. And the structure of this justification is best captured by experiential foundationalism, not by intuitionism.

This result may seem surprising, since 'intuitionism' has so frequently and indifferently been used to cover both the pluralistic theory and the claims about its epistemic justification. But this is not the most surprising result of our argument, for we can now usher onto the stage the irony which has been waiting impatiently in the wings.

The thought that we have intuitions about self-evident, necessary, a priori, and certain moral truths is ultimately Platonic in inspiration. In contrast, the justification I have suggested for pluralism is, of course, fundamentally Aristotelian. It is a non-consequentialist but value-grounded view of reasons; it adopts a biological conception of value; it is pluralist, as in a certain way was Aristotle's own theory. Its appeal to reflective equilibrium is also akin to Aristotle's own dialectical method of reasoning about morality, which appeals to common opinions and seeks to adjudicate conflicts between them. This Aristotelian view is, I have argued, a better justification for pluralism than that which Ross embraced. And yet Ross was one of the great Aristotelian scholars of his day: editor of the Oxford translations of Aristotle's works between 1908 and 1931; translator of the *Metaphysics* and *Nicomachean Ethics*; the author of the textbook *Aristotle*. Aristotle's influence is of course to be found at several points in Ross's moral works.[39] Yet Ross never managed to shake off the intuitionist epistemology which he inherited from a fundamentally Platonic source, nor did he embrace the Aristotelian account of value which, I have suggested, would have better served his pluralism. Ross the Aristotelian scholar never made sufficient contact with Ross the moral theoretician. So though, in rejecting Ross's justification for pluralism, we have severed Ross the moral theoretician from Ross the epistemologist, it is satisfying that in doing so, we have managed to reunite Ross the moral theoretician with Ross the Aristotelian scholar. Pluralism, I suggest, should follow Ross the scholar, and return to its Aristotelian roots.

---

[39] Notably, Ross quotes Aristotle on the necessity of *aisthesis* when the moral situation is complex, and he cites the passage from the *Nicomachean Ethics* on dialectical method before setting out his own version of reflective equilibrium (*The Foundations of Ethics*, 1–2).

Intuitions and Moral Theorizing

7

Brad Hooker

What is Moral Intuitionism?

The term 'moral intuitionism' gets attached to a range of different views. Some of these views are more widely held than others are. Here is a list of views often referred to as intuitionism, and a ranking of them in terms of popularity:

Reflective equilibrium method. Moral theories are better to the extent that they accord with moral claims that are attractive in their own right—i.e. apart from any inferential support they receive from other moral claims. Most philosophers currently accept this theory.

Moral pluralism. There is an irreducible plurality of fundamental moral considerations, which are not all ordered in a strict hierarchy. Many philosophers currently accept this theory.

Faculty intuitionism. Intuition is a special faculty capable of apprehending moral truths. Few philosophers currently accept this theory.[1]

The popularity of a view cannot establish its truth, nor can the unpopularity of a view establish its falsity. Nevertheless, I shall focus on the two more popular forms of intuitionism.

Robert Audi, Gerald Dworkin, Andrew Moore, Michael Smith, and Jay Wallace commented extensively on a draft of this paper. The end product is far better because of their generous aid. Others to whom I am grateful for helpful comments are Colin Cheyne, John Cottingham, Roger Crisp, Jonathan Dancy, Robert Frazier, Grant Gillet, Karen Jones, Rae Langton, Peter Leach, Sue Mendus, Alan Musgrave, Mark Nelson, Philip Pettit, Charles Pigden, Michael Ridge, Tim Scanlon, Philip Stratton-Lake, and David Ward.

[1] I believe that such intuitionists as Henry Sidgwick, G. E. Moore, and W. D. Ross were not committed to the existence of a special moral sense. See Sidgwick, *The Methods of Ethics* (London: Macmillan, 1907), 383 and 507; Moore, *Principia Ethica* (Cambridge: Cambridge University Press, 1903), p. x; D. Brink, 'Moral Realism and the Foundations of Ethics', *Social Philosophy and Policy*, 11 (1994), 107–13.

Brad Hooker

Most philosophers nowadays who mention 'moral intuitions' refer to a subset of moral beliefs, but this subset is not defined as the moral beliefs arrived at by some special faculty. Instead, a distinction is made between moral beliefs that are arrived at by inference from other moral beliefs and moral beliefs that are arrived at non-inferentially. A belief arrived at non-inferentially may also be accessible via inference. But a belief's status as an intuition consists in its being arrived at not by inference from other moral beliefs.

Pure coherentists hold that no belief can be at all justified except by its inferential relations with other beliefs. Consider some intuitively attractive moral belief that is well informed and carefully considered but does not connect with our other intuitively attractive moral beliefs. For coherentists, this carefully considered intuitively attractive moral belief is unjustified.

On the other hand, coherentists who are devotees of the reflective equilibrium method admit that a moral theory's according with this same intuitively attractive (i.e. non-inferential) moral belief can serve as an argument in favour of the moral theory.[2] As between two or more rival moral theories that are equally good in every other respect, the one that accords better with independently attractive beliefs is the better theory. So, for coherentists, an independently attractive moral belief, although itself unjustified unless or until it is connected to other moral beliefs, can play a decisive role in an argument for one moral theory as against another.[3]

That seems to me an awkward position to maintain. If some well-informed moral belief seems independently attractive to us, and if a moral theory's accordance with this belief counts in favour of the moral theory, why hold back from calling the belief justified?[4]

[2] See John Rawls, 'Outline for a Decision Procedure in Ethics', *Philosophical Review*, 60 (1951), 177–97; *A Theory of Justice* (Cambridge, Mass.: Harvard University Press, 1971), 19–21, 46–51; 'The Independence of Moral Theory', *Proceedings and Addresses of the American Philosophical Association*, 48 (1974–5), 7–8; N. Daniels, 'Wide Reflective Equilibrium and Theory Acceptance in Ethics', *Journal of Philosophy*, 76 (1979), 256–82; 'Reflective Equilibrium and Archimedean Points', *Canadian Journal of Philosophy*, 10 (1980), 83–110; 'Two Approaches to Theory Acceptance in Ethics', in D. Copp and D. Zimmerman (eds.), *Morality, Reason and Truth* (Totowa, NJ: Rowman & Littlefield, 1985); M. Holmgren, 'Wide Reflective Equilibrium and Objective Moral Truth', *Metaphilosophy*, 18 (1987), 108–25; 'The Wide and Narrow of Reflective Equilibrium', *Canadian Journal of Philosophy*, 19 (1989), 43–60; M. DePaul, 'Two Conceptions of Coherence Methods in Ethics', *Mind*, 96 (1987), 463–81; *Balance and Refinement: Beyond Coherence Methods of Moral Inquiry* (New York: Routledge, 1993); R. Ebertz, 'Is Reflective Equilibrium a Coherentist Model?', *Canadian Journal of Philosophy*, 23 (1993), 193–214.

[3] On the question of whether Rawls's reflective equilibrium method really was just a version of pure coherentism, see Ebertz, 'Is Reflective Equilibrium a Coherentist Model?'.

[4] Compare Sayre-McCord's line on 'permissively justified beliefs' in his 'Coherentist

Rejecting pure coherentism seems to me a lot easier now that Robert Audi has shown how accommodating and modest moral foundationalism can be.[5] Foundationalists can accommodate and indeed embrace the aspiration to consistency among one's beliefs. They can also (and I think should) accept that connectedness among moral beliefs is desirable. But this modest and accommodating foundationalism rejects the coherentist thesis that coherence is a necessary condition for justification. The claim is instead that a moral belief can be justified independently of its inferential relations with other moral beliefs.

If a moral belief can be justified by some feature other than its inferential relations with other beliefs, what is this feature? The traditional answer is self-evidence. As W. D. Ross writes, a self-evident proposition is 'evident without any need of proof, or of evidence beyond itself'.[6] Nothing more than adequate understanding of a self-evident proposition is required for being justified in believing that proposition (which is not to say that there cannot be other justification for believing it as well).[7]

Epistemology and Moral Theory', in W. Sinnott-Armstrong and M. Timmons (eds.), *Moral Knowledge? New Readings in Moral Epistemology* (Oxford: Oxford University Press, 1996), 161; and Gilbert Harman's 'Negative Coherentism' (*Change in View* (Cambridge, Mass.: MIT Press, 1986), 32); and the modest demands of Mark Timmons's 'contextualism' as explained in his *Morality without Foundations* (New York: Oxford University Press, 1999), 232–42.

5 See R. Audi, 'The Foundationalism–Coherentism Controversy: Hardened Stereotypes and Overlapping Theories', in Audi, *The Structure of Justification* (Cambridge: Cambridge University Press, 1993); 'Ethical Reflectionism', *Monist*, 76 (1993), 296–315; and 'Intuitionism, Pluralism, and the Foundations of Ethics', in W. Sinnott-Armstrong and M. Timmons (eds.), *Moral Knowledge? New Readings in Moral Epistemology* (Oxford: Oxford University Press, 1996).

6 Ross, *The Right and the Good* (Oxford: Clarendon Press, 1930), 29.

7 See Plato, *The Republic*; Aristotle, *Nicomachean Ethics*; J. Butler, *Fifteen Sermons Preached at the Rolls Chapel* (1726); S. Clarke, *A Discourse of Natural Religion* (1728); R. Price, *A Review of the Principal Questions of Morals*, 3rd edn. (1787); T. Reid, *Essays on the Active Powers of Man* (1788); Sidgwick, *The Methods of Ethics*, 199–201, 207–16, 338–42, 379–89; Moore, *Principia Ethica*, chs. 1 and 6; H. A. Prichard, 'Does Moral Philosophy Rest on a Mistake?', *Mind*, 21 (1912), 21–37; H. Rashdall, *A Theory of Good and Evil* (Oxford: Clarendon Press, 1929); C. D. Broad, *Five Types of Ethical Theory* (London: Routledge & Kegan Paul, 1930); W. D. Ross, *The Foundations of Ethics* (Oxford: Clarendon Press, 1939); E. F. Carritt, *Ethical and Political Thinking* (Oxford: Clarendon Press, 1947); A. C. Ewing, *Ethics* (London: Macmillan, 1947); *The Fundamental Questions of Philosophy* (London: Routledge & Kegan Paul, 1951); T. Nagel, *The View from Nowhere* (New York: Oxford University Press, 1986), ch. 8; *The Final Word* (New York: Oxford University Press, 1997), ch. 7; J. J. Thomson, *The Realm of Rights* (Cambridge, Mass.: Harvard University Press, 1990), 12–20; R. Audi, 'Intuitionism, Pluralism, and the Foundations of Ethics'; 'Self-Evidence', *Philosophical Perspectives*, 13 (1999), 205–28; *Epistemology: A Contemporary Introduction to the Theory of Knowledge* (London: Routledge, 1998), chs. 4 and 7; R. Dworkin, 'Objectivity and Truth: You'd Better Believe It', *Philosophy and Public Affairs*, 25 (1996), 87–139; J. Griffin, *Value Judgement: Improving our Ethical Beliefs* (Oxford: Clarendon Press, 1996), 13, 52, 125; R. Crisp, 'Griffin's Pessimism', R. Crisp and B. Hooker (eds.), *Well-Being and Morality: Essays in Honour of James Griffin* (Oxford: Clarendon Press, 2000), 116–20.

Brad Hooker

Self-evident propositions must be intellectually compelling independently of what they entail and of what entails them. If our justification for
believing a given proposition is that this proposition follows from more
general beliefs we have, then this justification does not come from the
proposition's self-evidence but rather from the proposition's inferential
relation to (the contents of) the more general beliefs. If our justification for
believing the proposition is that the proposition coheres with more specific beliefs that we already have, then this justification for the proposition is
again inferential.

To believe a proposition because of its self-evidence, we must understand
what it is we are believing, and this understanding must be the basis of the
belief.[8] Understanding a self-evident proposition provides justification for
believing it. The justification that understanding the self-evident proposition provides for believing the proposition is supposed to be non-inferential.
But can we adequately understand a proposition without drawing inferences? To answer this question, let us distinguish between inferences to a
proposition and inferences from it.

Consider first inferences to a proposition. Clearly, there are propositions
we can understand without drawing any inferences that lead to those
propositions.

Now consider inferences from a proposition. We need at least to be able
to draw some inferences from a proposition in order to understand it. Yet
we can understand a proposition (and find it intuitively attractive) before we
have drawn any inferences from it. Understanding requires the capacity to
draw inferences; it does not require that they already have been drawn or are
now being drawn.

I noted that moral foundationalists can be modest. First, they can deny
that self-evident propositions must be instantly compelling—i.e. on first
look.[9] One may have to think very carefully to find a moral proposition self-
evident. As Audi writes, 'One may require time to get it in clear focus, but
need not climb up to it on the shoulders of one or more premises.'[10]

Second, propositions that seem to be self-evident need not be beyond all
challenge or revision.[11] Further reflection may show us that these propositions are not self-evident and indeed untrue. Admittedly, popular moralists

---

[8] Audi, 'Intuitionism, Pluralism, and the Foundations of Ethics', 115.
[9] Ross, *The Right and the Good*, 29.
[10] Audi, 'Intuitionism, Pluralism, and the Foundations of Ethics', 115.
[11] Ewing, *Ethics*, ch. 8; *The Fundamental Questions of Philosophy*, 58–63; Audi, 'Intuitionism,
Pluralism, and the Foundations of Ethics', 107–8, 131.

who proclaim the self-evidence of various moral propositions often display an unreasonable degree of certainty, together with an unwillingness to provide any argument for the propositions claimed to be self-evident. But Audi has done much to rehabilitate the concept of self-evidence in moral philosophy by stressing that we can believe a proposition self-evident while admitting we might be mistaken and while taking seriously further argument for or against the truth of the proposition.

Nevertheless, because the term 'self-evident' has so often been misused by popular moralists to express an unreasonable degree of certainty and to silence further dispute, I myself feel more comfortable using a wider term that does not have those associations. I prefer the term 'independently credible'.[12] An independently credible belief is attractive without reference to evidence beyond itself and yet might turn out to be mistaken.

While independently credible beliefs arrive carrying some justification of their own, this does not mean they can accept none from other sources. On the contrary, they can accept support from their relations to other beliefs. For example, if two different moral beliefs are each non-inferentially credible, and one explains the other, this adds to the credibility of both these beliefs.

In short, the intuitionist view that some moral beliefs are independently credible is compatible with a moral epistemology that is partly coherentist. We search for a coherent set of moral beliefs and are willing to make many revisions so as to reach coherence. But, as the foundationalist stresses, we must start with moral beliefs that are attractive in their own right, i.e. independently of how they mesh with our other moral beliefs.[13]

Naturalism and Noncognitivism

The sort of reflective equilibrium methodology outlined above seems to me the least controversial sort of moral intuitionism. This sort of intuitionism is, I think, compatible with some kinds of moral naturalism and with some kinds of non-cognitivism, as well as of course with non-naturalism.

To be sure, some forms of naturalism claim to want nothing to do with intuitions. Consider, for example, the view identifying the individual's good with the natural property of satisfying the desires he or she would have after

[12] Cf. T. Scanlon, *What we Owe Each Other* (Cambridge, Mass.: Belknap Press, 1998), 70, and 382 n. 61.   [13] Cf. M. DePaul, *Balance and Refinement*.

both obtaining full empirical information and reasoning logically. Such a naturalistic view of individual good is often then combined with a similar view of moral rightness. For example, some have claimed that rightness is sometimes determined by the desires that an empirically informed and impartially benevolent observer would have. Alternatively, a naturalistic account of rightness might point to the code of norms that most empirically informed but otherwise normal people would want to be accepted by the society in which they had to live the rest of their lives.[14] These are forms of moral naturalism that advertise themselves as eschewing moral intuitions.

The problem with such forms of naturalism is that their attractive aspects are heavily outweighed by their counter-intuitive implications. Take first this sort of naturalism's desire-fulfilment account of individual good.[15] The problem is that, even after exposure to logic and all the relevant empirical facts, people might desire truly bizarre things—such as saucers of mud, or counting every blade of grass in the lawns on this street, etc. Such examples seem to me to render implausible the above naturalistic account of individual good.[16]

Consider now the naturalistic accounts of rightness I outlined above. First, if these naturalistic accounts of rightness depend upon implausible naturalistic accounts of individual good, then these naturalistic accounts of rightness will be unacceptable too. Second, quite apart from infection by the naturalistic accounts of goodness, both the two naturalistic accounts of moral rightness I mentioned have implausible implications. Ideal observer accounts of moral rightness have a strong tendency to yield act-utilitarianism, a theory with notoriously counter-intuitive implications. And the Brandtian focus on codes that most people (who know the relevant empirical facts and are thinking logically) would want for their society seems too relativistic.

So far I have been discussing forms of naturalism that try to eschew appeal to intuitions. I have suggested that they end up with counter-intuitive

---

[14] The sort of view I have in mind here is Richard Brandt's, as expounded in pt. 2 of his *A Theory of the Good and the Right* (Oxford: Clarendon Press, 1979).

[15] Brandt himself vacillated on whether a hedonistic account or a desire-fulfilment account of individual good is best for moral theory. Compare his *Theory of the Good and the Right*, ch. 8, with his *Facts, Values, and Morality* (New York: Cambridge University Press, 1996), 35–49. But given that it is a natural fact that people desire more for themselves than pleasure, I take it that the more natural position for naturalism is the desire-fulfilment theory.

[16] For some recent objections along these lines, see R. Crisp, *Mill on Utilitarianism* (London: Routledge, 1997); Audi, *Moral Knowledge and Ethical Character* (New York: Oxford University Press, 1997), 77 and 78.

implications. Other forms of naturalism, in contrast, hold that moral theorizing must begin with (rather than try to eschew) moral intuitions, and that moral judgements should be construed as referring to the natural properties picked out by the ultimately best moral theory.[17] Moral rightness would be constituted by these natural properties. This seems to me the best sort of naturalistic theory. It not only is compatible with intuitionism but also is really a form of intuitionism.

Turn now to non-cognitivism. Many non-cognitivists have wanted to attack intuitions. Think of Smart, Hare, Peter Singer, and Gibbard.[18] But there is no way to read these moral philosophers as completely turning their back on non-inferential first-order beliefs (or attitudes). On the contrary, they are often at their best when they are showing that their views are not as counter-intuitive as one might at first think.

A main problem for non-cognitivists is the question of mind-independence. If non-cognitivism claims that the universe really contains only non-evaluative natural properties in reaction to which we have various attitudes, then presumably non-cognitivists hold that there aren't *really* any evaluative properties for moral judgements to ascribe. But now what if everyone's attitudes change—for the worse? Suppose everyone went to sleep being against torturing animals for fun and woke up being in favour of torturing animals for fun. Non-cognitivists reply that it is a normative, or first-order, issue whether torturing animals would be morally right in a world in which no one disapproves of this.[19] Non-cognitivism is a second-order, meta-ethical view,

---

[17] Outlines of such a theory of moral value can be found in Nicholas Sturgeon's paper in this volume (Ch. 8). Cf. N. L. Sturgeon, 'Moral Explanations', in David Copp and David Zimmerman (eds.), *Morality, Reason, and Truth: New Essays on the Foundations of Ethics* (Totowa, NJ: Rowman & Littlefield, 1985); R. Boyd, 'How to be a Moral Realist', in G. Sayre-McCord (ed.), *Essays on Moral Realism* (Ithaca, NY: Cornell University Press, 1988); D. Brink, *Moral Realism and the Foundations of Ethics* (Cambridge: Cambridge University Press, 1989), chs. 2 and 6; F. Jackson, *From Metaphysics to Ethics* (Oxford: Clarendon Press, 1999), chs. 5 and 6. Some of these naturalists hold that their thorough coherentism rules out any place for non-inferentially justified beliefs. These naturalists nevertheless accord weight to systems of normative beliefs. This view is often thought of as minimally intuitionist.

[18] J. J. C Smart, 'Outline of a Utilitarian Ethics', in J. J. C. Smart and B. Williams, *Utilitarianism: For and Against* (Cambridge: Cambridge University Press, 1973); R. M. Hare, *The Language of Morals* (Oxford: Clarendon Press, 1952); *Freedom and Reason* (Oxford: Clarendon Press, 1963); *Moral Thinking* (Oxford: Clarendon Press, 1981); P. Singer, *Practical Ethics* (Cambridge: Cambridge University Press, 1979); A. Gibbard, *Wise Choices, Apt Feelings: A Theory of Normative Judgment* (Oxford: Clarendon Press, 1990). Contrast Simon Blackburn's *Ruling Passions: A Theory of Practical Reason* (Oxford: Clarendon Press, 1998), where making sense of intuitive reactions is much more explicitly and comprehensively embraced.

[19] See S. Blackburn, 'Rule-Following and Moral Realism', in S. Holtzman and C. Leich (eds.), *Wittgenstein: To Follow a Rule* (London: Routledge & Kegan Paul, 1981), 179; *Spreading the Word*

and, claim most non-cognitivists, does not entail the first-order, normative view that torturing animals is wrong only if people disapprove of it. Non-cognitivists claim their theory does nothing to prevent them from thinking that torturing animals is wrong whether or not anyone continues to disapprove of it.

Non-cognitivists had better be right about that. For if they aren't, their theory has a fatally counter-intuitive first-order implication, namely that torturing animals would become morally permissible if human attitudes changed. So, for the sake of argument, suppose non-cognitivists are right that their theory can accept that whether certain things are or would be morally permissible is completely independent of actual human attitudes. Then perhaps their theory does not have counter-intuitive implications about what is morally permissible and what is not.

Indeed, in so far as non-cognitivists try to make sure their theory has no counter-intuitive first-order implications, they are developing it in a way that I think is compatible with intuitionism. Certainly, non-cognitivists often seem to be seeking equilibrium between the moral attitudes they have at different levels of generality. At least some of the attitudes they are juggling are independently compelling, i.e. not merely on the basis of an inference from other attitudes. In according normative weight to those non-inferentially based attitudes, non-cognitivists look very like intuitionists.

(Second-Order) intuitions about (First-Order) Moral Theories

Some of the intuitions we have are about what constitutes benefit or harm to individuals. Some of our intuitions are about what is required, permitted, or supererogatory; some are about what natural facts are morally relevant, and how they are morally relevant. Some of these are more specific, and others less. I shall come back to these later. But first let me focus on the intuitions I think we have about moral theories:

(1) A moral theory cannot be correct unless it is internally consistent.
(2) A moral theory is better justified to us to the extent that it accords with the independently credible intuitions we have after careful reflection—including intuitions about what facts are morally

(Oxford: Clarendon Press, 1984), 217–19; 'Errors and the Phenomenology of Value', in T. Honderich (ed.), *Morality and Objectivity*, (London: Routledge & Kegan Paul, 1985), 6; *Ruling Passions*, 74 and 307.

relevant and about what is right overall when moral considerations conflict.

(3) Other things being at least roughly equal, a moral theory is better to the extent that it specifies a fundamental principle that not only underlies more specific moral truths, but also, ideally, provides impartial justification for them.

(4) Other things being at least roughly equal, a moral theory is better to the extent that it helps us deal with moral questions about which we are not confident, or do not agree.

(5) Other things being at least roughly equal, a moral theory is better to the extent that it starts from attractive general beliefs about morality.[20]

No one will deny that moral theories must be internally consistent (i.e. must satisfy (1) above). And I take it that all currently popular moral theories are internally consistent, as (1) demands. Unfortunately, many people deny that the moral theory I myself think best, i.e. rule-consequentialism, is internally consistent. But this is not the place to revisit that battle.[21]

Those who use the term 'moral intuition' without contempt will typically endorse (2) above. What is it for theory to accord with considered moral convictions? The standard way theories try to do this is by specifying intuitively plausible general principles from which the truth of our considered convictions can be derived.

But a theory can try to accord with considered convictions without trying to specify general principles. Consider moral particularism, according to which there really are no general principles compatible with the truth of all our considered moral convictions. Defenders of particularism think that the convictions we would have after careful consideration would be about particular cases only. Defenders of particularism also think their theory accords with all these convictions, in the sense that it concurs with them. So let us say that a moral theory accords with our considered moral convictions if it specifies general principles entailing the truth of these convictions, or if it merely concurs with the convictions.

The hard part in moral theorizing is not finding a theory that satisfies (2). The hard thing to do is to find a moral theory that, in addition to satisfying (2),

---

[20] I am grateful to Dale Miller for discussion of this point.

[21] See my 'Rule-Consequentialism, Incoherence, Fairness', *Proceedings of the Aristotelian Society*, 95 (1995), 19–35, esp. p. 29; my 'Ross-Style Pluralism versus Rule-Consequentialism', *Mind*, 105 (1996), 531–52, esp. pp. 538–9; and my *Ideal Code, Real World: A Rule-Consequentialist Theory of Morality* (Oxford: Clarendon Press, 2000), sect. 4.3.

articulates an underlying principle supporting all the other principles, ideally from an impartial point of view (that is, satisfies my (3)). In defence of (3), let me merely assert that the live question seems to me not whether, other things being equal, unity and simplicity in a theory are advantages.[22] The live question is, rather, how much weight to attach to unity and simplicity when other things are not equal. I also think fundamental impartiality is widely seen as desirable in a moral theory, if such impartiality does not then make implausible demands. I think few would deny that the features picked out by (1) and (2) are essential, and that the features picked out by (3), (4), and (5) are advantages.

Our Most Confident First-Order Moral Convictions are not the Most General Ones

Moral convictions come at many levels of generality. Some very general beliefs are very attractive, but they point in different directions. Furthermore, very general moral beliefs do not seem to be the moral beliefs in which we have most confidence.

Consider, for example, the Golden Rule 'Do unto others as you would have them do unto you'. I've regularly witnessed non-philosophers who have espoused this principle for decades nevertheless come to accept that it is mistaken within twenty seconds of hearing one of the textbook counter-examples to it. One such counter-example to the Golden Rule is that it is absurdly demanding. Joe, who is well-off, would like other well-off people to give him all their money. Since he would like well-off people to give him all their money, the Golden Rule seems to require him to give all his money to them! But, no matter what the Golden Rule says, no one really believes that morality really requires him to give all his money to the well-off.[23]

Another common criticism of the Golden Rule is that it is ambiguous. On one interpretation, the Golden Rule says:

> Morality requires us to do unto others as we would have them do unto us if we found ourselves in their position with our own tastes and preferences (and, perhaps, ideals).

---

[22] But such simplicity might be implausible if it implies that there are no deep moral dilemmas. Such simplicity needn't have this implication. See my 'Rule-Consequentialism, Incoherence, Fairness', 21.

[23] This example comes from Jeffrey Olen and Vincent Barry's Introduction to their *Applying Ethics* (Belmont, Calif.: Wadsworth, 1985), 9.

On the other interpretation, the Golden Rule says:

> Morality requires us to do unto others as we would have them do unto us if we found ourselves in their position with their tastes and preferences (and ideals).

The problem is that, whichever interpretation we choose, we can think of striking counter-examples to the Golden Rule. These counter-examples illustrate at least three further points. First, my treating you as I would like to be treated can be morally wrong when you have tastes and preferences different from mine (as noted by G. B. Shaw[24]). Second, my treating you as you would like to be treated can be morally wrong when you have evil preferences.[25] Third, my treating you as you would like to be treated can be morally wrong when my satisfying your innocent preferences happens to preclude my doing something else of greater moral importance—such as telling the truth, or keeping a promise, or helping someone else with more urgent needs.

As I said, I have been struck by how quickly non-philosophers will give up some cherished very general principle of morality when they are shown clear examples of its counter-intuitive implications. By 'give up' I do not mean to preclude attempts to revise the general principle so as to remove conflict with intuitions about specific kinds of cases. Certainly, most moral philosophers will try to amend a more general moral view in order to accommodate recalcitrant more specific intuitions.[26] But my general point here is that the very general principle is rejected or revised so as to fit with more specific intuitions.

Are Particular Moral Judgements Primary?

Well, if the most general moral beliefs are less secure than more particular ones, are moral beliefs about particular cases primary? General principles are certainly an important part of moral education. Particularists must admit this, since it would hardly be helpful to start off children's moral education by telling them that what matters morally depends always only on

---

[24] App. to *Man and Superman* (Westminster: Constable, 1903), 227.

[25] A point Sidgwick noted (*The Methods of Ethics*, 380).

[26] A recent example is Scanlon's shrinking of contractualism from a theory of the whole of morality to a theory of 'what we owe each other'.

the particular circumstances. Of course children start off learning about morality by learning general principles. They are told not to do 'that'— where the 'that' means not merely this act on this particular occasion, but this kind of act. Parents typically teach their children by saying such things as 'lying is bad', not 'lying is bad on this particular occasion'.

And children are grateful for general rules, as opposed to merely a series of particular prescriptions. Children naturally want to learn the general features marking off the acts that anger (or please) the powerful. They want rules so that they know what to expect.

Sometimes moral particularists say moral principles are really just indications of the way a fact can count morally. This seems an especially weak answer if conjoined with the thesis, which some particularists assert, that any fact can be morally relevant. True, children need to learn which facts can be relevant. But they understandably hope this is some (relatively small) subset of all possible facts. Moreover, ideally what they want to know is which facts are relevant in which kinds of case. They want to know, that is, some general principles.

Still, there is an argument we can imagine being put by particularists in favour of their view. This particularist argument starts with the claim that we have knowledge, in the first place, of how features of prospective actions count morally in particular situations.[27] For example, I see that, in the particular case I am considering, the fact that a certain act would keep my promise counts morally in favour of this action. I come to the same conclusion in a number of other cases. Reflection on these particular cases leads me to the general rule that the fact that an act would constitute keeping the agent's informed, uncoerced, morally permissible promise counts always morally in the act's favour. But if we can always see what is important in particular cases without reference to general rules, what use are general rules?

Furthermore, what authority could rules have as against dissenting intuitions? Suppose I now come across a new case about which I have the intuition that the fact that an act would keep my promise does not seem to count at all in its favour in this case. How could the rule favouring keeping the agent's informed, uncoerced, morally permissible promises have more authority than my conflicting intuition about the particular case? After all,

---

[27] This particularist foundation for moral epistemology appears in Ross, *The Right and the Good*, 33; *The Foundations of Ethics*, 168–71. While Ross was a generalist about moral pros and cons, his particularist epistemology has understandably been seized upon by Dancy. See Dancy's 'An Ethic of Prima Facie Duties', in P. Singer (ed.), *A Companion to Ethics* (Oxford: Blackwell, 1991), 225–6, 228; and his *Moral Reasons* (Oxford: Blackwell, 1993), 93–5.

the general rule was itself in effect merely a leap from the intuitions I had had about a string of previous cases.

In *The Right and the Good*, Ross wrote,

We find by experience that this couple of matches and that couple make four matches, that this couple of balls on a wire and that couple make four balls: and by reflection on these and similar discoveries we come to see that it is of the nature of two and two to make four. In a precisely similar way, we see the prima facie rightness of an act which would be the fulfilment of a particular promise, and of another which would be the fulfilment of another promise, and when we have reached sufficient maturity to think in general terms, we apprehend prima facie rightness to belong to the nature of any fulfilment of promise. What comes first in time is the apprehension of the self-evident prima facie rightness of an individual act of a particular type. From this we come by reflection to apprehend the self-evident general principle of prima facie duty.[28]

Note the stress at the beginning of this passage on finding out things 'by experience'. And note that near the end of the passage Ross specifies that the particular judgement 'comes first in time'.

Dancy observes that Ross's account of moral knowledge is 'essentially empiricist'.[29] Surely the general climate of respect for empiricism plus the acknowledged influence of H. A. Prichard persuaded many to hold that we apprehend particular moral truths before general ones. E. F. Carritt and C. D. Broad affirm almost the same thing about this as Ross does. For example, Carritt wrote,

I cannot persuade myself that I first morally apprehend the obligation of several rules, then intellectually apprehend one of alternative actions to be an instance of one and the other of another, and finally, by a second moral intuition, see which rule ought now to be followed. I rather think that I morally apprehend that I ought now to do this act and then intellectually generalize rules.[30]

Carritt's claim is merely autobiographical. The claim might be mistaken. Even if it is not, why think it of more than biographical interest? Is Carritt suggesting that this is the route others must also follow?

Ross offered a speculative story about human history. In *The Foundations of Ethics* he wrote,

We must suppose that when a certain degree of mental maturity had been reached, and a certain amount of attention had been . . . focused on acts which had hitherto been

---

[28] *The Right and the Good*, 32–3. [29] *Moral Reasons*, 94.
[30] E. F. Carritt, *The Theory of Morals* (London: Oxford University Press, 1930), 116. See Broad, *Five Types of Ethical Theory*, 271–2. Cf. J. Dancy, *Contemporary Epistemology* (Oxford: Blackwell, 1985), 220–1.

done without any thought of their rightness, they came to be recognized, first rather vaguely as suitable to the situation, and then, with more urgency, as called for by the situation. Thus first, as belonging to particular acts in virtue of a particular character they possessed, was rightness recognized. . . . the general principle was later recognized by intuitive induction as being implied in the judgements already passed on particular acts.[31]

This reduces to the claim that the first individuals to reach general principles must have already reached particular judgements. But why think this claim true, unless one thinks a general empiricism supports it? Even if, as a matter of historical fact, the first moral judgers did indeed make particular moral judgements before they espoused any general moral principle, why think this is more than a temporal contingency?

Virtually everyone after the first moral judges, I take it, learned general moral principles before making particular moral judgements. Again, children start off being told 'lying is bad', not merely 'lying on this particular occasion is bad'. The general principle is internalized before any particular judgements are made. But, again, this is merely temporal priority.

So, are particular judgements 'epistemically prior' to general moral judgements in some non-temporal sense? Consider these two propositions:

(Par)   That an act would keep one's informed, uncoerced, morally permissible promise is *in this case* a moral consideration in favour of one's doing the act.

and

(Gen)   That an act would keep one's informed, uncoerced, morally permissible promise is always a moral consideration in favour of one's doing the act.

There need be no logical error in believing (Par) while not believing (Gen), but there must be a logical mistake in believing (Gen) while denying (Par). Yet one can believe (Gen) while failing to believe (Par) because one has never considered (Par). Normally, one believes general truths without getting round to considering every individual particular truth that follows from them.

I cannot see how the arguments from Ross quoted above force us to the conclusion that our only, or best, access to moral truth is via the particular case. Acquisition of moral knowledge may begin with acquisition of beliefs about how certain properties count in certain kinds of case. These would be general moral beliefs, not particular ones. We can agree, I think, that sometimes more

---

[31] Ross, *The Foundations of Ethics*, 170.

specific truths are easier to discover than more general ones. Often, however, we have no intuition about what to do in a particular situation, except in so far as we see how some general moral principle of ours bears on the situation.

I will now try to list the moral intuitions in which I think we have greatest confidence after we have reflected carefully. These intuitions are general rather than particular. But they are not so general as such propositions as the Golden Rule, the categorical imperative, an act-consequentialist principle, or a contractualist account of moral wrongness. So let me refer to the intuitions I am about to list as 'fairly general'. If I am correct that we have these fairly general intuitions, then particularism does not accord with our beliefs.

Our Most Confident First-Order Moral Convictions are Ross-Style General Principles

The moral beliefs in which we have most confidence seem to me to take the form normally associated with Ross's list of 'prima facie duties'. A list of these beliefs might begin:

(A) That an act would kill or hurt someone is a strong moral consideration against doing it.

Do we need some exception clauses here? What about killing someone with that person's consent and when death is better for that person than continued life? I myself accept that euthanasia is sometimes right. But I also accept that in such cases there is a moral consideration against killing that needs to be outweighed. Another possible exception concerns cases where killing someone is the only way to prevent that person from intentionally harming someone else. Again, I agree that it can be morally right, all things considered, to kill or physically injure someone when this really is the only way to prevent that person from physically attacking innocent people. But, again in these cases, there seems to me to be a moral reason not to do this, albeit a reason that is outweighed in the circumstances.

Now consider:

(B) That an act would involve harming or taking someone else's property is a strong moral consideration against doing it.

Unlike (A), (B) requires little further comment.

A principle which will require further comment is the following:

(C) That an act would break your promise is a moral consideration against doing it (unless the promise was to do something immoral, or the promise was extracted from you via deception or via a threat of infringing someone's moral rights).

I assume here that once the promisee has released you from a promise, you can still keep it, and perhaps even ought to, but the moral force of the promise is greatly weakened, if not extinguished entirely. Likewise, the promise is extinguished if it becomes impossible to fulfil through no fault of the promisor. (Suppose you promise to help me paint my house on Saturday but it burns down before then.)

Are there any cases in which the fact that a particular act is the only way to keep your promise is not a moral consideration in favour of doing that act, although (i) the promise was morally innocent, (ii) the promise was not extracted by deception or by immoral threats, (iii) the promise has not become impossible to fulfil, and (iv) the promisee has not indicated that the promise is cancelled? Adapting O. Henry's short story, suppose I promise to buy expensive combs for a friend for her birthday in a few months, but she then loses all her hair between the date I made the promise and the birthday.[32] Does the fact that I made the promise give me any moral reason to buy the combs, once she has lost her hair? Of course I have a moral reason not to give her combs, namely that this would remind her of what she has lost. But is there nonetheless a (perhaps weaker) moral reason to give them to her in order to keep my promise?

If a promise is implicit by conditional, then the promise dies when the condition is not met. One condition that promisees often seek is that the promise is to be kept only if the promisee still wants it kept when the time comes.

To be sure, there are some kinds of case in which promisees do not want this condition. We may desire something to happen at a later time in our lives whether or not our present desire persists then. So we might seek a promise from someone to make sure that it will happen at that later time whether or not we then still have the same preference. Ulysses gets his crew to promise not to release him from the mast when they sail near the Sirens even though he will be screaming to be released then.

There are other kinds of case where the promise sought contains no condition that the promisee's desires persist. I might ask you for a promise to look after my sister after my death, though I believe none of my desires will persist beyond my demise. Indeed, presumably all promises to people about

---

[32] I am grateful to Gerald Dworkin for raising this objection.

what will happen after they are dead are to be taken as not conditional on their desires persisting beyond their deaths.

The presumption is different with promises about what will happen during the promisee's lifetime. Here, the default presumption must be that the promisee wants the promise to be conditional on his or her still wanting the promise to be kept when the time comes. Unless the promisee indicates otherwise when the promise is made, we are to assume the promisee seeks a promise that is conditional on the promisee's wanting the promise kept when the time comes.

Return now to my promise to buy combs for my friend. The default presumption is that, at the time I made the promise, she wanted me to buy combs for her birthday if but only if, when her birthday draws near, she still wants them. Once her hair has fallen out, I am extremely confident she does not want me to buy combs for her. (Given what I already confidently believe, I think it would be cruel even to ask her whether she still wants combs.) In this case, my promise exerts no moral pressure on me to buy her combs. But cases of this kind present no counter-example to my principle about promising above. We merely need to remember how promises are normally implicitly conditional on the persistence of the promisee's desires. If for some reason she did still want the promise kept, then there would be the *pro tanto* reason for me to buy the combs.

There are other complexities. What about a case where the promisee still wants the promise kept but we think keeping the promise would be very bad for her (because of changed conditions which she might not know about, or might know about while still making a mistake about her interests)? If on 13 March I promise you that I will do *x* on the 4 August, is this promise implicitly conditional on my believing on 4 August that my keeping the promise will achieve your ends? Promises are not normally conditional in this way. Even if I believe that keeping my promise to you will not be good for you, the fact that I made this promise is a moral consideration in favour of doing what I promised (unless you no longer want me to keep the promise). There might nevertheless be stronger moral reasons not to keep the promise—such as that my keeping the promise would harm you badly.[33]

---

[33] Some other complications are discussed in my 'Moral Particularism: Wrong and Bad', in B. Hooker and M. Little (eds.), *Moral Particularism* (Oxford: Clarendon Press, 2000). See Sidgwick, *The Methods of Ethics*, 305–11; H. L. A. Hart, *The Concept of Law* (Oxford: Clarendon Press, 1961), 192–3; C. Fried, *Contract as Promise* (Cambridge, Mass.: Harvard University Press, 1981), esp. ch. 7; Thomson, *The Realm of Rights*, ch. 12; Scanlon, *What we Owe Each Other*, ch. 7.

Let us turn now to:

(D) That an act would constitute lying is a moral consideration against doing it (except perhaps when there is a mutual agreement to try to deceive one another, as in games of bluff).

Ross held that the duty to tell the truth is derived from the more basic duty of fidelity, or perhaps the duty of fidelity and the duty not to harm others. If every declarative sentence (except those in jokes, fiction, and games of bluff) rides on the back of an implicit promise to try to tell the truth, then what is wrong with lying is that it breaks an implicit promise. I do not myself believe that there are always (outside jokes, fiction, and games of bluff) implicit promises to tell the truth. Perhaps there always should be such implicit promises, but if so then this might be because there is a *pro tanto* duty to tell the truth.

I now move to three further principles:

(E) That an act would promote justice is a moral consideration in favour of doing it.
(F) That an act would involve using your own resources to benefit someone with whom you have a special connection is a moral consideration in favour of doing it. (Those with whom you have special connections include not only family members and friends, but also those who have voluntarily helped you and those whom you have wronged.)
(G) That an act would benefit an innocent sentient being is a moral consideration in favour of doing it.

The principles (A)–(G) are not all exactly Ross's own principles. So I shall refer to them as Ross-style principles.

We could add other principles to the list above, but none I think we would be so confident about as the ones already listed. To mention just one possible addition, we might cite a 'duty to yourself':

(H) That an act would benefit you is a moral consideration in favour of your doing it.

Self-interest supplies reason to benefit yourself. But does morality also always generate some direct reason to benefit yourself? I think it does not. Assume you are choosing between x and y. If x would be more beneficial to you, then self-interest of course favours your choosing x. But suppose that, while x would be most beneficial to you, your choice would not affect anyone else.

Suppose you then choose y. Would your doing this be condemned by morality, because x would have benefited you more? I cannot believe that it would. Morality does not require you to do always what is best for yourself when others are not affected.

Another problem with the duty to yourself (H) is the existence of an asymmetry much emphasized by Michael Slote.[34] We typically think that it is not immoral to sacrifice something for yourself in order to benefit someone else, even when the cost to yourself is greater than the benefit to the other person. This is difficult to square with the idea of a moral duty to promote your own good.

But if there is not some such moral duty to yourself, how can we keep the moral duty to benefit others from usurping all your time and attention? Some philosophers have argued that you have the option or prerogative to pursue your own projects even when doing something else would benefit others more. The idea of a prerogative or option seems to me right. The difficulty is specifying just where the line is between the requirement to do good for others and the option to promote your own projects. Here is the formulation I tentatively think best:

(G*) That an act would benefit an innocent sentient being is a moral consideration in favour of doing it. But, apart from cases where the fate of humanity is at stake, morality cannot require you to sacrifice, for the sake of benefiting those to whom you have no special connection, more than a substantial amount in aggregate over the course of your whole life.[35] In addition, morality cannot require you to make a sacrifice, for the sake of benefiting someone to whom you have no special connection, when the benefit to the other person would be only slightly more than the loss to yourself.

Admittedly, (G*) does not seem on a par with the other Ross-style principles. I certainly would not suggest that (G*) is intuitively obvious, much less widely espoused! On the contrary, one of the things that is particularly unsettled now is where the limits of morality lie. My point here is not that we will find (G*) compelling, or indeed even familiar. My point is

---

[34] See e.g. M. Slote, *From Morality to Virtue* (New York: Oxford University Press, 1992), 13–17.

[35] As far as I know, the first person to defend in print a principle about aggregative rather than iterative sacrifice was Garrett Cullity. See his 'Moral Character and the Iteration Problem', *Utilitas*, 7 (1995), 293–5; see also Scanlon, *What we Owe Each Other*, 224. Let me add that 'those to whom you have no special connection' do not include those to whom you have made a relevant promise.

rather that (A)–(G) will be implausibly demanding unless either (A)–(G) are supplemented by (H), or (G) is replaced by (G*).

The list (A)–(G*) may need its principles fine-tuned. The list may need whole new principles added. It will certainly need lots of interpretation. Nevertheless, I think that the fairly general principles (A)–(G*), or something quite like them, are the normative moral ideas in which we have most confidence upon due reflection.

The principles (A)–(G*) are framed in terms of considerations in favour of or against—or, as we might say, moral pros and cons. But we can infer from (A)–(G*) many verdicts about what is, all things considered, morally right. Suppose, for example, that I could benefit you right now at absolutely no cost to anyone else, including me. Suppose also that I could not help anyone else (or any set of people) more right now than I could help you. In addition, suppose I have made no promises to anyone that helping you now would break. And suppose my helping you would not involve misrepresenting the truth. Further, suppose you are a meritorious person, indeed someone whose level of well-being is below her level of desert, in which case I would promote justice by raising your level of well-being closer to the level you deserve. Hence, here we have a case in which every moral consideration either favours my helping you or is silent.[36] In this case, clearly my helping you would be not only *pro tanto* good but downright right, overall.

How important is the verdict about this case? It generalizes to every case where the duties to benefit others and to promote justice favour an act that no other moral consideration opposes.

We can reach similar general verdicts with the other items in the list (A)–(G*). In any case in which some of these moral considerations favour one possible action over others and other moral considerations neither oppose that action nor favour some alternative action, then that action is morally right, overall.

This must be true in lots of cases. Often I can benefit someone when no alternative at the time would better serve any of (A)–(G) above and would cost me nothing (so (H) is irrelevant here). For example, I am about to walk up the three flights of stairs beside you when I notice you are carrying heavy bags. I could save you some pain and strain by sharing your load with you. The benefit to me of the exercise I would get out of helping you

---

[36] Here I am rejecting an incautious claim of Ross's. He wrote, 'moral acts . . . always . . . have different characteristics that tend to make them at the same time prima facie right and prima facie wrong; there is probably no act, for instance, which does good to any one without doing harm to some one else, and vice versa' (*The Right and the Good*, 33–4).

would cancel out the cost to me of the slight pain I would get at the time. Thus, on balance, helping you is no net sacrifice for me at all. Furthermore, I have not made any promise that my helping you will break. And I do not at this particular point in time have the opportunity to devote my energies to helping someone with whom I have some closer connection. And so on such that in this case, while there is a moral consideration in favour of helping you, there is none against. Or suppose I have too much food with me on the train. You are hungry for precisely the kind of food of which I have more than I want. I could give you my extra or throw it away. Or suppose I could steal or vandalize property without any benefit to anyone. In all such cases, i.e. when there is no conflict between moral considerations, the morally right thing to do is clear.

But what about cases where moral considerations conflict? To take one of Ross's own examples, suppose my keeping my promise to you would benefit you slightly less than my breaking my promise to you would benefit someone else.[37] Now suppose that the other considerations (i.e. (A), (B), (D)–(F*)) are silent or cancel one another out. Then my breaking my promise to you would be morally wrong because here (C) outweighs (G*).

To take another example, suppose my physically harming one person would somehow result in a small net gain in utility. Suppose further that the other considerations (i.e. (B)–(F*)) are silent or cancel one another out. In every case with these features, harming the person is morally wrong.

To be sure, there is enormous scope for interpretation in applying the Ross-style principles (A)–(G*). For example, even if we know a large amount of well-being is more important than a minor promise, there will be questions about what counts as a large amount of well-being and what counts as a minor promise. Such questions can be extremely difficult. Whether a given concept applies may be indeterminate or at least unknowable. This may even be true of the concept 'the act supported by the most important of the conflicting moral considerations in this case'.

Still, although our moral knowledge is limited, we shouldn't lose sight of its extent.

- We have what I am calling Ross-style principles about what counts morally in favour of an action and what counts morally against.
- We also have the general principle that, whenever at least some of these principles favour one alternative and none is against it, that alternative is morally right.

---

[37] Ibid., 34–5.

- And we also have general principles about some kinds of case where moral considerations conflict.

We have quite a lot that counts as general moral knowledge.

The Relation between Ross–Style Principles and Proposed even more General, Underlying Principles

I turn now from the relation between Ross-style general principles and particular judgements to the relation between Ross-style principles and the most general principles that might be thought to serve as the single foundational principle. Rule-consequentialism, contractualism, the Golden Rule, Aristotle's doctrine of the mean, and other conceptions have each been put forward from time to time as the single foundational principle of morality. Yet we have more confidence in the set of Ross-style principles than in any such proposed single principle. To see this, consider potential conflicts between such single principles and the principles (A)–(G*). Then see which we find most compelling.

A great deal of normative ethics has consisted in just this sort of reasoning. We have the general act-consequentialist idea that it cannot be wrong to do what produces the most good. Then someone asks us to consider the class of cases in which breaking a promise would produce only a tiny amount more good overall, and would benefit someone other than the promisee, and in which other moral considerations are silent or cancel one another out. Or we embarrass certain forms of contractualism by pointing to the class of cases in which someone could save some animal from excruciating pain without incurring any cost to any human.

I've tried to suggest the epistemological priority that Ross-style principles have in my intuition (2):

(2) A moral theory is better justified to us to the extent that it accords with the independently credible intuitions we have after careful reflection.

Contrast the strength of (2) with (3):

(3) Other things being at least roughly equal, a moral theory is better to the extent that it specifies a fundamental principle that not only underlies more specific moral truths, but also, ideally, provides impartial justification for them.

It may turn out that no theory whose implications accord with considered first-order moral convictions is able to specify some single principle that can ground our Ross-style principles. In this case, what I've been calling the Ross-style principles are, as Ross contends, the foundational principles of morality. And, in this case, the moral convictions in which we have most confidence and thus are the starting point for our moral epistemology turn out to be the foundation of our normative ethics.

But of course epistemic priority (order of discovery) can part company with explanatory priority (order of explanation).[38] Our theory of physical reality starts from our confidently held beliefs about 'mid-sized dry goods' but takes us to beliefs about an underlying level of molecules and atoms and subatomic properties. Likewise, our epistemological route into morality could be at a level that turns out not to be the most fundamental.[39] It could be in ethics that what we are most confident about, namely the Ross-style general principles, do indeed turn out to be foundational, because there is not any single deeper principle underlying and unifying them. As I see it, the most exciting research programme in moral philosophy is to see whether, on the contrary, there is some deeper unifying principle. Part of what makes this research programme so exciting is that we cannot prejudge that there is something there to find, or that there is not.[40]

---

[38] John Cottingham pointed out to me that Descartes noted this distinction in his 'Conversation with Burman' (1648). See *Œuvres de Descartes*, ed. C. Adam and P. Tannery (Paris: Vrin/CNRS, 1964–76), v. 153; or *The Philosophical Writings of Descartes*, III, ed. J. Cottingham, R. Stoothof, D. Murdoch, and A. Kenny (Cambridge: Cambridge University Press, 1991), 338.

[39] This is a theme of David Brink's superb 'Common Sense and First Principles in Sidgwick's Methods', *Social Philosophy and Policy*, 11 (1994), 179–201.

[40] But consider an argument for thinking that there is no more fundamental principle underlying the Ross-style duties. This is an argument against contractualism, rule-consequentialism, and most other moral theories. The argument is that propositions stating Rossian *pro tanto* duties are necessary truths, but any supposed deeper principle underlying these duties would have to maintain that they are only contingent. I reply to that argument in the final two sections of 'Reflective Equilibrium and Rule Consequentialism', in B. Hooker, E. Mason, and D. Miller (eds.), *Morality, Rules and Consequences* (Edinburgh: Edinburgh University Press, 2000).

Ethical Intuitionism and Ethical Naturalism

8

Nicholas L. Sturgeon

I

It is common for philosophers discussing ethical issues to appeal to what they freely call intuitions—their own and, they hope, their audience's—about real or imagined cases. Only rarely do they treat such intuitions as indefeasible: typically, they are prepared to play off intuitions against one another, revising or abandoning some for the sake of a more coherent theoretical picture, deferring also to the perceived plausibility of various general principles, themselves treated as defeasible and approximate. Is this procedure ever a way of actually justifying a moral belief, or of coming to know something? In my view the answer is yes, on both counts.

Does this answer make me an ethical intuitionist? That will depend on what we understand by ethical intuitionism, a complex topic as we shall see. We can make this question more pointed if we recall some of the doctrines often gathered under the intuitionist banner, either by defenders or opponents, and recall also the regard in which many of these doctrines have been held during the last half-century of analytic metaethics. For William Frankena was only speaking for many when he noted in 1963 that intuitionism, with its commitment, as he saw it, to 'simple properties . . . of a peculiar non-natural sort, [to] a priori or non-empirical concepts, intuition, self-evident or synthetic necessary propositions, and so on' was, as he temperately

I am grateful for helpful discussion at the University of Keele conference on Re-evaluating Ethical Intuitionism, held on 3–5 June 1999, and subsequently at Union College; the University of California, San Diego; the University of California, Los Angeles; the University of California, Riverside; and California State University, San Bernardino. I have also benefited from extensive comments from Richard Boyd and from Pekka Väyrynen.

put it, 'hard to defend in the present climate of opinion'.[1] So we might ask: Does my answer commit me to any of *these* things—and, if it did, would that be sufficient to refute it? It is not hard to find writers who will think that the answer to both these questions is yes. The procedure I have described is, generically, just John Rawls's method of reflective equilibrium.[2] But R. M. Hare has labeled Rawls, for advocating this method, an ethical intuitionist, making clear that by intuitionism he understands the thesis that we possess a 'special faculty' for discerning synthetic moral truths a priori.[3] Nor is Hare alone in his suspicion that reliance on any method like Rawls's would require an intuitionism committed to at least some of the tenets on Frankena's list, and suspect for that reason.[4]

My position is unlikely to look any better to these critics when we turn from examples in which we form moral impressions of cases considered in thought to ones in which we confront them before our eyes. In seeing some action take place, can we ever just see that it is wrong? As part of a larger argument for moral nihilism, the view that there are no moral facts, Gilbert Harman once claimed that we cannot: at least, not really, and not in any way that would provide moral knowledge.[5] In my own earlier discussions of Harman's argument I put this question about observation to one side because I did not think (and still do not think) that an affirmative answer to it is required in order to respond to his deeper challenge, which questions the supposed explanatory relevance of moral facts.[6] But once that deeper

---

[1] W. K. Frankena, *Ethics* (Englewood Cliffs, NJ: Prentice-Hall, 1963), 86–7. Verdicts in this fashion are not entirely a relic of times past. Allan Gibbard has written more recently, about an intuitionist view he calls 'Platonist', that 'it is not strong in ordinary thought. To the naïve ear, the claims of Platonism sound fantastic: their appeal comes chiefly from a lack of anything to put in their place' (*Wise Choices, Apt Feelings: A Theory of Normative Judgment* (Cambridge, Mass.: Harvard University Press, 1990), 154). And Stephen Darwall suggests that 'when we . . . try to think philosophically about what ethics and ethical judgment can be, we—along with many philosophers—may find intuitionism simply incredible' (*Philosophical Ethics* (Boulder, Colo.: Westview Press, 1998), 54).

[2] J. Rawls, *A Theory of Justice* (Cambridge, Mass.: Harvard University Press, 1971), 46–53.

[3] R. M. Hare, *Moral Thinking* (Oxford: Clarendon Press, 1981), 75–8.

[4] See e.g. P. Singer, 'Sidgwick and Reflective Equilibrium', *Monist*, 58 (1974), 490–517, and R. B. Brandt, *A Theory of the Good and the Right* (Oxford: Clarendon Press, 1979), 18–20.

[5] G. Harman, *The Nature of Morality* (New York: Oxford University Press, 1977), 3–9. The qualifications are needed because Harman does allow that there are 'moral observations,' but only in the sense of moral judgments made 'immediately and without conscious reasoning' (p. 7); they need not be true and they are not, on the argument of these pages, instances of knowledge.

[6] N. L. Sturgeon, 'Moral Explanations', in David Copp and David Zimmerman (eds.), *Morality, Reason, and Truth: New Essays on the Foundations of Ethics* (Totowa, NJ: Rowman & Allanheld, 1985); repr. in G. Sayre-McCord (ed.), *Essays on Moral Realism* (Ithaca, NY: Cornell University Press, 1988). Also N. L. Sturgeon, 'Harman on Moral Explanations of Natural Facts', *Southern Journal of Philosophy*, 24, suppl. (1986), 69–78.

challenge is met, then it does seem to me obvious that there can be moral observations. As Harman himself puts it, in describing what we might be tempted to think: 'If you round a corner and see a group of young hoodlums pour gasoline on a cat and ignite it, you do not need to *conclude* that what they are doing is wrong; you do not need to figure anything out; you can *see* that it is wrong.'[7] But this description seems to me, as I suspect it does to many readers, just about right; and I would take seeing the action to be wrong to be a way of knowing that it was wrong.

Of course, the two-part suspicion to which I have been referring—that they are committed to ethical intuitionism, and that this spells their doom—has been applied to views far less intuitionist-sounding than mine. John Mackie, for example, claims that 'the central thesis of intuitionism is one to which any objectivist view of values is in the end committed: intuitionism merely makes unpalatably plain what other forms of objectivism wrap up'.[8] I have dwelt on the details of my own position, however, partly to show why Mackie might well think that I have not even done a good job of 'wrapping up' its intuitionist implications, but even more to add interest to what I propose to say in its defense. For I do not think that my views on moral epistemology in fact commit me to anything unpalatable, or to anything that ought to prove impossible to defend in a reasonable climate of philosophical opinion.

Since the suspicion I am responding to comes in two parts, I could elaborate my defense in either of two ways. I could deny that I am committed to intuitionism. Or I could admit to being an intuitionist, but argue that intuitionism need not commit one to anything so very implausible. Now, in fact, my preferred response is the former of these. My position is a version of ethical naturalism. On a common understanding that would make my choice an easy one, for intuitionism and naturalism have often been taken to be opposed almost by definition, either because intuitionism is understood to come with a metaphysical component, a commitment to nonnatural properties,[9] or because naturalism is thought to have an epistemological one, the denial of an *is-ought* gap. I shall question both of these

---

[7] Harman, *The Nature of Morality*, 4.

[8] J. L. Mackie, *Ethics: Inventing Right and Wrong* (Harmondsworth: Penguin, 1977), 38.

[9] Beyond Frankena's entirely typical characterization, one can note that to find a discussion of intuitionism in Richard B. Brandt's *Ethical Theory* (Englewood Cliffs, NJ: Prentice-Hall, 1959) one has to go to a chapter called 'Nonnatural Properties'. A recent defender of intuitionism who thinks it is not tied to the nonnatural is Robert Audi, in 'Intuitionism, Pluralism, and the Foundations of Ethics', in Audi, *Moral Knowledge and Ethical Character* (New York: Oxford University Press, 1997), 64 n. 46.

common understandings. Still, I shall claim that my view is not a version of intuitionism. Part of my project in this paper is to explain why it isn't, despite its accommodating moral observations and what we call ethical intuitions. I shall also explain why I think that the features that distinguish it from intuitionism are reasons for preferring it.

My discussion would be seriously incomplete, however, if it did not also consider replies in the second style, that hold that a view can be intuitionist and none the worse for it. For although I shall argue that there are in the end good reasons not to be an intuitionist, I am also sure that intuitionism need not be implausible in all the ways that Frankena and a chorus of others have alleged. This is partly because some of the features he associates with that doctrine may not be as indefensible as he supposes. A more recent climate of philosophical opinion looks more kindly on synthetic necessary truths, for example, even if not on a priori knowledge of them, than did the one to which Frankena refers. But it is also because intuitionism may not be committed anyway to all the doctrines that he lists. I see no reason why an intuitionist must believe in simple ethical properties, or even in a distinction between simple and complex properties. The question of whether an intuitionist must believe in nonnatural properties—a commitment that I as an ethical naturalist would agree with Frankena in finding implausible—is moreover a more complex one than commonly supposed. I take intuitionism to be primarily an epistemological position, one that holds at its core that we possess some genuinely noninferential ethical knowledge (and noninferentially warranted ethical beliefs). And despite the important historical links between this epistemology and a metaphysics of the nonnatural, my verdict will be that an intuitionist could dodge this commitment—though only, I shall suggest, by incurring a different sort of cost. Similar, though simpler, doubts can also be raised about other alleged commitments on lists like Frankena's—for example, to a special faculty of ethical intuition,[10] or to intuited truths that can be

---

[10] I suppose that this must be what Frankena means in putting 'intuition' on his list; it is otherwise hardly news that intuitionists believe in it. One might distinguish here the question whether there is a special faculty from the question whether there is an infallible one. G. E. Moore denies that there is a faculty of ethical intuition on the grounds that any way in which we can 'cognize' a true proposition is also a way in which we can cognize a false one (*Principia Ethica*, rev. edn., ed. Thomas Baldwin (Cambridge: Cambridge University Press, 1993), 36); A. C. Ewing makes a similar disclaimer (*Ethics*. New York: Free Press, 1953), 122). This bears on the question of whether there is an infallible faculty but not on whether there is a topic-specific one. One might note that, like synthetic necessary truths, dedicated modular faculties are back in fashion; but rational intuitionists (W. D. Ross, more recently Audi in 'Intuitionism, Pluralism, and the Foundations of Ethics') disown this commitment as well.

known *only* by intuition.[11] Clearly, then, there is no way for me to weigh the plausibility of my own position against an intuitionist one without considering the extent to which intuitionism can escape charges like these.[12] So that is another task for my discussion.

I should say how I am understanding the question of what a doctrine such as intuitionism is committed to. I am not just concerned with what the doctrine entails, but, more dialectically, with what one would have to believe in order to give the doctrine its best defense or, at any rate, a plausible defense. Thus, to take an extreme example, and from an opponent rather than a defender of intuitionism, I think that for all his emphasis Mackie leaves it less than clear exactly why he believes that any objectivist position about values must be committed to intuitionism. But his words suggest some intimate connection between this epistemological liability (as he counts it) of objectivism and a corresponding metaphysical difficulty: that, as he argues, objective values would have to be impossibly weird or 'queer' entities. And on the simplest reading—I come to a subtler one below—he takes objectivism to be committed to intuitionism because he does not see how knowledge of anything that weird could be obtained in any other way.[13] Of course, this is not a very plausible inference: twentieth-century physics has supplied us amply with weird objects, but neither Mackie nor most others have thought that knowledge of these things would have to be noninferential.[14] Still, imagine a defender of objective

---

[11] Moore is emphatic that intuited ethical truths have this property (*Principia Ethica*, 34). Audi disagrees, in 'Intuitionism, Pluralism, and the Foundations of Ethics', 47. A. C. Ewing says that 'even if what presents itself intuitively cannot be proved or disproved, inference may be used to cast doubt on it or partially to confirm it' (*Ethics*, 116).

[12] I shall not address here every charge that has been raised against intuitionism, however. One that must await another occasion is from Paul Edwards: 'Intuitionism and, more generally, all forms of non-naturalism from Plato to Ross, have fundamentally had one and only one purpose: to help support the morality of self-denial and sin . . . the moralities of the fuddy-duddies and sourpusses' (*The Logic of Moral Discourse* (New York: Free Press, 1955), 240).

[13] Mackie suggests such a connection when he summarizes the two parts of his 'argument from queerness' in successive sentences: 'If there were objective values, they would be entities or qualities or relations of a very strange sort, utterly different from anything else in the universe. Correspondingly, if we were aware of them, it would have to be by some special faculty of moral perception, utterly different from our ordinary ways of knowing anything else' (Mackie, *Ethics*, 38). David Brink is one writer who, quite understandably, adopts what I call the simplest reading of this passage: *Moral Realism and the Foundations of Ethics* (Cambridge: Cambridge University Press, 1989), 180.

[14] Nor does Mackie help his case by using Plato's forms to illustrate how strange objective values would have to be, since—even if forms are strange, itself a disputed issue—there are plausible readings of Plato as a coherentist who thinks that knowledge of the forms is gained through dialectic rather than by intuition. See e.g. G. Fine, 'Knowledge and Belief in Republic V–VII', in

values who is convinced by Mackie that they must be metaphysically weird, and who agrees that for this reason they must be known by intuition. Then that intuitionist would certainly be committed to metaphysically mysterious entities; and if that were the only plausible defense of intuitionism available I would have to take intuitionism itself to be committed to metaphysical mysteries. In fact, however, I am sure that there are other routes to intuitionism far more plausible than this one; and, as I have said, I think that the question of whether they require anything metaphysically mysterious is a complex one. Therefore, in my view, the question of intuitionism's metaphysical commitments is equally complex. I shall consider it in detail below.

II

What are the other arguments for intuitionism, then? There are several, and among them, to be sure, are some that would import the sort of features about which some critics are so dismissive. In *Principia Ethica*, for example, the only argument that G. E. Moore actually offers for his intuitionism, almost as an aside, derives that view entirely from his first-chapter conclusion that intrinsic goodness is simple: relying, it appears, on the principle, which he never states, that all knowledge of simple properties must be non-inferential.[15] Any proponent of this argument would of course have to agree that there are simple ethical properties.

Any route to intuitionism that goes by way of the alleged simplicity of goodness or of some other ethical property would have to be highly contentious, however.[16] That is one reason why I propose to focus instead on a

---

S. Everson (ed.), *Companions to Ancient Thought*, i: *Epistemology* (Cambridge: Cambridge University Press, 1990), ch. 5.

[15] The argument occupies one sentence in §46: 'Of any answer to *this* question [namely, of what things or qualities are good] no direct proof is possible, and that, just because, of our former answer, as to the meaning of good, direct proof *was* possible.' The 'former answer' has just been summarized as the thesis 'that "good is indefinable", and that to deny this involves a fallacy'. Strictly speaking, Moore's inference relies not just on the principle stated in the text, but also on his unquestioned assumption that we do know things about intrinsic goodness.

[16] If the claim that a property is simple is understood as a metaphysical one, then (*a*) there will be dispute about whether we know what this means, and (*b*) there will in any case be doubts about whether thought experiments like Moore's open question argument (*Principia*, §13) can establish any such metaphysical conclusion. If the claim is instead really about the *concept* of the property (as seems more appropriate if the implication is to be an epistemological one), to the effect that it lacks a certain sort of analytic definition, then doubt will shift to the unstated epistemological principle. For, following the work of Kripke and Putnam, it has been widely held that natural kind concepts,

different and probably more familiar argument, with premises that would be far more widely accepted. I think of it as the standard argument for intuitionism, partly because it has clearly influenced most intuitionist writers, partly because even those who (like Moore) take a different route to the doctrine nevertheless accept its premises.[17] The argument has mattered not just for its influence on intuitionists, moreover, but for its role in the thinking of their critics. For it is a valid argument, which means that anyone who wants to reject intuitionism will have to deny one of its premises; and, on the natural way of dividing the premises, the choice of which to deny becomes a choice among the major alternatives to intuitionism in metaethics. Consideration of the argument thus proves useful for sorting out the premises, along with the critics of intuitionism who would deny them, as well as for seeing what that doctrine might commit its proponents to. Since I am one of the critics, this will also help me locate my own view with respect to familiar alternatives.

On that natural division of the premises, there are three of them. (1) The most important, in my view, but the one least often thought to require explicit statement, is foundationalism about knowledge and justified belief. These are different topics, but it will simplify my exposition to formulate it as a doctrine about knowledge: the application to justification will be parallel, and I shall return below to some separate issues it may raise. I understand foundationalism, then, to comprise two claims: first, that all knowledge we have of truths must either be based by reasonable inference on other things we know, or else be based on no inference at all; and, second, that if we have any knowledge of the first sort, the kind based on inference, that knowledge must all ultimately be based entirely on knowledge of the second sort, on the things we know without inference. (2) The second premise, which by contrast with the first is usually the one most emphasized, is what is often called the autonomy of ethics: the thesis that from entirely nonethical premises there is no reasonable inference to any ethical conclusion. From these two premises there is a quick argument that, if we have any ethical knowledge at all, then some of that knowledge must be

---

for example, lack analytic definitions; but it is not plausible that our knowledge of natural kinds must be noninferential.

[17] Moore clearly accepts the first and third premises of the argument, foundationalism and the view that there is moral knowledge. And although he does not argue for his intuitionism by appeal to the autonomy of ethics, he does believe that ethics is autonomous. For he holds (*a*) that there are only two sorts of ethical propositions, (*b*) that there are no proofs whatever of the first sort, and (*c*) that proofs of the second sort must include premises of the first sort. *Principia Ethica*, 34.

noninferential. For if we have any ethical knowledge based on inference, that knowledge (according to foundationalism) must ultimately be based, by reasonable inference, entirely on things we know without inference; and (according to the autonomy of ethics) some of that noninferential knowledge must be ethical. If we then add our third premise, (3) that we do have some ethical knowledge, it follows that some of that knowledge must be noninferential—that is, that the core thesis of ethical intuitionism is true.[18]

One benefit of bringing this argument to the fore is that thinking about it can throw light not only on its conclusion but on its premises. The thesis that ethics is autonomous, for example, owes its philosophical interest entirely to its role in this standard argument and in closely related arguments in moral epistemology. But it has often been debated in isolation, and in ways that leave it unclear exactly how large a gap between *is* and *ought* its proponents mean to assert or its critics to deny. The proponents clearly mean at least that no *ought* can be *deduced* from an *is*, but it is often less clear whether they mean to claim more.[19] Should they mean more? If they intend their thesis to figure in the standard argument, there is a straightforward answer: namely, that this will depend on what they believe about another large issue in epistemology. For any version of foundationalism—indeed, virtually any epistemological theory, foundationalist or not—will recognize certain kinds of inference as knowledge-generating, as ones by which someone may base new knowledge on things already known. In formulating foundationalism,

[18] It is by now standard to explain the route to intuitionism in approximately these terms. See e.g. W. Sinnott-Armstrong, 'Intuitionism', in L. C. Becker (ed.), *The Encyclopedia of Ethics*, (New York: Garland, 1992), i: 628–30, and R. L. Frazier, 'Intuitionism in Ethics', in E. Craig (ed.), *Routledge Encyclopedia of Philosophy*, (London: Routledge, 1998), iv: 853–6, as well as my 'Metaphysics and Epistemology', in Becker (ed.), *The Encyclopedia of Ethics*, i: 798–804, and my 'Naturalism in Ethics' in Craig (ed.), *Routledge Encyclopedia of Philosophy*, vi. 713–17. Although the argument clearly influences intuitionist writers, as I shall show, it is surprisingly hard to find a clear statement of it with no premises suppressed. See, however, H. Sidgwick, *The Methods of Ethics*, 7th edn. (Chicago: University of Chicago Press, 1962), 98, and Ewing, *Ethics*, 119–20.

[19] Hare's vindication in *The Language of Morals* (Oxford: Clarendon Press, 1952) of 'Hume's celebrated observation on the impossibility of deducing an "ought"-proposition from a series of "is"-propositions' (p. 29) is a prominent example of a discussion that focuses entirely on whether ethical conclusions are ever entailed by nonethical premises. Hare has never supplemented this highly influential argument with an explanation of how it might extend to inferences other than entailments (even if it is true that the extension could somehow be made). A. J. Ayer's discussion in *Language, Truth, and Logic* 2nd. edn. (London: Gollancz, 1946), ch. VI, is incomplete in a different way. Adapting Moore's open question argument, Ayer argues that ethical and nonethical terms are never synonymous; this does duty as his entire argument that ethical propositions are unverifiable by inference. But although Ayer explicitly recognizes weak (that is, nondeductive) as well as strong verification (ch. I), he provides no explanation of how this argument is to apply even to all deductive inferences, let alone to nondeductive ones.

Nicholas L. Sturgeon

I have called these 'reasonable' inferences. And as my corresponding word-
ing indicates, what the autonomy of ethics has to deny, for the standard
argument to be valid, is that any of *these* inferences, the reasonable inferences, ever leads from entirely nonethical premises to an ethical conclusion.
Thus, if only deductive arguments can be reasonable, it will suffice for a version of the autonomy of ethics to deny that an *ought* can be deduced from an
is.[20] If, however, as many believe, other forms of inference can also generate
knowledge (for example, inference to the best explanation), then the doctrine will have to cover them, too. I do not believe that this point has ever
been entirely lost from view in debates about moral epistemology, but neither has it always been emphasized when it matters. I shall return to it below.

Perhaps an even more interesting feature of this argument, for our purposes, is that although its premises are controversial, none of them is at all
crazy. The first two, foundationalism and the autonomy of ethics, continue
to have sophisticated, even tough-minded defenders. Some of the tough-
minded seem to have more qualms about ethical knowledge. But all I mean
to be noting here is that, however it may have been in the climate of opinion
of which Frankena wrote, skeptics who deny such knowledge now standardly acknowledge the considerable attractions of the view they oppose:
they acknowledge, for example, that failure on their part to construct a reasonable facsimile, some form of 'quasi-knowledge', would significantly
compromise their own position. And it is far from clear that any such facsimile is available.[21] So the three premises can certainly look reasonable

[20] One legitimate reason why some discussions of the autonomy of ethics have focused on
deductive inference, is that there are recognized technical problems in formulating the doctrine for
such inferences so as to avoid trivial counterexamples. The earliest mention I know of this problem
is in J. G. Kemeny and P. Oppenheim, 'On Reduction', *Philosophical Studies*, 7 (1956), 18 n. 5. Their
brief diagnosis anticipates the more complex ones in, for example, A. N. Prior, 'The Autonomy of
Ethics', *Australasian Journal of Philosophy*, 38 (1960), 199–206; D. R. Kurtzman, ' "Is," "Ought," and
the Autonomy of Ethics', *Philosophical Review*, 79 (1970), 493–509; and F. Jackson, 'Defining the
Autonomy of Ethics', *Philosophical Review*, 83 (1974), 88–96. If nondeductive inference were better
understood, we might see a similar need to refine the doctrine for that topic; I am assuming that, as
in the case of deductive inference, a philosophically interesting version would survive.

When I speak in the text of the autonomy of ethics, I mean an appropriately qualified version.
This means that in the standard argument the third premise must also be modified correspondingly.
We might call the inferences from nonethical premises to ethical conclusions that an appropriately
modified autonomy of ethics would allow 'the trivial exceptions'. Then the third premise will say
that we possess ethical knowledge beyond any that could be inferred from nonethical premises just
by way of the trivial exceptions. These qualifications will matter again when I speak, below, of other
areas of thought being autonomous; but for ease of exposition I leave them understood in the text.

[21] See e.g. S. Blackburn, *Spreading the Word* (Oxford: Clarendon Press, 1984) and *Essays in
Quasi-Realism* (New York: Oxford University Press, 1993); and Gibbard, *Wise Choices, Apt Feelings*.
I have criticized Blackburn's proposals in 'What Difference does it Make whether Moral Realism

enough taken individually. That does not of course guarantee that it would be reasonable to combine them. But it does, I think, leave an intuitionist in a good position to ask exactly what it is that would make the resulting position so questionable.

For, such an intuitionist might well note, it is at least at first glance unclear what there is in the standard argument to commit a proponent to any of the eyebrow-raising features associated with intuitionism by Frankena and others. Thus, on the epistemological side, there is no implication that intuitive ethical knowledge must be of a uniform subject matter—all about intrinsic goodness, for example, or prima facie duties—or that it must be obtained by a special faculty. To be sure, there are some epistemological implications worth noting, that I think are important for understanding intuitionism, but they are not ones that critics have normally singled out in rejecting the doctrine. For the standard argument implies not just that we possess noninferential ethical knowledge, but also that such knowledge is required as a (partial) foundation for any other ethical knowledge we may have. If intuitionism were just the thesis that we have some intuitive ethical knowledge, then it might be combined with a denial of the autonomy of ethics, and even with a concession that we might have got all our ethical knowledge just by inference from nonethical facts instead; or with a denial of foundationalism, and so with the concession, not just that any given piece of ethical knowledge that we have by intuition, we might have had by inference instead—a possibility the standard argument *does* leave open—but that we might instead have possessed *only* ethical knowledge based on inference. By including foundationalism and the autonomy of ethics among its premises, the standard argument precludes these possibilities. It seems a measure of the influence of the standard argument, moreover, that these possibilities, and the corresponding concessions, are not ones to which any intuitionist writers have been attracted. We might want, therefore, to build their rejection into the definition of intuitionism. I shall at any rate speak of *standard* intuitionism as precluding them.[22]

Of course, more embarrassing epistemological commitments might emerge from a more specific version of the premises. For example, if the best version of foundationalism turned out to require all noninferential knowledge to be of truths not knowable in any other way, then an intuitionism

is True?', *Southern Journal of Philosophy*, 24, suppl. (1986), 115–41, and in 'Contents and Causes: A Reply to Blackburn', *Philosophical Studies*, 61 (1991), 19–37. For Gibbard, see my critical study of *Wise Choices, Apt Feelings*, *Noûs*, 29 (1995), 402–24.

[22] This is an important point that I failed to mention in the two surveys cited in n. 18.

backed by the standard argument would have to require the same of intuitive ethical knowledge. However, since it seems a strength, not a weakness,
of recent versions of foundationalism to allow that truths known noninferentially might also be known by inference, it seems unlikely that an intuitionist could be held to such a commitment.

When we turn to metaphysical commitments the situation becomes both
more complicated and more interesting. For, on the one hand, the premises of the standard argument are entirely epistemological; they say nothing
at all about metaphysics. On the other hand, metaphysical commitments
might still emerge if they were needed to establish one or more of the
premises. I doubt that there could be trouble of this sort from the direction
of foundationalism. Someone might of course hold, though I think not
plausibly, that the best version of foundationalism would have to require all
noninferential knowledge to be of simple properties.[23] There might be
more plausibility, however, and at least as much historical resonance, in the
suggestion, about the autonomy of ethics, that it has to be understood as a
doctrine laden with metaphysics. For it might be maintained that the only
reasons for believing this doctrine are also reasons for thinking that there
would have to be an ontological divide between the subject matter of any
nonethical premises and that of any ethical conclusion, between the realms
of (nonethical) fact and of value.

This is a suggestion we need to explore seriously, but we should distinguish a simpler from a more complex version. A simple version might focus
just on the distinction between the two realms and, in a fashion familiar
from Mackie, on the alleged mysteriousness of that of value. But I doubt
that this could by itself look like the best defense of the autonomy of ethics:
for one thing, as a general principle, that the mysterious cannot be inferred
from the mundane seems no more plausible than the epistemic principle we
were tempted to ascribe to Mackie above, that the mysterious can only be
known by intuition. A more complex proposal, however, and one requiring
more attention, might also serve as a more charitable reading of that claim
of Mackie's, that any objectivist about value must be an intuitionist. For it
seems to me entirely possible that Mackie's reason for making this charge
lies simply in the standard argument. On this suggestion, he takes the first
two premises, foundationalism and the autonomy of ethics, to be so obvious as not to need stating; and if an objectivist then supplies the third
premise, that there is ethical knowledge, the objectivist must in his view be

---

[23] This would be the converse of the principle on which Moore appears to rely; see n. 15.

at least an implicit intuitionist. But, on this reading, what becomes of the link Mackie apparently sees with the metaphysical costs of objectivism? That would come, I now suggest, in the understood rationale for thinking ethics autonomous. For that would just be the idea, familiar from Hume and especially influential among noncognitivists, that it is distinctive of ethical thought to be intrinsically action-guiding, and that, as Hume remarks, 'an active principle can never be founded on an inactive'.[24] This principle, which we may call the internalist rationale, is not in itself metaphysical, and in the hands of either a noncognitivist or an error theorist would have no untoward metaphysical implications. But if it is combined, as by an objectivist, with the thesis that there is ethical knowledge, and hence that there are ethical truths, then it appears to require the instantiation of ethical properties that would have to be intrinsically action-guiding—a kind of property that Mackie of course finds exceedingly strange.

And not only Mackie. For whether or not this is the best reading of Mackie—a point on which I remain uncertain—it surely identifies what has become a common reason, among other writers, for thinking ethical intuitionism committed to something metaphysically doubtful. These writers could be wrong. It could be a mistake to think that properties represented by an intrinsically action-guiding mode of thought would have to be intrinsically action-guiding properties. Or it could be that that action-guiding properties can after all be natural properties. Assumptions to the contrary are plausible enough, though, and widely enough held, to make it an interesting question what would follow if they were correct, that is, if the internalist rationale really did commit an intuitionist to nonnatural properties.[25] For the purposes of my discussion, therefore, I shall assume that the

---

[24] D. Hume, *A Treatise of Human Nature*, 2nd edn., ed. L. A. Selby-Bigge, rev. P. H. Nidditch (Oxford: Clarendon Press, 1978), 457. For the record, I doubt that this remark represents Hume's own best, considered reason for believing in an *is–ought* gap (as he says he does at the conclusion of this section). I consider this issue in 'Moral Skepticism and Moral Naturalism in Hume's *Treatise*', *Hume Studies*, 27 (Apr. 2001), 3–83.

[25] I am here eliding a distinction that for some purposes might matter a great deal. Moore distinguishes the ethical property of intrinsic goodness both from natural properties and from 'metaphysical' or supernatural ones. (See *Principia Ethica*, §25. 'Metaphysics' he characterizes as aimed at 'giving us such knowledge as can be supported by reasons, of that supersensible reality of which religion professes to give us a fuller knowledge, without any reasons'; §66.) So his nonnatural properties are not supernatural any more than they are natural. Mackie, however, despite his praise for Moore's insight into the failure of ethical naturalism, apparently thinks there would be no difficulty in identifying ethical properties with supernatural properties, like Plato's forms, if there were any such properties; his objection to ethical naturalism, unlike Moore's, is that ethical properties would have to be supernatural. I really ought to say, therefore, that our question is whether intuitionism is committed to either supernatural or nonnatural properties. That is clumsy, however; and since my

internalist rationale does carry this cost; my question is then whether an intuitionist can find an alternative rationale for thinking ethics autonomous.

A glance at the early twentieth-century intuitionists might suggest that there is an easy answer. For why not put the internalist rationale to one side and defend the autonomy of ethics just by appeal to Moore's open question argument, to establish that there are no synonymies or analytic equivalences between ethical and nonethical terms? One worry about this proposal, for our purposes, is that the historical intuitionists, who were fond of Moore's argument, thought that it *also* showed, when conjoined with the view that we possess ethical knowledge, that ethical properties must be nonnatural. If that were right, this alternative defense would be no help when our interest is precisely in seeing whether intuitionism might be freed from a commitment to the nonnatural. I am confident, however, that on this point the historical intuitionists were wrong: from the fact that two terms are not synonyms it does not follow that they represent different properties, still less that one of them represents something nonnatural. A more telling worry about this proposal derives, however, from a point I mentioned above, that any version of the autonomy of ethics that is to function in the standard argument must rule out, not just some inferences from nonethical premises to ethical conclusions, but all reasonable inferences that threaten to cross this line. This is a serious problem for the proposal that we just rely on Moore, because it is not plausible that the only reasonable inferences we make are ones that depend on synonymy between terms in the premises and the conclusion. There is no obvious route from the denial of synonymies between ethical and nonethical terms, for example, to the verdict that in no reasonable inference to an explanation could the conclusion be ethical and the premises not. The intuitionist needs a defense of the autonomy of ethics that is not limited in this way;[26] and, in addition, we are assuming, would benefit from one that would not force her into a nonnaturalist metaphysics.

Is there a rationale for the autonomy of ethics that meets these specifications? My answer is, cautiously, that there may be. What I am sure of is that

---

sole concern here is with whether intuitionism conflicts with naturalism, which as I understand it rejects both the supernatural and the nonnatural, I shall convenience just use 'nonnatural' for any property that is not natural.

[26] Of course, the internalist rationale too has been discussed in detail only (as by Hare) for cases in which some nonethical premise is alleged to entail an ethical conclusion: see n. 19. But it at least gestures at a general difference between ethical and nonethical claims that might perhaps be developed into a rationale for a general ban on inferences to the latter solely from the former.

there is a plausible alternative rationale for believing in the autonomy of ethics, that extends to all reasonable inferences, and makes the internalist rationale I have cited quite unnecessary. My caution, for reasons I shall explain, is about how easily available this alternative rationale really is to the intuitionist. If an intuitionist can use it, that will be good news for the intuitionist. But even if it is not available to the intuitionist, it will be good news that it is available to me. For my own version of ethical objectivism, though as I have said not a form of intuitionism, is like intuitionism in affirming both that ethics is autonomous and that we have ethical knowledge—just the combination of views that threatens to force the intuitionist into nonnaturalism. So this problem is not *uniquely* a problem for intuitionism; I need a reply to it too.

III

I can best explain my view, including my way around this challenge, by locating it among the alternatives to intuitionism. And, as I have suggested, a helpful way of laying out those alternatives is to catalogue their ways of rejecting the standard argument for that doctrine. Thus, an ethical skeptic will obviously reject the final premise, that there is ethical knowledge. It is common for skeptics to be quite happy about the argument up to that step, however, and indeed to rely on it. For the first step of the argument, as we saw, relies on foundationalism and the autonomy of ethics to force a choice between skepticism and intuitionism. A familiar skeptical strategy has been to follow the argument this far, but then to argue for skepticism by rejecting intuitionism.[27] Whether intuitionism can be rejected quite as easily as the adherents of this strategy often suppose is of course one of the questions we are now considering.

Another familiar alternative is to deny the autonomy of ethics. Until quite recently this option has often been presented as the only nonskeptical

---

[27] With the foundationalism left entirely implicit, this variation of the standard argument can be found in chs. 2 and 3 of Hare's *The Language of Morals*. Ch. 2 affirms that no 'ought' can be derived from an 'is', and ch. 3 argues that no 'Cartesian' (that is, intuitionist) procedure is available for ethics. With the epistemology closer to the surface, but with the thesis that ethics is autonomous replaced merely by the claim that ethical terms lack analytic naturalistic definitions, the argument is also in ch. 6 of Ayer's *Language, Truth, and Logic*. What I above called the 'charitable reading' of Mackie's charge that any ethical objectivist must be an intuitionist attributes the same argument to him. (On that reading, the argument is almost entirely implicit, of course.)

alternative to intuitionism: a mistake, but an understandable one, as a glance at the standard argument will confirm, for anyone taking foundationalism for granted. The resulting position has standardly been called ethical naturalism. There seem to me more than one reason for finding this usage unfortunate, but the one I want to emphasize here is that it seems too narrow.[28] For I think of the most interesting form of ethical naturalism as primarily a metaphysical doctrine, not tied to a specific epistemology. It holds that there are ethical facts and that they are entirely natural facts; as a nonskeptical view it also says that we can gain knowledge of these facts, but it is compatible with a variety of views about how we do this. My own adherence to this metaphysical view is either what explains, or else what is explained by, my suspicion of nonnatural ethical properties, and my consequent interest in whether there is a form of intuitionism that can avoid them. If there is, then it would be possible on the understanding I am proposing for a metaethical view to be at once naturalist and intuitionist. My own preference, as I have said, would be to conjoin this metaphysics with an epistemology that is not intuitionist, but which agrees with intuitionism in honoring the autonomy of ethics.

Although my definition ties ethical naturalism to no one epistemology, there is still an obvious epistemological constraint that any version must meet. This is, speaking generally, that its account of ethical knowledge should fit with a plausible overall epistemology; and, more specifically, that since it says that ethical facts are natural facts, its account of how we know ethical facts ought to look a lot like its story about how we know other natural facts. This constraint is vague but not without content; though, of course, different writers will apply it differently, depending on their other

---

[28] It is also too broad. For, if we are to infer *oughts* from *is's*, the candidate *is's* can include premises about supposed theological facts as well as about natural ones—remarks, as Hume says, about 'the being of a God' as well as 'observations about human affairs' (*A Treatise of Human Nature*, 469). And, however interesting the question of whether ethics could be founded on a religious metaphysics, if such a view were correct, that does not seem to me a question about the prospects for ethical *naturalism*, which I take to hold at a minimum that we must find a place for ethics in a purely natural world.

This broad usage traces to Moore, who, despite being explicitly aware of the distinction between viewing goodness as a natural property and viewing it as a 'metaphysical' one, thought the difference dialectically unimportant because both views rest on the same generic mistake, which he calls 'the naturalistic fallacy' in both applications (*Principia Ethica*, §25). To my knowledge he never refers to metaphysical ethical views themselves as naturalistic. But it is certainly under Moore's inspiration that C. D. Broad takes the further step of calling theological theories of ethics naturalistic (*Five Types of Ethical Theory* (London: Routledge & Kegan Paul, 1930), 259) and it is with explicit reference to Moore that Hare does so (*The Language of Morals*, 82).

views about epistemology and especially about our knowledge of the natural world. Indeed, the best reason I can offer for defining naturalism in this primarily metaphysical fashion is that we can then see how writers with very different epistemological views, but all respecting this constraint, could end up attributing such different epistemological commitments to a single doctrine, some of them taking it to deny the autonomy of ethics while others, like me, see it as perfectly compatible with that doctrine.

Consider, then, two representative philosophers, one a critic of naturalism and the other a proponent, who agree that it conflicts with the autonomy of ethics. Moore thinks in *Principia Ethica* that we have a simple a priori test for property identity. This is not just a doctrine about natural properties, but it applies to them. We could use it, for example, to address such apparently scientific questions as whether biological properties are simply chemical or physical ones: an affirmative answer would imply the a priori reducibility of biology to the latter disciplines. And if we thought the test reliable in that application, we would of course understand ethical naturalism to be making a claim that could be addressed in the same way, and thus as committed to denying the autonomy of ethics: indeed, as committed to the a priori reducibility of ethics to other naturalistic disciplines.[29]

Or, putting Moore to one side, consider the sort of view Philippa Foot once described as standard, and appeared to subscribe to herself, about how we settle questions of (natural) fact.[30] We do this, she says, by relying on standards of evidence that are fixed by the meanings of the terms used to frame the question. As her examples make clear, this means that if we have some description of an observation O, and some conclusion C, and we want to know whether O supports C (and if so, how much) all we need to know are the meanings of C and (presumably) O. If the answer is yes, then 'someone who went on questioning whether the evidence was evidence could eventually be shown to have made some linguistic mistake'.[31] We could liberalize this view a bit, while retaining its spirit, by tying standards of evidence less closely to linguistic

[29] As I have explained elsewhere ('Moral Explanations'), this oversimplifies. Even granting Moore his view that true property identities must be analytic, the view that ethical properties are natural will not promise an analytic reduction for ethics unless we also know that we have nonethical terms for all the natural properties there are. However, an exactly parallel point applies to the example about biology. So we can say that Moore's view makes it just as likely in the one case as in the other that a metaphysical reduction would require that there also be an analytic reduction.

[30] P. Foot, 'Moral Beliefs', in Foot *Virtues and Vices and Other Essays in Moral Philosophy* (Berkeley: University of California Press, 1978), 110–11. Foot here describes what she takes to be a standard contrast between questions of fact and questions of value, in order to reject it; but her criticisms of the distinction are all directed entirely at its account of questions of value. I am taking it, therefore, that she accepts its account of questions of fact. [31] Ibid. 110.

meaning: it will be enough if they are fixed by our concepts, and so accessible to us just by reflection, whether or not we have language to express all we think. But it should be clear that on a reasonable understanding this view has the implication that Foot intends: that if this is how we settle questions of natural fact, and if ethical naturalism is the view that ethical questions are questions of natural fact[32] and that we do sometimes settle such questions, then it has to say that ethics is not autonomous. For in that case there will be reasonable inferences, certifiable a priori, from our nonethical evidence to ethical conclusions.

By contrast, my own view is that both these pictures of how we know about the natural world are seriously mistaken. The objections to Moore are by now familiar and I have already alluded to them. It is highly doubtful that his supposed a priori test for property identities is reliable: too many plausible identifications fail the test. There is no reason, therefore, for understanding the ethical naturalist to be proposing reductive property identities (on the order of 'goodness = pleasure') that are intended to pass that test. And, consequently, there is also no reason for seeing the naturalist as proposing an analytic reduction for ethical discourse, or as challenging, in this way, the autonomy of ethics.

I also claim little originality for my criticism of the essentially verificationist account of confirmation endorsed by Foot. But since the problems with this view seem to be less often cited in the literature of metaethics, I have more excuse for elaborating. The main reason why questions about evidence cannot be answered just by understanding some fact and the conclusion for which it may or may not be evidence is that assessments of evidence are, as the jargon has it, theory-dependent. What this means is that in deciding, on the basis of some candidate piece of evidence, what to think about a specified conclusion, we typically find ourselves having to rely not just on our understanding of the fact and the conclusion but also on a large body of further assumptions, often so complex that we are unlikely to be able fully to articulate them. When our reasoning crosses one of those 'divides' that have animated philosophers' skeptical worries, moreover—for example, if it is scientific reasoning that proceeds from observed facts to a conclusion about something unobservable—then the additional assumptions we rely on

---

[32] Foot resolutely avoids formulating ethical naturalism in the metaphysical way I favor: it is never about facts or truths or properties, in her discussion, but about our practices of justification. But I believe that I here provide a fair translation into her idiom. (This counts of course as a modest qualification to my claim that we can see Moore, Foot, and me as all attaching different epistemological implications to the same doctrine.)

inevitably include some that concern the far side of the divide: in this case, further assumptions about unobservables. I would claim that the same is true when the divide comes in other familiar places: between present evidence and conclusions about the past, or present and past evidence and conclusions about the future, for example, as well as between observations of behavior and ascriptions of psychological states. As this last example suggests, there may be more controversy about some of these cases than others. But I think a strong case can be made that theory-dependence of this sort pervades our reasoning about the world.

There is, it should be clear, an equivalent way to put this conclusion: namely, that our thought about the natural world is highly populated by areas that are autonomous with respect to the evidence we bring to bear on them. If what I have said concerning reasoning about unobservables is correct, for example, then there is no reasonable inference to any conclusion about unobservables from premises that are entirely about observables.[33] This denial is not just about deductive inferences, or about inferences that depend on synonymous expressions appearing in the premises and conclusion, moreover; it covers all the standard patterns of nondeductive inference, since those are the ones whose theory-dependence it has been the most interesting to establish. That is why, if ethical thought dealt with natural facts, it would on the epistemology I have sketched be no surprise at all if ethics turned out to be an autonomous area of thought, in just the same sense. For it would simply be one more area in which our reasoning about evidence for natural facts has to be theory-dependent.

This is what I have had in mind in saying that there is a purely naturalistic rationale for believing in the autonomy of ethics. Obviously, by a rationale I don't mean a proof. I have no way of demonstrating that ethics, even with a naturalistic subject matter, could not have turned out to be an exception, a nonautonomous discipline. Nor have I quite offered an explanation: what I have suggested is just that the explanation for the autonomy of ethics is probably the same as the explanation for the autonomy of many other areas of thought. But even this limited point is dialectically important. For if the autonomy of ethics were an exceptional phenomenon, then it might require an exceptional explanation, such as, for example, the internalist one. This thought seems to have influenced Foot, for example: she appears to have agreed with her opponents that if ethics were autonomous, that fact would provide important support for internalism. Internalism is a complex

---

[33] With the same trivial exceptions that have to be allowed in the ethical case: see n. 20.

and difficult issue about which I have said almost nothing here. The only point I wish to make now is that, in a debate with the kind of ethical naturalism I have been describing, there is no form of internalism that gains any extra credibility from its promise to explain the otherwise puzzling fact that you can't derive an *ought* from an *is*. For there is no need to find that fact otherwise puzzling.

Is this naturalistic rationale for thinking ethics autonomous, which fits so nicely into a position like mine, also available to an ethical intuitionist? The answer is that it is—but only at a cost, for a reason we are in a good position to appreciate. For our intuitionist, or at least our standard intuitionist, is a foundationalist. And accepting this rationale for the autonomy of ethics requires seeing a number of areas of thought about the natural world as autonomous. But combining foundationalism with the view that a certain area of thought is autonomous forces a choice, with respect to that area, between skepticism and intuitionism.[34] We saw this in examining the standard argument, as applied to ethics: foundationalism, conjoined with the autonomy of ethics, forces a choice between ethical skepticism and ethical intuitionism. But nothing special about ethics mattered to that argument; it would work just as well for any area held to be autonomous. So, although an ethical intuitionist who adopted my suggested rationale for the autonomy of ethics would thereby have dodged some metaphysical commitments, she would at the same time have acquired some in epistemology. For unless she wants to be a skeptic about the past, the future, the unobservable, and a variety of other topics, she will have to be an intuitionist about them. That is, she will have to hold that we have, in each area, some noninferential knowledge, and that that noninferential knowledge serves as a necessary partial basis for everything else that, in that area, we know.

I call this commitment a cost because it seems to me not very plausible. I doubt that we have noninferential knowledge about, especially, the future or unobservables; I especially doubt that we have enough noninferential knowledge in these areas to provide a needed basis for all the rest we know. To be sure, it is true, with respect to scientific unobservables, that physicists value what they call physical intuition and accord it epistemic weight. So someone might claim that what they call intuition really is, or at least includes, noninferential knowledge about unobservable physical reality.

---

[34] Or, more precisely, between intuitionism, on the one hand, and, on the other, skepticism about all knowledge in the area beyond what can be inferred by way of the 'trivial exceptions'; see n. 20. I am taking it that, in every area, this would still amount to a very extensive skepticism.

But I find it more plausible to think that what is here called intuition is actually a product of inference in a broad but epistemologically well-motivated sense. Judgment here outruns the ability to articulate reasons; but we need some account of why the only people with physical intuition worth trusting are those with extensive knowledge of highly sophisticated, approximately true physical theory and a lot of experience in applying it. Indeed, to return to a question I raised at the beginning of this paper, my view of what philosophers call their ethical intuitions, when they rely on them in ethical discussion, is very similar. I think that these 'intuitions', too, are a product of inference in a broad but reasonable sense, that they tend to be most reliable when the background assumptions on which they rest are true, and that when they are well justified by their overall fit in one's beliefs, other beliefs can owe a great deal of their justification in turn to fitting well with them. One of the best reasons I have to offer for this view, moreover, follows a suggestion from Richard Boyd and simply points to the considerable similarity of what we call ethical intuition to physical intuition.[35] And, in offering this argument, I am of course assuming that it is implausible that physical intuition embodies genuine noninferential knowledge.

Perhaps these considerations are not decisive. An intuitionist might suggest that we turn from the discussion of knowledge to that of justification, which I have for convenience been leaving aside, although foundationalism can be formulated about both topics.[36] Justification comes in degrees: and an intuitionist might begin with the claim that some *part* of the justification of some of our most general beliefs, about, say, unobservable physical reality, is noninferential. This would be a hard claim to refute just going case by case, for we of course have many beliefs we regard as justified without being confident about the source of their justification.

I have not finished with my discussion of intuitionism, for I have some further points to urge against it. But I have now completed my discussion of a large preliminary question, which is whether intuitionism can simply be dismissed on the basis of the metaphysical and epistemological extravagances that are commonly charged against it. The easy part of my answer is that it is not committed to all of those normally listed. For example, I can see no reason why an intuitionist must believe in simple ethical properties, a dedicated ethical faculty, or ethical truths that can be known or justified

---

[35] R. Boyd, 'How to be a Moral Realist', in G. Sayre-McCord (ed.), *Essays on Moral Realism* (Ithaca, NY: Cornell University Press, 1988), 192–3, 206–8.

[36] The proposal, I assume, would include eventually returning to the topic of knowledge, since I am taking the intuitionist to be a foundationalist about both knowledge and justification.

only noninferentially. But on the question of whether intuitionism carries an implausible commitment to the nonnatural my answer is more complicated. Strictly it does not. I have argued, however, that intuitionism does create a disjunctive commitment that some could find unpalatable: it forces a choice between an implausible metaphysics within ethics and an implausible epistemology outside it. My argument for this conclusion is tentative in ways I have tried to make explicit, and neither option is beyond defense. But the difficulties are perhaps serious enough to add to the attraction of alternatives to intuitionism, if reasonable candidates are available.

IV

I have not quite completed my survey of the alternatives to intuitionism. But my discussion should have made clear both what the one remaining alternative is and that it is my preferred option. Since I am neither an ethical skeptic nor an intuitionist, I must reject either the autonomy of ethics or foundationalism. But I agree that ethics is autonomous. So it is foundationalism that I reject.[37] In brief, justification for a belief seems to me always a matter of its resting on the right sort of inference, where inferences include unconscious ones: so I do not think that any beliefs are self-justifying. If knowledge had to be justified belief this would commit me already to denying foundationalism about knowledge, too, but I am not sure that knowledge has to be justified as opposed to, in the right circumstances, reliably caused and regulated belief. I resist foundationalism about knowledge, however, in two ways. First, I think that many beliefs claimed to count as noninferential knowledge are in fact based on inference. Second, I take advantage of the fact that foundationalism is not just the view that we have some noninferential knowledge, and thus that it can be denied without denying that view. For, notice, in the standard illustrations of the ways in which the assessment of observed evidence for scientific theories is theory-dependent, it would make no difference to the point at issue if one allowed

---

[37] This was for a long time a nearly invisible option in metaethics, as shown not just by the fact that no one adopted it, but that in statements of the standard argument and related arguments, foundationalism regularly entered as an implicit premise, too obvious to need stating. But more recently this alternative has received interesting defenses: e.g. Brink, *Moral Realism and the Foundations of Ethics*, ch. 5; G. Sayre-McCord, 'Coherentist Epistemology and Moral Theory', in W. Sinnott-Armstrong and M. Timmons (eds.), *Moral Knowledge? New Readings in Moral Epistemology* (Oxford: Oxford University Press, 1996); and Boyd, 'How to be a Moral Realist'.

204

that all our knowledge of empirical evidence is noninferential; it would still be true that an inference from that evidence to a theoretical conclusion depended on still more theory, so that if we have any theoretical knowledge or justified theoretical beliefs, foundationalism must be false.[38]

A full treatment of the debate between intuitionism and a view like mine would have to address, at much greater length, this large issue in general epistemology between foundationalists and their opponents. I have offered some relevant if brief remarks about the epistemology of science, but my ambitions here are otherwise more modest. Noting the larger issue and its importance, but bracketing it as much as possible, I shall conclude by considering in order three key points of detail that might be thought to count for or against intuitionism.

1. First, then, let me return to the other question I raised at the beginning of this paper, about moral observation. I there agreed that people can observe—that is, see with their eyes—that good or bad things are happening, that someone is doing something wrong, and the like. Why isn't this ethical intuition?

My answer is unoriginal and probably unsurprising, but I want to say something about why I find it plausible. Harman, when he describes his imagined case in which you, as it seems, observe the wrongness of some children's action, makes two claims about it: (a) that your observation is 'theory laden' in that 'what you see depends to some extent on the theory you hold, consciously or unconsciously',[39] and (b) that if the observation is a moral one, any supposed moral facts would be 'completely irrelevant' to the explanation of your making it.[40] I have argued elsewhere that Harman is mistaken about the second point. But I think he is right about the first. Given my broad understanding of inference, moreover, I take this to mean that moral observation, even when it doesn't require stopping to 'figure anything out', always does involve inference, automatic and unconscious, and that among the premises are moral views one already has. Once Harman's second claim is disposed of, furthermore, I don't see why the first should look like any kind of invitation to skepticism, nihilism, or relativism about morality. It can hardly look that way to Harman, since he holds that *all* observation, scientific as well

---

[38] In a similar way, ethical intuitionism, or at any rate standard intuitionism, is not just the view that we have noninferential ethical knowledge; so it could be false even if we did have such knowledge. I make no appeal to this point in my argument, however.
[39] Harman, *The Nature of Morality*, 4.
[40] Ibid., 7.

as moral, is theory-laden, but he is not a skeptic, nihilist, or relativist about science.

Richard Werner and David McNaughton have objected that if moral observation is always theory-laden, then there is no room for the sort of moral observation that leads to a moral conversion: to put it less dramatically, no room for surprises.[41] Harman's way of putting his point may invite this criticism. If the idea is that what you see is always determined by your preconceptions, how can what you see ever confound your preconceptions? But the reasonable answer, which strikes me as plausible and psychologically realistic, is that our preconceptions about morality—as about many other topics—come at different levels of consciousness and of generality, as well as from different sources, and are by no means of a piece. They include things we simply take for granted, plus others that we know when we really stop to think but that otherwise fade out of view, especially if they fit poorly with some long-standing and comfortable stereotype. Any number of events, from a conversation to a dream to a perceptual encounter, can precipitate the kind of shake-up in such a system in which a new order emerges and new connections come to the fore. Some of these reorderings I count as inferences, and when they occur because they introduce a more coherent fit among the various pieces, I call them rational inferences. So there is ample room for surprises.[42] Harman certainly misleads when he speaks of all this as our carrying a 'theory' in our heads, making it sound as if we just had a few exceptionless principles that we apply to cases as we meet them. But on a fair reading he can hardly be held to such a simplistic picture. For, again, he thinks that scientific as well as moral observations are theory-laden, but certainly knows that scientific observation can surprise.

---

[41] R. Werner, 'Ethical Realism', *Ethics*, 93 (July, 1983), 653–79; D. McNaughton, *Moral Vision* (Oxford: Blackwell, 1988), 102–3.

[42] Both Werner and McNaughton try to describe cases in which moral observations produce changes in belief and plausibly are not theory-laden. Werner's case suffers from being terribly unrealistic, a serious flaw in an argument about how the psychology of perception actually works. (He imagines Fred, who is such a thoroughgoing utilitarian that he harbors *no* moral ideas that might conflict with that doctrine, but who then rejects it after watching *Roots*. I do not believe that there are any people remotely like Fred; it is worth noting that defenders of utilitarianism join their opponents in *hoping* that there are none, since they standardly applaud people's nonutilitarian modes of thought and motivation, on grounds of their contribution to happiness.) McNaughton's case is by contrast an actual one, George Orwell's description of a hanging in which he suddenly saw the 'unspeakable wrongness' of killing. But the case seems to me, if not to McNaughton, to fit rather well the characterization I give in the text, in which noticing something small—that a condemned man is still capable of valuing such ordinary things as keeping his feet dry—breaks a stereotype that had been keeping one from adding together all sorts of things that one in a way already knew. (In any case, I do not think that McNaughton can mean that Orwell brought to the case absolutely no prior moral views that might count against killing.)

2. The cases I have raised as a problem for my view—ethical observation, and what we refer to as our ethical intuitions—are ones in which the phenomenology seems to favor the intuitionist. For we don't seem here to be relying on inference: it is I who have had to argue in reply, I hope plausibly, that we really are doing so. I want to point out, therefore, that there is another side to this coin, in that there are ways in which intuitionists have to discount the apparent role of inference—this time, what most would agree was inference—in shaping our moral outlooks. Of course, the intuitionist may have a defense of doing so; my point is just that some theoretical defense is certainly needed.

It will help in making my point to begin with a stronger form of intuitionism than we have been considering. I have mentioned that intuitionism as I define it is not committed to the thesis that all our noninferential ethical knowledge is of facts that could only be known noninferentially, or that our noninferentially justified ethical beliefs could be justified in no other way. But some historical intuitionists did accept these claims, and it is worth recalling why it could look like a step forward to have left them behind. Moore is a useful figure to cite here, partly because he is so emphatic about the point. For claims about intrinsic value, he says, 'no relevant evidence whatever can be adduced'; any ethical philosopher who offers for (or against) such propositions 'any evidence whatever', therefore, may be suspected 'of the error of confusion'.[43] Readers who get beyond this proclamation in the preface to the first edition of *Principia Ethica* may thus be surprised to find the book full of argument for and against various accounts of intrinsic value. Some of these arguments are quite famous: there are Moore's arguments against Mill's and Sidgwick's versions of hedonism and his critique of ethical egoism, among others,[44] arguments of considerable cogency rightly credited with raising the costs of holding the positions attacked, even if not with refuting them so decisively as Moore claims. But what can Moore be thinking of himself as doing in offering such arguments? The answer is that there turns out to be, in Moore as in Mill, a larger meaning of the word 'proof' in which it covers 'indirect proof', as Moore calls his own reasoning, as well as direct proof. The only difference between the two modes of reasoning is in the alleged status of their premises—direct proof relying on intuited premises, indirect not—and in the alleged status of their conclusions, since direct proof, according to Moore, really establishes something, whereas indirect proof does not.[45]

---

[43] *Principia Ethica*, pp. 34–5. [44] Ibid., §§45–63.
[45] Ibid., §§45–6. The difference does not correlate, as one might be tempted to think, with the

Nicholas L. Sturgeon

This distinction strikes many readers as implausible. Moore's arguments, and other arguments about intrinsic value, seem to carry some weight, as do arguments about any other sort of topic in ethics.[46] If reflecting on this and similar cases does not push one all the way to coherentism, it can easily prompt at least the sort of weakening of intuitionism I have mentioned. This will involve admitting that ethical propositions that can be known or justified noninferentially can also be known or justified by inference. Almost surely, it will also mean giving up another view Moore also held, that noninferential knowledge or justification attaches to only one kind of topic (on Moore's theory, intrinsic value). For once an intuitionist admits that arguments to as well as from propositions about some topic can be justificatory, she is pretty well forced to say that noninferential knowledge and justification are found not just in beliefs about that topic but in beliefs about others as well.

There is nothing inconsistent about the resulting position, but I do think that it leaves the intuitionist with a disadvantage to be surmounted. For compare this situation with the one that would have obtained if a position like Moore's had been right *and* had turned out to match our argumentative practice in discussion and debate. Suppose, that is, that it had been our practice to take some kinds of ethical claim only as premises, never as conclusions, whereas for others these roles were reversed. In such an imagined situation, there might have been room for skepticism about the premises, and so for wondering whether we really know anything in ethics. But it would have seemed pretty obvious that if we did have knowledge or justified belief in ethics, the correct account of it would have to be intuitionist. We can imagine an eccentric coherentist critic trying out the idea that we really do reason about the premises, too, but there would be little purchase for such a position if it had to admit that this happened only unconsciously and that it never showed up in rational public debate.

---

distinction between deductive and nondeductive inference. The sort of dialectical argument that Moore calls indirect can include finding contradictions among one's opponent's views (§46), so can make use of deduction; while direct proofs in ethics all rely in part on causal generalizations (pp. 34–5), the support for which can hardly be entirely deductive. (Notice, incidentally, that once 'indirect' proof is recognized, we lose the textual warrant I cited in n. 17 above for saying that Moore accepts the autonomy of ethics, for the passage I noted applies that doctrine only to direct proof. It seems clear that Moore does honor the doctrine even in his dialectical arguments, but a reader does not find a general statement of it.)

[46] Many have had similar thoughts about Sidgwick's dialectical arguments in *The Methods of Ethics*, as compared with his claimed intuitions.

Contrast this imagined case, then, with what the weakened version of intuitionism, unlike Moore's, openly admits to be our actual situation. There are no propositions serving only as premises or only as conclusions; every kind of consideration we reason from we also reason to, and vice versa. The intuitionist maintains that we are in our discussions relying on noninferential knowledge and justification, all the same: but if asked for a reason why we should believe this, she will have to reply not by pointing to our practice, which has a suspiciously coherentist look to it, but by citing fairly abstract arguments in epistemology.[47] Now, I don't mean to denigrate abstract arguments; they can establish surprising things. All I mean to point out is that this argument will have to be bearing a lot of weight, since in the respects I have described it is running against the appearances.

3. My third and final point addresses an issue I have alluded to several times: how broadly to understand the notion of inference, and of a belief's being based on inference. As should be clear, I construe the notion generously. I apply it to cases in which someone is unable to articulate the premises, and also to cases in which someone is unconscious of making an inference and perhaps even of accepting the premises. A critic may think it no surprise that someone who locates inferences by standards as lax as these will find correspondingly few intuitions; but she may see that mainly as a good reason to insist on a tighter usage.

My understanding of the concept undoubtedly extends it beyond its common-sense boundaries. In a full discussion of foundationalism and its rivals, I would defend it as a philosophically well-motivated extension, justified by its role in a plausible epistemology. Putting that larger issue to one side, what I want to press here is a dialectical point targeted more specifically at the ethical intuitionist. It will also be my final illustration of a lesson I have tried to emphasize in this paper, the usefulness of thinking about intuitionism and its implications in light of the standard argument for the doctrine. I pointed out above that because two premises in that argument, foundationalism and the autonomy of ethics, both use the notion of reasonable inference, an intuitionist is required to understand that concept in appropriately corresponding ways in the two occurrences,[48]

---

[47] Ewing notes that it is sometimes difficult to tell whether apparent intuitions are due instead to inference, but he insists that this could not be true of all of them. His reason for so thinking does not appeal to our practices of justification or even to the phenomenology, however; it is simply the standard argument (*Ethics*, 119–20). (Ewing does not hold unambiguously that intuited truths could also have been known inferentially; see n. 11.)

[48] It need not be the *same* way. For the standard argument to be valid, the autonomy of ethics must deny that there exist, between nonethical premises and ethical conclusions, any inferences

Nicholas L. Sturgeon

a point that matters in assessing the implications of the doctrine. Now I want to point out that the simpler fact that both principles employ the notion of inference puts some pressure on the intuitionist to interpret that notion liberally.

For consider how the doctrine of the autonomy of ethics is applied as a critical tool by virtually everyone who believes in it. Someone puts forward an argument, the expression of an inference, with an ethical conclusion, but with premises that are entirely nonethical. Friends of the autonomy of ethics will of course think that the inference as stated is not a reasonable one. But almost invariably they think more than this. For they also think that the person who makes such an inference must in fact be assuming, be relying on, have been influenced by, further assumptions beyond those stated—specifically, some further ethical assumption or assumptions. As we all know, however, discussion may reveal that the person making the inference was entirely unaware of relying on any further assumptions, including ethical assumptions: that is why elementary instruction about *is* and *ought*—even rather crude instruction—can actually show people something about their own reasoning. Furthermore, the content of the ethical assumption may prove quite elusive, even for someone aware of it. Attempts to state it may be demonstrably inadequate, for example, if they provide no intelligible bridge from the nonethical premises to details of the conclusion of which the reasoner is firmly convinced. There can be good reason, moreover, to think that the ethical assumptions cannot always be fully articulated: at least that this would be very difficult, perhaps that the difficulty is closer to one of principle. The moral I draw is this. Anyone who accepts the autonomy of ethics and applies it in the familiar manner I have described is already working with a generous notion of what counts as relying on a premise in one's reasoning; the step from there to allowing that an entire piece of reasoning might be unconscious, or else not fully articulable, does not seem so large as to involve a distinction of principle. And ethical intuitionists, or at any rate standard intuitionists, do accept the autonomy of ethics.[49]

But must they apply it in the familiar way? There is room for this question because the autonomy of ethics, while it says something about what it

(beyond the trivial exceptions) that foundationalism would count reasonable. But there is no harm if it denies *more* than that.

[49] Philosophers of a Davidsonian bent may see us, when we do this, as constructing a social world of rational agents by doing this; the more realistically minded, like me, will think that we have lots of evidence that people are at least minimally rational, at least on topics like this one, which warrants us in interpreting them as if they were.

takes for an inference to be reasonable, says nothing further about what to make of the psychology of reasoners. It strictly leaves it open, therefore, that, confronted with our enthymematic reasoner, a friend of the autonomy of ethics might say, 'What terrible reasoning! Here is someone who drew an ethical conclusion from nonethical premises, without in any way relying on any ethical assumptions.' It is a striking fact, however, that although we of course recognize unreasonableness and imperfect reasoning in one another, we do not easily interpret one another as so flagrantly violating important principles of rationality, such as its proponents take the autonomy of ethics to be. Even when they reason badly, we understand people to be somewhere in the neighborhood of what good reasoning would require— as when we apply the autonomy of ethics in the familiar way.

Unless they are prepared to offer reasons for diverging from this quite standard practice, therefore, I think that proponents of the autonomy of ethics, including standard intuitionists, are under considerable dialectical pressure to accept a broad notion of inference, and of baring a belief on inference.

A central point that I have tried to illustrate in this paper is that in assessing a contested doctrine like ethical intuitionism, it helps a lot to keep in view the doctrine's underlying motivation, as captured in this case by the standard argument. I have relied on this background in evaluating a handful of familiar objections to intuitionism, and especially in thinking about its relation to ethical naturalism. Perhaps my most important conclusion is that although some of the familiar charges against intuitionism are exaggerated, it nevertheless seems committed to some conclusions that a philosophical and ethical naturalist will find implausible. I have also suggested that a nonintuitionist moral epistemology can deal adequately with some cases that appear to favor intuitionism; and I have pressed a couple of difficulties for intuitionism that might favor a more coherentist theory of moral knowledge and justification.

Knowing What to Do, Seeing What to Do

9

Allan Gibbard

'Normative' concepts, we can say, are concepts 'fraught with ought'—the phrase is Wilfrid Sellars'. Here is a broad hypothesis on how these concepts work: Normative concepts get their character from their place in a broad kind of planning we do, in our thinking how to live. Roughly, questions of what we *ought* to do are questions of *what to do*.

G. E. Moore argued that good is a simple, non-natural object of thought. His doctrines are often put like this: Good is a simple, non-natural property. It supervenes on natural properties, but is itself distinct from any natural property. And it is known to us by 'intuition'.[1] Moore himself might welcome such a formulation, but his arguments, I maintain, support non-naturalism and intuitionism in a different, emended form. What's non-natural, on this emended doctrine, is not a property but a concept. The *property* of being good is a natural property, though perhaps a complex one, a property shaped by organic wholes, trade-offs of desiderata, and the like. The *concept* of being good, though, is special, and what's non-naturalistic is this concept. This is not how Moore would have put the matter, but it does have affinities with Moore's claims as he put them.

Moore, on this free reading, got matters right—or so I'll assume. If he did, I contend, then we can explain the special behaviour of normative concepts, and do so without anything non-natural in our metaphysics. As a preliminary move, let me shift the discussion: I'll talk not of good but of ought, since it's with an ought, I'd maintain, that normative concepts are basically fraught. To say that something is good is to say, roughly, that it ought to be desired. For this ought, I'll start with a slogan: Ought questions are questions of what to do.

---

[1] Moore, *Principia Ethica* (Cambridge: Cambridge University Press, 1903); see esp. pp. 5–21.

This slogan we can class as a form of expressivism for 'ought', as the term 'expressivism' is used in current meta-ethics. Now from such an expressivistic starting point, many things follow. There follows, I would claim, a version of what Simon Blackburn calls quasi-realism: Starting without the materials of normative realism, without supposing that there's a property oughtness, we can end up showing why we legitimately talk of oughts in realistic style, in much the way we talk of rocks and chairs. Starting as expressivists, we end up sounding like realists.[2] And our talk will act the way a non-naturalist would claim, a non-naturalist like my revised Moore. Blackburn perhaps won't agree to some of the ways I develop this programme, but I myself think of what I'm doing as filling the programme in.

Is this story still a form of intuitionism, or does it mimic intuitionism? Knowing what you ought to do must amount, if the slogan is right, to knowing what to do. Is there such a thing, then, as knowing what to do— and if so, how can you know? Intuitionists argue traditionally that when you push ought questions far enough, their answers must rest on a kind of 'seeing': just seeing what you ought to do, or seeing something from which it follows what you ought to do. These arguments can transfer to knowing what to do, and so it seems that my expressivistic quasi-realism has just fled one kind of mysterious appeal to powers of intuition for another. Well, it is right, I'll claim, that expressivists need intuition. But that's no embarrassment: An expressivist can explain, in expressivistic terms, what claims to intuition mean—and we can see why anyone who thinks what to do, in any sustained way, must be committed to claiming powers of intuition. That is what I'll be arguing in the course of this paper.

What did Moore Show?

Begin with Moore emended; the aim will be to construct a well-founded target theory, a target which an account of ethical concepts might hit or miss. Moore, I think, displayed the special behaviour of a class of concepts, the concepts we now call 'normative'. Many features of his picture were correct, and we can test hypotheses about the meanings of normative terms by seeing if they match these features.

---

[2] S. Blackburn, *Essays in Quasi-Realism* (New York: Oxford University Press, 1993), 3–9, 15–34. I attempt part of such a programme in my *Wise Choices, Apt Feelings: A Theory of Normative Judgment* (Cambridge, Mass.: Harvard University Press, 1990), 153–219.

Allan Gibbard

What carries persuasion in Moore is not the confused details of his arguments, but his examples, along with the rough uses he makes of them. Two interrelated lines of argument in Moore are the ones I find most convincing: one asks 'What's at issue?' in a debate; the other appeals to coherent states of mind. My purpose in reviewing these familiar arguments is to ask what conclusions they support, and so I'll be rendering them freely with an eye to their import.[3]

First, then, the 'What's at issue?' test. Two philosophers debate. One—call him Désiré—claims that 'good' means desired, and we want to test his claim. Another philosopher, Hedda, thinks that pleasure and pleasure alone is good, whereas Désiré rejects the claim that pleasure alone is good. What's at issue? Two assertions are in play:

(H)   Only pleasure is good. —Hedda
(*H) Not only pleasure is good. —Désiré

Désiré and Hedda, Moore thinks we can see, disagree when they say these things. But Desiré can't express his disagreement with Hedda by saying this:

(*D) Not only pleasure is desired. —Desiré

For Hedda can agree with this, though she still asserts (H), that only pleasure is good. The first two statements contradict each other, Moore thinks we can see: (*H) contradicts (H). The first and the last do not: (*D) does not contradict (H). It follows that Désiré's two claims (*H) and (*D) don't mean the same thing. Désiré can see that himself: he makes both claims, but as he tracks the conversation, he realizes that only his claim (*H), not (D*), directly contradicts what Hedda is saying. Whether or not what's desired must always be good, 'good' doesn't mean 'desired'.

This argument ties in closely with a second test, a test of conceptual coherence. Hedda cannot both think (H), that only pleasure is good, and (*H), that not only pleasure is good—she can't think both these things and remain coherent. She can, though, coherently think (H) and (*D): she can think that only pleasure is good, but that not only pleasure is desired. The two-person question of whether Hedda and Désiré are at odds in a set of claims boils down, then, to a one-person question: whether she could, without giving up her own claims, accept his claims and stay coherent.

These tests place a great explanatory burden on two notions: (i) one

---

[3] Moore, *Principia Ethica*, 11.

214

person's accepting or rejecting a claim of another, and (ii) a state of mind's being conceptually coherent. Notion (i), we should note, comes also in a one-person variant spanning time; we have the notion (i*) a person's sticking to a claim he previously held, as opposed to rejecting it. Moore's arguments require claims that can be accepted or rejected at different times and by different people, and coherence or incoherence in accepting a set of claims. With Hedda and Désiré, after all, Moore's argument starts from the finding that Hedda and Désiré aren't strictly disagreeing when she says 'Only pleasure is good' and he says 'Not only pleasure is desired'—and that's because it is coherent to accept both claims at once. Tracking their conversation requires appreciating, implicitly at least, what claims are coherent together and what ones aren't. It's this ability in us that Moore relies on for the uptake of his arguments.

I'll now offer my free—or emended—reading of Moore, and then say that it's on this reading of his doctrines that his arguments support them. First, note that by some accounts of what 'naturalism' is, Moore, for good, is a naturalist. '*The* good', he tells us, or 'that which is good', is not indefinable. By '*the* good' he means 'the whole of that to which the adjective will apply, and the adjective must *always* truly apply to it'.[4] 'I do most fully believe that some true proposition of the form "Intelligence is good and intelligence alone is good" can be found.'[5] A true proposition of this form, he explains, would not be a definition of good, but would be a definition of *the* good.

What, then, does Moore mean by '*the* good'? On one apparent reading, it is the extension of the adjective 'good', the set of all and only those things that are good. For all Moore's purely conceptual arguments tell us, Hedda the hedonist might be right about what this extension is. She thinks that all and only pleasant things are good, and nothing in Moore's study of concepts alone is meant to refute her.

Moore, though, demands something stronger than this of *the* good. Suppose that Hedda is right, and suppose too that, in fact, only terrestrial beings experience pleasure. Then 'pleasure' and 'terrestrial pleasure' have the same extension: all and only terrestrial pleasures are pleasant, and so all and only they, on Hedda's view, are good. But *the* good is pleasure, according to Hedda, not terrestrial pleasure. Being pleasant makes something good; being terrestrial doesn't. It might, after all, have been the case, though in fact it isn't, that extraterrestrial beings—beings, say, on a planet of Alpha

---

[4] Ibid., 9.   [5] Ibid.

Centauri—experienced pleasure too. This might have been the case, even if in fact, in the universe, there happen to be no non-terrestrial beings that are capable of pleasure, even if there never have been and never will be. *The* good, Moore tells us, is the whole of 'that to which the adjective must *always* truly apply'; he thus uses the modal construction 'must always'. For pleasure to be *the* good, then, we require that all and only pleasant things are good not only as things in fact stand, but in every possible situation. In this sense, 'pleasant' and 'good' must be coextensional necessarily.

Is Moore, then, a believer in simple, non-natural properties? For the real Moore, the answer is doubtless yes, but suppose we distinguish properties and concepts. Is it the property of good or the concept of good that Moore's arguments address? If concepts, properties, and extensions are distinct, then a term like 'pleasant' will indicate each in a different sense. I'll adopt the following terminology for these relations: The term 'pleasant', I'll say,

- *designates* its *extension*, the set of actually pleasant things,
- *signifies* the *property* of being pleasant, and
- *expresses* the *concept* of being pleasant.

Purported examples of a property–concept distinction abound in recent philosophy.[6] The property of being me, I can say, is just the property of being Allan Gibbard. The two concepts I can entertain, though, are distinct: suffering amnesia but happening upon a set of bizarre philosophical writings, I might deny being Gibbard. Still, so long as I keep my logical cogency, I won't deny my self-identity: 'Of course I'm me, but I am not Gibbard.' The same can go for the concepts of being water and being H_2O, having a certain chemical structure: opponents of Lavoisier didn't deny that water is water, but they denied that water is H_2O—and, though wrong, they weren't in this being incoherent. The concepts are distinct, at least for chemists of old and for naive beginners in chemistry. As it turns out, though, the property of being water just is the property of being H_2O.

Properties go with necessity: in any possible situation in which I existed, I would be Allan Gibbard. I might not be called that, had my parents chosen differently, but I, as things turned out, can say of any non-actual

---

[6] See, among others, S. Kripke, 'Naming and Necessity', in Donald Davidson and Gilbert Harman (eds.), *Semantics of Natural Language* (Dordrecht: Reidel, 1972), and H. Putnam, 'The Meaning of Meaning', in Putnam, *Mind, Language and Reality: Philosophical Papers*, ii (Cambridge: Cambridge University Press, 1975).

situation in which I would exist, 'Allan Gibbard is who I would be.' Likewise, in any possible situation, water would be H_2O; if something other than H_2O behaved exactly as water behaves in everyday experience, that stuff still wouldn't be water. Identity of properties, however, though it yields necessary equivalence, doesn't yield a priori equivalence. Chemists, after all, required evidence that water is H_2O—just as I, were I amnesiac, might require evidence that I am Gibbard.

These glosses on the phenomena doubtless still require debate, but here I'll assume them, and ask how to read Moore's views into such a picture. What position might his arguments and tests support? Hedda thinks that the terms 'good' and 'pleasant' are necessarily coextensive. Need she think, according to Moore, that the two terms signify different properties? Nothing in Moore's tests forces that conclusion, so long as the two terms express different concepts. Being pleasant is being good, Hedda thinks, but Désiré denies that only pleasant things are good, and in this, she must recognize, he is at least conceptually coherent—just as opponents of Lavoisier were conceptually coherent in denying that all and only water is H_2O. He can disagree with the claim that something is good while agreeing that it is pleasant. These tests show that the *concepts* of being good and of being pleasant are distinct. They don't show that two distinct *properties* are in play. Moore's tests show distinctness of concepts, not of properties.

If two terms stand for the same property, then they are necessarily coextensive. Does the converse hold: if two terms are necessarily coextensive, does it follow that they signify the same property? Different accounts of properties say different things on this score—but in any case, we can say this: Nothing in Moore's arguments *forces* a conclusion that more than one property is in play. The most ontologically economical upshot, the view that a hedonist like Hedda can take after applying Occam's razor, might therefore be that a single property can do all that's needed. The property of being good and the property of being pleasant, she can claim, are one and the same.

Try emending Moore, then, as a non-naturalist for concepts but not for properties. This fits his tests: what his tests support is claims of distinct concepts, not properties. Why leave Moore with a class of entities—non-natural properties—that have ever since seemed mysterious, and that his arguments do nothing to establish?

In reading Moore, then, we can close our eyes at the right points, and then find him proclaiming not non-natural properties, but non-naturalistic concepts. All *properties* are *natural*, but some *concepts* are *non-naturalistic*.

Concepts of What to Do

We humans are planners, inescapably, and in the course of our planning we commit ourselves to concepts that behave as Moore expects. We commit ourselves to such concepts, whether or not they are concepts we actually use, concepts we have words to express. We are each of us committed to such planning content, whether or not the languages we speak give us means to voice this content—or so I shall maintain.

As I've said, the normative concept that is basic, on my view, is not that of good but of a kind of ought; for this ought, *questions of what we ought to do are questions of what to do.* From this slogan, all else falls out: the structure I have foisted on Moore of non-naturalistic concept and natural property, and the features of normative concepts that Moore's arguments lay open to view.

First, non-naturalism: that non-naturalism for concepts falls out of the slogan is fairly obvious. Questions of what we ought to do are questions of what to do. The question what to do is distinct from any question of how matters stand naturalistically. Naturalistic findings matter, of course: if I find that the building's on fire and we'll all be burned to a crisp unless we get out, I won't find it hard to settle what to do. My conclusion to get out of the building, though, doesn't follow in strict logic from my naturalistic findings; someone crazy enough or depressed enough could coherently agree with my naturalistic findings but disagree on what to do. Questions of what to do aren't purely questions of natural fact, it seems clear, and so planning concepts—oughts that capture conclusions on what to do—are not descriptive, naturalistic concepts.

Second, naturalism for the properties signified by the oughts of planning. My argument for this I'll only sketch, since it raises many questions along the way. In the first place, let's put the planning *ought* that figures in conclusions on what to do as follows: If I settle, say, on now going swimming, I conclude that, as things stand for me right now, swimming is *the thing to do.*[7] (A more careful treatment would allow ties in my deliberations, broken arbitrarily; I'd then need a notion of concluding that something's all right or okay to do, or something of the sort. But I'll ignore this, and speak just of being 'the thing to do'.) We are to prove, then, the following: there is a natural property that constitutes being the thing to do.

The argument I'll sketch is transcendental: the aim is to prove that, as

---

[7] Peter Railton suggested this term to me.

planners, we are all committed to its conclusion. We must all, as planners, agree that there is a natural property that constitutes being the thing to do. As a first step, suppose that a person were fully decided in life, hyperdecided. (Hyperdecided states of mind are of course idealizations, like the states of mind that figure in theory of subjective probability. To discern the logic of a set of concepts, it is often helpful to consider ideal deployers of the concept, shorn of human limitations.) Hera, let's imagine, has settled what to do in every possible situation a person could be in. She thus has an ideally complete contingency plan for living. This plan must amount to planning to do all and only acts with a certain natural property—perhaps an infinitely complex property, but natural in the sense that it is composed of naturalistically conceived materials. Hera plans to do act A_1 in circumstance C_1, act A_2 in C_2, and so on, and so in effect she plans always to do the act with this property: being A_1 in C_1, or A_2 in C_2, or . . . . How else but in naturalistic terms, after all, would she recognize which act realizes her plan in any given circumstance? She plans always to do precisely what has this property; call it property N. Property N is natural in the broad sense I have indicated: it is composed, perhaps infinitely, of naturalistically conceived materials. In terms of the planning concept of being the thing to do, then, Hera could put her view like this: The thing to do is always the thing with property N. She will think this for any possible circumstance, and so think: 'In any possible circumstance, the thing to do is whatever has property N.' In this sense, she will think that property N is the property of being the thing to do. She thus accepts a claim of natural constitution: that there is a natural property that constitutes being the thing to do. Or if she hasn't thought matters through to this conclusion, at least she is committed to it by things she already accepts.

I now say that we too are committed to this claim of natural constitution. We, most of us, are far from hyperdecided on what to do. As a matter of general logic, though, we are committed to those things we would accept if we did become hyperdecided. That is to say, suppose there is a conclusion that I would accept no matter how I came to be hyperdecided, so long as I didn't change my mind about anything. Then I'm already committed to this conclusion. I can't now coherently reject it, because if I did, then I couldn't settle the things I'm undecided about without changing my mind about something. But the claim of natural constitution satisfies this requirement: we've already seen that if, like Hera, I were hyperdecided, I would accept this claim. And so as a thinker and planner, I'm already committed to it: I am committed to the claim of natural constitution. By the same line of argument, so are you, and so is any planner.

Now for the transcendental move: I proclaim what I've argued we're all committed to. *There is a natural property that constitutes being the thing to do.* If we disagree on what to do, we'll disagree on what this property is. But in that case, at least one of us will be wrong: that too is something we'd agree about in any hyperdecided state.

That's a quick sketch of some of the realistic-sounding conclusions that follow from thinking that ought questions are questions of what to do. I'll now ask what follows in certain regards from all this. First, what is the relation between this kind of position—a quasi-realistic expressivism—and standard, non-naturalistic intuitionism? Second—but here I'll more be raising questions than offering answers—what kind of account must I give of practical knowledge, of knowing what to do?

Intuitions too Many?

A classic argument convinced Henry Sidgwick that to know an ought, I need an intuition.[8] I mean here the argument I sketched at the outset, an argument that convinces many others along with Sidgwick. It rests, in effect, on Hume's claim that no *ought* follows from any naturalistic *is* by itself—or from any number of them. Argument must lead back to at least one ought premiss that isn't itself established by further argument. This premiss we'll trust only if we find it self-evident, if we're willing to rely on it without further reason. Now if we do think we know this premiss, then we must think we have some capacity to know such things—and this capacity we call intuition.

I put this in foundationalist terms, but the same applies to a form of coherentism, the view that various considerations stand in relations of mutual support.[9] I may find a conclusion credible because of a network of considerations I find evident each on its own to some degree, which support each other and support the conclusion. For this to warrant a conclusion, I don't, perhaps, need a capacity to know a premiss for sure on no further basis. Still, I do need some capacity to 'see' what's credible. When I treat a consideration as having some credibility beyond what it draws from other

---

[8] Henry Sidgwick, *The Methods of Ethics*, 7th edn. (London: Macmillan, 1907), 338–42.

[9] The term 'coherentism' is often used for a far less plausible view, that any system of beliefs is justified so long as it is coherent. The view proposed here, that self-evidence may be partial, seems to me better to capture the coherentist's vision of beliefs' lending support to each other.

considerations, this must warrant me in doing so; it must justify me in according this consideration some independent degree of credence. This capacity to recognize a degree of independent credibility we can likewise call intuition. No one intuition is then decisive by itself, but each bears some weight. Any warranted ought conclusion must still rest on at least one ought intuition. So goes the argument.

What, though, is the conclusion that an *ought* intuition supports? Is it an answer to the question of what to do? To answer a question of what to do is to form a plan for what to do; to settle on what to do right now is to acquire motivations—the kinds of motivation involved in acting on a plan one accepts. If the *ought* conclusions that *ought* intuitions yield are conclusions of what to do, they are planning conclusions. Intuitionism, then, turns out to be the kind of theory I have been advocating. I can be happy with this kind of intuitionism, and an intuitionist of this kind can be happy with what I am saying. Or at least, we haven't, in this discussion, uncovered any points of disagreement.

Suppose, however, that what I *ought* to do is one question and what *to do* is another. Suppose that what a person ought to do is one question—a question of non-natural fact, of which acts have a certain non-natural property—and the practical question of what to do, if in that person's shoes, is another. Classic intuitionists like Prichard, Moore, and Ross didn't much talk about what to do as such; they thought it went without saying. Perhaps, then, they are best read as expressivists like me: they may in effect have agreed that the ought questions they were addressing were questions of what to do. Suppose, however, a non-naturalistic intuitionist denies this: denies that ought questions could be answered directly by saying what to do. Such a position would commit us to superfluous concepts and superfluous intuitions. Classic intuitionists, I have said, may not best be read as taking the two kinds of questions as distinct. If we read them as not doing so, though, we must remember this: their position requires only questions of what to do, and not additional questions about the layout of non-natural properties. Talk of 'non-natural properties' amounts to familiar talk of what to do. Suppose, though, we read them as saying that apart from questions of what to do, there are questions of which acts have a certain non-natural property—and these are the *ought* questions proper. Such a position would call for an intuition too many.

Concede that we swallow all qualms about the non-natural, finding them misdirected, prissy, or scientistic. Or perhaps, on due consideration, we find we just have no such qualms; some philosophers, once they reject ethical naturalism in all its forms, live happily with the non-natural. Still, though, it is baffling how non-natural facts could help with ethics. What good is a non-natural property? Settling what's good settles what to go for, or so it's meant to; we're to further the good and oppose the bad. Why, though, further one non-natural property and oppose another? Settling what I ought now to do settles what to do, or so it's meant to; I'm to do that act. Why, though, do whatever turns out to have a certain non-natural property? Perhaps we are just supposed to 'see' that the good is the thing to promote. For this, however, we would need intuitions of two different kinds: one to establish what's good, and another to reveal that what's good is to be pursued. Perhaps we just 'see' that what we ought to do is the thing to do. Here again, we need two distinct intuitions: one for what we ought to do, and one telling us to do what we ought to do.

Why leave a burning building? Because to stay risks quick and painful death, whereas to leave offers normal prospects for life. That seems the full answer, but strictly speaking, I have agreed, it leaves an obvious step implicit. Intuitionism in this non-expressivist form, however, would attribute one implicit step too many. To conclude for getting out, on this view, I must accept two items: (i) the normative one, the claim that normal prospects for life are better than quick and painful death, and (ii) the practical one, the injunction to choose what is better. Is it intuition, then, that delivers the second finding, so that we need an intuition for (ii) as well as for (i)? That's one more obvious finding than we need; what's obvious is to choose life over death.

Descriptivism, we could say, is the doctrine that ought claims describe rather than prescribe. To tell myself, seeing the fire, 'Get out while you can' is not to describe, and a descriptivist, in the sense of the term that draws my complaints, thinks that telling myself that I ought to get out amounts to something different from telling myself to get out. This downplays choice: at stake in ought inquiry, surely, is what to do. Non-naturalists agree with my suspicion that no natural property will settle what to do, and that may be why Moore speaks of a non-natural property, a property just assumed to fit the job description of settling what to do. When, though, I leave a burning building because otherwise I'd die, it's hard to see what thoughts of a non-natural property add to my reasoning. 'Avoid dying!' seems a good practical premise in my situation. Why trace this back to two distinct putative thoughts, 'I ought to avoid dying' and 'Do what I ought to do!'

Some 'naturalists', on the other hand, agree that no purely naturalistic description of my plight logically settles what to do, but they are hyperexternalists: they believe in the possibility of 'sensible knaves' who know full well what they ought to do, but don't see that as greatly bearing on what to do. Could a non-naturalist be such a hyperexternalist? Suppose Xanthippe is rational in every way. Then she will form correct fundamental beliefs as to what she ought to do, and as rational, she will go on to do what she is convinced she ought to do. She combines two distinct kinds of rationality, on the story we're now trying out: she is rational in forming her ought convictions, and rational in seeing that the thing to do is what she ought to do. These forms of rationality, says this kind of hyperexternalist, are separable—if not with us humans as we are, with beings we might coherently imagine. Alcibiades, imagine, has perfect command of the concept of ought, and is fully rational in forming his convictions as to what he ought to do. In these matters of belief, he is altogether rational. Still, he does not regard what he ought to do as bearing systematically on what to do. In this he is irrational, perhaps, but it is fully coherent to describe him this way: fully rational in belief as to what he ought to do, but irrational in matters of what to do.

This typology would attribute distinctions where common sense won't find them. Tweedledum rationally forms all the right convictions of what he ought to do, and he reliably acts on them. His brother Tweedledee, though, is a convinced egoistic hedonist: he thinks that one ought always to do what most furthers one's own prospects for pleasure and lack of displeasure. This is not the rational view to have, let's imagine. (If you think it is, you can invent another view, irrational by your lights, to attribute to Tweedledee.) Fortunately, though, Tweedledee has another deep irrationality: he doesn't see that what you ought to do has anything much to do with what to do. Indeed his views on what to do coincide amazingly with those of Tweedledum. The two argue at great length about what a person ought to do, but on questions of what to do, they are in full accord.[10] (They differ, to be sure, on what to say about actions, but set that aside.)

Hyperexternalists take Tweedledee's disagreements with his brother at face value: the two, they say, disagree sharply and systematically on what a person ought to do. I myself think they are alike pretty much: they agree remarkably on how to live, and their only disagreement is verbal. They disagree only on what to say about their alternatives and on words with which to think about those alternatives—no great issues.

My own view is that questions of what to do need discussing; what to do

---

[10] James Lenman offers a similar argument to the same effect.

isn't always an afterthought. Naturalistic findings won't settle what to do beyond all need for thinking and discussion. We need, then, language for all this, language with all the power and flexibility of descriptive language—but with its tie to what to do built in. We need a predicate that conveys 'to-be-doneness'. With it we capture all the power of logic and reasoning that predicates give us. Our natural languages may have such a predicate: 'ought' in English on certain readings, perhaps, or 'is the thing to do'. But whether human languages have such a predicate or not, for crystal-clear thought about what to do, we would need such a predicate. If such language doesn't exist, we'll have to invent it. (And then we'll have a language that looks so much like our old one that it will be hard to say why we should judge that our language has changed. We've perhaps been speaking expressivism all along.) This, I suggest, is the truth behind non-naturalistic intuitionism.

Do we Intuit What to Do?

Suppose we accept that *ought* questions are questions of what to do. There are no two separate intuitions about what we ought to do, and whether to do what we ought. This still seems to leave us with intuitions; now, they are intuitions on what to do. The argument for this is the classic one: The building's on fire, I realize, and we'll all be burned to a crisp unless we leave. I then know what to do: the thing to do is to get out. How do I know? I can't deduce what to do purely from the natural facts of my situation, conceived naturalistically—even though, to be sure, the natural facts that bear on what to do include a multitude of further background facts that I rely on, facts that I haven't bothered to mention. Escape holds out prospects of a life I'll find rewarding on the whole, perhaps even promoting the happiness of others on the whole as well. Still, from any number of these facts, a decision to leave doesn't follow with the sheer force of logic. I need another kind of premiss to establish that life beats death in such a case. And this claim that life is better than death amounts to a plan, a plan to go for life in preference to a quick and painful death.

How can I settle on this plan? Perhaps on the basis of other planning conclusions I've already reached. But again, this regress can't go on forever; it comes to an end, or it circles around in coherentist style. If it comes to an end, the starting points for my planning can't then stem from prior premisses. I'm confident of them, on no further ground; I find them self-evident. Or if the support I give these planning features goes in circles, I've got to find some parts of these circles to some degree credible on their own. Thinking pain bad is thinking pain a thing to avoid, and thinking this amounts to planning, for any course of action open to me, to treat whatever painful prospects it carries as weighing against that course of action. To do this, and to do it on no further grounds, we can say, is to find it *intuitive* that pain is bad. That's a technical label for this familiar psychic state that I'm in.

Does this mean that I know what to do by intuition? That must be a stronger claim. In a parallel way, I might, say, find it intuitive that God exists, accepting confidently that he does, on no further grounds. Whether I then have intuitive knowledge, though, that God exists will be controversial. The atheist and agnostic won't agree that I know this by intuition, and many theists won't either—though they all can admit that, in this psychological sense, I do find it intuitive. To say that I find it intuitive is to describe my state of mind. To say that I *know* by intuition is to claim something stronger.

What is knowledge? Justified true belief, tradition has it, along with some further requirement to ensure that one's way of coming to this belief is somehow reliable—that the truth of the belief is no fluke. Epistemology attains heights of refinement on how to formulate this last part, and this part may indeed hold the key to the whole concept of knowledge; I won't, though, claim any great idea as to how this part should be filled in. Instead, to inquire whether a person can know what to do, we can ask whether concluding what to do will sometimes parallel clear cases of knowledge. Does coming to a view on what to do parallel coming to a view on how things stand—so that what constitutes knowing how things stand carries over to matters of what to do?

A view of what to do is not, perhaps, a belief precisely, a belief in something that can be literally true or false. Against this, however, we can take minimalist positions: If getting out, say, is the thing to do, then it's *true*, we can proclaim, that getting out is the thing to do. If I come to that view, then I *believe* that getting out is the thing to do. As for belief and truth in any more substantial sense, it's hard to put our fingers on what this sense might be; perhaps minimal truth and belief are all the truth and belief there are.[11]

---

[11] P. Horwich, *Truth* (Oxford: Oxford University Press, 1990; 2nd edn. 1998). In *Wise Choices, Apt Feelings*, unlike here, I claim that there is a more substantial sense of truth in which normative claims are neither true nor false. I no longer find this position convincing, and so settle for minimalist truth in this paper without addressing whether 'true' has a more substantial, demanding sense.

And further, if I believe that getting out is the thing to do, this belief can be justified or not. The concept of justification we can explain by repeating old expressivist slogans in new variants: questions of what beliefs are justified are questions of what to believe, and a view on what to believe, a normative epistemology, amounts to a contingency plan for when to believe what. All this carries over to thinking what to do: we can plan for our deliberations on what to do, and settle, in our contingency plans, what to conclude in which circumstances. What goes for knowing how things stand, then, transfers— at least so far—to concluding what to do.

That leaves the problematic final clause in a definition of knowing, the 'no fluke' clause. Claims to knowledge license reliance, not just on the verdict but on the process. If you say that I know to get out of the building, you are not just agreeing with me that, in my plight, the thing to do is to get out; you are saying to rely on the process by which I came to think this. Settling what a person knows is, in part, settling what sorts of judgements to rely on.[12] For this notoriously difficult part of an account of knowledge, I can't quickly say much more. But we can see already, even on the rough account I've been using, that judgements of reliability will be plan-laden. Reliability is a normative notion, an ought-laden notion, and ought thoughts consist in plans. To judge a process of coming-to-accept reliable will be, in effect, to plan to rely on such a process. Fill all this in for matters of how things stand, and the account, we may expect, will transfer over to matters of what to do.

Here, then, is a programme for explaining attributions of knowing what to do. Do we, then, sometimes know what to do; are such attributions sometimes true? Consider: How could I coherently think not? In my planning, I reach conclusions on what to do: doubtless, given the fire and my danger, the thing to do is to get out of the building. Could I think this, and deny that the thought is true, or justified, or reliably formed? That seems incoherent: if the thought isn't justified or reliably formed, why go on maintaining it? If I do, though, regard my thought that I'd better get out as justified, then I can be led to an intuitionism for what to do. My justification must lead back to bases known or supported by intuition, to things I would find evident, at least to some degree, on no further basis. If my conclusion to get out is warranted, then so are these ultimate grounds—to some degree, at least, on no further basis.

---

[12] Blackburn discusses knowledge and reliability in his *Essays in Quasi-Realism*, 35–51. In *Ruling Passions: A Theory of Practical Reason* (Oxford: Clarendon Press, 1998), 318–19, he considers first-person claims to ethical knowledge as placing one's judgement beyond revision.

Questions of what we ought to do are questions of what to do; that was the starting point of this inquiry, a form of the doctrine known as expressivism for ought. We might have thought that this led us away from quaint old talk of intuitive knowledge of oughts. It leads instead, though, we seem to be finding, to intuitionism in another form: intuitionism for what to do.

I find it intuitive that pain is to be avoided. That's a psychological feature of mine, an aspect of my psychic state: I aim to avoid pain, on no ground beyond that it hurts. Is this intuition then valid; do I know, by this intuition, that pain is bad? I can't deny that I do; I can't deny it plausibly and coherently. Pain is a thing to avoid, say I; this I can't give up without dropping my plans to shun pain. On what ground is pain a thing to avoid? Often I can find other aims that pain would stymie, but these can't account for the full urgency of avoiding pain. Planning coherently, as I do, to shun pain, I take myself to know that pain is a thing to avoid. I know this not entirely by deriving it from further things I know—this I can't coherently reject without changing my mind about what to do and why. I come to know that pain is bad by finding it intuitive, finding it clear on no further ground.

In saying that I know this by intuition, I'm not saying to trust intuitions indiscriminately. I'll think that in some cases, a person's finding a thing intuitive isn't to be relied on. (To think this amounts to planning not always to accept things on the grounds that someone finds them intuitive.) My plans for when to rely on someone's finding a thing intuitive of course are not well worked out. But Henry Sidgwick, for instance, did work out careful plans, and we can imagine that I might do so, without changing my mind about anything. In claiming intuitive knowledge that pain is bad, I'm committing myself to a feature of plans for when to rely on a person's judgement. Such plans are constrained by the requirement that they include reliance on the particular way in which I find it intuitive that pain is bad. If my future plans rule out this feature, I'll have changed my mind.

What makes, then, for genuine, reliable intuitions? Opponents of intuitionism claim that they never experience such things—whereas a proponent will think that these opponents just misconstrue what she is talking about.[13] By the account of intuitive knowledge or justification that I am proposing, any coherent planner must agree that he has intuitions, and that his thoughts on what to do rest, many of them, on valid intuitive bases. He thinks, say, 'I've got to get out of this building.' Coherence in thinking what to do, everyday coherence, then commits him to accepting the following:

---

[13] See e.g. P. F. Strawson, 'Ethical Intuitionism', *Philosophy*, 24 (1949), 23–33.

that his plan to flee could be part of some well-grounded pattern of thoughts that is ideally coherent, and which he, apart from normal human limitations, is in a position to have. 'You couldn't coherently think that and be justified' is, after all, a criticism, decisive if established—although faced with the fire, to be sure, he won't take time to ponder the criticism. Now in this ideally coherent pattern of thoughts, the conclusion to get out of the building leads back, in its rationale, to at least one thought—a thought given some degree of credence on no further grounds—about how to weigh considerations in one's planning, or some such matter. This must be a normative thought, an ought thought or a reason thought. The ideally coherent planner has this thought as an intuition, and in relying on the intuition, he regards it as valid.

Part of coherent planning how to plan, then, is settling when to rely on the thoughts one finds credible on their own. To settle this is to come to a view as to what kinds of thinking make for valid intuitions. Even in advance of coming to such a view, however, we are committed as planners to there being such a thing as a valid intuition concerning what to do, an intuition that yields knowledge.

Expressivism too, then, needs intuitions. Normative knowledge rests in the end on intuitions; on this, expressivists can agree with non-naturalists. To think such a thing, however, we don't have to believe in non-natural properties; non-naturalistic concepts of natural properties will do the job. We don't have to believe in an *ought* that is distinct from being the thing to do, or in normative thought that is distinct from planning. Intuition figures in thinking what to do, and *oughts* in conclusions of what to do. Neither requires a mysterious metaphysic or mysterious psychic powers.

Prichard on Duty and Ignorance of Fact

10

Jonathan Dancy

Introduction

I am contributing this paper to a volume intended to re-evaluate ethical intuitionism for two reasons, one historical and the other not. The historical reason is that Prichard's paper 'Duty and Ignorance of Fact' caused a complete volte-face in Ross. Ross's first book, *The Right and the Good*, expounded the view that Prichard's paper was intended to undermine, and Ross was so completely persuaded by Prichard that he included in *The Foundations of Ethics* a ten-page summary of Prichard's argument, often word for word. (Nonetheless, he managed, as I will suggest below, to make a couple of significant errors.) This interesting example of the influence that Prichard had over Ross is worth re-examination. I suggest that Prichard's arguments were not really as powerful as Ross supposed.

The non-historical reason is that intuitionism is often thought of as a highly objective view, under which there are normative (and non-natural) features of the world in virtue of which certain actions are demanded of us. Certainly that was the standard intuitionist position. We find it in Broad's conception of rightness as a sort of fittingness that can hold between action and situation,[1] which was adopted by both Ross and Ewing.[2] Prichard argues, by contrast, that whatever may be the case about rightness, agents' *obligations* depend not on features of the situation but on features of their perspectives. The arguments he offers would, I think, serve to suggest that reasons, too, are grounded in features of the agent's thought rather than

---

[1] C. D. Broad, *Five Types of Ethical Theory* (London: Routledge & Kegan Paul, 1930), 164–5.
[2] See the discussion in W. D. Ross, *The Foundations of Ethics* (Oxford: Clarendon Press, 1939), 51 ff., and in A. C. Ewing, *The Definition of Good* (New York: MacMillan, 1947), 132–6.

given us by the nature of the situations we find ourselves in. If sound, then, Prichard's arguments support a far less 'objectivist' position than the one we standardly associate with him. This 'subjectivist' form of intuitionism remains to be assessed.[3]

It is not, however, as if the issue is one that only affects intuitionists. It at least reminds one of a familiar debate within consequentialism. What divides 'objective' consequentialists from 'subjective' consequentialists (at least those of the 'act' rather than the 'rule' variety) is the question whether the rightness of an act is to be determined by its actual consequences or by the consequences it may reasonably be expected to produce. Of course this is not quite the same as the question whether moral reasons are grounded in features of the agent's thought. For what can reasonably be expected is not necessarily the same as what the agent reasonably expects. Still, some of the pressures that drive people towards subjective consequentialism are also visible in Prichard; I will be suggesting that thinking about Prichard should help us to resist those pressures.

1

In his 1932 Henrietta Hertz Lecture 'Duty and Ignorance of Fact'[4] Prichard's initial question is 'If a man has an obligation, i.e. a duty, to do some action, does the obligation depend on certain characteristics of the situation in which he is,[5] or on certain characteristics of his thought about the situation?'[6] And the apparent answer that Prichard gives to this question is that the obligation depends on characteristics of the agent's thought, not on characteristics of the situation. Prichard appears, that is, to adopt what he calls throughout 'the subjective view' as opposed to 'the objective view'. However, the version of 'Duty and Ignorance of Fact' that is printed in the posthumous collection *Moral Obligation* contains a sort of appendix

---

[3] I make a much more substantial attempt to argue the objectivist case in ch. 3 of my *Practical Reality* (Oxford: Clarendon Press, 2000). Ewing rejects the subjectivist position roundly in *The Definition of Good*, 122–5. E. F. Carritt also offered an extended discussion of the issue in his *Ethical and Political Thinking* (Oxford: Clarendon Press, 1947), ch. 2.

[4] This lecture was originally published in the *Proceedings of the British Academy* (1932), and was included in the posthumous collection of Prichard's work *Moral Obligation*, ed. W. D. Ross (Oxford: Clarendon Press, 1949). References here are to the reprinted version.

[5] Later: characteristics of the action; later again: characteristics of the activity.

[6] 'Duty and Ignorance of Fact', 18.

that was not included in the original 1932 publication,[7] and in which Prichard expresses second thoughts about various aspects of his own paper, including apparently some dissatisfaction with the initial question referred to above. It may even be that the right way to think of his final 'resolution' of the difficulty (contained in the appendix) is to take it as an attempt to collapse the question rather than as the adoption of one horn of the dilemma and the rejection of the other. I return to this issue at the end of my paper.

Prichard says that the main difficulty with the objective view is a sceptical one: that, if it were true, then 'although we may have duties, we cannot know but only believe that we have; and therefore we are rendered uncertain whether we, or anyone else, has ever had, or will ever have, a duty'.[8] To reach this conclusion, Prichard first appeals to a certain result in the philosophy of action, namely that the only things that we 'strictly speaking' do are things that we can, as he puts it, do directly. For 'where we bring about something by causing something to cause it, the result is not wholly due to us'.[9] Causing that effect, then, is not something that we have done 'directly'; the thing we did directly was the action that resulted in that effect. According to Prichard, it seems, strictly speaking we only have duties to do what we can strictly speaking do, i.e. do directly. So our duties are all to be expressed in the following form:

When the situation in which a man is contains a thing of the kind A capable of having a state of the kind X effected in it, and when also it is such that some state or combination of states Y which the man can bring about directly would, if brought about, cause a state of the kind X in A, the man ought to bring about that state or combination of states.[10]

Prichard adds to this account of the nature of our duties an epistemological position that he inherited from Cook-Wilson and which leads him to claim that we can never know what our action will cause. Put these two results together and a blanket form of moral scepticism emerges. We can know that there are duties in a conditional sense; we can know that *if* we are in a situation where an action we can do directly would have certain effects, we ought to act in that way. But we can never know unconditionally, either of ourselves or of anyone else, that we or they are in fact bound to act in that way, for our incurable ignorance of the future effects of our actions means that we can never know that we are in a situation of that sort.

There is a doubt about Prichard's thinking here. For his official claim is

---

[7] I imagine that Ross found these notes among the papers that Prichard left after his death, but I have no evidence that this is so.   [8] 'Duty and Ignorance of Fact', 24.
[9] Ibid., 20.   [10] Ibid., 21.

that on the objective view we can never know that anyone has ever had or will ever have a duty. Part of this is in the past tense, and for that part to hold good one of two things must be the case. Either Prichard's scepticism about knowledge of consequences must be a fully general causal scepticism, and apply to knowledge of the effects of some past event or action as much as to those of a present or future one. Or, more plausibly, he is supposing that I cannot have a duty unless it is possible for me to know that I have it at the moment of action. Since, he would say, this is never possible, nobody can know later that I had a duty at that earlier time if it was not possible for me to know it then.

This is sufficient to establish Prichard's claim that we are rendered uncertain whether anyone has ever had or will ever have a duty, so long as we take that claim in a certain way. Suppose, however, that I know that I have two conditional duties, with contradictory antecedents. I know that if my action would have a certain effect, I ought to do it, and if it would not have that effect, I ought to leave well alone. In this case, despite Prichard's argument, I know that there is something that I should do, though I do not know what it is. His claim that we are rendered uncertain whether we, or anyone else, has ever had, or will ever have, a duty, has to be understood as meaning that there is no duty that we can be sure that anyone had, has, or will have. So understood, the argument is reasonably water-tight.

Prichard then says that there is only one alternative to the view that our obligations rest on the facts of the situation, and that is that the obligation depends on our being in a certain attitude of mind towards the situation;[11] and he says that the most plausible account of the required attitude of mind is as that of thinking certain things likely. Here I want to say that there are surely other possibilities, for all that has yet been said. There are three contrasts that we can use to generate other options, those between:

(1a) what is the case v. (1b) what is likely to be the case
(2a) what is likely given available evidence v. (2b) what is likely given what the agent believes
(3a) what is actually likely (on whatever basis) v. (3b) what the agent believes to be likely.

Take the first contrast, between what is the case and what is likely to be the case. The objectivist who goes for the latter of these has to give some account of the contrast between the facts and the 'probable facts'. Relative

---

[11] 'Duty and Ignorance of Fact', 25.

to what are the probable facts probable? This takes us to the second contrast. Suppose that we opt for the view that duty is determined by the probable facts, and that those probable facts are determined by available evidence. They are determined not by the beliefs of the agent, which can be false, misconceived, etc., but only by a selection of the actual facts, those that are in some suitable sense available to—to whom? We have a choice between saying 'available in general' and 'available to the agent'. Let us allow, since we cannot keep everything in the air, that we should be thinking here about availability to the agent. This would give us a position (the combination of (1*b*), (2*a*), and (3*a*)) that would have some defence against Prichard's sceptical worry. If the ground of duty always consists in facts available to the agent, it would be harsh to insist that we never know that we have a duty, or indeed what that duty is, even if we still doubt that we know this of anyone else.

Still, we should note that what Prichard has done is to opt immediately for (3*b*), the second option of my third contrast, in expressing the subjective view in terms of what the agent believes to be likely. This makes it plausible to suppose that of my second contrast, he has opted for (2*b*), and thinks of likelihood as determined relative to the beliefs of the agent, rather than in terms of available evidence. The significance of this is that on Prichard's view the ground for obligation includes things that are not the case—false beliefs of the agent's (understanding 'beliefs' here as things believed)— while on the other view it does not. That is, on Prichard's view, obligation is determined by what the agent believes would be likely given what else he believes, whether what he believes is the case or not.

There are all these difficulties, then, in agreeing with Prichard that there is only one alternative to the objective view, namely the combination of (1*b*), (2*b*), and (3*b*). But Prichard needs to be handled carefully. He often fails to put his reasoning in at all, saying such things as 'when we reflect, we see'. It may be that there are arguments against these other alternatives that he has just not mentioned yet.

So far we have had a sceptical argument against the objective view, which I don't think many of us will find very persuasive. I will just mention two reasons for not finding it persuasive. First, I do not see any reason to allow that I can never know what the consequences of my actions will be. Obviously with many actions this will be true. But don't I know that when I have torn this paper (i.e. moved my arms in a certain way while holding the paper), the paper will end up in two or more pieces? Second, I see no reason to suppose that we can only strictly speaking have obligations to do what we can strictly speaking do. The 'strictly speaking' operator need not behave in this way. Prichard uses the terms 'strictly speaking do' and 'directly do' indistinguishably, and says that we 'indirectly do' any action whose result is 'not wholly up to us'. He would say, for instance, that my persuading you to come to the party is something that I do not do directly, and therefore I do it 'in a less strict sense'.[12] The idea is that I only really do that for which I am not beholden to anyone or anything else; the appeal here is to a sort of pure agency. I directly or strictly speaking only do those things that there is no chance I should fail to do if I set myself to do them. This is the principle that leads him later in the paper to announce that the *only* thing that I can strictly speaking do is to 'set myself' to act in one way rather than another (and, hence, that one can only be morally obliged to set oneself to achieve certain things, never actually to achieve them). My own view about this is that the things that require the cooperation of others may be harder to achieve, but still their cooperation may be something that I do achieve, something that I can be rightly proud of having achieved, and something that I may have a duty to achieve. I see no reason to suppose that just because I cannot do it 'directly', I cannot strictly speaking have a duty to do it.[13]

I suspect we are much more likely to be impressed by a different argument against the objective view which for Prichard appears to be somehow secondary, since he offers it only to show that much of our ordinary thought is in direct conflict with that view. (The sceptical argument that he prefers could hardly be said to be an appeal to what we ordinarily think, and indeed I think that Prichard prefers it because it rests on a philosophical conclusion, and that he takes that to be firmer ground for argument.) The two examples that he offers on pp. 29–30 are, as he puts it, examples of cases where we ought to do something as an insurance. The first raises the question 'Ought we to stop, or at least slow down, in a car, before entering a main road?' The second, which Prichard got from Collingwood, asks whether, if a car is heading towards a fork one branch of which leads to a road that has collapsed in a landslide, we have a duty to stop the car, assuming that we do not know which fork the driver is intending to take. The objective view is committed to saying that we only have such a duty if in fact

---

[12] 'Duty and Ignorance of Fact', 20.

[13] There is a second principle that only emerges later, which is that if I do B by doing A, I do A in some more direct sense than that in which I do B. Prichard asks, 'By directly causing what, did I cause what I did?' (ibid. 32). This appeal to the by-locution should not be taken as evidence that if I do B by doing A, my duty can never strictly speaking be a duty to do B. I may signal by waving my hand, but my duty is to signal (in some way or other), not to wave my hand.

the driver was intending to take the dangerous fork, and if he was not, our stopping him is an action that we have no obligation to do. Similarly, if we do slow down thinking it likely that there is traffic, we are only entitled to think that it is likely that we ought to slow down, and if we find there to be no traffic, we should conclude that we had no obligation after all.

The natural response to this is to claim that the ground of the duty to slow down is the fact that there might be traffic—the chance of traffic—and that this ground remains even if there is in fact no traffic. But Prichard's reply to this is that 'there are no such things as probabilities in nature. There cannot, e.g., be such a thing as the probability that someone has fainted, since either he has fainted or he has not. . . . the fact which we express . . . by the statement: "X has probably fainted" . . . must consist in our mind's being in a certain state or condition.'[14]

There are various things to be noticed here. The first is that this is surely a very dubious and throwaway conception of the meaning of a probability statement, open to all sorts of objections.[15] The second is the weakness of Prichard's argument against objective probabilities, which consisted merely in the claim that 'there cannot, e.g., be such a thing as the probability that someone has fainted, since either he has fainted or he has not'. For how would the existence of objective tendencies in nature be incompatible with the Law of Excluded Middle? Perhaps the problem lies only in objective probabilities about the past, or about the past and present (though I doubt it). But as far as the future is concerned, the existence of an objective tendency in nature to produce a certain result (if indeed the idea of such a thing is coherent in the first place) is perfectly compatible both with that result's occurring and with its not occurring, as well as with the thought that it must either occur or not.

A further issue, however, is whether Prichard's own example is consistent with his conception of the meaning of a probability statement. Note

---

[14] Ibid., 30.

[15] See Ewing, *The Definition of Good*, 125–8, where Ewing objects to this passage on predictable grounds, very similar to his objections to subjectivist accounts of moral judgement. Ewing's general view about Prichard's paper is that 'Prichard's difficulties . . . arise mainly from (a) ignoring the third sense of "right", (b) assuming that probability cannot be objective' (p. 125 n.). The third sense of 'right' is that under which the rightness of an act will depend on what is really probable, given our data. The first sense of right takes rightness to be determined by what is in fact the case. The second sense takes it to be determined by what we judge probable on the evidence available. Ewing allots a certain priority to the first sense of right, but says he generally prefers to use 'ought' in the third sense (p. 128). Ross, taking Prichard to have destroyed the supposed first sense, opts for the second and a 'double dose of subjectivity' (*The Foundations of Ethics*, 164).

that this conception is run in terms of some state of mind of the speaker, not in terms of some state of mind of the agent; Prichard claimed that the fact which *we* express when we say that someone has probably fainted must consist in *our* mind's being in a certain state. As a result, Prichard seems to be unable to give an account of what could be meant by *our* saying of the driver that *he* should slow down because there might be traffic. It does not mean, on Prichard's account of probability statements, that he should slow down because *he* is in a certain state of mind. But neither does it in fact mean what officially it should on Prichard's account, that he should slow down because *we* are in a certain state of mind. Prichard's account only works if the speaker is identical with the agent.

But even if Prichard were right on all these points, I think there would still be a further response available to the objectivist. This is to say that among the reasons for one to slow down is that one does not know that there is no traffic. If one knew that there was traffic, what one knows would give one a reason to slow down. In this case, then, what one knows, rather than the knowing of it, gives one a reason. But if one does not know that there is no traffic, it is one's not knowing this, together with the disaster there would be if one failed to slow down and there were traffic, that gives one a good reason to slow down.

Someone else's not knowing something can be a perfectly ordinary, objectivist reason for action—e.g. for telling them whatever it is that they don't know. In this sense, so can the agent's not knowing something, without this breaching any objectivist defences. My not knowing something can give me a reason to go and look it up. Someone else's knowing something can be a good reason for action. And so can the fact that one knows something oneself, e.g. that there is no traffic. (And so, of course, can the fact known.) Further, if this person's knowing that p is capable of being a reason, so is her not knowing that p. None of this does anything to show that reasons emerge from the perspective of the agent, in the sort of way that Prichard seems to be intending to suggest. It just shows that facts about the agent are often included among the reasons for or against action, and some of those facts concern what the agent believes or knows (or hopes or fears or wants or dislikes). All reasons are given us by facts of one sort or another, and none by our false conceptions of how things are.

It is with thoughts like these that one begins to wonder whether Prichard's original question was a good one. The reasons I have just been talking about are that she knows that p or believes that q, and they are, let us suppose, her reasons. If she knows that her friend is in distress, she has special reason to go round and engage in a bit of support. Is this a reason over and above that grounded in the distress itself? I suggest that if I know that she is in distress and you merely wonder whether she might be, though both of us have a reason to go round, I may have a stronger reason than you do. In these cases, that the agent knows, believes, or suspects that p is to be understood as part of the situation. But it could also be thought of as a characteristic of the agent's thought. In which case Prichard's dilemma fails to get a grip.

It is beginning to look as if we were offered a choice between two views:

(1) None of an agent's reasons is grounded in the agent's beliefs.
(2) All of an agent's reasons are grounded in that agent's beliefs, maybe probability beliefs.

And we think that neither of these things are true. Some reasons are grounded in the agent's beliefs, and others are not, and that is an end of it. All are, in the relevant sense, objective. If we want to say this, of course, we have to be sure that the way in which we do so does nothing to support the inference that if some reasons are grounded in the agent's beliefs, all are.

II

In this section I consider a potential difficulty for the version of the objective view that has begun to emerge. This is that it fails to address the tension between two questions:

(1) What ought he to do, given the facts?—the objective question
(2) What ought he to do, given his beliefs?—the subjective question

The second of these surely appeals to the situation as the agent conceives it, not to the fact that the agent so conceives. If so, then though the subjective question makes manifestly good sense, the objective view seems to lack the resources to address it. Indeed, that view announces that no obligations depend on the agent's perspective in the sort of way that the subjective question seems to suppose.

There is a tension between the two questions because the answers to them can differ; indeed, they can even be opposed. When they are opposed, we want some account of how to deal with the situation. Could both answers be true? If so, how? If not, why not?

One way of addressing the tension is to announce that there are two

Jonathan Dancy

senses of 'ought'—a subjective sense and an objective sense. This appeal to different senses in order to resolve a philosophical tension was a common manoeuvre among the intuitionists; we find it in Ewing, in Joseph, in Broad, and in Ross, in one form or another.[16] But I find it deeply unsatisfying. One way in which it fails to satisfy is that it fails to retain any sense of tension or opposition between the answers to the two questions at all. Of course we gain the advantage of being able to say that opposing answers to the two questions could both be true. But the loss of any sense of tension is too high a cost to pay for this.

A second and more popular way of addressing the tension is to suppose that a univocal 'ought' is used to express two distinct sets of constraints. If the 'ought' is a moral one, the agent on this account has two complete sets of moral reasons—or, better, of moral constraints. First, there are those deriving from the situation. Second, there are those deriving from the agent's perspective—from the agent's take on things. The term 'rational' is often used to mark constraints of the second, 'internal' kind, in the analogous debate within the theory of ordinary practical rationality. Derek Parfit writes that there are two questions: what there is most reason for me to do and what it would be most rational for me to do.[17] Parfit was thinking about the relation between two questions about ordinary, non-moral reasons for action. But presumably the same distinction should be available in the moral case. If so, we have to say something about the relation between these two questions. But it seems to me hard to suppose that there are just two sets of moral constraints covering, as it were, the same territory, each with its own ground. In fact I think that this idea is untenable. The problem, as I see it, lies in the difficulty of putting together the prescriptions of each. How are we to assess against each other the claims of objective and subjective duty? This will be no problem for the agent, of course, since the agent is unable to distinguish in other than an abstract and general way between how he takes things to be and how they in fact are. But *we* can distinguish between these things, as can the agent in retrospect. And I just don't see how to put together the demand that he do it, grounded in the nature of the situation, and the demand that he not do it, grounded in his beliefs. This is not the normal case where there are reasons of the same general type in favour and against.

---

[16] See Ewing, *The Definition of Good*, 120–1; also his *Ethics* (London: English Universities Press, 1953), 145. See also H. W. B. Joseph, *Some Problems in Ethics* (Oxford: Clarendon Press, 1931), 61 and 104; Broad, *Five Types of Ethical Theory*, 162–3; Ross *Foundations of Ethics*, 46–7.

[17] D. Parfit, 'Reasons and Motivation', *Proceedings of the Aristotelian Society*, suppl. vol. 71 (1997), 99.

There would be no special difficulty if it were. It is a most peculiar situation altogether.

There is a 'refined' version of the approach we are currently considering, which announces that the two questions are concerned with different objects. The objective question concerns which *action* ought to be done. The subjective question concerns what the *agent* ought to do. This looks as if it should be some improvement on the unrefined version above, since we no longer have two sets of moral constraints covering the same territory. But I can make no sense of the sort of distinction between action and agent that would be required to make the approach work.[18] The idea, I suppose, is that if there are two distinct objects here, action and agent, remarks about one are hardly capable of conflicting with remarks about the other. But agent and action do not seem to be separable objects in the kind of way that this seems to require. And even if they were, being told that the action I ought to do is one thing (a remark about the action) and the way in which I ought to act is another (this is the remark about the agent) seems more or less incoherent to me. The tension between the answers to our two questions has been garbled by the attempt to understand it in terms of some metaphysical distinction between action and agent.

There remain, however, two further moves we can make in trying to understand the tension. The first of these involves an appeal to the distinction between the deontic and the evaluative. Deontic concepts are such as 'ought', 'right', 'obligation', 'duty', 'wrong', 'permissible', 'required'. Evaluative concepts are such as 'good', 'bad', and maybe 'evil'. But the point here is not so much this sort of distinction between concepts as an analogous distinction between two types of thought. The objective question is answered by saying what the agent ought to do, or, equivalently, what action the agent should take. The subjective question addresses itself to a different issue: how well should we think of the agent for acting as she did? The first question is a deontic one, and the second an evaluative one. Our evaluative answer to this second question need not interfere with our deontic answer to the first. It may be that we are not to think too badly of the agent for having acted as she did, even though in fact she did not do what she should have done in the situation (i.e. she did not do what the situation in fact called for). Such a case might be one where the agent was misinformed, through no fault of her own.

---

[18] I complained about this sort of use of a distinction between action and agent in my *Moral Reasons* (Oxford: Blackwell, 1993), ch. 13.7.

Jonathan Dancy

It is tempting, though mistaken, to marry this third strategy with the second, supposing that evaluative thought applies properly to agents rather than to actions, while deontic thought applies properly to actions. This manoeuvre inherits all the problems of the second strategy, with some added ones of its own. These last include the ban on evaluating actions and on asking 'did he act rightly?'

But even if we don't make this mistake, the third strategy faces difficulties. The main difficulty is that the two questions seem to be addressed to the same *deontic* issue, namely what should the agent do. (They differ on what is allowed to count as deciding that issue.) The attempt to understand the subjective question as evaluative rather than deontic really involves the suggestion that its deontic form is misleading. In this sense, the idea is that there are really no 'subjective *oughts*'—no deontic question that is somehow relative to the agent's conception of the situation. This seems to me to be more a dissolution than a resolution of the problem.

There is, however, a fourth possibility that does not make this mistake. I presented matters as if the objective question runs in terms of a supposed relation between features of the situation and action, while the subjective question runs in terms of a different relation between beliefs and actions. But it seems to me possible to understand answers to the supposedly subjective question in a different way, seeing them as specifying an objective constraint on a combination of belief and action rather than as specifying a subjective constraint on action, grounded in the agent's beliefs. That there are objective constraints on combinations of this sort seems to me to be shown by thinking about what we might call 'hypocrisy', namely the ban on thinking that others should not do this sort of thing while doing it oneself. My view about this is that this ban is genuinely on a combination, and that it does not permit one to detach a ban on one element once the other is in place. What we have here, then, is a ban on believing that others should not do it while doing it yourself, which does not convert (or 'detach') into a direct ban on the belief, given the action, nor into a direct ban on the action, given the belief. Doing it yourself does not make believing that others should not act likewise wrong, any more than that belief makes the action wrong. There is nothing wrong with the belief, nor with the action; what is wrong is having both at once. So we can hear the phrase 'believing this, you should do that' as meaning 'you should not both believe this and fail to do that'. But this 'should' is an objective one, just the same sort of 'should' as is at issue with the first question.

The idea driving this approach is that it is much easier to hold together

240

simple objective constraints on actions and complex objective constraints on combinations of beliefs and actions than it is to hold together two distinct types of constraint, each with its own sort of ground. We get a set of questions, all using the same sense of 'ought', to which our answers may differ. But when they do differ, this is just another instance of the familiar situation in which there are different demands on us not all of which we can satisfy at the same time. That is quite different from the sort of situation generated by the first or second approaches, where the 'oughts' we are putting up against each other are of quite different sorts.[19]

I find this way of reading the subjective question persuasive in its own right, then, and this leaves me asking whether I should add the third approach to the fourth one, or whether the fourth one should be thought of as adequate all on its own. I think that the answer to this is that we do need to add use of the deontic–evaluative distinction to the structural distinction between 'if he believes this, he ought to act thus' and 'he ought, if he believes this, to act thus'. For something not too damning should be able to be said about the agent who acts in good faith and with good intentions, in a case where that agent is misinformed through no fault of her own. Just saying that she did the wrong thing seems inadequate. We want to be able to find something to say, not so as to diminish the sense that what she did was wrong, but so as to diminish our condemnation of her for having acted wrongly. Of course the complex objective requirement is one that she did satisfy, and that is already something. But she might satisfy that requirement even if she ought not to have believed as she did. Among those who fail the simple requirement, then, there are better and worse. The worse is the one who *merely* satisfies the complex objective requirement. The better might be one who both satisfies that requirement and believes irreproachably even though mistakenly. Deontic conceptions give out at this point, and we need the evaluative if we are to draw the relevant distinctions.

III

How does Prichard purport to resolve the tension between objective and subjective questions? Officially, he abandons the objective question entirely, so far as obligation is concerned. There is no objective question about

---

[19] For further discussion of this issue, see my *Practical Reality*, ch. 3.

Jonathan Dancy

what one ought to do. Interestingly, however, there is for Prichard a perfectly good objective question about what it is right to do. In fact, Prichard would read the objective question as about what it is right to do and the subjective question as about what one ought to do. The first of these is determined by looking at the situation, and the second by looking at features of the agent's thought.

He makes this position possible for himself by arguing that though rightness is a property of the action, there is no such property as 'ought-to-be-doneness'. Obligations belong to agents, not to actions.[20] There is a property of 'being obliged', and it belongs to agents. There is no property of obligatoriness. Prichard takes this idea to give him the answer to his original question. The idea is that since obligations are features of ourselves rather than of our actions, there is no bar on those obligations being grounded in features of our thought about the situation. This is important because it causes our prejudices against the subjective view to subside. Those prejudices largely depended on the thought that our obligations must depend on the fact that our action would have a certain character, not on our thinking it likely that it would. But once we understand that obligatoriness, to the extent that there is such a thing at all, is a feature of us rather than of our action, Prichard thinks that our resistance to the subjective view will subside.

He might be right about this, but he should not be. For the question whether obligatoriness belongs to the agent or to the action is irrelevant to the battle between the objective and the subjective view. Prichard himself came to see this later, as he confesses in the notes that are printed at the end of the later version of 'Duty and Ignorance of Fact', and which I consider in the Appendix to this paper. The point is that even if we allow that obligation depends on features of the agent rather than on those of the action, we still have to choose between the question whether those obligations depend on features that the agent actually has or merely those that he takes himself to have. Locating obligation inside the agent leaves this objective–subjective choice still to be made. So Prichard's supposed resolution of the question with which he started is irrelevant.

Why then was he so impressed with it? The answer lies in his idiosyncratic reason for supposing that duties must be objective. In a revealing passage, he writes: '[the subjective view] seems impossible. For an obligation to do some action seems to be a character of that action; and therefore, it

[20] This doctrine had already been propounded by Joseph in his *Some Problems in Ethics*, 61–2.

would seem, it must depend on the fact that the action would have a certain character if it were done, and not on our thinking it likely that it would.'[21] The point, of course, is that this metaphysical reason for preferring the objective view if we can get it is not likely to be *our* reason. We are likely to think that assessing obligation entirely through the perspective of the agent is likely to let the immoral off the hook—a sort of thought that seems to have been entirely foreign to Prichard, and one that would not be addressed by his 'discovery' that obligatoriness is properly a feature of the agent rather than of the action. It turns out that when we begin to read Prichard's paper and come across his original question on the first page, we misunderstand its purport. For Prichard, it is a question driven by metaphysical considerations; for us, by moral ones.

The view that Prichard has now reached is that the objective question, so far as it makes sense at all, is concerned with which action is right, while the subjective question is concerned with which is the action that the agent ought to do. But this could hardly count as a resolution of the tension between the objective and the subjective question. The difficulty faced by an agent who is told that one action is right but another is the one that he ought to do has simply not been addressed, indeed cannot be addressed, and this is surely a reliable sign that something has gone wrong in the theory. But Prichard's view seems to me to cause considerable trouble for the relation between the right and the obligatory in a further and more general way. For on his own showing rightness remains a feature of the action, and hence incapable of being grounded in features of our thought, while obligatoriness is entirely grounded in features of our thought. But whatever the relation between what is right and what we ought to do, it surely cannot be the case that the grounds for rightness are utterly distinct from the grounds for obligation, as on the present account they would have to be. They would have to be distinct because, as Prichard sees it,

while the truth could not be expressed by saying: '*My setting myself to do so-and-so* would *be* right, because *I think* that it would have a certain effect'—a statement which would be as vicious in principle as the statement '*Doing so-and-so* would *be* right because *I think* it would be right'—there is nothing to prevent its being expressible in the form '*I* ought to set myself to do so-and-so, because I think that it would have a certain effect'.[22]

This quotation is the evidence that Prichard retains the standard intuitionist view that rightness is an intrinsic feature of actions, while he has

---

[21] 'Duty and Ignorance of Fact', 36.   [22] Ibid., 37.

abandoned the attempt to define 'ought' in terms of 'right' or vice versa. This makes it all the stranger that Ross, in his slavish account of Prichard's article, never once draws any distinction between rightness and obligatoriness. (This is one of the two errors I referred to in my Introduction; the other can be found in footnote 13 above.)[23]

What is more, there are various possible accounts of the relation between rightness and obligation other than the one that Prichard eventually adopts, and which do not have the awkward consequence of making the ground for rightness necessarily distinct from the ground for obligation. Prichard's view is, effectively, that one has an obligation to do that which would be right if the world were as one supposes, even if it is not in fact right. But we might say instead that the ground for obligation includes the ground for rightness, in the sense that rightness *plus* relevant features of the agent, e.g. opportunity, together ground obligation for that agent. Or we might say that the ground for rightness includes the ground for obligation, in the sense that obligation is grounded only in accessible right-making features. This last view has it that some right-making features, i.e. the inaccessible part of the ground for rightness, cannot stand as part of the ground for obligation. The former view has it that obligation is grounded in agent-relative features, among others, but that the sort of agent-relativity concerned is not accessibility. Finally, there could be a combined view, which took obligatoriness to be grounded in accessible parts of the ground for rightness *plus* other relevant features of the agent. My main point in listing these alternative views is that none of them has the awkward consequence that Prichard's view has for the relation between rightness and obligation. Of course these views still have to face the difficulty that the agent may be told that one action is right and another is the one that he ought to do. This is the difficulty that I tried to approach in the previous section by understanding the subjective question in terms of objective requirements on combinations of beliefs and actions.

There is a further potential difficulty with Prichard's view, and that is that the argument that forces us to abandon ought-to-be-doneness may force us to abandon rightness, as a feature of the action, as well. I mention this worry without being sure that it is a genuine one. But consider Prichard's actual argument for taking obligatoriness to be a feature of the agent rather

---

[23] Of course it would be far better if Prichard had given the same general treatment of rightness as he does here of obligation, and elsewhere in his corpus (largely unpublished) he does indeed seem to take that more defensible position. But the sentence quoted above from p. 37 seems conclusive evidence that here, at least, he does not take it.

than of the action: 'For since the existence of an obligation to do some action cannot possibly depend on actual performance of the action, the obligation cannot itself be a property which the action would have, if it were done'.[24] If I fail to do the right thing, there is no right action which I have failed to do. So we can say 'if I had done that I would have done a right action', but we cannot say that what I did was not the right action in the situation. In this sense, nobody ever does a wrong action.

Perhaps this last point is wrong. My main suggestion, however, has been that, though there is a significant matter at issue, namely how we are to understand the relation between the objective and the subjective question, Prichard's official resolution of this question leaves matters worse than it found them, quite apart from being irrelevant. This is harsh criticism, but what I really think is that Prichard's general understanding of the issue was defective. He felt that he had to plump entirely either for the subjective or for the objective understanding of what is going on in this area. My own position is that there are ways of finessing the matter so as to retain traces of both views, even if the overall style of the eventual mixture will be objectivist.

APPENDIX: ON PRICHARD'S RECANTATION

I consider here Prichard's eventual attempt to solve what he sees as the main difficulty for the subjective view. This matter is confusing (to me at least). Prichard's first idea, the one in the original lecture, is that obligations are characters of the agent rather than of the action (or, rather, of the activity) and so our obligations must depend on some fact about ourselves. This, as he later acknowledges, and as we saw above, is irrelevant to the issue. For it remains an open question whether those facts need to be believed by us, and this was what was supposed to be at issue between the objective and the subjective view.[25]

Prichard offers in the later note a quite different 'resolution' of the objection to the subjective view that it makes our obligations 'turn not on the nature of the situation but on that of our thought about it'.[26] Consider the objectivist claim:

---

[24] 'Duty and Ignorance of Fact', 37.

[25] Ross, in his exposition of Prichard's paper, ends by claiming that 'even if we think that there is a character of rightness that attaches to an activity, it will, on the subjective view as now restated, be a character which belongs to the activity not because of the activity's being thought to have a certain character, but because of its actually being of a certain character, the character of being the setting oneself to bring about a certain effect. This character it actually has, and there is in principle no reason why it should not be the ground of a further character of rightness' (*The Foundations of Ethics*, 156). But this seems to be an expression of the objective view, not of the subjective view that Ross is trying to support.

[26] 'Duty and Ignorance of Fact', 38.

the obligation to bring about X must depend on some character that bringing about X would have, and not on our thinking that it would have that character.

Now substitute 'willing X' for 'bringing about X', as Prichard suggests in line with his earlier conclusion that when we act, our activity really consists in setting ourselves, or willing, to effect a certain change. This yields:

the obligation to will X must depend on some character that willing X would have, and not on our thinking that it would have that character.

Prichard then says that our thinking X likely to effect something else Y enters into the character of that activity which we have an obligation to do, on this account. For the thought that X is likely to produce Y is part of the willing of X. This thinking, then, enters into the character of the willing, i.e. of that which is obligatory for us. It follows, then, that the intrinsic nature of the obligation necessarily depends on some features of our thought. The idea here, I think, is that the character that willing X would have, in virtue of which we have an obligation to do it, is (partly) that of being thought by us likely to produce Y.

What sort of a resolution is this? In the main text Prichard presents things as if we should be persuaded that the subjective view is true and the objective view therefore false. Is he still sticking to that picture? I think he is now suggesting that the contrast between the objective and the subjective view is a false contrast, for the character that willing X would have, in virtue of which we are obliged to do it, is that of being thought by us to have a certain character.

But if so, the suggestion is a failure. If the character that willing X would have, in virtue of which we ought to do it, is our thinking it to have some character, the character which grounds the obligation is not the character which we think that willing X would have, but a character which it has, namely our thinking it to have some other character. And if this is right, what we emerge with is the objective view in a rather peculiar form, rather than the subjective view. And the contrast between the two views remains in force.

What has I think created the confusion here is the apparently tiny difference between two versions of the contrast between the objective and the subjective view:

1st (better) version: the obligation to will X must depend on some character that willing X would have, and not on our thinking that it would have *that* character.[27]

2nd (worse) version: the obligation to will X must depend on some character that willing X would have, and not on our thinking that it would have *some* character.

In terms of the second version, Prichard's resolution amounts to a deconstruction of the issue. In terms of the first, it does not. And it is the first that we really want. For after all the question, as I take it, is whether the rightness of an action is grounded in features of the situation, including the agent—perhaps only those that pass the sort of epistemic filter that we refer to with the phrase 'available evidence'—or whether the obligation is grounded in features of the situation as the agent takes it to be. The idea that so perplexes Prichard, that it is abhorrent that the obligation to do an action should be (partly?) grounded in features of our thought, is only disturbing if the phrase 'features of our thought' is taken in the latter sense, as 'features of the situation as we maybe falsely suppose it to be'. I have argued that, taken in that sense, Prichard provides no effective argument that obligation is subjectively rather than objectively grounded.

---

[27] Cf. 'Duty and Ignorance of Fact', 28 lines 12–15, 26–9, and p. 38, end of penultimate para.

There is an explanation of what has gone wrong here. I argued earlier that Prichard misdiagnoses the ground of the apparent impossibility that obligation be grounded in features of the agent's thought. It is this misdiagnosis that leads him to see no difference between the better and the worse version of the initial contrast. He is really only interested in the question whether the obligation is a character of the action or of the agent.[28] The idea that causes the trouble is the idea that obligatoriness is (at least capable of being) an intrinsic feature of the action, and therefore cannot derive, even partly, from features of other objects. Once Prichard has seen this idea off, he doesn't care *which* features of the agent's thought might be the ground for obligation. His misunderstanding of the problem leads him to be blind to the defects of his own resolution.

[28] Ibid., 36.

247

Ethical Intuitionism and the Motivation Problem

11

Stephen Darwall

> In order, therefore, to prove that the measures of right and wrong are eternal laws, obligatory on every rational mind, it is not sufficient to shew the relations upon which they are founded: we must also point out the connexion betwixt the relation and the will; and must prove that this connexion is so necessary, that in every well-disposed mind, it must take place and have its influence.
>
> (David Hume, A Treatise of Human Nature)

1. Hume's challenge

Hume issues this famous challenge to his rationalist opponents in the process of a larger argument that 'moral distinctions' are 'not deriv'd from reason'.[1] Moral features could be cognized by reason, Hume argues, only if

This paper was initially prepared for the 'Re-evaluating Ethical Intuitionism' conference at the University of Keele, June 3–5, 1999, and versions have also been presented at Johns Hopkins University, Bowling Green State University, the University of Saskatchewan, and Universidad Torcuato di Tella, Buenos Aires, Argentina. I am indebted to audiences on these occasions, and especially to Robert Audi, John Broome, David Copp, Jonathan Dancy, Allan Gibbard, Philip Pettit, Susan Wolf, and Nicholas Zangwill for their comments and suggestions.

[1] The rationalists Hume addresses were either rational intuitionists, such as Samuel Clarke and John Balguy, or reductive rationalists, like William Wollaston. Hume was in no position to consider the sort of rationalism of practical reason that Kant would advance. The rational intuitionists held that fundamental moral truths are 'eternal and immutable', independently of our cognitive capacities, and are cognizable by reason a priori. Wollaston held that moral properties can be reduced to the truth or falsity of the propositions that actions express and can, therefore, be known by reason. For example, acts of theft invariably express the falsehood that someone else's property belongs to the agent and can be known to be wrong on that basis.

they were either 'matters of fact' apprehensible through empirical investigation or 'relations susceptible of certainty and demonstration'.[2] If the rationalists are to defend the latter alternative, he says, they face two formidable tasks. They must first identify some certain or demonstrable relations that hold just where moral relations do.[3] And they must then 'prove a priori, that these relations, if they really existed and were perceived, would be universally forcible and obligatory', that is, that their perception would move the will. However daunting the first task might prove, Hume remarks that the second will be 'more difficult' still.[4]

But why must this second challenge be met? The burden of explaining such a strong connection between moral judgment (or apprehension) and motivation arises only if such a connection exists in the first place. Why couldn't Samuel Clarke and his followers have denied that there is any necessary connection between apprehending a moral relation through reason and motivation? Or, more cautiously, why couldn't they simply have avoided the question? The 'more difficult' Humean challenge seems to require an assumption of either judgment internalism (that anyone who judges he should do something is necessarily given some motivation to do it, or would under specifiable conditions) or perceptual internalism (that anyone who sees that he should do something necessarily is, or would be, moved to do it).[5] Why should the rationalists have accepted either of these assumptions?

Perhaps nothing this strong is required to motivate Hume's challenge,

---

[2] D. Hume, *A Treatise of Human Nature*, 2nd edn., ed. L. A. Selby-Bigge, rev. P. H. Nidditch (Oxford: Clarendon Press, 1978). Although he does not distinguish them, there are actually two aspects of Hume's claim that 'moral distinctions' are 'not deriv'd from reason.' One is that just mentioned: moral features are not distinguished by reason—they are not known, perceived, or judged by reason. The other is that moral distinctions are neither based on nor identical to rational distinctions; they are not distinctions of reason—nothing is immoral because it is 'contrary to reason' or irrational. This latter claim follows 'directly', Hume argues, from the fact that no action or passion can be contrary to reason, since, lacking any 'representative quality', none can be either true or false (pp. 458–9).

[3] 'As moral good and evil belong only to the actions of the mind, and are deriv'd from our situation with regard to external objects, the relations, from which these moral distinctions arise, must lie only betwixt internal actions, and external objects, and must not be applicable either to internal actions, compared among themselves, or to external objects, when placed in opposition to other external objects' (ibid., 464–5).   [4] Ibid., 465.

[5] Another form, existence internalism, holds that if someone ought to do something, then necessarily she must be capable of having some motivation to do it (perhaps under certain hypothetical conditions). On these distinctions, see S. Darwall, 'Reasons, Motives, and the Demands of Morality: An Introduction', in S. Darwall, A. Gibbard, and P. Railton (eds.), *Moral Discourse and Practice* (New York: Oxford University Press, 1997), 306–10; and *Impartial Reason* (Ithaca, NY: Cornell University Press, 1983), 54–5. For convenience, I will sometimes use 'internalism' to refer to either or both of these positions. Context should make my meaning clear.

however. After all, Hume himself never claims a conceptually or meta-physically necessary connection between motivation and either moral judgment or perception.[6] He does say that a central feature of the human psychology of moral thought is its going 'beyond the calm and indolent judgments of the understanding' and 'influenc[ing] our passions and actions'.[7] But this can be explained, he evidently believes, by contingent psychological processes of sympathy and sentiment that link moral thought and action causally. These, however, would be insufficient to connect motivation to morality as the rationalists understand it. Contingent connections of human psychology are not projectible to every possible rational being, and the rationalists believe that moral distinctions are valid a priori for 'every rational mind'.[8] Given their conception of ethics, Hume must believe, the rationalists must establish a connection between the rational apprehension of moral distinctions and the will that is necessary and a priori in order to establish a general connection of any kind between moral thought and practice.

Of course, the rationalists might still have avoided Hume's challenge by denying that there is any such general connection, except, perhaps, for the relatively trivial fact that a morally good person does what she judges it right to do. Remarkably, however, the eighteenth-century rational intuitionists refused to take this position. To the contrary, they took precisely the view that Hume suggested they must. Thus Richard Price proclaimed it 'not conceivable' that a person perceiving that an action ought to be done might 'remain uninfluenced, or want a motive'.[9] And Clarke's follower John Balguy maintained that the recognition that an action is 'right and fit' necessarily gives rise to a motivational state he called 'approval', which leads to action 'where-ever it is not over-ruled' by a more powerful motive.[10] Clarke's own position was more equivocal. But he also claimed that the rational apprehension of necessary moral relations brings with it

---

[6] On this point, see C. Brown, 'Is Hume an Internalist?', *Journal of the History of Philosophy*, 26 (1988), 69–87. Since the sentiments from which Hume believes moral distinctions derive are feelings of an observer contemplating motives and characters, rather than those of a deliberating agent contemplating eligible alternatives, it is not at all obvious how Hume can himself hold that apprehending moral distinctions is able to motivate action directly. I discuss this feature of Hume's view, with special relation to the case of justice, in *The British Moralists and the Internal 'Ought': 1640–1740* (Cambridge: Cambridge University Press, 1995), 288–318.　　　[7] *Treatise*, 457.

[8] Ibid., 465.

[9] 'Excitement belongs to the very ideas of moral right and wrong, and is essentially inseparable from the apprehension of them' (R. Price, *A Review of the Principal Questions in Morals* (1758), in D. D. Raphael (ed.), *British Moralists 1650–1800*, ii (Oxford: Clarendon Press, 1974), 186).

[10] J. Balguy, *The Foundation of Moral Goodness* (1728), facs. edn. (New York: Garland, 1978), 45.

an awareness of the distinctive 'force' of an obligation to do what is eternally 'fit'.[11]

As it has turned out, not only early modern intuitionists have been attracted to this position. Sidgwick, 'philosophical intuitionism's' most careful and sophisticated defender, espoused it.[12] And something close to it seems implicit in Prichard's early writings also. Of course, not all intuitionists have been internalists. Ross is the best example of an externalist intuitionist, holding that ethical intuition must combine with an independent desire to motivate morally good action. Prichard sometimes takes this view also, as does Moore, although Moore doesn't focus on the issue sufficiently to clarify what his considered view would be.

Since it exposes them to Hume's challenge, it is worth asking what has led intuitionists to be internalists to the extent that they have. Which, if any, of the intuitionists' core commitments lead in internalism's direction?[13] An answer, I shall argue, can be found in the central intuitionist claim that moral thought has an irreducibly normative element in virtue of which, they argue, it is intrinsically action-guiding. This is what creates the dialectical situation with which we began. To the extent that they are committed to the fact of moral judgment's being action-guiding, intuitionists face the Humean challenge of showing how it can be action-guiding. In what follows, we shall consider how the intuitionists have attempted to meet this challenge. I shall argue that their attempts have failed and, consequently, that Hume's challenge remains a substantial obstacle to a plausible formulation of intuitionism.

Before we begin, however, we should remove a possible source of confusion. For our purposes, the familiar distinction between moral norms, conceived narrowly in terms of right and wrong, and norms of rationality or practical reason is irrelevant. Our concern will be with claims that intuitionists make about the nature and apprehension of ethical, or normative practical, principles conceived in the broadest possible way.[14] So what is at

---

[11] S. Clarke, *A Discourse Concerning the Unalterable Obligations of Natural Religion* (1706), i.3; repr. in *Works of Samuel Clarke*, 4 vols. (1738), facs. edn. (New York: Garland, 1978), ii. 614.

[12] 'Philosophical intuitionism' is Sidgwick's term. For a discussion of Sidgwick's internalism, see Sect. 6 below.

[13] In the direction, that is, of judgment or perceptual internalism. Intuitionists are united in denying the forms of existence internalism (constitutive or metaphysical internalism) which hold that motivation (at least, partly) constitutes the truth-makers for normative (practical) propositions. On these points, see Darwall, 'Reasons, Motives, and the Demands of Morality', and *The British Moralists and the Internal 'Ought'*, 9–14, 325–8.

[14] For convenience, I will generally use 'moral' in this broad sense, that is, as interchangeable with 'ethical', 'normative practical', or 'rational', except where context makes a narrower reading evident.

issue for us is not the relation between intuitionism and internalism in another of its senses, namely, the thesis that (narrow) moral demands necessarily create normative reasons for acting (morality–reasons internalism).[15] What we want to understand is the relation between, on the one hand, the intuitionist doctrine that, as fundamental normative practical principles are necessarily valid a priori for every rational agent, they must be apprehensible by rational intuition and, on the other, whether and why such an apprehension is necessarily motivating.[16] What, if anything, in the intuitionist doctrine exposes them to Hume's challenge. And what, if anything, might enable them to respond to it.

2. Varieties of Intuitionism

First, some preliminaries about what I shall mean by 'intuitionism'. Intuitionists of all stripes agree that ethical knowledge derives from a form of apprehension or 'intuition' that is neither inferential nor empirical. They generally accept that there can be moral reasoning (except, perhaps, for those Sidgwick calls 'perceptional' or 'ultra-intuitionists'), but believe that it ultimately requires premises that are accepted, not because they follow from further premises, but because they seem, on reflection, to be self-evident. Second, as I shall be understanding the position, intuitionists hold that fundamental ethical principles are necessarily valid for every rational agent and, consequently, that they can be known only by a form of awareness that is a priori. Unlike 'moral sense' theorists such as Hutcheson and Hume and 'sensibility' theorists like Wiggins and McDowell, intuitionists hold that ethical apprehension differs from any form of sense perception and from any emotion or sensibility whose objects are contingent or response-dependent features. Intuitionists thus deny that fundamental normative properties are like secondary qualities or that, like such features as the humorous or the embarrassing, they depend upon human sensibility in any way. Recent defenders have pointed out that intuitionists need not hold that intuitive moral knowledge

---

[15] I discuss these distinctions in 'Reasons, Motives, and the Demands of Morality', 305–12.

[16] That is, what is the relation between intuitionism and 'reasons–motives' judgment (or perceptual) internalism, i.e. the claim that if one judges (or perceives) that one ought (has normative reason) to do something, then, necessarily, one has some motivation to do it. For these distinctions, see my 'Reasons, Motives, and the Demands of Morality'.

requires a 'special rational faculty'.[17] But however they conceive moral reflection, intuitionists agree in claiming that it involves awareness of truths that are necessary and a priori.

Intuitionists deny that fundamental moral truths are analytic—that they are true by definition—as Moore argued most forcefully. But they also deny, as against constructivists or practical reason theorists, that these are synthetic truths or norms that are constructed or presupposed by the exercise of practical reason.[18] According to intuitionism, reason is more like the ability to discern physical shape. It is a power to see something that is independent of, and not either made true by or presupposed in, its own exercise.

Finally, as I shall understand it, intuitionism is a form of cognitivism. Noncognitivists agree with intuitionists in holding that moral judgments are irreducible to empirical or other non-normative claims. And they may agree that some must be fundamental and intuitive. But whereas intuitionists believe that these can be genuine apprehensions of moral truths, noncognitivists deny this.

What, however, do intuitionists mean by the form of awareness they call 'intuition.' Sidgwick lists four conditions[19] First, the terms of the apprehended proposition must be 'clear and precise'. Second, the proposition must be ascertained to be self-evident by 'careful reflection' and distinguished from 'mere impressions or impulses' as well as from stable opinions that result only from 'frequent hearing and repetition'.[20] Third, self-evident intuitions must be mutually consistent. And fourth, because conflicting intuitions cannot both be correct, intersubjective disagreement must be explained away.[21]

[17] R. Audi, 'Intuitionism, Pluralism, and the Foundations of Ethics', in *Moral Knowledge and Ethical Character* (New York: Oxford University Press, 1997), 37.

[18] There is an element of Clarke's thought that runs against this grain, namely, his view that inequity involves a kind of rational absurdity or contradiction (*Works*, ii. 619). However, Clarke's principle of equity is only a formal principle that requires moral consistency (we should treat others as we 'would reasonably expect others should in like circumstances deal' with him) (ibid.). Substantive moral duties (of benevolence, gratitude, and so on) are, for him, a matter of eternal 'fitnesses' and 'unfitnesses' that are apprehended by reason, not created by the exercise of reason.

[19] Satisfaction of these 'would establish a significant proposition apparently self-evident, in the highest degree of certainty attainable' (H. Sidgwick, *The Methods of Ethics*, 7th edn. (London: Macmillan, 1967), 338–9).

[20] So it may not be self-evident that a belief is a self-evident intuition. Results of empirical psychology, for example, might bear on the question.

[21] Robert Audi also lists four, somewhat overlapping conditions. First, an intuition must be 'non-inferential'. At the time it is intuitively held, it must not be based on some further premise. Second, like Sidgwick's second requirement, an intuition must be a 'moderately firm cognition', rather than a 'mere inclination to believe'. Third, like Sidgwick's first condition, intuitions must be

Sidgwick distinguishes three different forms of intuitionism: 'perceptional intuitionism', 'dogmatic intuitionism', and 'philosophical intuitionism'. Perceptional intuitionism holds that we can immediately intuit 'the rightness or wrongness of particular acts', that is, of act-tokens rather than act-types.[22] More plausible, Sidgwick thinks, is dogmatic intuitionism, which holds that certain act-types can be seen self-evidently to be right or wrong. Sidgwick calls this 'dogmatic' because it takes the 'morality of common sense' more or less for granted. It holds that certain general rules are 'implicit in the moral reasoning of ordinary men', and that, because they are objects of 'really clear and finally valid intuition', they are not susceptible to further review or subject to further grounding.

This is the form of intuitionism we are familiar with from the writings of Prichard and Ross. Ross believed that we apprehend self-evidently 'certain types of act' to be 'prima facie' right and others to be prima facie wrong.[23] An act-type is a prima facie duty, according to Ross, if, and only if, a token of that type would be a duty all things considered were it not also a token of some other act-type that is a conflicting prima facie duty.[24] As an example, Ross says, '[that] an act qua fulfilling a promise . . . is prima facie right is self-evident . . . in the sense that . . . when we have reached sufficient mental maturity and have given sufficient attention to the proposition it is evident without any need of proof, or of evidence beyond itself . . . just as a mathematical axiom . . . is evident'.[25]

When Mill opposes the ethics of the 'intuitive school', in utilitarianism, this is also the form of intuitionism that he had in mind. Perceptional intuitionism, Mill says, has been rejected by everyone with 'any pretensions to philosophy'.[26] The only live debate, he thinks, is between those who hold

formed in light of an 'adequate understanding' of their 'propositional objects', including the terms and concepts with which the intuition is framed. Finally, intuitions are pretheoretical in the sense of neither depending evidentially on theories nor themselves being 'theoretical hypotheses'. In sum, then, intuitions are stable, clear, consistent, pretheoretical, putative apprehensions of self-evident moral propositions, which are formed on the basis of careful reflection, and which can survive intersubjective reflection with others ('Intuitionism, Pluralism, and the Foundations of Ethics', 41–2).

[22] *The Methods of Ethics*, 100.

[23] W. D. Ross, *The Right and the Good* (Oxford: Clarendon Press, 1967). Significantly, Ross held that while it is self-evident that certain act-types (e.g. keeping promises, telling the truth, etc.) are moral duties, other things being equal, it is not self-evident in any particular case what one should do, for example, when such duties conflict. Thus Ross was not a perceptual intuitionist (pp. 29, 31, 33).

[24] There are problems of detail here since it seems to be possible for what Ross classifies as prima facie duties to be defeated as well as overridden. [25] Ibid.

[26] 'Our moral faculty, according to all those of its interpreters who are entitled to the name of thinkers, supplies us only with the general principles of moral judgments; it is a branch of our

that the principles of 'popular morality' are 'evident a priori, requiring nothing to command assent, except that the meaning of the terms be understood', and those, like Mill, who believed that moral common sense is acceptable only to the extent that it can be justified by a more fundamental principle.

Sidgwick followed Mill in opposing dogmatic intuitionism and in holding that common sense requires grounding in a fundamental principle. And he followed Mill also in holding that the requisite foundation is provided by the principle of utility. But Sidgwick disagreed profoundly with Mill about the metaphysics and epistemology lying behind this fundamental principle. According to Mill, the only alternative to the intuitive school's dogmatic acceptance of common-sense morality was to treat issues of right and wrong as 'questions of observation and experience'.[27] Sidgwick, however, agreed with the 'intuitive moralists' that moral questions cannot be reduced to questions of empirical fact. Mill had been wrong to attempt 'to establish a logical connexion between psychological and ethical principles' and to make an empirical argument for the principle of utility on that basis.[28] This amounted to changing the subject from ethics to psychology. The only way to counter dogmatic intuitionism, Sidgwick believed, was with a deeper, philosophically more sophisticated form of intuitionism, one he called philosophical intuitionism. In order to make the 'utilitarian methods—which [he] had learnt from Mill . . . coherent and harmonious', they had to be based on a fundamental intuition.[29]

For our purposes, however, philosophical intuitionism shares the main features of the common-sense, pluralist-deontological approach of Prichard and Ross that is more usually called intuitionism these days. Both hold that fundamental moral principles are necessary truths, and both hold that these can be known a priori through a non-inferential apprehension.

3. Early Modern Intuitionism and Motivation

We can return now to the early modern forms of intuitionism that provoked Hume's challenge. How did the challenge arise? And what resources did the intuitionists have to respond to it?

---

reason, not of our sensitive faculty' (J. S. Mill, *Utilitarianism*, ed. G. Sher (Indianapolis: Hackett, 1996), 2).

[27] Ibid., ch. I.   [28] Ibid., 85.   [29] Ibid., pp. xvi–xvii.

Stephen Darwall

Historically, the rational intuitionism that Hume opposed grew out of a reaction to early modern forms of voluntarism, both the theological voluntarism of the early modern natural lawyers, like Pufendorf and Locke, and more secular versions, like Hobbes's.[30] Cudworth's critique was the most powerful.[31] Against the view that moral truths are, as the voluntarists claimed 'positive' or 'factitious', Cudworth argued that terms like 'moral good and evil, just and unjust' must be either (i) 'names for nothing else, but willed and commanded', (ii) terms that refer to something whose nature is independent of will, or (iii) 'names without any signification'.[32] Voluntarists can hardly accept the third alternative, and accepting the second amounts to giving up voluntarism. That leaves the first alternative, but Cudworth argues that it is not a happy position either, since it deprives voluntarists of the ability to assert the rightness of obeying sovereigns as a substantive ethical doctrine. It becomes a mere tautology. 'It was never heard of', Cudworth writes, 'that any one founded all his authority of commanding others, and others['] obligation or duty to obey his commands, in a law of his own making, that men should be required, obliged, or bound to obey him'.[33]

The central move here, which the rationalists deployed repeatedly against different reductionist opponents, is a version of the style of argument Moore would make familiar for the twentieth century.[34] Any attempt to define moral vocabulary in nonnormative terms must fail since, as Price put it, 'our ideas of right and wrong are simple ideas'; they cannot be reduced to or analyzed into others.[35] So it doesn't matter whether a philosopher attempts to identify moral right and wrong with God's commands or with those of the sovereign, or whether, like Mill, he identifies them with empirical facts about desire and happiness. So long as he attempts to reduce

[30] On this point, see J. B. Schneewind, 'Voluntarism and the Foundations of Ethics', *Proceedings and Addresses of the American Philosophical Association*, 70 (1996), 25–42.

[31] Put forward in R. Cudworth, *A Treatise Concerning Eternal and Immutable Morality*, ed. S. Hutton (Cambridge: Cambridge University Press, 1996). Although it was not published until 1731, Cudworth composed this work in the 1670s or 1680s. Cudworth is normally interpreted as a rationalist intuitionist, like Clarke or Price. I believe this view to be mistaken. In *The British Moralists and the Internal 'Ought'* I argue that Cudworth holds a rationalism of practical reason that is more like Kant's view than Clarke's or Price's (see pp. 109–48). Nevertheless, Cudworth's critique of voluntarism was common ground with intuitionists like Clarke, Balguy, and Price.

[32] Cudworth, *A Treatise Concerning Eternal and Immutable Morality*, I. ii. 1.

[33] Ibid., I. ii. 3.

[34] A. N. Prior discusses Cudworth's argument in the context of a study of G. E. Moore's presentation of the naturalistic fallacy and its historical antecedents in *Logic and the Basis of Ethics* (Oxford: Oxford University Press, 1949), 13–25.

[35] *A Review of the Principal Questions in Morals*, 41.

intrinsically normative, moral features to those he identifies by going outside of the moral vocabulary, he changes the subject from ethics to something else like psychology or theology.[36]

A main motivation of early modern intuitionism, therefore, is anti-reductionism. Indeed, Price moves almost at once from the claim that right and wrong are simple, irreducible ideas to the conclusion that they must be apprehensible by an immediate 'intuition' of reason or 'the understanding'.[37] But not quite, since Price realizes that the first philosopher to have claimed explicitly that moral ideas are simple in Locke's sense of not being analyzable into a complex of other simple ideas was Francis Hutcheson, who was a moral sense theorist rather than an intuitionist. Hutcheson had argued against Locke that the ideas of moral good and evil could not be analyzed into those of divine command and sanctions, and that all moral ideas contained as an irreducible core the simple, distinctively moral ideas of approbation and condemnation. In fact, this, along with a Lockean concept empiricism (all simple ideas come from some sense), is what led Hutcheson to the conclusion that there must be a moral sense.[38]

So anti-reductionism does not lead immediately to intuitionism. To take the next (and final) step, Price argues directly against Hutcheson's view that moral qualities can be apprehended by a form of sensibility that, like ordinary sense experience, responds to contingent features. In doing so, Price turns back against Hutcheson an argument that Hutcheson had used against the voluntarists. Hutcheson had complained that voluntarism reduced morality to something positive and arbitrary, but Price argues that Hutcheson's theory of the moral sense was ultimately no different since it made morality depend on a 'positive constitution of our minds', an 'implanted and arbitrary' 'taste' 'similar to the relishes . . . created by any of our other senses'.[39] The problem with Hutcheson's moral sense theory, Price believed, was that it failed to appreciate that morality is nonarbitrary in two ways. Not only do right and wrong not result from an arbitrary fiat, they are also nonarbitrary in the further sense of being necessarily true. Morality is 'necessary and immutable'.[40] And because it is, it cannot be

---

[36] Obviously, this overlooks the problem, often pointed out in connection with Moore's 'open question' argument, that the proposed reduction may be synthetic rather than analytic. See e.g. W. K. Frankena, 'The Naturalistic Fallacy', *Mind*, 48 (1939), 464–77.

[37] *A Review of the Principal Questions in Morals*, 41.

[38] By which Hutcheson simply meant an aspect of our sensibility that 'receives' the simple ideas of approbation and condemnation.   [39] Ibid., 14–15.

[40] Ibid., 85.

apprehended a posteriori by any sense, but must be grasped a priori, by what Price calls an 'intuition' of the mind.[41]

These, then, were the main features of early modern intuitionism. Because moral ideas are simple and irreducible to nonnormative notions, they must be apprehensible immediately, without reliance on reasoning from further premises. And because moral truths are 'eternal and immutable', this immediate apprehension cannot be a direct perception of any contingent sense or sensibility. It followed, the intuitionists argued, that fundamental moral truths must be apprehensible as self-evident a priori by some form of rational intuition.

But why would such an apprehension necessarily move the will? Why did the intuitionists believe, as Price put it, that it was 'not conceivable' that someone might perceive an action and yet 'remain uninfluenced, or want a motive'? And how did they think that Hume's challenge could be met?[42]

The answer lies, in large part, in an analogy the rationalists drew between the way reason gives rise to belief and the way it must be able, similarly, to move the will. Balguy provides the clearest example, although Clarke says something very similar.[43] 'The same necessity', Balguy wrote, 'which compels men to assent to what is true, forces them to approve what is right and fit.'[44] When we are convinced by an argument that something is true, we believe the conclusion for the reasons contained in the premises. No one who has followed a geometrical demonstration 'can forbear giving his assent', as Clarke puts it.[45] Moreover, this seems not merely to be a contingent truth. It seems to be necessarily true. By analogy, Balguy argued, we necessarily are moved to do whatever we apprehend to be right and fit.

But why should it be true? The concept of a (normative) reason for believing something (in the sense of a ground of the fact that one ought to believe it) is a different concept from that of something that makes the belief (i.e. what is believed) true or from the concept of evidence of its truth. Of course, we believe that evidence for p necessarily provides a reason to believe p. But why is that? And what explains why taking something as evidence for p or as establishing p's truth necessarily tends to give rise to that belief?

---

[41] *A Review of the Principal Questions in Morals*, 13–41. In this section Price follows closely Cudworth's argument in the *Treatise*, esp. bk. IV.

[42] I do not mean that the rationalists saw themselves as responding to a challenge posed by Hume. Both Balguy and Clarke wrote well before Hume's *Treatise* was published, and although Price refers to Hume in various places, he does not mention him in this connection.

[43] See n. 11.

[44] Again, approval is a motivational state for Balguy, one which gives rise to action 'where-ever it is not over-ruled' by a more powerful motive. See n. 10.

[45] *Works of Samuel Clarke*, ii. 614.

The answer has to do with the nature of belief. Intrinsic to belief as a state of mind is its distinctive 'direction of fit'.[46] Beliefs 'aim' to track the truth by their very nature—this is their 'constitutive aim' or 'object'. In this way beliefs differ from other doxastic or epistemic attitudes such as, for example, assuming something's truth or pretending that it is true. If a state of mind doesn't respond (within an appropriate range) to acknowledged evidence, then it simply does not count as a belief. That is why it is necessarily true that beliefs respond to evidence as they do.

In the same way, the rationalists argued, the will has its own distinctive constitutive aim or object. 'The intellectual nature', Price says, 'is its own law. It has within itself a spring and guide of action which it cannot suppress or reject' that is like the irrepressible 'spring and guide' of belief.[47] But whereas the constitutive aim of belief is truth, Price claims that the object of our practical intellectual nature, the will, is 'rectitude'.[48] Similarly, Balguy says that 'the end of rational actions, and rational agents, consider'd as such, is reason or moral good'.[49] This is the 'proper object of our moral capacity'.[50]

If it is the nature of the will to track rectitude or moral good, as it is intrinsic to belief to track the truth, then just as acknowledging evidence of p's truth necessarily tends to give rise to a belief that p, so perhaps might acknowledging that A would be right or morally good necessarily tend to motivate a person to will A. Just as we do not count mental states that generally fail to meet the former of these conditions beliefs, so also might we not count states that generally fail to meet the latter as states of will, intention, and volition.

There is, however, a disanalogy between the ways this line of thought treats belief and the will, respectively, that creates a significant problem with using it to respond to Hume's challenge. We can put the problem this way.[51] Belief has both a formal, explicitly normative constitutive aim and a substantive, nonnormative constitutive aim. The formal aim of belief is explicitly normative, to believe whatever we ought to believe (or equivalently, what it is reasonable, or there is good reason, to believe). Our beliefs 'succeed' formally when they match the norms for belief, whatever these might be.

[46] See e.g. Lloyd Humberstone, 'Direction of Fit', *Mind*, 101 (1992), 59–83. In what follows I am very much indebted to J. D. Velleman, 'The Possibility of Practical Reason', *Ethics*, 106 (1996), 694–726.   [47] *Review of the Principal Questions in Morals*, 187.
[48] Ibid.   [49] *The Foundation of Moral Goodness*, 48.   [50] Ibid.
[51] Here again I am indebted to Velleman, 'The Possibility of Practical Reason'. See also P. Railton, 'On the Hypothetical and Non-Hypothetical in Reasoning about Belief Action', in G. Cullity and B. Gaut (eds.), *Ethics and Practical Reason* (Oxford: Clarendon Press, 1997).

Stephen Darwall

But belief, by its very nature, also has a substantive aim or standard of success, namely truth. Truth is a substantive aim or standard for belief in the sense that it is a substantive norm or normative claim, rather than a mere redundancy or tautology, that we ought to believe what is true. The concept of truth is not identical with the concept of what we ought to believe, so that we ought to believe what is true is a substantive normative claim that differs from the tautology that we ought to believe what we ought to believe. Thus, while belief's formal aim is explicitly normative (what we ought to believe), its substantive aim, truth, is not. If it were, the claim we ought to believe whatever is true would be a mere tautology.

Although they don't put it this way, the fact that belief has truth as substantive aim is implicit in the rationalists' explanation of belief formation. According to the rationalists, what leads rationally to a belief that p is seeing convincing evidence of p's truth, not apprehending that p is something we ought to believe. In our terms, we are moved directly to a belief, not by seeing that so believing would achieve belief's formal aim, but by seeing that it would achieve belief's substantive aim.

For example, when I follow a geometrical demonstration, say, of the theorem that two tangents drawn to a circle from an external point must be congruent, I move from beliefs in the premises to a belief in the conclusion by seeing that if the premises are true, then the conclusion must be true also. In the instance at hand, I see that two triangles can be constructed, each formed by a line from the external point to the center of the circle, a radius drawn to the respective points of tangency, and the respective tangents. I then see that these two triangles must be congruent, since their respective radii are congruent, the angles formed by the respective radii and tangents are congruent (since both are right angles), and they share a common hypotenuse. And if the respective triangles are congruent, then the respective legs formed by the tangents must be congruent also. QED. Having followed the proof, necessarily, I believe the theorem or, at least, have a strong tendency to do so.

Compare now the case of the will. Suppose we say that the aim of the will is reasonable, morally good, or right, action. As Balguy puts it, these are 'the end of rational actions, and rational agents, consider'd as such'.[52] But this explicitly normative aim—willing what we ought or have good reason to do—is the aim of the will in exactly the same sense that believing what

---

[52] Obviously, I am making the rationalist assumption that these are all the same. If they are not, if, say, the morally right is distinguishable from the rational, then the argument would apply only to the perception that conduct is rational. This is a significant issue in its own right, but it is orthogonal to our current concerns, so I will ignore it.

we ought or have good reason to believe is the aim of belief. It is will's formal aim, just as the latter is belief's formal aim. What, then, might be the will's substantive aim? The rationalists do not identify one. We might wonder, indeed, whether the will, in fact, has a substantive aim in the same way that belief does. Moreover, even if the will were to have a substantive aim, the rationalists would be poorly positioned to acknowledge this for reasons that will become clear presently. In any case, it is because believing what is true is belief's substantive aim that being convinced by an argument of p's truth is necessarily connected to a tendency to believe p. For there to be an analogous process with the will, therefore, it would have to proceed, not via an apprehension of the normative proposition that something is what I ought to will or do—that is, that so willing would achieve the will's formal aim. It would have to proceed via the apprehension of a relation between so willing and some nonnormative feature that supplies the will's substantive aim.

The sense in which belief's substantive aim is nonnormative, again, is that the claim that some proposition p is true differs from the claim that we ought to believe p or from any other explicitly normative claim. Of course, we ought to believe what is true, but that normative claim differs from the claim that p is true, since otherwise the former would simply reduce to the tautology that we ought to believe what we ought to believe. As we have been taking it, it is because belief has truth as substantive constitutive aim that we ought to believe what is true. Because belief has this substantive aim, moreover, normative epistemology can be effectively reduced to the theory of evidence and probability. In figuring out what we ought to believe (which beliefs would satisfy belief's formal aim), we can effectively focus on which beliefs are best supported by our evidence (that is, which beliefs would satisfy belief's substantive aim). For the case of belief, satisfying the (nonnormative) substantive aim is what counts as satisfying the formal (normative) aim.

Suppose that the rationalists were to try to press the analogy and say that the will has a substantive aim, like belief. They would then have to accept that determining what we ought to will (what would satisfy will's (normative) formal aim) can be accomplished by determining what would achieve the will's nonnormative substantive aim. This would put the rationalists in the difficult position of having to accept that, just as normative epistemology can be effectively reduced to the theory of evidence and probability, so also can normative ethics be reduced to something whose subject is not explicitly normative. It would mean that the fundamental premises from which we make inferences in moral reasoning would not themselves be normative propositions. That, however, would undercut the intuitionists' anti-reductionist argument

Stephen Darwall

for the immediate apprehensibility of fundamental moral premises. They would no longer be in a position to argue that 'moral axioms' must be immediately apprehensible because they are irreducibly normative. It is hard to imagine anything that runs more directly against the tenor of rational intuitionist thought.

Reflection on the case of belief actually highlights the problem the intuitionists face in responding to Hume's challenge. The intuitionists maintain that fundamental normative propositions are like mathematical axioms in being objects of self-evident, a priori intuition. If that were so, it would explain why we have a strong tendency to believe them when we contemplate them reflectively. But it wouldn't begin to explain how rational intuition can move the will, in ethics any more than in mathematics.[53]

4. A Different Theoretical–Practical Analogy?

Perhaps, however, the intuitionists might have exploited a different analogy between theoretical and practical reasoning. When I follow the geometrical

[53] T. M. Scanlon argues that desires might best be understood as the appearance of normative reasons for acting. (See *What we Owe to Each Other* (Cambridge, Mass.: Belknap Press, 1998), 33–55.) According to Scanlon, a desire might be a state such as the painfulness of an impending trip to the dentist appearing to one as a reason not to go. This might suggest that the acceptance of normative propositions can be intrinsically motivating. However, there is an important difference between desires, understood in the way Scanlon suggests, and the acceptance of such fundamental normative principles as the intuitionists propose. Thus, compare the difference between the desire just mentioned and its seeming self-evident to one on reflection that the fact that an experience would be painful is a reason for the person who might suffer it to avoid it. Even if seeing its painfulness as a reason to avoid a trip to the dentist (i.e. not just believing that it is a reason, but having the trip's painfulness appear to one as a reason to avoid it, casting the trip in an unfavorable light) is intrinsically motivating, it would not follow that pain's seeming, on reflection, a reason for anyone to avoid it is similarly motivating.

Or consider Sidgwick's axiom of prudence. Sidgwick says that it is self-evident that 'the mere difference of priority and posteriority in time is not a reasonable ground for having more regard to the consciousness of one moment than to that of another' (*The Methods of Ethics*, 381). That something would give me 'desirable consciousness' now is no reason, in itself, to prefer it to something that would give me the same desirable consciousness at some time in the future. However, even if seeing the fact that something would give me desirable consciousness as a reason to pursue it is intrinsically motivating, it doesn't follow that acknowledging, on reflection, that pure time preference is irrational is intrinsically motivating.

Of course, such an acknowledgment might still be intrinsically motivating, but that would not be because desires are, but because accepting a norm is. What the intuitionists require is some cognitivist, nonconstructivist account that might explain this. (For a noncognitivist account, see A. Gibbard, *Wise Choices, Apt Feelings: Theory of Normative Judgment* (Cambridge, Mass.: Harvard University Press, 1990).)

262

demonstration described above, my reasoning follows the logical principle of modus ponens. It is because I believe that if the two tangents are corresponding sides of congruent triangles, then they are congruent, and that they are corresponding sides of congruent triangles, that I conclude that the two tangents are congruent. My beliefs follow this principle. Indeed, they must follow this principle in so far as I reason correctly or rationally. Something similar is true, a number of philosophers have pointed out, about an apparently analogous form of practical reasoning, namely, inferences from ends to means that are necessary to achieve them.[54]

Since the adoption of an end involves the idea of 'my causality as an acting cause', as Kant put it, when I adopt E as end, I commit myself to bringing it about by some means or other.[55] If, then, I believe that M is the only way of realizing E, then I must either will M or relinquish E. What, however, is the force of this 'must'? It is the same as the 'must' in 'If I believe that if p, then q, and I believe that p, then I must believe that q'. It is a rational must. The point is not, in the latter case, that my believing q follows from my believing p and my believing if p, then q. It is not logically impossible that I have the latter beliefs and lack the former. It is just incoherent or irrational. That is, it is irrational to continue to believe p, believe that if p, then q, and fail to believe q. Rationally, one must either give up the belief that p, give up the belief that if p, then q, or form the belief that q. Similarly, in the practical case, though it is logically possible to have E as end and fail to will M when one believes M is the only means to E, it is irrational. Rationally, one must either give up E as end, give up the belief that M is necessary to bring about E, or will M.

Here we find an analogy between theoretical and practical reasoning that carries through. Moreover, the analogy illustrates a way in which reasoning can itself contribute to the formation of belief and intention that, in the practical case, outstrips the motivational force of desire or intention taken by itself. Since it is possible to intend to bring about E and believe that M is necessary to do so, yet fail to will M, but not possible rationally to do so, practical reasoning must be capable of adding some motivation itself or,

---

[54] For further discussion here, see J. Broome, 'Normative Requirements', *Ratio*, 12 (1999), 398–419; C. Korsgaard, 'The Normativity of Instrumental Reason', in G. Cullity and B. Gaut (eds.), *Ethics and Practical Reason* (Oxford: Clarendon Press, 1997); Darwall, *Impartial Reason*, 15–17, 43–50; and Railton, 'On the Hypothetical and Non-Hypothetical in Reasoning about Belief and Action'.

[55] I. Kant, *Groundwork of the Metaphysic of Morals*, ed. M. Gregor, introd. C. M. Korsgaard (Cambridge: Cambridge University Press, 1998), 28: Ak. p. 417.

at least, of transferring the motivation involved in accepting its premises. What's more, it must do so in a way that a desire to do what is rational or right could not adequately explain. As Lewis Carroll pointed out for the case of belief, believing further conditional premises are no substitute for rules of inference and the disposition to follow them. If I believe p and if p, then q, it is reasoning (a disposition to follow modus ponens) that takes me to the belief that q. Neither the beliefs that p and if p, then q, nor even additional beliefs, such as if (if p, then q) and p, then q, can, without rule-governed dispositions of reasoning, produce an inferred belief that q, either by themselves or together.

Similarly, in the practical case. Without practical reasoning—in this instance, the rule-governed disposition to move from what I accept in having E as end and the belief that M is the only means to E to the intention to undertake M (or renounce E)—no set of intentions, beliefs, and desires can lead to this inferred intention. Adding in the further desire or intention to take the necessary means to one's ends, or to be rational, or whatever, only leaves us with a parallel Lewis Carroll problem. Unless I am disposed to reason practically, to infer an intention either to undertake M or renounce E from my intention to achieve E and my belief that M is necessary to achieve E, then no addition of further beliefs, desires, and intentions can help.

Here, then, is a way in which all parties might agree that pure reason can be practical.[56] The problem for the intuitionists, however, is that this practicality comes through inference or reasoning, not through any rational intuition of fundamental moral (or practical) truths. So even if reason is in this respect an active principle in the formation of desire and intention, no less than in the formation of belief, this will not help intuitionists to show how rational intuitions can be action-guiding themselves. The most the analogy can do for them is to give assurance that if they can show that the acceptance of fundamental moral premises has practical force, then this force can be preserved by a form of practical inference.

5. The Motivation Problem in Ross and Prichard

This leaves the eighteenth-century intuitionists without an adequate response to Hume's challenge. What alternatives have emerged since? I

[56] This, I take it, is the upshot of C. Korsgaard, 'Skepticism about Practical Reason', *Journal of Philosophy*, 83 (1986), 5–25.

mentioned earlier that it might be possible simply to avoid the challenge by denying internalism, as Ross did.[57] Ross's position may actually seem more equivocal, however. He undoubtedly holds that morally good action always includes a desire to do what is right in addition to the belief that the action before one is the right thing to do. But Ross also says that it should be no more mysterious that 'the thought of an act as right can arouse a desire to do it' than it is 'that thought of an act as pleasant, or as leading to pleasure, should arouse an impulse to do it'.[58] This might seem to suggest that Ross allows the possibility that the desire necessary for morally good action is not an independent desire, but a 'motivated' one.[59] And it is consistent with that that the apprehension that an act is right always and necessarily gives rise to a desire to do it. Were he to accept this, Ross would be a judgment internalist.

However, for Ross, morally good actions are motivated by the desire to do whatever is right. Plainly Ross doesn't think that the belief that this action is right can cause a desire to do whatever is right. What he must think is that the thought that this action is right can give rise to a desire to do this action because of a desire to do whatever is right. And he clearly thinks that the latter is a desire one can lack, even, apparently, when one has the capacity to apprehend moral rightness.[60] So Ross is indeed a judgment externalist.

To the extent that intuitionists are prepared to adopt this position, they can avoid Hume's challenge.[61] But this may not be an entirely happy position. Many find Ross's externalism unattractive on philosophical and on ethical grounds.[62] It seems to make ethics into just another classificatory schema rather than something essentially concerned with guiding action. And it makes moral goodness into something approaching a fetish rather than the property of a deeply integrated moral personality.

Michael Smith makes a version of the second objection when he argues

---

[57] And Prichard also in 'Duty and Interest', in H. A. Prichard, *Moral Obligation and Duty and Interest: Essays and Lectures*, with introd. by J. O. Urmson (London: Oxford University Press, 1968), 224–5.   [58] *The Right and the Good*, 157–8.

[59] In the sense that Thomas Nagel discusses in *The Possibility of Altruism* (Oxford: Clarendon Press, 1970), 29–30.

[60] 'Human nature being what it is, the latter thought [that this action would be pleasant] arouses an impulse to action much more constantly than the former [that this action would be right]' (*The Right and the Good*, 158).

[61] In this connection, see D. Parfit, 'Reasons and Motivation', *Proceedings of the Aristotelian Society*, suppl., 71 (1997), 99–130.

[62] The classic discussion is W. D. Falk's ' "Ought" and Motivation', *Proceedings of the Aristotelian Society*, 118 (1947–8): 111–38. See also Nagel, *The Possibility of Altruism*, 3–12; Korsgaard, 'Skepticism about Practical Reason'; Darwall, *Impartial Reason*, 54–5.

that good people 'care non-derivatively' about what is morally right and not just about doing whatever is right.[63] They care nonderivatively, for example, about honesty, justice, and helping others, and not just about 'one thing: doing what they believe to be right, where this is read de dicto and not de re'.[64] The point is not that morally good people don't care about doing whatever is right, but that they also have intrinsic concerns for things that are right. Such concerns may be antecedent to any explicit apprehension of their moral status, but they may also arise in the process of apprehending it. This last point is important, since we may want to agree with Kant (as rational intuitionists generally have) that the morally good person is governed by a concern to do whatever is right. The problem is that in so far as I have only the desire to do what is right de dicto, without any desire to do what is right de re, I seem to be lacking in important elements of moral character. There will be a solution to this problem, however, only if the apprehension of moral rightness itself involves (or engages) desires to do what is right de re.

Rossian externalism avoids the Humean challenge, then, but at too high a cost, since it distorts the relation between moral reflection and motivation. Moreover, the problem is not, as some have suggested, that Ross holds that only desires, and not beliefs, can motivate.[65] As far as the problem we have just noted goes, it wouldn't matter if Ross held that the belief that there are right actions, and that this is one of them, can give rise to action directly. So long as the resulting motivation is only de dicto and not (also) de re, it would seem to express an insufficiently integrated moral character.

I believe that some appreciation of these points lies behind Prichard's remark in 'Does Moral Philosophy Rest on a Mistake?' that we recognize the 'nature of the demand which originates the subject' of moral philosophy when we 'feel the force of the various obligations in life', and when he says that 'to feel that I ought to' do something 'is to be moved towards' doing it.[66] The picture this suggests is not Ross's externalist model. It suggests that de re motivation is somehow already involved in the forming of an intuitive moral belief itself. Significantly, Prichard says that we feel the force of 'various' obligations, as though these were distinct, not just the force of obligation, considered abstractly. As suggestive as these remarks are, however, Prichard never developed them. By the time of 'Duty and

---

[63] M. Smith, *The Moral Problem* (Oxford: Blackwell, 1994), 75.   [64] Ibid.

[65] J. Dancy, 'Intuitionism', in P. Singer (ed.), *A Companion to Ethics* (Oxford: Blackwell, 1993), 415–16.

[66] H. A. Prichard, 'Does Moral Philosophy Rest on a mistake?', in Prichard, *Moral Obligation: Essays and Lectures*, ed. W. D. Ross (Oxford: Clarendon Press, 1949), 1 and 7.

Interest' he seems to have adopted a thoroughly externalist account of moral motivation.

I should stress, again, that the problem with the externalist picture is not its supposition that the de dicto desire to do what is right has an important role to play in moral reasoning and deliberation. It is reasonable to suppose, indeed, that deliberation is actually governed by such a desire. Although we can, of course, deliberate idly without any commitment to doing what we determine we should do, it is very difficult to see how any account of serious deliberation can dispense with a desire (or practical commitment of some other kind) to doing whatever (we determine) is right. The problem arises from supposing that the motivation that results from moral deliberation comes entirely from this desire. An adequate account should explain how moral reflection and deliberation can give rise to de re desires for the things we judge to be morally right, regulated, albeit by the governing concern to do whatever is right.

To see how this might happen, compare what Ross says about the thought of an act as pleasant giving rise to a desire to do it. Consider two different ways this might happen. In one, I desire to do something enjoyable and become convinced by a trusted friend that I will find an activity enjoyable even though I can't now imagine what could possibly be enjoyable about it. In another, I imagine an activity and intrinsically like and am attracted by various aspects of it in imagination. I predict that I will enjoy it, because of what I imagine it will be like, my current assessment, and my belief that my imaginative assessment will coincide with my real one when I actually engage in the activity. In both cases, I believe that I will enjoy the activity and form a desire to engage in it. But otherwise the cases are very different. In the first, I develop no desire to engage in the activity for its own sake, no de re desire to engage in it. Rather it is because I have a desire to do whatever I will enjoy (within limits) and am convinced that I will enjoy this activity that I form the derivative desire to engage in it. In the latter case, however, I come to believe that I will enjoy the activity by (imaginatively) apprehending its enjoyable qualities in a way that gives rise to a positive regard for that specific activity and a de re desire to engage in it.[67]

---

[67] Compare here what Hobbes says about the identity of 'desire' and 'love', and Mill about desire and enjoyment being the same 'psychological fact'. What both mean is that desire and the sort of intrinsic liking involved in enjoyment are the same positive regard, the difference between them being that with desire it is for some nonactual possibility considered in prospect, and with enjoyment it is for some actual aspect of our experience. T. Hobbes, *Leviathan* (1651), ed. E. Curley (Indianapolis: Hackett, 1994), VI.iii; Mill, *Utilitarianism*, ch. IV.

Stephen Darwall

Were moral reflection to involve something similar to the latter process, it might explain how, in the process of forming the judgment that something is morally right, one can acquire de re desires to do what is (as one judges) right. We have, in fact, theories of moral judgment that fit this model, but they are no help to the intuitionist. For a sensibility theory, like McDowell's for example, there is a conceptual connection between the response-dependent features that correct moral perception defects and the motivation-laden forms of sensibility necessary for this apprehension. When the virtuous person sees that kindness is called for, for example, she sees things in a light that both expresses and encourages a de re concern to be kind.[68] But a sensibility theory explains the practicality of moral judgment by response-dependence, and intuitionists are bound to reject this as inconsistent with their central claim that fundamental moral truths are necessary and a priori.[69]

A Kantian practical reasoning approach provides a different picture of practical thought that might explain how moral reflection can generate de re moral concerns, while maintaining the intuitionist tenet that fundamental moral truths are synthetic a priori. The categorical imperative procedure brings the practical force of will inside moral reflection. In determining that it is wrong, for example, to refuse to participate in practices of mutual aid, I see that not participating is inconsistent with what I would will for all from a perspective I attempt actually to occupy in moral reflection. A de re concern that people (myself included) cooperate for reciprocal advantage is itself involved and generated in determining that not cooperating would be wrong. The problem for the intuitionist, however, is that the Kantian approach holds fundamental moral truths to be, in this way, truths of practical moral reasoning, not independent truths that reason apprehends. And this the intuitionist is bound to reject.[70]

6. Sidgwick on Irreducibility and Action-Guidance

Even if externalism is in some ways an unattractive position, it might still be the intuitionists' best alternative. Lacking a convincing direct response to Hume's challenge, intuitionists might not be able to do better than

---

[68] J. McDowell, 'Virtue and Reason', *Monist*, 63 (1979), 331–50; 'Values and Secondary Qualities', in T. Honderich (ed.), *Morality and Objectivity: A Tribute to J. L. Mackie* (London: Routledge & Kegan Paul, 1985).   [69] See Sect. 2.
[70] See Sect. 2.

attempting to avoid it altogether. In this concluding section, however, I will present some reasons for thinking that intuitionists are not well positioned to pursue this strategy. Intuitionists are united in their opposition to all forms of reductionism in ethics. But what underlies their confidence that every reduction must fail? What makes them so sure that no empirical, or other metaphysical, inquiry can decide fundamental questions of ethics?

Some insight into this question can be gained, I believe, by taking note of what Sidgwick says in a fascinating passage from the 'Ethical Judgments' chapter of *The Methods of Ethics*. Sidgwick ends the passage with a statement of the intuitionists' doctrine of irreducibility. 'The fundamental notion represented by the word "ought" or "right"', he says, is 'essentially different from all notions representing facts of physical or psychical experience.'[71] How does Sidgwick get to this claim?

The preceding paragraphs concern the role of reason and desire in motivation or, as Sidgwick also calls it, 'the influence of the intellect on desire and volition'.[72] Everyone is familiar, he says, with conflicts between irrational (or 'non-rational') desires, on the one hand, and deliberate judgment, on the other.[73] There is, however, a substantial issue regarding the nature and extent of these conflicts. In exactly what ways can 'the intellect' influence desire and volition?

Some philosophers (Sidgwick clearly has Hume in mind) hold that reason's influence is exhausted by two roles: (*a*) enabling 'new perceptions and representations of means conducive to the desired ends', or (*b*) enabling 'new representations of facts actually existing or in prospect . . . which rouse new impulses of desire or aversion'.[74] But these conflicts, Sidgwick says (again echoing Hume) are not 'properly conceived' as between reason and desire. They are rather 'among our desires and aversions; the sole function of reason being to bring before the mind ideas of actual or possible facts, which modify . . . the resultant force of our various impulses.'[75]

Sidgwick had already made it clear two chapters before that he rejects this view. As he describes it here retrospectively, he had already contrasted ' "non-rational" desires and inclinations' with 'the motive to action supplied by the

---

[71] *The Methods of Ethics*, 25.　　　[72] Ibid.　　　[73] Ibid., 24.

[74] Ibid. Compare Hume: 'According to this principle, which is so obvious and natural, it is only in two senses that any affection can be called unreasonable. First, When a passion, such as hope or fear, grief or joy, despair or security, is founded on the supposition of the existence of objects, which really do not exist. Secondly, When in exerting any passion in action, we choose means insufficient for the designed end, and deceive ourselves in our judgment of causes and effects' (*Treatise of Human Nature*, 415).　　　[75] *The Methods of Ethics*, 25.

recognition' that an act is 'reasonable' or 'right', that is, that it ought to be done.[76] What is remarkable about the current passage, however, is that Sidgwick here identifies the claim that 'ordinary moral or prudential judgments' have an 'influence on volition' with the claim that they are irreducible to 'facts of physical or psychical experience' (i.e. the facts which, according to the Humean view, are the only ones that can move the will when rationally apprehended, and then only by engaging desire).[77] What leads Sidgwick to make this identification, I think, is that he believes that the central difference between psychological and ethical judgments is that only ethical judgments are intrinsically action-guiding, only they concern regulation of conduct and choice by their very nature. Thus in the earlier chapter Sidgwick distinguishes disciplines like psychology and sociology, which are 'positive' and seek 'to understand human action', with ethics, which is 'practical' and seeks 'to regulate it'.[78]

If, however, what stands behind the intuitionists' irreducibility claim is the thesis that ethical judgments are intrinsically action-guiding, then it may be difficult for them to avoid Hume's challenge. For the question will naturally arise how on an intuitionist picture ethical judgments can be action-guiding and move the will.[79] This leaves intuitionism with a substantial burden to overcome. To the extent that its irreducibility claim is grounded in the thesis that ethical thought and discourse is essentially action-guiding, intuitionism will owe us some (presumably a priori) account of how intuitive ethical judgment can move the will. But it is unclear what resources, if any, intuitionism has to meet this challenge. The attempts I have canvassed here do not give cause for optimism.

[76] *The Method of Ethics*, 23.

[77] 'I hold that this is not the case; that the ordinary moral or prudential judgments which, in the case of all or most minds, have some—though often an inadequate—influence on volition, cannot legitimately be interpreted as judgments respecting the present or future existence of human feelings or any facts of the sensible world; the fundamental notions represented by the word "ought" or "right," which such judgments contain expressly or by implication, being essentially different from all notions representing facts of physical or psychical experience' (ibid., 25).

[78] Ibid., 2.

[79] Sidgwick gives little help with this question himself. At points he suggests a version of the analogy between belief and will. He grants that although 'we cannot help believing what we see to be true', 'we can help doing what we see to be right or wise', but he nonetheless explains this practical gap as being due to conflicting 'irrational' impulses which 'prevent' the 'practical realization' of our ethical knowledge (ibid., 5). Lacking contrary impulses, he appears to imply, the apprehension that an action is right is, necessarily, sufficient to motivate it. At other points he relies on the fact that in any 'serious' deliberation the agent 'assumes in himself a determination to pursue whatever conduct may be shown by argument to be reasonable' (p. 5). As we have seen, however, neither of these lines of thought can provide a satisfying answer to Hume's challenge. The former analogy breaks down at the critical point, and the latter desire cannot explain moral deliberation's giving rise to desires to do what is right de re. See Sect. 3 and 5, respectively.

A Wittgensteinian Approach to Ethical Intuitionism

12

Robert L. Arrington

My thesis in this paper is that W. D. Ross's principles of prima facie duty are best understood as instances of what Wittgenstein calls grammatical propositions. If this view is correct, it will show us the importance of these principles and help us see why they are important. At the same time, my interpretation will require a substantial revision of Ross's conception of these principles, especially his epistemological claims about our knowledge of them. I begin in Section 1 with an exposition of what Ross has to say about the principles of prima facie duty or rightness, and then I point to some problems I have with Ross's theory. In Section 2 I challenge the epistemological assumptions Ross makes, and in doing so I maintain that the principles in question are the object of neither knowledge nor belief. Section 3 puts before us Wittgenstein's conception of grammatical propositions, and the concluding section shows us how Wittgenstein's perspective illuminates the actual role of Ross's principles—and similar propositions—in our moral lives.

1. Ross's Intuitionism

Ross's theory is a familiar one,[1] and so I shall be very brief in my presentation of those aspects of it that are of interest to me. According to Ross, as a

---

[1] See W. D. Ross, *The Right and the Good* (Oxford: Clarendon Press, 1930).

result of various relationships we have with other people, and with ourselves, we come to have certain prima facie duties toward them or ourselves. For instance, as a result of having promised something to someone, I have a prima facie duty to do what I promised; as a result of an offensive remark I made to someone, I have a prima facie duty to apologize. Thus there are various types of prima facie duty, and types of varying orders of generality. There are, for example, the prima facie duties of promise-keeping, and, more generally, of fidelity. The duty to apologize is a species of the prima facie duty of reparation, and so on. Ross calls a statement to the effect that a certain kind of act is a prima facie duty a principle of prima facie duty.

Ross claims that we apprehend the prima facie rightness of certain types of acts, and in doing so we come to an awareness that it is self-evidently the case that any act of one of these types is prima facie right or prima facie our duty. No independent evidence is needed to detect the truth of this principle, nor is any proof needed. Our reason reveals that, in and of itself (self-evidently), the principle is true. In a word, we have a rational intuition of its truth, a direct, unmediated awareness by the faculty of reason that an act of this type is indeed prima facie right or one's duty. Ross draws an explicit analogy between our rational apprehension of the truth of the principles of prima facie duty and the apprehension of the truth of mathematical axioms and the validity of certain forms of inference. Reason, of the intuitive variety, is involved in all three cases, and we have as much right to trust reason in the moral case as in the mathematical and logical ones. Granted, not all people, at all times of their lives, will be able to apprehend the truth of one or more of the principles of prima facie duty, but this is equally true of the mathematical and logical principles. What is required in all of these cases is a mature and attentive mind. When a person with such a mind grasps the truth of the principles of prima facie duty, she is acknowledging a 'part of the fundamental nature of the universe'. These principles reflect some of the universal and necessary features of the universe—the moral order, Ross calls them.

Ross, of course, is quick to contrast the knowledge we have of the principles of prima facie duty with our grasp of what is actually our duty in a particular case. The latter grasp which, according to Ross, should not be called apprehension at all—is directed toward one's actual or absolute duty, not one's prima facie one. One's actual duty is a toti-resultant attribute, a duty that is a function of all the moral features of a particular situation, whereas one's prima facie duty is a parti-resultant attribute reflecting only one moral aspect of the situation. Among the many features of a particular

272

situation may be various relationships one has with others or oneself, each one of these relationships giving rise to a prima facie duty. Unfortunately, life being as it is, these prima facie duties may conflict, in the sense that doing one of them may make it impossible to do one or more of the others. In such a complex situation involving conflict among our 'conditional' duties, how do we determine what our actual duty is? For Ross, apprehension of self-evidence is out of the question here, as is any form of certainty. We must rely, as Aristotle told us long ago, on 'perception', or what today we might wish to call judgment. Such judgment involves an assessment of the relative stringency of the conflicting prima facie duties and leads to the conclusion that, all things considered, one's actual or absolute duty is to do thus and so.

Another aspect of Ross's theory should be noted. When we reach a conclusion about our absolute duty and this conclusion requires us not to fulfill one of the conflicting prima facie duties arising out of the situation, it does not follow that this prima facie duty is no longer a duty, at least conditionally. And even as defeated, it continues to exert its pull on us, to impose a moral burden. Violating a prima facie duty, even when it is our actual duty to do so, involves doing something morally unsavory and leads us to feel compunction. This act of violating the conditional duty also, in Ross's eyes, gives rise to another duty, perhaps prima facie, namely to 'make up for' or compensate for the violation. Prima facie obligations must occasionally be broken, but doing so places a moral burden on the one who is morally required to break them.

In presenting the above outline of some parts of Ross's moral theory, I have avoided his controversial use of the notion of 'tendency' to express prima facie duty. I have wanted to concentrate on those aspects of his theory that, in the eyes of many philosophers who agree with him, reflect our actual moral thinking. I would summarize these aspects as follows, characterizing them, to be sure, in a fashion congenial to what I want to say later about them: (a) there are principles of prima facie duty which have a distinctive epistemological status in our moral lives; they express intrinsic necessities and are known intuitively to be true; (b) these general principles are distinct from the particular judgments we make in concrete situations about what (absolutely) we ought to do, the latter judgments being far more problematic than the general principles; and (c) the general principles are still operative, in a special way, even when we judge that they are not to be followed.

Although it is easy to be sympathetic with Ross's view that the above theoretical claims reflect the manner in which everyday, ordinary moral thinking takes place, there are aspects of the theory that are hard to accept. First, do we really have a rational intuition showing us that the principles of prima facie duty are self-evident? Is there really an analogy between the cases of mathematics and logic and the case of morality? Many philosophers and students of philosophy would be reluctant to answer these questions affirmatively. One reason for this is as follows: in the realms of logic and mathematics there is, at the end of the day, consensus; in the realm of morality there is considerable disagreement. Have philosophers like Mill simply been blind to the fact that we have a self-evident prima facie duty to keep a promise, independently of the question whether doing so promotes the general welfare? It is difficult to see many of the great moral philosophers as being guilty of something like moral blindness. Maturity and attentiveness abound among moral philosophers—yes, there are exceptions—and yet many of them disagree with Ross. How so? We need a philosophical characterization of morality that will accommodate the fact that there is disagreement over its fundamental nature and content. Ross's intuitionism makes it difficult to understand this fact.

Second, Ross's claims about what kinds of moral proposition can be known intuitively are puzzling. In *The Right and the Good* he tells us that we come to apprehend the truth of the principles of prima facie duty or rightness only after we directly apprehend the rightness of a particular act: 'What comes first in time is the apprehension of the self-evident prima facie rightness of an individual act of a particular kind.'[2] And later, in *The Foundations of Ethics*,[3] he argues that we first recognize rightness as belonging to particular acts; we do not, he claims, deduce the rightness of particular acts from a general principle of rightness: 'But when I reflect on my own attitude toward particular acts, I seem to find that it is not by deduction but by direct insight that I see them to be right, or wrong.'[4] I apprehend the rightness as a resultant attribute of the particular act, and so the 'direct insight' is a rational insight into the self-evident connection between the resultant property of rightness and the properties of the individual act on which it supervenes. Subsequently, the general principle is 'recognized by intuitive induction as being implied in the judgements already passed on particular acts'.[5]

There are three things that puzzle me about these claims. First, if we can

---

[2] *The Right and the Good*, 33.
[3] *The Foundations of Ethics* (Oxford: Clarendon Press, 1939).   [4] Ibid., 171.
[5] Ibid., 170.

directly apprehend the rightness of a particular act, why make such a fuss over the general principles of prima facie rightness? They seem to play no useful—certainly no basic—role in moral knowledge; we don't need them if we can directly intuit that particular acts are right or wrong. Second, if, as Ross suggests, the general principles are the result of 'intuitive induction', how can they be necessarily true? If I intuit that several individual acts of kind F are right, the inference to 'All acts of kind F are right' is subject to all the woes of induction. Of course, I must grant that I don't know exactly what Ross means by intuitive induction. Third, can we really understand what is involved in grasping directly and self-evidently the rightness of a particular act? Doesn't self-evidence require some generality, something that 'reason' can catch hold of?

A final and, for me, more important comment on Ross is the following: Clearly Ross thinks we have knowledge of the principles of prima facie rightness and of the prima facie rightness of individual acts. And in denying that we have an intuitive apprehension of the absolute rightness of a particular act, he seems to suggest that at most we can claim to believe that an individual act is absolutely right—he speaks in this context of 'probable opinion'.[6] Such a belief might well prove to be false, and any certainty we might entertain as to its truth would be misplaced. It is with Ross's characterizations of the epistemological status of judgments about prima facie rightness that I want to begin my criticism of his theory. In doing so, I shall consider only the principles of prima facie rightness, but I shall undertake the discussion in light of an example of my own which is not one of Ross's principles—the judgment 'it is wrong to tell a lie'. This judgment is, I think, suitably close in nature to the principles, and it is, for me, a clearer case.

2. Reflections on 'It is wrong to tell a lie'

[O]ne thinks that the words 'I know that . . .' are always in place where there is no doubt, and hence even where the expression of doubt would be unintelligible.[7]

What role does 'It is wrong to tell a lie' play in our lives? And, likewise, what is the role of such similar sentences as 'It is one's duty to keep one's promises'

---

[6] *The Right and the Good*, 33.

[7] L. Wittgenstein, *On Certainty*, ed. G. E. M. Anscombe and G. H. von Wright, trans. D. Paul and G. E. M. Anscombe (Oxford: Blackwell, 1969), §10.

and 'It is wrong to hurt another person'? More specifically, what is the epistemological context in which we find these sentences? Do they express beliefs? Do they express knowledge? Or, we must surely ask, are they expressions of neither belief nor knowledge but rather of some noncognitive feelings, attitudes, or commitments to principle? Or, finally, are they beyond belief and knowledge by virtue of playing some special role that cannot be characterized in any of the above traditional ways? I shall argue for the latter characterization of them. In doing so, I shall attempt to abide by the rules for the use of epistemic expressions in everyday, concrete contexts, and thus I shall follow in the spirit of Wittgenstein, who writes in *On Certainty* that he wishes 'to reserve the expression "I know" for cases in which it is used in normal linguistic exchange'.[8]

It is tempting to say that we believe whatever is expressed by the above sentences. Surely I believe it is wrong to tell a lie. I am certainly ready to affirm it—many is the time I have told my children that it is wrong to tell a lie, and in conversations with adults I have no hesitation to say that it is wrong to tell a lie as I censure someone who has done precisely this. But does the fact that I willingly affirm it show that I believe it? Consider an analogous case in basic arithmetic. I tell my young children that two plus two equals four, but I am not sure I want to say that I believe this proposition. 'I believe that two plus two equals four' does not sound strong enough. In fact, it seems more appropriate to say that I know that this is so. But, then, how do I know it? About all I can say is that early in life I was taught that two plus two equals four and thereafter never doubted it, and these seem pretty weak epistemological credentials.

To get back to the moral case: do I believe it is wrong to tell a lie or do I know it? Talk of believing something, at least in some contexts, implies a bit of uncertainty, as if I think so but am not quite sure—as if I might become more certain of it later on. In a nonmoral case, if asked, say, 'Is John in his office?' I might reply 'I believe that he is'. But it does not seem right to preface 'It is wrong to tell a lie' with this use of 'I believe'. There is no uncertainty about the matter on my part, and it is difficult to imagine any circumstances in which my confidence in 'it is wrong to tell a lie' would increase or decrease.[9]

In some contexts, to be sure, an affirmation of one's beliefs implies no

[8] *On Certainty*, §260.
[9] As Wittgenstein puts it, to say that I believe something expresses 'my readiness for my statement to be tested' (Ibid., §355), and I am not at all ready for 'It is wrong to tell a lie' to be tested. When moral philosophers do try to test it, they and I do not share the same wavelength.

uncertainty at all, but, instead, absolute conviction. The religious believer's 'I believe that all human beings are born in sin'; the political activist's 'I believe that the evils of the present day are the direct result of international capitalism'; and the baseball addict's 'I believe Joe DiMaggio is the greatest baseball player ever'—all of these seem to express beliefs that are unquestioned. At the same time, however, the person who expresses one of them is usually all too ready to defend it—by pointing to sayings in the Bible, by discussing socialist economic doctrine, by citing baseball statistics. I'm afraid I can't do any such thing regarding 'It is wrong to tell a lie'. If someone responded with 'It is not wrong to tell a lie', I would not quite know what to say. Beliefs, even the strongest ones, need defense; our (at least my) moral proposition appears not to be capable of it or to need it.

So, then, do I know that it is wrong to tell a lie? I do assert it in full confidence, but it is not clear to me that this is an expression or claim of knowledge. As I asked a moment ago about the arithmetical case, so I can ask about this moral proposition: how did I come to know it? How did I get into a position to do so? What compelling grounds have been adduced in its favor?[10] How was the contradictory proposition 'It is not wrong to tell a lie' shown to be false? If knowledge is what we have here, it is a fairly strange type of it, since there was never any process of coming to know this proposition and there are no grounds that I am ready to provide in order to demonstrate its truth, to show how I know and that I am in a position to know it—all these being things we stand ready to do in normal cases of claiming to know. Early on I simply accepted the proposition, not on the basis of the realization that it, and not its contradictory, was supported by compelling evidence, but on the basis of the fact that my parents and early teachers drilled it into my head. To this day I can't give you any indication of the grounds that support 'It is wrong to tell a lie' and overturn 'It is not wrong to tell a lie'. Knowledge claims, however, require a certain kind of context: the overcoming, or at least conceivable overcoming, of ignorance or error by the citation of compelling grounds for knowledge. If proof must back up claims to knowledge, it is inappropriate to say that I know that lying is wrong. So 'It is wrong to tell a lie' doesn't fall into either the belief or the knowledge category.

---

[10] Again Wittgenstein: ' "I know" often means: I have the proper grounds for my statement' (ibid., §18), and also, 'One says "I know" when one is ready to give compelling grounds. "I know" relates to the possibility of demonstrating the truth' (ibid., §243). To claim that one knows, one must be ready to give someone else grounds 'that satisfy him that I am in a position to know' (ibid., §438). Finally, 'Whether I know something depends on whether the evidence backs me up or contradicts me' (ibid., §504).

Not all moral propositions are like this. I believe, for example, that some, but certainly not all, late-term abortions are wrong, and I am ready to claim knowledge that the American war in Vietnam was morally wrong. So there are moral beliefs and moral knowledge (or appropriate claims to such)—it is just that 'It is wrong to tell a lie' does not express a moral belief or a claim to moral knowledge.

And, of course, there is another big problem here. I don't think that it is always wrong to tell a lie. There are occasions, few and far between, to be sure, when I think that one ought to do so. If I were in the situation Kant describes in his infamous example, it seems that the morally appropriate thing to do would be to lie to the likely assailant at the door about the presence of my friend in the house. So, do I think that it is sometimes wrong to tell a lie, or even that it is usually so? The former is clearly too weak, but so is the latter. My parents didn't tell me that it is usually wrong to tell a lie, but, emphatically, that it is wrong to do so. But they probably would have agreed with me about what to do when the likely assailant appeared at the door.

I believe it is wrong to tell a lie but that sometimes one ought to do so.[11] How can I have it both ways? Unless I am simply inconsistent here and guilty of an obvious logical incoherence in my moral convictions, I must find a way of reconciling these two convictions. Well, this much seems true: I don't believe that it is always wrong to tell a lie, at least in the sense of believing that there are never occasions on which one ought to do so. So I am not committed to the inconsistent duo 'It is always wrong to tell a lie' and 'Sometimes it is not wrong to tell a lie'. It follows that 'It is wrong to tell a lie' is not equivalent to 'It is always wrong to tell a lie'. Kant seemed to accept the equivalence, and that's what got him in trouble. But what is 'It is wrong to tell a lie' saying if not 'It is always wrong to do so'?

It helps here to note that we often say something like 'Well, there are times in life in which one is forced to tell a lie'. In saying this, one is not, of course, claiming that sometimes one is physically compelled to do so. Rather, it is more like this: from a moral point of view, on occasion one doesn't have any choice. In the situation encountered, one option is clearly the one morally demanded and the others are morally impermissible. If it is clear that as a result of my telling the truth in a particular situation someone will be harmed in a serious way, then—no other options affording themselves—I

---

[11] A good question: How can I speak of belief here, as it seems very natural to do? And the answer is: What I believe in this case is that there are exceptions to my duty to tell the truth, and, in agreement with Ross, I take this to be a matter on which there is never any great certainty. Hence it is appropriate to speak of belief in this context.

think I ought to lie. Indeed, I feel morally compelled to do so. Of course, and this is another part of the familiar story, I regret having to do so, I do it reluctantly, and I may feel considerable remorse over my action. Therefore I don't tell the lie willingly—I would much rather not do so—and therein lies the source of my feeling forced in the situation to tell a lie.

Being required morally to tell a lie in a certain situation does not, it seems to me, constitute a particular exception to the claim that it is wrong to tell a lie. Therefore 'It is wrong to tell a lie' is not a generalization, or at least not the kind that would be undermined by an occasion on which I am morally compelled to do so. Indeed, in some indirect way, this particular occasion instantiates the fact that it is wrong to tell a lie. How, otherwise, could we explain the 'being forced' aspect of the situation and the moral unsavoriness of my action?

What we need is a philosophical characterization of 'It is wrong to tell a lie' and similar propositions which recognizes the peculiar epistemological characteristics of them that I have stressed and likewise recognizes the peculiar status they have in moral dilemmas. The characterization I shall now attempt to provide comes from Wittgenstein—or, I should hasten to say, from my understanding of that dark thinker.

3. Wittgenstein and Grammatical Propositions

I wish to suggest that 'It is wrong to tell a lie' is a grammatical proposition. In doing so I am making use of Wittgenstein's grammatical–empirical distinction. The explanation of this distinction begins most easily with the latter part of it. Empirical propositions, as one might surmise, are assertions that are subject to the court of experience. They may be true or false, and we believe that they are the one rather than the other, or probable or improbable, on the basis of the evidence available to us regarding them. 'Evidence' here should be construed in a fairly broad sense, but propositions resulting from observation or the data of sense would be paradigm cases of evidence favoring one empirical proposition over another. The important thing about empirical propositions is their contingency: given what they mean, their truth value is undetermined, and this truth value is something we must find out or discover.

It seems clear to me that there are some empirical moral propositions in this sense. 'It would be wrong for Jack and Jill to engage in premarital sex' is, I think, an example; the generalization 'Premarital sex is wrong' is another, as is 'Gambling is wrong' and 'Marital infidelity is wrong'. Whether these propositions are true or false depends on the evidence and arguments that can be mustered in their favor or against them. In my part of the world some people (fortunately very few) still think that dancing and playing bridge are wrong. I strongly disagree and would be willing to engage in a debate on the matter if called on to do so. I don't think that premarital sex is wrong in general, but there may well be particular cases (Jack and Jill) in which it is. Argument and evidence are clearly appropriate in all of these instances. Moreover, the notion of belief 'fits' these contingent propositions, and, when the individual case is compelling, so does the notion of knowledge.

To my mind, the contrast between 'It is wrong to tell a lie' and 'Marital infidelity is wrong' is sharp. I believe most cases of marital infidelity are wrong, and I am willing to defend this belief. If asked to defend the assertion that lying is wrong, I wouldn't know what to say—other than simply to rephrase the matter by saying that it is wrong to deceive other people in what you tell them. If it is said that it is wrong to lie to others because it will hurt them, I don't know what 'hurt' means in this context. Surely lying to someone usually won't physically hurt them, and if it is said that it will psychologically hurt them, this notion needs to be explained. If it means causing them mental anguish, this will occur only if the lie is found out—but surely the lie is wrong even if it is not found out. All one can say is that lying to others is treating them with disrespect, but this comes to little more than treating them in ways in which one ought not—i.e. Lying is wrong. As I see it, 'lying is wrong' is one of my basic moral commitments. It is not a contingent proposition and does not stand in need of defense.

In fact, this commitment defines, at least in part, what the moral dimension is for me. Just as 'Red is a color' goes some way toward defining what a color is, and 'Yellow is a color', 'Blue is a color', and 'Green is a color' continue the process, so 'Lying is wrong', 'Breaking promises is wrong', 'Hurting other people is wrong', and similar propositions spell out, at least for me, what morality is all about. I don't have any more general concept of morality against which I can test and judge whether 'Lying is wrong' is true or false. Being moral just is not lying, not breaking promises, not hurting others unnecessarily, and the like.[12]

---

[12] See my *Rationalism, Realism, and Relativism: Perspectives in Contemporary Moral Epistemology* (Ithaca, NY: Cornell University Press, 1989), ch. 6.

Nor do I possess the full concept of lying before I understand that lying is wrong. 'Lying is wrong' is a grammatical proposition in that it characterizes the nature or essence of lying. Wittgenstein asserts that 'Essence is expressed by grammar'[13] and 'Grammar tells us what kind of object anything is.'[14] If I don't accept that lying is morally questionable, I don't have anything like an adequate understanding of lying—I don't know fully what it is. It may appear that the word 'lying' can be defined in a morally neutral way, namely to lie is intentionally to tell someone something one believes not to be true. But the inadequacy of this expression of the concept would come out if someone asked what was meant by 'intentionally to tell a falsehood', to which one might well reply: to try to deceive—and the moral quality is then on the surface. Lies, in their very nature, are morally tainted.

'Lying is wrong', then, is constitutive of my concept of a lie. And it is, as we have seen, partially constitutive of my concept of morality. Propositions which are constitutive of concepts are, in Wittgenstein's terms, grammatical propositions.[15] He would want to say that they express or reflect rules for the proper use or application of words, since for him a concept just is a set of rules for properly employing a word.[16]

Grammatical propositions, as distinct from empirical ones, are necessary, not contingent. They are not of such a nature that observation or evidence could show them to be false. Does this make them necessarily true? Wittgenstein thinks it is misleading to talk this way. Necessarily true of what? Characterizing them as necessarily true makes them seem like descriptive propositions, but descriptions which have the queer property that they can't even be conceived to fail to describe correctly their subject matter. Any description surely can be understood to fail to apply to its subject matter. Instead of saying that grammatical propositions are necessarily

---

[13] L. Wittgenstein, *Philosophical Investigations*, 3rd edn., trans. G. E. M. Anscombe (London: Macmillan, 1958), §371. [14] Ibid., §373.

[15] See my 'The Grammar of Grammar', in R. Haller and J. Brandl (eds.), *Proceedings of the 14th International Wittgenstein Symposium* (Vienna: Holder-Pichler-Tempsky, 1990).

[16] A couple of other grammatical remarks, from outside the sphere of morality: 'Only of a living human being and what resembles (behaves like) a living human being can one say: it has sensations; it sees, is blind, hears, is deaf, is conscious or unconscious' (*Philosophical Investigations*, §281), and '. . . "The room has length" can be used as a grammatical statement. It then says that a sentence of the form "The room is —— feet long" makes sense' (L. Wittgenstein, *The Blue and Brown Books* (Oxford: Blackwell, 1958), 30). The virtue of these examples of grammatical remarks (statements, propositions) is that they make clear how they are rules of language and specifically of sense. Some other examples: 'Every rod has a length' (*Philosophical Investigations*, §251); 'Believing is not thinking' (ibid., §574); and 'White is lighter than black' (*Remarks on the Foundations of Mathematics* (Oxford: Blackwell, 1964), 30).

true, it is better to say that they have a different function from empirical ones. The latter are to convey information about how things are, information that clears up ignorance or error. Empirical propositions are debatable, and it is very important to get them right, since not to do so is to be guilty of error. Grammatical propositions, on the contrary, set out rules for the proper use of words. What looks like a necessarily true description of some essential feature of the world turns out, for Wittgenstein, to be a rule of language. As he puts it: 'Consider: "The only correlate in language to an intrinsic necessity is an arbitrary rule. It is the only thing which one can milk out of this intrinsic necessity into a proposition".'[17] These arbitrary rules are norms of representation; in effect they tell us how to use correctly the words that occur in those empirical propositions which can be either true or false. Failure to abide by the rules generates, not falsehood and error, but senselessness and conceptual confusion. As standards of sense, the rules are the constant norms that give our words abiding meaning for ourselves and for others.

One likely objection to my claim that 'It is wrong to tell a lie' is a grammatical proposition is that grammatical propositions tell us how to talk (with sense) whereas 'It is wrong to tell a lie' tells us how to act. According to this objection, 'It is wrong to tell a lie' is a principle of action, not, as my account suggests, merely a linguistic principle of speech.

But is 'It is wrong to tell a lie' a moral principle which tells us how to act? If so, it is a principle that not only has numerous exceptions but also one that is subject to open-ended exceptions. There are many situations which might morally override the fact that an act is one of truth-telling: that it might harm someone in a serious way, that it might involve the breaking of a significant promise, that it might infringe upon proper gratitude, etc. And there seems to be no a priori limit we can place on the possible exceptions, other than that they must involve some other moral feature that, in the particular case, conflicts with truth-telling. Rather than being a principle that always, or for the most part, guides a person in her actions, 'It is wrong to tell a lie' comes across more as a vital consideration that goes into the determination of whether a particular act is the right thing to do. It identifies a factor that must be taken into account in judging that a particular act is one's duty or not. Some people may have 'Always tell the truth' as one of their moral principles—they would believe that one ought always tell the truth come what may. But in confronting the complex world in which we

---

[17] *Philosophical Investigations*, §372.

live, others—most of us, I think—are more cautious, even while admitting that truth-telling always has moral relevance for judging whether a particular action is our duty or not.

Moreover, for an action to be one having moral worth, it must be based on reasons and rational considerations, i.e. on judgment. If I tell the truth on a particular occasion and my action is morally commendable, it is because I think and judge that this action is my duty, and act accordingly. My thinking it my duty involves understanding that it is so by virtue of its being an act of truth-telling, by virtue, that is, of one of the criteria for moral duty or right action being met. My thinking it the right thing to do also involves the judgment that there are no overriding considerations that trump the act's right-making characteristic, namely, its being a case of truth-telling. All of the considerations that play a part in my doing something because it is an act of truth-telling involve an application of the conceptual rule that telling the truth is right and telling a lie wrong. Thus determining that an act is one that I ought or ought not to do involves appeal to a rule of moral grammar. When I acknowledge this rule in making my moral judgment and then act accordingly, my action has moral worth. It follows that the idea of an action having moral worth cannot be defined without appeal to the rules of moral grammar.

To return to our grammatical characterization of 'It is wrong to tell a lie' and the concept of morality, let us acknowledge that in general concepts may not be very precise, and thus the rules or grammatical propositions that constitute them may be a bit indeterminate and ragged at the edges. Such, I think, is the case with the concept of morality. There are activities and aspects of life that do not clearly fall either within or without the concept of morality. But there are central features of this concept, and telling the truth and keeping promises certainly are found among these central features. To abandon the grammatical propositions 'Telling a lie is wrong' and 'It is one's duty to keep one's promises' would be to change the concept of morality in a very basic way.

But, of course, we could change it. Utilitarians, I think, have been trying to change it—or reject it—for ages. In their minds being moral just is maximizing benefits.[18] Thus for them lying and breaking promises are only contingent features of the moral life, which is to say that the proposition 'Lying is wrong' is an empirical one for them. They don't share my concept of morality. To be sure, that people have the concepts they do is a contingent

---

[18] Or, alternatively, to be rational, as opposed to being moral, just is maximizing benefits.

fact. (To admit this is different from saying that the grammatical rules that constitute these concepts are contingent, i.e. that the rules themselves might be true or false.) The concepts people have today may not be the ones they operate with tomorrow, and different people may have different concepts attached to the same word, i.e. different rules for its proper use. Grammatical propositions are not about Platonic forms; they reflect the current standards of human language practices. These practices are fairly fragile; they undergo change as a result of many conditions; indeed, they may disappear altogether. Two or more practices may come into conflict with one another, especially when they use the same word or words differently, i.e. according to different grammatical rules.

A central question for Wittgenstein is whether we can justify any of these concepts or grammatical rules—and invalidate others. And his answer is negative, as we see from the remark quoted above in which he says that arbitrary rules are all that is left of intrinsic necessities.[19] We also see from his comments on the autonomy of grammar how and why he rejects any notion of validating or invalidating grammar. These comments, found in *Philosophical Remarks*, *Philosophical Grammar*, and *Philosophical Investigations*, demonstrate that various putative ways of justifying or invalidating grammar do not succeed, either because they beg the question in favor of, or against, the concept or grammatical rule in question, or because they fail to realize the kind of rule that is in question.[20] For instance, Wittgenstein denies that one can justify grammar by pointing to language-independent logical forms or structures of reality which the grammar might be thought to reflect, since any attempt to describe these forms or structures would incorporate the very grammar up for validation. In another instance, Wittgenstein shows that those who engage in pragmatic attempts to justify linguistic rules fail to see that these rules are part of language-games that have their own internal purposes or goals; only rules, like cooking rules, that are designed to yield a result independent of the activity—a result like tasty food—can be validated on the grounds that in point of fact following them does produce such results. The upshot of these considerations is that no concept can be shown to be true (or false), justified (or unjustified), valid (or invalid). Language, its grammar, and its concepts are autonomous.

[19] *Philosophical Investigations*, §72.

[20] L. Wittgenstein, *Philosophical Remarks*, ed. R. Rhees, trans. R. Hargreaves and R.White (Oxford: Blackwell, 1975); and *Philosophical Grammar*, ed. R. Rhees, trans. A. J. P. Kenny (Oxford: Blackwell, 1974). Also see my 'The Autonomy of Grammar', in S. G. Shanker and J. V. Canfield (eds.), *Wittgenstein's Intentions* (New York: Garland, 1993).

The autonomy of grammar combined with the idea that language-games and their concepts are contingent yields an interesting result. People who use a certain language are guided constantly and rigidly by the rules of grammar that are constitutive of the language or its concepts ('the hardness of the logical must'). These rules are the norms of representation which determine sense in the language in question. Within that language, there can be no escaping the rules. They guide one unalterably, providing fixed points of reference that make it possible to ascertain the truth or falsity of contingent claims made with the concepts whose sense they fix. At the same time the language or language-game, with its fixed and autonomous grammatical rules, is as a whole in no sense necessary. People need not talk that way, and if they do, they may at some point cease to do so. Moreover, gradual changes can be made within the grammatical rules, not on the grounds that they have been discovered inadequate in some way, but because interests, needs, general facts of nature, etc. change and prompt people to talk differently.

Different people may have different languages—different ways of dividing up the color spectrum, of keeping time, of selling things like wood, of prescribing and proscribing behavior. Similarly, they may have different concepts of morality—we would say this if they used something like the same terms 'moral', 'duty', 'right', and the like in different ways from ours. Or they may have ways of prescribing behavior so different from ours that we would not want to call what they have morality. If such a difference in morality, or in ways of prescribing behavior, were to exist, if we were to have different concepts of morality or 'proper' behavior, there would be no way to justify one of these over against the other—that is the message of Wittgenstein's autonomy theme. The participants in one morality could not legitimately be accused by participants in the other of making an epistemological error with regard to their concepts. Both sets of participants would be guided unalterably by the grammatical standards that are constitutive of their concept of morality. Those standards would define where they stand firm. And in standing firm in their respective ways, they might well come to odds practically— talking right by one another while at the same time cursing or shooting at one another. They could not legitimately accuse one another of making mistakes, but only of being so different— 'evil,' 'abominable'— that they cannot share the same physical space. As Wittgenstein puts it, 'one might simply say "Oh, rubbish!" to someone who wanted to make objections to the propositions that are beyond doubt. That is, not reply to him but admonish him.'[21] In thoughts such as these, we find an illumination, I think, of the conflicts among deontologists, consequentialists, and virtue ethicists—and possibly among opponents in such practical arenas as the abortion debate.

4. Once Again: 'It is wrong to tell a lie'

Now we can return to the proposition that was giving us so much trouble. Now we can understand its epistemological peculiarities. And now we can see how Ross's intuitionism comes close, but not quite close enough, to understanding these peculiar propositions.

'It is wrong to tell a lie' is a grammatical rule partly constitutive of my concept of morality. Your concept may be different. I doubt very much that all Westerners, even all Americans, even all current-day Atlantans, even all students in a classroom on any given day, share this concept, but I am equally convinced that many do. It is a central plank in what many of us call morality. And it is so basic that for us it is removed from the arena of doubt. As Wittgenstein puts it, it has been placed in the archives. For those who accept and operate with this concept of morality (and the grammatical remarks expressing it), it is something they take as a matter of course, without question.

But this exalted status doesn't mean that we who accept this grammatical proposition claim to know it.[22] On the contrary, because it has this 'archival', matter-of-course status, it is inappropriate to speak of knowing it. Knowledge requires proof, evidence, observation—precisely what we do not have in this case. People who are 'ignorant' of the proposition simply have not had a good moral education—it is not that they have missed out on the evidence or failed to grasp the proof. Hence there is operative here nothing like what Ross calls rational apprehension; nothing like self-evidence as a mode of proof. It is not difficult, however, to understand why Ross

---

[21] *On Certainty*, §495.

[22] Wittgenstein explicitly makes this point about mathematical and logical propositions, which, if not themselves grammatical propositions, are the closest of kin. He writes, for example, 'If you know a mathematical proposition, that's not to say you yet know *anything*. i.e., the mathematical proposition is only supposed to supply a framework for a description' (*Remarks on the Foundations of Mathematics*, 160). And about logical propositions he has this to say: 'one needs to remember that the propositions of logic are so constructed as to have no application as information in practice. So it could very well be said that they are not propositions at all' (ibid., 53).

thought there was such a thing as the apprehension of self-evident moral truth. Propositions like 'It is wrong to tell a lie' have been placed beyond doubt. It is not that we cannot as a matter of fact doubt them but that it makes no sense to do so. They function, not as disputable claims about human action, but as the standards which give sense to our way of speaking morally about action. Philosophers like Ross have confused the distinctive function and character of these propositions with epistemological necessity. They have invented a form of knowledge—rational apprehension of self-evidence—in order to accommodate these propositions within an epistemological context.

The grammatical propositions definitive of morality can be seen at work in arguments over contingent moral claims. In investigating a case of marital infidelity, for example, we are on the lookout for deceit, for the breaking of promises, and for harm and hurt. If a person and his spouse have an understanding with one another, if neither feels betrayed by the infidelity, if neither is hurt or depressed over it, and if the acts of unfaithfulness work to promote a high level of, let us say, physical satisfaction for one or both persons—even while their marriage provides other benefits for them—then it would be hard for me to understand how the infidelity is wrong in this instance. To be sure, I find it difficult to believe that this combination of circumstances often exists, and so I believe that marital infidelity is usually wrong. But, using the grammatical rules that define morality for me as my guide, I am prepared to investigate the individual case and prepared to exempt it from moral censure, even while experience shows me—once again in light of moral grammar—that almost always marital infidelity is wrong.

In other words, the characterization of 'It is wrong to tell a lie' as a grammatical proposition allows one to illuminate the difference between it and a contingent moral claim like 'Marital infidelity is wrong'. This characterization also reveals the relationship between the two kinds of proposition: how the grammatical one figures as a standard of sense in the investigation of the truth or falsity of the contingent empirical one. It does not, however, figure therein as a premise from which a particular or general conclusion is derived. Given what 'lying' and 'immoral' mean—which any mature participant in my language-game of morality will grasp without having to be given a definition (a grammatical proposition)—then finding acts of lying at the center of most cases of marital infidelity is enough to mount a prima facie condemnation of it as immoral.

In thoughts like these we find an explanation of why Ross wants to speak of a direct apprehension of the rightness of particular acts and denies that

Robert L. Arrington

we deduce this rightness from a general moral principle. He is right: there is no deduction; we do directly see that some acts are right. But neither is there any rational apprehension going on here. There is simply the manifestation of our ability to use the word 'right' in our moral language-game—to use it consistently with the grammatical propositions that define it, usually without actually appealing to these propositions in the concrete application. (To be sure, they could be appealed to if there were disagreement over a particular application of 'right'.) All we need to explain this appropriate application are the normal operation of our sense faculties and our mastery of the moral language of 'right'. These Wittgensteinian thoughts can also explain why we need something like Ross's general principles of prima facie duty or rightness. Ross himself does not need these principles—as he conceives of them. But understanding them, not as substantive moral principles, but as grammatical propositions regulating the language of right and duty, shows us both their nature and our need for them. They are the norms of representation presupposed by the individual acts of language-use involved in seeing and saying that a particular act is one I ought or ought not to do. They are the rules that give sense to our moral language.

Let me turn, in conclusion, to the difficult question of how 'It is wrong to tell a lie' can be one of my constant moral guideposts even while I grant that sometimes it is wrong not to tell a lie. Recognizing that I am using a metaphor that needs a lot of unpacking, I want to say that 'It is wrong to tell a lie' defines a significant dimension of moral space. It identifies a moral value, or, in this case, disvalue. Lying is morally repugnant, come what may, even when my situation is one in which it becomes, regrettably, the right thing to do.

Wittgenstein is thought by many of his readers to have developed a useful technical notion of a criterion as a means of conveying the distinctive relationship between certain forms of behavior and the attribution of mental states.[23] The forms of behavior are part of the concept of what they govern. According to one way of understanding criteria, they are conceptually based evidence for the existence of mental states; according to another way, they are situation-sensitive sufficient conditions for the existence of these states. In both interpretations, they are defeasible: an otherwise warranted assertion of the existence of a mental state—an assertion based on the

[23] See M. Addis, *Making Sense of Other Minds* (Aldershot: Ashgate, 1999). Also see P. M. S. Hacker, *Insight and Illusion* (Oxford: Clarendon Press, 1972; rev. edn. 1986), ch. x; and J. V. Canfield, *Language and World* (Amherst: University of Massachusetts Press, 1981), chs. 3–8.

288

occurrence of the criterial behavior—can be defeated by unusual circumstances. As defeasible claims, however, the burden of proof is on someone who denies one of these claims in the face of the satisfaction of the criteria—this person must show, not the possibility, but the actuality of a defeating condition.

The definitive contours of moral space, I suggest, function very much like criteria—in this case criteria for the assertion of moral judgments about whether particular acts, or general classes of them, have a certain moral property. If an act is an instance of a lie, then one of the criteria for an immoral act—that it is a lie—has been met. This criterion is set forth in the proposition we have been discussing all along: 'It is wrong to tell a lie'. A moral judgment based on the satisfaction of one of the criteria for applying the moral term in the judgment, is, however, defeasible. It can be defeated, but only by the assertion that another dimension of moral space is satisfied, one which overrides the dimension specified in the criterion first employed. Understood as expressing multiple criteria for an act being morally wrong, statements like 'It is wrong to tell a lie' and 'It is wrong to break a promise' do not themselves conflict—it is always morally inappropriate both to tell a lie and to break a promise. Nor do these statements have exceptions—they always specify an aspect of moral space. Even when their applications conflict as a result of the facts of particular situations, the grammatical statements remain unsullied, since defeasibility is built into their applications.

Clearly this is a complicated story. I hope only to have suggested a way in which we can understand 'It is wrong to tell a lie'—a way that accommodates much that Ross had to say about our prima facie duties and principles of right action without accepting his epistemological characterization of the propositions expressing them. But the characterization of these propositions as grammatical remarks shows how easy it would be to take them as Ross does—it identifies the temptation to this particular form of philosophical confusion. This characterization illuminates how 'It is wrong to tell a lie' is beyond both belief and knowledge, but not, for all that, a matter of affective or conative states that render it noncognitive.

A Wittgensteinian approach to any philosophical subject matter is unpopular these days, and so I know full well that I have not convinced all of the readers of this essay—perhaps not any of them—that it serves us beneficially in this area of ethical theory. I have only tried to show what a Wittgensteinian approach to ethical intuitionism might look like and to give some very general reasons why I think it holds promise.

Bibliography

ADDIS, M., *Making Sense of Other Minds* (Aldershot: Ashgate, 1999).

ALSTON, W. P., 'Foundationalism', in J. Dancy and E. Sosa (eds.), *A Companion to Epistemology* (Oxford: Blackwell, 1992).

ARISTOTLE, *Nicomachean Ethics*.

ARRINGTON, R., *Rationalism, Realism, and Relativism: Perspectives in Contemporary Moral Epistemology* (Ithaca, NY: Cornell University Press, 1989).

—— 'The Grammar of Grammar', in R. Haller and J. Brendl (eds.), *Proceedings of the 14th International Wittgenstein Symposium* (Vienna: Holder-Pichler-Tempsky, 1990).

—— 'The Autonomy of Grammar', in S. G. Shanker and J. V. Canfield (eds.), *Wittgenstein's Intentions* (New York: Garland, 1993).

—— 'Structural Justification', repr. in R. Audi, *The Structure of Justification* (Cambridge: Cambridge University Press, 1993).

ATTFIELD, R., *A Theory of Value and Obligation* (London: Croom Helm, 1987).

AUDI, R., 'Ethical Reflectionism', *Monist*, 76 (1993), 295–315.

—— 'The Foundationalism–Coherentism Controversy: Hardened Stereotypes and Overlapping Theories', in Audi, *The Structure of Justification* (Cambridge: Cambridge University Press, 1993).

—— 'Intuitionism, Pluralism, and the Foundations of Ethics', in W. Sinnott-Armstrong and M. Timmons (eds.), *Moral Knowledge? New Readings in Moral Epistemology* (Oxford: Oxford University Press, 1996); repr. in Audi, *Moral Knowledge and Ethical Character* (New York: Oxford University Press, 1997).

—— *Moral Knowledge and Ethical Character* (New York: Oxford University Press, 1997).

—— 'The Axiology of Moral Experience', *Journal of Ethics*, 2 (1998), 355–75.

—— *Epistemology: A Contemporary Introduction to the Theory of Knowledge* (London: Routledge, 1998).

—— 'Moderate Intuitionism and the Epistemology of Moral Judgment', *Ethical Theory and Moral Practice*, 1 (1998), 14–34.

—— 'Self-Evidence', *Philosophical Perspectives*, 13 (1999), 205–28.

—— *The Architecture of Reason* (Oxford: Oxford University Press, 2001).

AYER, A. J., *Language, Truth, and Logic* (2nd edn. London: Gollancz, 1946; Harmondsworth: Pelican, 1971).

BAIER, K., *The Rational and the Moral Order* (La Salle, Ill.: Open Court, 1995).

BALGUY, J., 'The Foundations of Moral Goodness', in L. A. Selby-Bigge (ed.), *The*

Bibliography

British Moralists: Being Selections from the Writers Principally of the Eighteenth Century (New York: Dover, 1965).

—— *The Foundation of Moral Goodness* (1728), facs. edn. (New York: Garland, 1978).

BLACKBURN, S., 'Rule-following and Moral Realism', in S. Holtzman and C. Leich (eds.), *Wittgenstein: To Follow a Rule* (London: Routledge & Kegan Paul, 1981).

—— *Spreading the Word* (Oxford: Clarendon Press, 1984).

—— 'Errors and the Phenomenology of Value', in T. Honderich (ed.), *Morality and Objectivity* (London: Routledge & Kegan Paul, 1985).

—— *Essays in Quasi-Realism* (New York: Oxford University Press, 1993).

—— *Ruling Passions: A Theory of Practical Reason* (Oxford: Clarendon Press, 1998).

BLANSHARD, B., *Reason and Goodness* (London: George Allen & Unwin, 1961).

—— 'Sidgwick the Man', *Monist*, 58 (1974), 349–70.

BONJOUR, L., *In Defence of Pure Reason: A Rationalist Account of A Priori Justification* (Cambridge: Cambridge University Press, 1998).

BOYD, R. 'How to be a Moral Realist', in G. Sayre-McCord (ed.), *Essays on Moral Realism* (Ithaca, NY: Cornell University Press, 1988).

BRADLEY, F. H., *Ethical Studies*, 2nd edn. (Oxford: Clarendon Press, 1927).

BRANDT, R. B., *Ethical Theory* (Englewood Cliffs, NJ: Prentice-Hall, 1959).

—— *A Theory of the Good and the Right* (Oxford: Clarendon Press, 1979).

—— *Facts, Values, and Morality* (New York: Cambridge University Press, 1996).

BRINK, D., *Moral Realism and the Foundations of Ethics* (Cambridge: Cambridge University Press, 1989).

—— 'Common Sense and First Principles in Sidgwick's Methods', *Social Philosophy and Policy*, 11 (1994), 179–201.

—— 'Moral Realism and the Foundations of Ethics', *Social Philosophy and Policy*, 11 (1994), 107–13.

BROAD, C. D., *Five Types of Ethical Theory* (London: Routledge & Kegan Paul, 1930).

BROOME, J. 'Normative Requirements', *Ratio*, 12 (1999), 398–419.

BROWN, C., 'Is Hume an Internalist?', *Journal of the History of Philosophy*, 26 (1988), 69–87.

BUTLER, J., *Fifteen Sermons Preached at the Rolls Chapel* (1726).

CANFIELD, J. V., *Language and World* (Amherst: University of Massachusetts Press, 1981).

CARRITT, E. F., *The Theory of Morals* (London: Oxford University Press, 1930).

—— *Ethical and Political Thinking* (Oxford: Clarendon Press, 1947).

CASULLO, A., 'Revisability, Reliablism, and A Priori Knowledge', *Philosophy and Phenomenological Research*, 49 (1988), 187–213.

CHANG, R. (ed.), *Incommensurability, Incomparability, and Practical Reason* (Cambridge, Mass.: Harvard University Press, 1997).

CLARKE, S., *A Discourse of Natural Religion* (1728), in D. D. Raphael (ed.), *British Moralists 1650-1800*, i (Oxford: Clarendon Press, 1974).

—— *A Discourse Concerning the Unalterable Obligations of Natural Religion* (1706); repr. in *Works of Samuel Clarke*, 4 vols. (1738), facs. edn. (New York: Garland, 1978).

CRISP, R., *Mill on Utilitarianism* (London: Routledge, 1997).

—— 'Griffin's Pessimism', in R. Crisp and B. Hooker (eds.), *Well-Being and Morality: Essays in Honour of James Griffin* (Oxford: Clarendon Press, 2000).

—— and HOOKER, B. (eds.), *Well-Being and Morality: Essays in Honour of James Griffin* (Oxford: Clarendon Press, 2000).

CUDWORTH, R., *A Treatise Concerning Eternal and Immutable Morality* (1731), ed. S. Hutton (Cambridge: Cambridge University Press, 1996).

CULLITY, G., 'Moral Character and the Iteration Problem', *Utilitas*, 7 (1995), 289–99.

—— and GAUT, B. (eds.), *Ethics and Practical Reason* (Oxford: Clarendon, 1997).

DANCY, J., *Contemporary Epistemology* (Oxford: Blackwell, 1985).

—— 'An Ethic of Prima Facie Duties', in P. Singer (ed.), *A Companion to Ethics* (Oxford: Blackwell, 1991).

—— 'Intuitionism', in P. Singer (ed.), *A Companion to Ethics* (Oxford: Blackwell, 1991).

—— *Moral Reasons* (Oxford: Blackwell, 1993).

—— 'On the Logical and Moral Adequacy of Particularism', *Theoria*, 3 (1999), 212–24.

—— 'The Particularist's Progress', in B. Hooker and M. Little (eds.), *Moral Particularism* (Oxford: Clarendon Press, 2000).

—— *Practical Reality* (Oxford: Clarendon Press, 2000).

DANIELS, N. 'Wide Reflective Equilibrium and Theory Acceptance in Ethics', *Journal of Philosophy*, 76 (1979), 256–82.

—— 'Reflective Equilibrium and Archimedean Points', *Canadian Journal of Philosophy*, 10 (1980), 83–110.

—— 'Two Approaches to Theory Acceptance in Ethics', in D. Copp and D. Zimmerman (eds.), *Morality, Reason and Truth* (Totowa, NJ: Rowman & Littlefield, 1985).

DARWALL, STEPHEN, *Impartial Reason* (Ithaca, NY: Cornell University Press, 1983).

—— *The British Moralists and the Internal 'Ought': 1640–1740* (Cambridge: Cambridge University Press, 1995).

—— 'Reasons, Motives, and the Demands of Morality: An Introduction', in Stephen Darwall, Allan Gibbard, and Peter Railton (eds.), *Moral Discourse and Practice* (New York: Oxford University Press, 1997).

—— *Philosophical Ethics* (Boulder, Colo.: Westview Press, 1998).

—— GIBBARD, ALLAN, and RAILTON, PETER (eds.), *Moral Discourse and Practice* (New York: Oxford University Press, 1997).

DEPAUL, M., *Balance and Refinement: Beyond Coherence Methods of Moral Inquiry* (New York: Routledge, 1993).

—— 'Two Conceptions of Coherence Methods in Ethics', *Mind*, 96 (1987), 463–81.

DESCARTES, R. *Œuvres de Descartes*, ed. C. Adam and P. Tannery (Paris: Vrin/CNRS, 1964–76), vol. v.

—— *The Philosophical Writings of Descartes*, vol. i, ed. J. Cottingham, R. Stoothof, and D. Murdoch (Cambridge: Cambridge University Press, 1985); and vol. iii, ed. J. Cottingham, R. Stoothof, D. Murdoch, and A. Kenny (Cambridge: Cambridge University Press, 1991).

Bibliography

DONAGAN, A., 'Moral Rationalism and Variable Social Institutions', in P. A. French, T. E. Uehling, Jr., and H. F. Wettstein (eds.), *Midwest Studies in Philosophy*, 7: *Social and Political Philosophy* (1982).

DWORKIN, R., 'Objectivity and Truth: You'd Better Believe It', *Philosophy and Public Affairs*, 25 (1996), 87–139.

EBERTZ, R., 'Is Reflective Equilibrium a Coherentist Model?', *Canadian Journal of Philosophy*, 23 (1993), 193–214.

EDWARDS, P., *The Logic of Moral Discourse* (New York: Free Press, 1955).

EWING, A. C., *The Definition of Good* (New York: MacMillan, 1947).

—— *Ethics* (London: Macmillan, 1947; New York: Free Press, 1953).

—— *The Fundamental Questions of Philosophy* (London: Routledge & Kegan Paul, 1951).

FALK, W. D. ' "Ought" and Motivation', *Proceedings of the Aristotelian Society*, 118 (1947–8), 111–38.

FINE, G. 'Knowledge and Belief in Republic V–VII', in S. Everson (ed.), *Companions to Ancient Thought, i: Epistemology* (Cambridge: Cambridge University Press, 1990).

FLETCHER, J., *Situation Ethics* (London: SCM Press, 1966).

FOOT, P., 'Moral Beliefs', in Foot, *Virtues and Vices amd Other Essays in Moral Philosophy* (Berkeley: University of California Press, 1978).

FRANKENA, W. K., 'The Naturalistic Fallacy', *Mind*, 48 (1939), 464–77.

—— *Ethics* (Englewood Cliffs, N. J.: Prentice Hall, 1963; 2nd edn. 1974).

—— 'Sidgwick and the History of Ethical Dualism', in B. Schultz (ed.), *Essays on Henry Sidgwick* (Cambridge: Cambridge University Press, 1992).

FRAZIER, R. L., 'Intuitionism in Ethics', in E. Craig (ed.), *Routledge Encyclopedia of Philosophy*, vi (London: Routledge, 1998).

FRIED, C., *Contract as Promise* (Cambridge, Mass.: Harvard University Press, 1981).

GAUT, B. 'Moral Pluralism', *Philosophical Papers*, 22 (1993),17–40.

—— 'The Structure of Practical Reason', in G. Cullity and B. Gaut (eds.), *Ethics and Practical Reason* (Oxford: Clarendon Press, 1997).

—— 'Rag-Bags, Disputes and Moral Pluralism', *Utilitas*, 11 (1999), 37–48.

GIBBARD, A., *Wise Choices, Apt Feelings: A Theory of Normative Judgment* (Cambridge, Mass.: Harvard University Press; Oxford: Clarendon Press, 1990).

GRIFFIN, J., *Well-Being* (Oxford: Clarendon Press, 1986).

—— *Value Judgement: Improving our Ethical Beliefs* (Oxford: Clarendon Press, 1996).

GROTE, J., *Exploratio Philosophica*, ii (Cambridge: Cambridge University Press, 1900).

HACKER, P. M. S., *Insight and Illusion* (Oxford: Clarendon Press, 1972; rev. edn. 1986).

HARDIN, 'Common Sense at the Foundations', in B. Schultz (ed.), *Essays on Henry Sidgwick* (Cambridge: Cambridge University Press, 1992).

HARE, R. M., *The Language of Morals* (Oxford: Clarendon Press, 1952).

—— *Freedom and Reason* (Oxford: Clarendon Press, 1963).

—— 'Rawls' Theory of Justice', in N. Daniels (ed.), *Reading Rawls: Critical Studies on Rawls' 'A Theory of Justice'* (Oxford: Blackwell, 1975).

—— *Moral Thinking* (Oxford: Clarendon Press, 1981).

HARMAN, G., *The Nature of Morality* (New York: Oxford University Press, 1977).

—— *Change in View* (Cambridge, Mass.: MIT Press, 1986).

HART, H. L. A., *The Concept of Law* (Oxford: Clarendon Press, 1961).

HEGEL, G. W. F., *The Phenomenology of Spirit*, trans. A. V. Miller (Oxford: Oxford University Press, 1977).

HOBBES, T., *Leviathan* (1651), ed. E. Curley (Indianapolis: Hackett, 1994).

HOLMGREN, M., 'Wide Reflective Equilibrium and Objective Moral Truth', *Metaphilosophy*, 18 (1987), 108–25.

—— 'The Wide and Narrow of Reflective Equilibrium', *Canadian Journal of Philosophy*, 19 (1989), 43–60.

HOOKER, B., 'Rule-Consequentialism, Incoherence, Fairness', *Proceedings of the Aristotelian Society*, 95 (1995), 19–35.

—— 'Ross-Style pluralism vs. Rule-Consequentialism', *Mind*, 105 (1996), 531–52.

—— *Ideal Code, Real World: A Rule-Consequentialist Theory of Morality* (Oxford: Clarendon Press, 2000).

—— 'Moral Particularism: Wrong and Bad', in B. Hooker and M. Little (eds.), *Moral Particularism* (Oxford: Clarendon Press, 2000).

—— 'Reflective Equilibrium and Rule Consequentialism', in B. Hooker, E. Mason, and D. Miller (eds.), *Morality, Rules and Consequences* (Edinburgh: Edinburgh University Press, 2000).

HORWICH, P., *Truth* (Oxford: Oxford University Press, 1990; 2nd edn. 1998).

HUMBERSTONE, L., 'Direction of Fit', *Mind*, 101 (1992), 59–83.

HUME, D., *A Treatise of Human Nature*, 2nd edn., ed. L. A. Selby-Bigge, rev. P. H. Nidditch (Oxford: Clarendon Press, 1978).

—— *An Enquiry Concerning the Principles of Morals*, ed. T. Beauchamp (Oxford: Clarendon Press, 1998).

IRWIN, T. H., 'Eminent Victorians and Greek Ethics', in B. Schultz (ed.), *Essays on Henry Sidgwick* (Cambridge: Cambridge University Press, 1992).

JACKSON, F., 'Defining the Autonomy of Ethics', *Philosophical Review*, 83 (1974), 88–96.

—— *From Metaphysics to Ethics* (Oxford: Clarendon Press, 1999).

JAMES, W., 'The Will to Believe', in James, *The Will to Believe and Other Essays in Popular Philosophy* (New York: Dover, 1956).

JOSEPH, H. W. B., *Some Problems in Ethics* (Oxford: Clarendon Press, 1931).

KANT, I., *Groundwork of the Metaphysic of Morals*.

KATZ, J. J., 'Some Remarks on Quine on Analyticity', *Journal of Philosophy*, 64/2 (1967), 36–52.

—— *The Metaphysics of Meaning* (Cambridge, Mass.: MIT Press, 1990).

KEMENY, J. G., and OPPENHEIM, P., 'On Reduction', *Philosophical Studies*, 7 (1956), 6–19.

KORSGAARD, C., 'Skepticism about Practical Reason', *Journal of Philosophy*, 83 (1986), 5–25.

—— *The Sources of Normativity* (Cambridge: Cambridge University Press, 1996).

Bibliography

—— 'The Normativity of Instrumental Reason', in G. Cullity and B. Gaut (eds.), *Ethics and Practical Reason* (Oxford: Clarendon Press, 1997).

KRIPKE, S., 'Naming and Necessity', in D. Davidson and G. Harman (eds.), *Semantics of Natural Language* (Dordrecht: Reidel, 1972).

KURTZMAN, D. R., ' "Is," "Ought," and the Autonomy of Ethics', *Philosophical Review*, 79 (1970), 493–509.

MCDOWELL, J., 'Virtue and Reason', *Monist*, 63 (1979), 331–50.

—— 'Values and Secondary Qualities', in T. Honderich (ed.), *Morality and Objectivity: A Tribute to J. L. Mackie* (London: Routledge & Kegan Paul, 1985).

—— 'Projection and Truth in Ethics', in S. Darwall, A. Gibbard, and P. Railton (eds.), *Moral Discourse and Practice* (New York: Oxford University Press, 1997).

MACINTYRE, A., *After Virtue: A Study in Moral Theory* (London: Duckworth, 1985).

—— *A Short History of Ethics: A History of Moral Philosophy from the Homeric Age to the Twentieth Century*, 2nd edn. (London: Routledge, 1998).

MACKIE, J. L., *Ethics: Inventing Right and Wrong* (Harmondsworth: Penguin, 1977).

MCNAUGHTON, D., *Moral Vision* (Oxford: Blackwell, 1988).

—— 'An Unconnected Heap of Duties?', *Philosophical Quarterly*, 46 (1996), 443–7.

—— and RAWLING, P., 'On Defending Deontology', *Ratio*, 11/1 (1998), 37–54.

MILL, J. S., *Utilitarianism*, ed. G. Sher (Indianapolis: Hackett, 1996); and ed. R. Crisp (Oxford: Oxford University Press, 1998).

MOORE, G. E., *Ethics* (London: Oxford University Press, 1966).

—— 'The Conception of Intrinsic Value', in Moore, *Principia Ethica*, rev. edn. (Cambridge: Cambridge University Press, 1993).

—— *Principia Ethica* (Cambridge: Cambridge University Press, 1903), rev. edn., ed. T. Baldwin (Cambridge: Cambridge University Press, 1993).

NAGEL, T., *The Possibility of Altruism* (Oxford: Clarendon Press, 1970).

—— *The View from Nowhere* (New York: Oxford University Press, 1986).

—— *The Final Word* (New York: Oxford University Press, 1997).

NOWELL-SMITH, P. H., *Ethics* (Harmondsworth: Penguin, 1954).

OLEN, J. and BARRY, V., *Applying Ethics* (Belmont, Calif.: Wadsworth, 1985).

O'NEILL, O., 'Instituting Principles: Between Duty and Action', *Southern Journal of Philosophy*, 36, suppl. (1997), 79–96.

PARFIT, D., 'Reasons and Motivation', *Proceedings of the Aristotelian Society*, suppl., 71 (1997), 99–130.

PLATO, *Republic*, trans. D. Lee, 2nd edn. (Harmondsworth: Penguin, 1974).

PRICE, R., *A Review of the Principal Questions in Morals* (1758), in D. D. Raphael (ed.), *British Moralists 1650–1800*, ii (Oxford: Clarendon Press, 1974).

PRICHARD, H. A., 'Does Moral Philosophy Rest on a Mistake?', *Mind*, 21 (1912), 21–37; and in Prichard, *Moral Obligation: Essays and Lectures*, ed. W. D. Ross (Oxford: Clarendon Press, 1949).

—— 'Duty and Ignorance of Fact', in Prichard *Moral Obligation*, ed. W. D. Ross (Oxford: Clarendon Press, 1949).

—— *Moral Obligation: Essays and Lectures*, ed. W. D. Ross (Oxford: Clarendon Press, 1949).

—— 'Duty and Interest', in Prichard, *Moral Obligations and Duty and Interest: Essays and Lectures*, with introd. by J. O. Urmson (London: Oxford University Press, 1968).

PRIOR, A. N., *Logic and the Basis of Ethics* (Oxford: Oxford University Press, 1949).

—— 'The Autonomy of Ethics', *Australasian Journal of Philosophy*, 38 (1960), 199–206.

PUTNAM, H., 'The Meaning of Meaning', in Putnam, *Mind, Language and Reality: Philosophical Papers*, ii (Cambridge: Cambridge University Press, 1975).

—— *Reason, Truth and History* (Cambridge: Cambridge University Press, 1981).

RAILTON, P., 'On the Hypothetical and Non-Hypothetical in Reasoning about Belief and Action', in G. Cullity and B. Gaut (eds.), *Ethics and Practical Reason* (Oxford: Clarendon Press, 1997).

RAPHAEL, D. D., 'Sidgwick on Intuitionism', *Monist*, 58 (1974), 405–19.

—— *Moral Philosophy* (Oxford: Oxford University Press, 1981).

RASHDALL, H., *A Theory of Good and Evil* (Oxford: Clarendon Press, 1929).

RAWLS, J., 'Outline for a Decision Procedure in Ethics', *Philosophical Review*, 60 (1951), 177–97.

—— *A Theory of Justice* (Cambridge, Mass.: Harvard University Press, 1971; Oxford: Clarendon Press, 1972).

—— 'The Independence of Moral Theory', *Proceedings and Addresses of the American Philosophical Association*, 48 (1974–5), 5–22.

—— 'Kantian Constructivism in Moral Theory', *Journal of Philosophy*, 77 (1980), 515–72; repr. rev. in Rawls, *Political Liberalism* (New York: Columbia University Press, 1993).

REID, T., *Essays on the Active Powers of Man* (1788), in D. D. Raphael (ed.), *British Moralists 1650-1800*, ii (Oxford: Clarendon Press, 1974).

ROSS, W. D., 'The Basis of Objective Judgements in Ethics', *International Journal of Ethics*, 37/2 (1927), 113–27.

—— *The Right and the Good* (Oxford: Clarendon Press, 1930; repr. 1967; Indianapolis: Hackett, 1988).

—— *The Foundations of Ethics* (Oxford: Clarendon Press, 1939).

RUSSELL, B., *The Problems of Philosophy* (London: Oxford University Press, 1913).

SAYRE-MCCORD, G., 'Coherentist Epistemology and Moral Theory', in W. Sinnott-Armstrong and M. Timmons (eds.), *Moral Knowledge? New Readings in Moral Epistemology* (Oxford: Oxford University Press, 1996).

SCANLON, T. M., 'Contractarianism and Utilitarianism', in A. Sen and B. Williams (eds.), *Utilitarianism and Beyond* (Cambridge: Cambridge University Press, 1982).

—— *What we Owe to Each Other* (Cambridge, Mass.: Belknap Press, 1998).

SCHNEEWIND, J. B., *Sidgwick's Ethics and Victorian Moral Philosophy* (Cambridge: Cambridge University Press, 1977).

—— (ed.), *Moral Philosophy from Montaigne to Kant*, 2 vols. (Cambridge: Cambridge University Press, 1990).

Bibliography

—— 'Voluntarism and the Foundations of Ethics', *Proceedings and Addresses of the American Philosophical Association*, 70 (1996), 25–42.

SEXTUS EMPIRICUS, *Outlines of Pyrrhonism*, trans. J. Annas and J. Barnes as *Outlines of Scepticism* (Cambridge: Cambridge University Press, 1994).

SHAW, G. B., *Man and Superman* (Westminster: Constable, 1903).

SIDGWICK, H., *The Methods of Ethics*, 7th edn. (London: Macmillan, 1907; repr. 1967; Chicago: University of Chicago Press, 1962).

—— *Outlines of the History of Ethics for English Readers* (London: Macmillan, 1954).

SINGER, M. G., 'The Many Methods of Sidgwick's Ethics', *Monist*, 58 (1974), 420–48.

SINGER, P., 'Sidgwick and Reflective Equilibrium', *Monist*, 58 (1974), 490–517.

—— *Practical Ethics* (Cambridge: Cambridge University Press, 1979).

SINNOTT-ARMSTRONG, W., 'Intuitionism', in L. C. Becker (ed.), *The Encyclopedia of Ethics*, i (New York: Garland, 1992).

SLOTE, M., *From Morality to Virtue* (New York: Oxford University Press, 1992).

SMART, J. J. C., 'Outline of a Utilitarian Ethics', in J. J. C. Smart and B. Williams, *Utilitarianism: For and Against* (Cambridge: Cambridge University Press, 1973).

SMITH, M., *The Moral Problem* (Oxford: Blackwell, 1994).

SOBER, E., *Philosophy of Biology* (Oxford: Oxford University Press, 1993).

STRATTON-LAKE, P., 'Can Hooker's Rule-Consequentialist Principle Justify Ross's Prima Facie Duties?', *Mind*, 106 (1997), 51–8.

—— 'Why Externalism is not a Problem for Ethical Intuitionists', *Proceedings of the Aristotelian Society*, 99 (1999), 77–90.

—— *Kant, Duty and Moral Worth* (London: Routledge, 2000).

STRAWSON, P. F., 'Ethical Intuitionism', *Philosophy*, 24 (1949), 23–33.

STURGEON, N. L., 'Moral Explanations', in D. Copp and D. Zimmerman (eds.), *Morality, Reason, and Truth: New Essays on the Foundations of Ethics* (Totowa, NJ: Rowman & Allanheld, 1985); repr. in G. Sayre-McCord (ed.), *Essays on Moral Realism* (Ithaca, NY: Cornell University Press, 1988).

—— 'Harman on Moral Explanations of Natural Facts', *Southern Journal of Philosophy*, 24, suppl. (1986), 69–78.

—— 'What Difference does it Make whether Moral Realism is True?', *Southern Journal of Philosophy*, 24, suppl. (1986), 115–41.

—— 'Contents and Causes: A Reply to Blackburn', *Philosophical Studies*, 61 (1991), 19–37.

—— 'Metaphysics and Epistemology', in L. C. Becker (ed.), *The Encyclopedia of Ethics*, i (New York: Garland, 1992).

—— 'Critical Study of *Wise Choices, Apt Feelings*, *Noûs*, 29 (1995), 402–24.

—— 'Naturalism in Ethics', in E. Craig (ed.), *Routledge Encyclopedia of Philosophy*, vi (London: Routledge, 1998).

—— 'Moral Skepticism and Moral Naturalism in Hume's *Treatise*', *Hume Studies* (forthcoming).

THOMSON, J. J., *The Realm of Rights* (Cambridge, Mass.: Harvard University Press, 1990).

—— 'The Right and the Good', *Journal of Philosophy*, 94 (1997), 273–98.

TIMMONS, M., *Morality without Foundations* (New York: Oxford University Press, 1999).

URMSON, J. O., 'A Defence of Intuitionism', *Proceedings of the Aristotelian Society*, 75 (1975), 111–19.

VELLEMAN, J. D., 'The Possibility of Practical Reason', *Ethics*, 106 (1996), 694–726.

WARNOCK, G. J., *Contemporary Moral Philosophy* (London: Macmillan, 1967).

WARNOCK, M., *Ethics since 1900* (Oxford: Oxford University Press, 1968).

WERNER, R., 'Ethical Realism', *Ethics*, 93 (July 1983), 653–79.

WILLIAMS, B., *Ethics and the Limits of Philosophy* (London: Fontana, 1985).

—— 'What does Intuitionism Imply?', in Williams, *Making Sense of Humanity and Other Philosophical Papers 1982–1993* (Cambridge: Cambridge University Press, 1995).

WITTGENSTEIN, L. *Philosophical Investigations*, 3rd edn., trans. G. E. M. Anscombe (London: Macmillan, 1958).

—— *The Blue and Brown Books* (Oxford: Blackwell, 1958).

—— *Remarks on the Foundations of Mathematics* (Oxford: Blackwell, 1964).

—— *On Certainty*, ed. G. E. M. Anscombe and G. H. von Wright, trans. D. Paul and G. E. M. Anscombe (Oxford: Blackwell, 1969).

—— *Philosophical Grammar*, ed. R. Rhees, trans. A. J. P. Kenny (Oxford: Blackwell, 1974).

—— *Philosophical Remarks*, ed. R. Rhees, trans. R. Hargreaves and R. White (Oxford: Blackwell, 1975).

ZIMMERMAN, M., 'On the Intrinsic Value of States of Pleasure', *Philosophy and Phenomenological Research*, 411–2 (1980), 26–45.

—— *The Nature of Intrinsic Value* (Totowa, NJ: Rowman & Littlefield, 2001).

Index

action
  distinguished from agent 239
  direct 231
Addis, M. 288n
agent-relative reasons/principles 50–1,
  146–7
Alston, W. P. 140n
analytic/synthetic 8, 24
a priori and self-evidence 18, 22ff, 59,
  71, 141, 184, 187, 252, 258
Aristotle 47, 56, 58, 68, 69, 72, 74, 75n,
  149, 159–60, 163n
Attfield, R. 77n
Audi, R. 18, 19, 23n, 58n, 59n, 60n, 61,
  66n, 71n, 72n, 86, 115n, 116n, 139n,
  143, 163–5, 166n, 186n, 187n, 188n,
  253–4
autonomy
  epistemic 48–9.
  of ethics 190–211

Ayer, A. J. 64, 191n, 197n
Baldwin, T. 5n, 6n
Balguy, J. 15n, 248n, 250, 258, 259–60
Barry, V. 170n
Bentham, J. 71
bias 113–14, 119, 122, 134–5
Blackburn, S. 13n, 167n, 192n, 213,
  226n
Blanshard, B. 56
BonJour, L. 22n, 25n, 114n
Boyd, R. 167n, 203, 204n
Bradley, F. H. 101–2, 110–11
Brandt, R. B. 147n, 166, 185n, 186n

Brink, D. 21n, 161n, 167n, 183n, 204n
Broad, C. D. 6n, 56n, 71n, 103, 163n,
  173, 198n, 229, 238
Broome, J. 263n
Brown, C. 250n
buck-passing account
  of goodness 12, 150–1
  of rightness 15
Butler, J. 163n

Canfield, J. V. 288n
Carritt, E. F. 163n, 173, 230n
Carroll, L. 264
Casullo, A. 25n
categorical imperative 268, 38–45
clarity 70, 74
Clarke, S. 2, 3n, 4–5, 56, 60, 69n, 97,
  163n, 248n, 150, 151n, 253n, 256n,
  258
cognitivism/non-cognitivism 1, 6, 23–4,
  104, 165, 167–8, 195, 253
coherence/coherentism 116–18, 140,
  147, 162–3, 208–9, 220
Collingwood, R. G. 234
common sense 1, 3ff, 26–7, 56, 67–70,
  72n, 75, 77, 78, 93, 97, 101, 109–12
concepts and properties 8–11, 216–17
consensus 71–2
consequentialism 45ff, 76, 84, 146, 159,
  169, 182, 229–30
consistency 71, 74, 116
contractualism/constructivism 99–101,
  149–51
Cook-Wilson, J. 231

Index

Index

Lightning Source UK Ltd.
Milton Keynes UK
17 February 2010

150242UK00002B/13/A

9 780198 250982